DAUGHTER
of PERSIA

DAUGHTER
of PERSIA

A Woman's Journey from Her Father's Harem Through the Islamic Revolution

SATTAREH FARMAN FARMAIAN
with DONA MUNKER

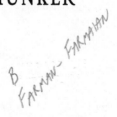

B
FARMAN-FARMAIAN

THREE RIVERS PRESS • NEW YORK

The line from Ferdowsi's *Book of Kings* in Chapter 1 is translated by Reuben Levy in *The Epic of the Book of Kings* (University of Chicago Press, 1967, p. 69); the prose translations of Sa'adi's poetry in Chapters 5, 8, and 12 are taken from Mehdi Nakosteen's *The Maxims of Sa'adi* (University of Colorado Press, 1977; pp. 99, 101, and 98, respectively); the lines from Ibn Khaldun in Chapters 13 and 16 are translated by Franz Rosenthal (*The Muqaddimah: An Introduction to History,* edited and abridged by N. J. Dawood, Princeton University Press, 1967, pp. 253 and 257, respectively); in Chapter 17, the lines from Rumi are taken from the R. A. Nicholson translation of his poems (*Selected Poems: Divani Shamasi Tabriz,* Cambridge University Press, 1952); the lines from Omar Khayyam's *Rubaiyat* in Chapter 7 are from the classic Edward Fitzgerald translation. The phrase by Arthur M. Schlesinger, Jr., referred to in the Afterword appeared in "War in the Gulf: Counsel of Ignorance," the *New York Times*, December 17, 1990.

Published in the United States by Three Rivers Press, an imprint of the Crown Publishing Group, a division of Random House, Inc., New York.
www.crownpublishing.com

Three Rivers Press and the Tugboat design are registered trademarks of Random House, Inc.

Originally published in slightly different form in hardcover in the United States by Crown Publishers, an imprint of the Crown Publishing Group, a division of Random House, Inc., New York, in 1992.

Library of Congress Cataloging-in-Publication Data

Farman-Farmaian, Sattareh.
Daughter of Persia : a woman's journey from her father's harem through the Islamic Revolution / Sattareh Farman Farmaian with Dona Munker.
p.   cm.
Includes index.
1. Farman-Farmaian, Sattareh.   2. Women—Iran—Biography.
3. Iran—Biography.   I. Munker, Dona.   II. Title.
CT1888.F37A3   1993
955.05'092—dc20
[B]   92-40640
CIP

ISBN-13: 978-0-307-33974-4
ISBN-10: 0-307-33974-2
Printed in the United States of America

Design by Shari de Miskey

10   9   8   7   6   5   4

First Three Rivers Press Edition

To my daughter, Mitra,
and my grandchildren,
Kayvon and Juni

CONTENTS

PART THREE: KHANOM

PART FOUR: EARTHQUAKE

ACKNOWLEDGMENTS

*W*HILE THIS IS A WORK OF NONFICTION, TO PROTECT THEIR safety and privacy the identities of Sattareh Farman Farmaian's original students, some persons on her staff, and her revolutionary interrogators have been disguised.

The authors wish to acknowledge the kindness of Professors Amin Banani, Richard Cottam, and Mark Gasioworski in reading the manuscript, as well as the efforts of our capable and enthusiastic editor at Crown, Jane Meara. We are also grateful to others who have contributed to this book in important ways: Dr. John Milner, who brought us together; our original editor, Lisa Healy, who was among the first to understand what we wanted to do; our invaluable literary agent, Joy Harris; and copy editor Miriam Hurewitz.

For help of various kinds, Dona Munker is much indebted to Ruth Britton, Mary Ann Eckels, Elena Eskey, Laura Foreman, Dr. Maurice Hamovitch, Marian Krauskopf, Françoise Poyet, Dr. Alan Roland, Toni Sciarra, and Myra Turoff; to colleagues in the New York University Biography Seminar who have shown interest and offered comments, especially Paul Alexander, Deirdre Bair, David Hoddeson, Kenneth Silverman, and Lois Underhill; and to Vartan Gregorian, formerly of the New York Public Library, for believing that popular history can also be good history. Finally, for extending the support, encouragement, and patience that the work of a long and complex book demands of others, she thanks her mother, Professor Frances Lomas Feldman, not only a great social worker but a first-rate proofreader; and her husband, a first-rate listener.

TO THE READER

*T*HIS BOOK BEGINS IN THE TIME OF MY REMARKABLE FATHER, Shazdeh—a man born to a power and privilege which, in his place and time, would have been enough for most men of his class, but whose active and forceful personality made him exceptional, and whose forward-looking temperament has profoundly affected my own outlook. If my recollections can contribute to greater understanding between my Western and Iranian friends and add something to their awareness of the rich diversity of human cultures, I will feel that I have succeeded in doing something tangible. But I hope also that my American friends will find in these pages cause to reflect on the consequences of their own well-meaning efforts to remake the world in their image.

I speak here of the journey I and my country took as we stumbled into the modern world, and have set down many facts and events of my own life in Iran and the West, as well as my own opinions concerning those events and persons involved in them. My interest has been to record what happened to me—and only to me; the opinions and experiences of others regarding any part of what I describe, however similar or different from mine, are not my concern. My account reflects my views and no one else's, not even others in my family, and I alone bear responsibility for the substance of what is said here.

My purpose is neither to pass judgment nor to escape it. This is not a journalist's or a scholar's history but a personal memoir of things that I, an Iranian like many others of my generation, witnessed during my lifetime. The memories presented and the thoughts, opinions, or intentions ascribed to others—especially my father and other public figures—are what I clearly recollect myself, or firmly believe to be true from my own observation, from discussions with others having close knowledge of the events in question, or from documents that I have read. As for the political matters recalled here, they are widely known to historians, and have been written about often by experts far more learned than I. Anyone who is curious to know more of the momentous events of which I speak, or who wishes to verify that what I have related about them is true, will find it easy to do so.

From the day I was born I have always loved action more than words. But now only words are left. This story and these words, therefore, are for my daughter, Mitra, my grandchildren Kayvon and Juni, and all young Iranians who, like them, live in foreign countries and ask their elders, "What did you do wrong there, that we too must live in exile, far from our own land?" For the present, at least, the failure of my generation has dispossessed them of their Persian heritage. I want them to know what *I* think we did wrong. And I want them to know what I remember there.

I wish to thank Joan Palevsky, Elizabeth Dawson, and Morgan Walters for all their encouragement in this endeavor.

SATTAREH FARMAN FARMAIAN

PART ONE

IN SHAZDEH'S REALM

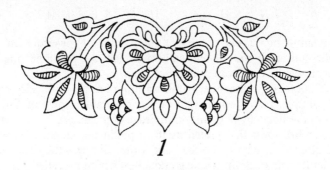

1

BREAD AND SALT

I wish to go to Iran, to see my much-praised father.

—The tale of Rustam and Sohrab, from THE BOOK OF KINGS

*W*HEN MEMORY HAUNTS ME, ABOVE ALL IT IS HIM THAT I RE-
member. He was more than sixty when I was born, and
old when I knew him—a dauntless, aged lion of the fallen dynasty,
troubled by the griefs and ailments of many years. But in the world
in which I moved and lived, he ruled supreme.

I was born in rose-perfumed Shiraz, the capital of the ancient province from which the Persian Empire sprang, and a city famous for its
gardens, wines, and poets. My father, who had been a military commander and governor all his life, had been sent to take charge of the
restless province during the First World War. I was the fifteenth of
his thirty-six children, and the third child of my mother, Massumeh,
who was the third of his wives.

At the time of my birth, the Qajar dynasty still ruled Iran, and my
father, though a political moderate and a firm supporter of the democratic Iranian constitution, was closely related to the throne by ties
not only of blood but of marriage, his first wife being a royal princess.
Well into his later years, he looked much as he did when young:
handsome and virile, domineering and vigorous—not tall, but with
a cleft chin, a full white mustache, and piercing, hawklike eyes of
light green, a most unusual color for an Iranian. In the whole gigantic

3

royal family he was one of the wealthiest and most powerful men, and to the end of his days he carried himself with the proud bearing of a general who comes from a house of kings.

My mother, on the other hand, was not of noble birth. Her family were simple, pious people from the central Iranian town of Tafresh, west of the holy city of Qom, on the edge of the desert; it was a small, ancient hill town that prided itself on producing clerks, secretaries, and other men who could read and write. She was the daughter of my father's steward, my gentle grandfather, whom we called Aghajun, and had been born in Tehran not long before our constitutional revolution and the terrible civil war that followed. Her marriage to my father was the third of the eight he made during the course of his long life. She went to join him in Shiraz just after the end of World War I, and I am told that I was born there two years later.

I did not, however, grow up in Shiraz, but in Tehran, for I came into the world close to the time of the Qajars' downfall in the British-engineered coup d'état of February 1921, which brought Reza Khan to power. (He was later called Reza Shah Pahlavi. Nineteen twenty-one, of course, is the date given for this fateful event in the West. The Iranian calendar is different from the Western. By Persian reckoning, the coup responsible for the establishment of the Pahlavi dynasty took place not in 1921, but in the year 1299.) As bad luck would have it, when Reza Khan's forces marched into Tehran my father had just completed his Shiraz assignment and had returned to the capital ahead of us. He and two of his prominent elder sons were arrested and imprisoned, and for three long months our mothers suffered the agony of knowing neither their husband's fate nor their own. Not until Reza Khan had himself proclaimed war minister and made certain that no one was strong enough to oppose him were my father and his sons released, with my father forced to spend the remainder of his days under the watchful eyes of the future shah's secret police.

Certain that Reza Khan's clemency would continue only so long as he and his family made no trouble for the new regime, my father ordered his harem conveyed back to the capital and settled his younger wives and us, their children, in a compound on Sepah Avenue, in the quarter known as the Shah's Garden. Here Qajar cabinet ministers, diplomats, generals, and other high servants of the throne had long resided. In this new home, which he expected to be his last, my father devoted himself entirely to running what lands and villages he still possessed and supervising his younger children's upbringing and education. So it happened that I came to spend childhood in a compound ringed about by shimmering pools and splendid green gardens, laid down like flowering carpets in the dusty lap of the Alborz Mountains by the now disenthroned, and frightened, Qajars.

I can never forget this marvelous home of my childhood, whose like has surely vanished from Iran forever. In it my father watched over the welfare of more than a thousand people whose very survival depended entirely on him: wives, children, countless paid servants, secretaries, craftsmen, and laborers, as well as many faithful elderly retainers and old soldiers who had served him in the past. For the shelter and protection of all these people, as well as of their families, he alone was responsible.

This had become a heavy burden for him to bear. Under Reza Khan's regime his eldest sons had once again become men of importance and distinction. But the new ruler was confiscating for his own use the property of numerous Qajar noblemen, and no one could predict his future plans for my father or any of his male children.

All Qajar families knew that Reza's secret police were everywhere. "When you pray," my mother would instruct us, "always ask God to let Shazdeh live one hundred and ten years." This was her way of saying, "Pray that your father lives forever, for when he dies, we and all these people will be nothing." Being nothing meant having no father, brother, husband, or son to protect you. In our country, if you were not yourself strong, wealthy, or powerful, or if you did not have somebody strong to protect you, you were nobody, and you did not survive.

Yet my father's compound was also a place of enchanting tranquility and beauty. Its center was a great oval park or garden bordered by poplar trees, and the entire compound, which was about half a mile long, was surrounded by a ten-foot wall whose iron-studded wooden gate on Sepah Avenue was guarded by liveried watchmen. Inside, circling the gravel carriage road around the central garden, like stones on a giant's necklace, were my father's home and the walled subcompounds of his younger wives, along with storehouses, a carpentry shop, and even a garage, for my father's dark blue Essex sedan was one of the country's few motorcars. There were a smithy, a dairy, a bathhouse, a greenhouse, and a big kitchen where food was prepared each day for my father, his staff, and his servants, and where his Persian chef supervised the daily concoction of pastries and French delicacies for my father and his Persian and foreign luncheon guests.

The subcompounds where we and our mothers lived were known collectively as the *andarun*, the "inner" quarter, or harem; everything else, including the central garden and the other buildings surrounding it, was the *biruni*. This was the "outer," or public, quarter where my father lived, and was the realm of men. It reflected the greater world beyond, which was also a realm of men.

At the northernmost end of the great garden of the biruni stood a sparkling blue reflecting pool in which a fountain murmured throughout the long hot season. Bright tiles of Persian blue surrounded the pool, and from its sides stretched ornamental flower beds of roses and narcissus among which my father in his enforced retirement might stroll, chat with old political and diplomatic friends and military comrades, or sip tea under the shade of pines and cypresses, poplars and old sycamores.

Only four of the eight wives my father married in the course of his long life lived in our compound: my mother; two other ladies, Batul and Fatimeh, whom my father had married at about the same time as my mother and who lived across the park from us; and, after about 1928, another lady, Hamdam, whom we did not often see because she lived at the opposite end of the park. His second wife, a Kurdish chieftain's daughter, had long since died, but his first wife, the Qajar princess Ezzatdoleh, who was much older than the rest, had an establishment of her own next door to our compound, as did their four adult sons, while two more ladies whom my father married late in life had houses elsewhere in the city. All the wives in the compound looked upon each others' children as their own, and Batul and Fatimeh were my mother's best friends. We also regarded the princess Ezzatdoleh and her sons as part of our family. She was extremely fond of my mother, who was an exceptionally kind and compassionate person, and they saw each other often, for the princess and my father, though on good terms, had long been separated, and Ezzatdoleh, who was lonely, frequently needed my mother's soothing company.

My father did not allow our mothers to leave home often, but they did not often need to. Both the biruni and the andarun were places of ceaseless activity. Droshkies constantly rattled up the gravel road carrying visitors to our mothers' homes, as well as the Persian and foreign guests of my father or men who had come to see him on business. Male servants traveled continually back and forth, bearing messages from my father to his wives' homes or from one wife to another, or lugging baskets of charcoal and firewood for them, or prodding donkeys laden with bricks to repair their houses and courtyards, or carrying bolts of cloth for them to sew our clothing and their servants' on the Singer sewing machines my father had given each of them for this purpose. In their walled-off subcompounds, which were closely guarded and where no men other than near relatives were permitted entry, women servants in snug embroidered bodices, narrow trousers, full swinging skirts, and flowing head scarves or gaily colored *chadors* (a chador is simply any veil covering the whole body) brought bedding or preserved foods to and from storage, prepared meals in courtyard kitchens, washed clothes in outdoor brick pools, and laid out branches of turmeric and other herbs and spices to dry in the patios.

So it is engraved on my heart, a bustling, almost completely self-contained world inside the encircling wall. Everyone there was linked with everyone else, for "family" in our small universe meant not only our father and mothers and brothers and sisters and other relatives who lived in and around the compound, but all the other people inside our walls: our nannies, our *lalehs* or male caretakers, the cooks, guards, porters, stewards, secretaries, artisans, old military pensioners, and everyone else my father supported. They and we all belonged to him, and were fed, protected, and cared for by him. This supreme bond with our benefactor, which Iranians call "the bond of bread and salt," gave us all an indissoluble connection. No one in the compound, from the most decrepit ex-sergeant to the youngest schoolchild, ever forgot this allegiance for a single moment. I seemed myself to remember it almost hourly.

As I was the only girl of my age group among my father's many offspring, I had no playmates of my own sex. From the moment of birth I was full of energy, and while my mother, who was extremely religious, was terribly strict in her views about girls, she was also a practical person. To give me some companionship and get me out of her hair, she had arrived at the unconventional solution of letting me leave the andarun at will to play with my younger brothers and half-brothers and the servants' sons in the biruni, all of us under the watchful eye of my laleh, Mashti, who guarded her gatehouse. That a woman as devout as my mother saw nothing improper in this was less strange than it might seem. My father had ordered our mothers to make sure that all of us, including the girls, got plenty of exercise, and although this was quite a radical idea, our mothers, who considered their husband the wisest man on earth, would not have dreamed of disobeying him.

My mother therefore sealed my fate as a part-time boy by sewing me a pair of yellow felt trousers, and I was constantly out of doors, reigning along with my next younger half-brother Abol over a small gang of rapscallions with all the authority of an elder sister—daring my brothers to climb after me to the highest branches of the sycamore trees or challenging them to races up the house pillars, always making it a point to be faster and braver than they. My mother, a stern disciplinarian, never failed to give me a good paddling for my scuffed knees, scraped elbows, and ripped trousers, and as I always set my jaw and refused to cry when she did this, these spankings invariably exasperated her still more.

My willfulness was her despair, for Persian daughters are supposed to be meek and self-effacing, and I was an obstinate, contradictory square peg in her smooth round notions of what a real girl should be. But I had come to think of myself as neither more nor less than my brothers, and perhaps this helps to account for such unwonted stubbornness in a girl. Then, too, every day offered my eyes the supreme example of a determined will. Playing so often in the biruni, I could glance frequently toward the northern apex of the compound where, overlooking the reflecting pool, there rose a large, buff-colored brick mansion with a pillared portico—an imposing house in a commanding position: the house of my father, Shazdeh.

That was what everyone called him, and as a child I assumed that this was his name. His actual given name, however, was Abdol Hossein. "Shazdeh" was merely a title, and meant "king's son," or "prince." Before the Qajars' downfall, his full name with all its titles had been Abdol Hossein Mirza Shahzadeh Hazrat Aghdas Vala Farman-Farma, which means, roughly, "His Highness, Prince Abdol Hossein, the Eminent and Exalted One, the Greatest of All Commanders." When Reza Shah, who was trying to turn Iran into a modern, Western-style nation, ordered every Iranian to take a last name in the fashion of the West, my father decided to use the last of his titles as a surname. He called himself Abdol Hossein Mirza Farman-Farma, and the rest of us received the name of "Farman Farmaian," meaning "belonging to the Greatest of All Commanders."

But to me he was simply "Shazdeh," and his name meant both "father" and "all-powerful." I accepted his rule, as did everyone, with fear and reverence and distant adoration. He was the lodestar of our busy cosmos, and his will held it together. I knew that even our water, which in a desert country is a substance more precious than gold, came from Shazdeh. It bubbled into our reservoir pools from an underground clay aqueduct called a *qanat*, which he had caused to be built from the steep mountains years earlier to channel the melting snows to his estates, and thence southward to the common people of Tehran. This aqueduct was called by his surname, the Farman-Farma Qanat, and gave the purest and most delicious water in the city. To me, Shazdeh was like the qanat. He was the source of all wisdom, justice, and humanity. I yearned for his attention and approval. I would have done anything to please him.

On Friday, the Moslem holy day, our busy universe stopped turning for a few hours and we were permitted to draw near its center. This was the day when we and our mothers trotted up the white gravel road to the big house to pay a formal call on my father.

Our weekly "outing" to Shazdeh's house was a great event, and on Fridays the first breath of air from the garden below my window seemed more vivid than usual with the powerful breath of roses or narcissus or flowering pomegranate. At breakfast in the dining room down the hall, my mother would hurry us nervously along while she poured tea from the brass samovar and distributed white goat cheese, flat *taftoun* bread, and glasses of boiled milk to me, my older sister, and the smaller children as we sat tailor-fashion on the oilcloth that protected the carpet.

When she had wiped the little ones' noses and inspected everybody's hands and face to be sure that Shazdeh would have no uncleanliness to complain of, our mother would say, "All right, children, now let's go say *salaam* to your father," and, taking one end of her pretty white or yellow chador in her teeth to conceal her face from the glances of stray male employees in the biruni or Friday visitors to my father, she would lead us downstairs, out of the gatehouse at the low front wall, and up the carriage road to Shazdeh's.

Sometimes, as we passed the park, I would see petitioners encamped there, sharecropping villagers from the tiny hamlets on lands my father owned outside Tehran or hundreds of miles away in other provinces who had come to ask Shazdeh to settle a blood feud or protect them from the gendarmes. Sometimes it would be months before he could work out a solution, which might mean long-distance negotiations through intermediaries, or sending the petitioners home with a senior member of his staff to deal with the problem. In that case they would hunker patiently outside their tents for weeks, smoking their water pipes and talking and joking among their bedrolls and samovars under the trees near the reflecting pool.

I was fascinated by the lives of ordinary people. Over villagers such as these, landlords like my father had virtually limitless power. Despite his efforts to do right by them, I knew from Mashti and my mother that they often lived under the thumb of predatory bailiffs, soldiers, bandits, and others, whose greed, cruelty, and injustice could easily destroy them. The harshness of their existence was obvious from their thin, hungry-looking faces, and I would run to my mother saying,

"Oh, that man looks so old and weak; please give him lots of food!" I rejoiced when Mashti took them the big pots of meat and rice my mother cooked for them, and felt proud to know that Shazdeh was going to help solve their problem and see that they had justice. Everyone looked to Shazdeh for justice. There were never fights within our walls—everybody knew that they could rely on my father to find a fair solution to a problem. Besides, no one would have dared to steal or start a feud in Shazdeh's compound.

Once we were in the antechamber that led to my father's room, however, I would forget everything but the excitement and tension of the moment. If Delrobah, our father's black housekeeper, told our mothers that Shazdeh was still finishing breakfast or saying his morning prayers, or that he was not yet ready because his gout had troubled him the night before, I and my younger brothers and half brothers would jostle around the open door of the great chamber where he lived and worked to watch his progress. When the right moment came, my mother would shoo everyone inside.

I still have an old photograph that must have been taken around 1931, when I was about ten; Shazdeh loved all modern technology and often had a photographer attend these Friday inspections (for that was what they were). In the picture I am standing precariously atop a Victorian settee in the second row, surrounded by ten of my younger brothers and sisters: a dark-eyed, olive-skinned little girl with straight black bangs, wearing a white cotton dress with long, hot, tight sleeves. I am bending forward to peer at my year-old half brother Khodadad in the first row, who looks as though he might slide off the settee. But as I rarely betrayed what I felt even at that age, this distraction surely belies the excitement and anxiety inside me.

Although my father dropped in on us at home every ten days or so, these formal visits to his room were especially wonderful and fearful occasions. Having suffered in his lifetime from several political upheavals, Shazdeh, who had held many high posts in his career, had decided that we, his younger children, must have something more solid to depend on than politics after he was no longer there to watch over us. He was adamant that we learn to be self-reliant, and every day except Friday we were busy from dawn till dusk with school, homework, math tutors, Persian tutors, poetry tutors, and other pedagogical what-have-you's who swarmed in and out of the compound. My father tended each one of us carefully, individually, like a gardener fostering orchids, and as he cultivated each plant separately, he fully expected it to do its best for him.

Nothing is more important, he would admonish us, than your education. Don't think that you can go about with your noses in the air because of who your father is, as though you were everyone else's superior. Never mind if ignorant people like your lalehs and nannies call you "prince" or "princess"; all that sort of thing is over for us. Times are changing, and what counts nowadays is not who your father was but what you make of your own lives.

Thus, every Friday we would line up according to age, arms crossed reverently over our chests in front of his big European dining table for Shazdeh to inspect our ranks, quiz us about our schoolwork, and have us recite the often long passages of Persian poetry he commanded us to learn by heart every week. As he sat beside the table leaning on his cane, the bandage he wore on one gouty foot loomed as large in my eyes as a big white melon, but this in no way detracted from my reverence and fear.

I always stood between my older sister Jabbareh and my brother Abol, my stepmother Batul's son. I would fix my eyes respectfully on Shazdeh's face, as I had been taught, and when we had all bowed, I would pull myself up very straight and try to hide my nervousness as my father, leaning forward, began his questioning, starting with the oldest. Even though he had sent our elder brothers away to Europe, he still had so many other children in the compound, with more coming every year, that there might be as many as a dozen of us.

"Jaby," my father would begin.

My sweet and beautiful sister Jabbareh, four years my senior, always blushed when Shazdeh spoke to her.

"Your mother tells me," Shazdeh would say, "that Mademoiselle has praised your French."

Jaby shared a sour-faced governess named Mademoiselle Dupuiche with three of my older half sisters. France's refined and subtle language was admired as nearly the equal of the Persian, and French art and culture were accepted as supreme in Europe. My half sisters and Jaby also had to take lessons in French and Persian cuisine under the tutelage of Shazdeh's temperamental chef, Asghar. They were also taught painting and classical Persian music, the latter by a distant male relative of ours who was an army officer and always wore a sword when he came to give them their music lessons. This instruction, of course, was in addition to what Persian girls of our class were supposed to learn about sewing, embroidery, household management, and religion in their mothers' andaruns. If my father so required, we girls took extra tutoring in reading, math, poetry, Persian grammar, or any other academic subject, just like the boys, and we had to attend school six days a week. I was going to Tarbiat, a private elementary school near the compound, and Jaby attended the lycée Jeanne D'Arc, the French school for girls. Education, my father believed, was essential for preparing all his daughters for the life to which our birth inescapably destined us, the life of a society hostess.

In those days, about ninety-five percent of Persian adults, and nearly all women, were still illiterate. But my father, who always did exactly what he wanted to do, and did it with total and magnificent indifference to everyone else's opinion, had long entertained the highly unorthodox notion that education made women better wives. He had enforced this extraordinary idea not only by having my mother and his other wives learn to read and write when he married them, but by sending every one of his daughters to school—and the servants' sons and daughters, too, whenever he could sweet-talk their fathers into this. Jaby was an excellent student. She was also, in several important respects, my exact opposite: quiet, graceful, submissive, and a mirror of all that Persians hold to be the feminine virtues. My mother often remarked pointedly that she wished a few of these qualities would rub off on me.

My sister, still blushing, murmured something in response to Shazdeh's compliment. "Good, I'm glad to hear it," Shazdeh said. "A modern hostess must speak perfect French. But see to it," he added sternly, "that you do not neglect your cooking, if you want me to find you a husband."

Nothing anybody did was ever quite good enough for Shazdeh, especially where education was concerned. I, being very proud of my lovely sister's accomplishments, was sometimes a little pained that he was never really satisfied. My father rarely bestowed unqualified praise on anyone, which he must have thought would be bad for our character and make us less self-reliant.

My sister, however, never seemed hurt by these hints that she must work even harder to please him. She nodded obediently. "*Ghorban*, yes," she said. To show respect, we never addressed Shazdeh merely as *Agha*, "Sir." "Ghorban" is a word suggesting an almost untranslatable reverence on the part of the speaker. Although it is sometimes rendered in English as "Excellency," its truer meaning is "You for whom I sacrifice myself."

"Satti" was next. My name was really Sattareh, but usually no one called me this; as names went, it was a little strange. *His* children, my father declared, were not going to have names just like everybody else's. Consequently our mothers' new babies often ended up with names that were mildly eccentric. The normal form of my name in Persian is *Settareh*. This means "Star," and is an ordinary girl's name. But in the form in which Shazdeh had arbitrarily bestowed it, with an *a* at the beginning instead of *e*, the word sounded like "ruler"— not the royal kind, but the measuring stick. As far as I know, this peculiar name had no particular symbolism for him. Certainly he hadn't meant it to have any special meaning for its owner. My father was extremely self-centered, and it never occurred to him to consider how I or my mother might feel about my having such a strange name. Shazdeh's perfect egotism was a great cause of aggravation to our mothers. It particularly irked them that my father was not above dealing with their frequent pleas for more cash to buy necessities for their children and servants by pretending to have suddenly gone stone-deaf (indeed, he really was a little hard of hearing). Of course, they did not dare complain about it. I myself did not question my father's right to give me any name he wished. Nevertheless, I was grateful that nobody in the family, including Shazdeh, ever called me anything but "Satti."

"Satti."

Deeply impressed by Shazdeh's snow-white mustache and his military bearing, I struggled to keep my gaze fixed on his. His light green eyes were as bright as a falcon's. How distinguished he looked, I thought—just like a king's son. Then I caught my breath. His tone had indicated that something was amiss. But I did not dare speak to him unless he asked me a direct question.

"There is a smudge on your cheek. Didn't you go to the bath on Monday with your mother and sisters?"

Shazdeh entertained advanced and forceful opinions on the topics of modern hygiene, nutrition, and public health. We all had to bathe once a week, and he made his own doctor, an old friend and French-trained Iranian physician known to us as "Hadji Doktur Khan," look after everyone's health, including the servants'. Cleanliness was a very serious matter to Shazdeh. The blood rushed to my face. Horrified, I prayed that the flowery fields of the silk carpet beneath my feet would open and swallow me, like an earthquake.

"Ghorban, yes," I stammered, "and I washed this morning, too—"

Shazdeh smiled and patted my cheek affectionately. "All right, little scapegrace. But Koran says, 'God loves women who heed cleanliness.' "

Somebody snickered. Behind us, my mother fairly glowed with annoyance. "Now," Shazdeh went on, "you may recite that short poem I assigned you last week."

I breathed once more. Recently, on an informal visit to our house, he had brought me a collection of poems by the great thirteenth-century poet Sa'adi. Unlike other fathers in old Tehran families, who loaded their daughters with French clothes and jewelry, Shazdeh never gave his children anything but books. I was much more interested in these than in the sapphire and diamond rings I saw on wealthier friends or relatives. Studying, in contrast to tidiness, gave me no trouble at all; I was always first in my class at school. I recited flawlessly,

> *"Human beings are like parts of a body,*
> *created from the same essence.*
> *When one part is hurt and in pain,*
> *the others cannot remain in peace and be quiet.*
> *If the misery of others leaves you indifferent*
> *and with no feelings of sorrow,*
> *You cannot be called a human being."*

I loved Sa'adi, and I especially loved this poem, which always made me think of the common people in our compound: the petitioners in the park or the crippled old soldiers and nearly blind pensioners who sat all day under the trees, and who always had a hug and a few pieces of candy for any of us children who came along.

"Very good," said Shazdeh approvingly, and I was overjoyed to receive a small coin. "Do you know the meaning of the poem that Satti has just recited?" he would continue, addressing all of us. "It means that a country is a nation made of individuals. Every one of these individuals is important. Without seeing to people's welfare, a nation cannot become great. That is why it is your *dayn*, your duty, to work for the progress and well-being of others, so that our country can become a great nation again. Therefore you must study and be educated. Right now you are like raw iron. To become a sword, iron must pass through the forge, and the forge is education!"

Shazdeh would then move on to someone else, who might be found wanting in diligence in some subject, and would hang his head in shame. Our father's bright, fierce glance would flicker up and down our line. "All of you must study *hard*. Hard work is a virtue—no one heaps up treasure without hard work. When you grow up, you will realize that education is everything!"

Then he would go down our line, demanding more recitations, handing out more coins, praising and remonstrating, while I watched in simple awe. It amazed me that he could keep track of all our names, much less remember the weekly reports that our mothers gave him of our schoolwork, or recall what he had told us to memorize the previous Friday.

Finally, having given everyone his or her bit of recognition and patted all the babies' cheeks, Shazdeh would conclude with a final exhortation of the morning. This was designed to lodge the importance of education and our "dayn" firmly in our minds until the next Friday inspection, and was usually embellished with more quotations. "Education," he would say, alluding to Sa'adi, "makes old men's hearts young again." Or, quoting Sa'adi once more, "'A nation becomes more beautiful through its learned men.'"

On hearing glorious words like these, a shiver of joy and pride would course through me. Nothing was more important to me than being Shazdeh's daughter, and such noble sentiments, falling from his lips, were inexpressibly thrilling.

My mother cleared her throat. "Ghorban," she said. "Before we go, I need an extra hundred rials this month. The children's winter shoes are worn down to nothing, and Satti needs a new school satchel— Jaby's old one fell apart yesterday."

At this Shazdeh's snowy brows would draw together in a heavy frown, always a sign of his displeasure, while simultaneously his eyes would appear to glaze over. Grasping the head of his cane, he would stare straight ahead into space, as though he had not heard.

"Ghorban," said my mother wickedly, "Sa'adi also says: 'Silence is good, but timely speech is even better.'"

But although this, too, was a famous aphorism, and although my father's frown would deepen, he still made no reply. Instead, reaching for a silver dish full of small white candies that he kept on the table for us, he would merely signal that the inspection was over. Accepting our treat one at a time along with a treasured hug or kiss, and having each kissed our father's hand, we would file out, elbowing each other furtively and giggling with relief, I to eat lunch and spend the remainder of the one-day weekend holding sway over our little gang in the biruni. Those of us who were having problems at school knew that they and their mothers would soon be summoned for a private conference. Nothing was more important than our education. Why Shazdeh was so fervent on the subject I had no idea. But it went without saying that I would honor his wishes. One day I was going to be exactly like Shazdeh. I had already made up my mind. I would do something useful and important for our country, and make him proud of me.

If Shazdeh was the sun around which our lives revolved, my mother was the moon who made our tides roll in and out. Her greatness and authority were second only to his. We children addressed her with the most profound respect, and both to her face and each other called her not *Maman-jan*, "Mama," but *Khanom*, which simply means "Lady," or "Ma'am."

She had married Shazdeh about ten years before my birth. Her own father, my grandfather Aghajun, who was not only a trusted servant but my father's closest friend, was exactly Shazdeh's age. They were married when my father was in his middle fifties, for he had heard that Aghajun's eldest daughter was intelligent, sensible, witty, pious, and a gifted household manager. Of course, in theory it was not only an advantage but an honor for an ordinary family to have a daughter marry so lofty a member of the royal house, and naturally my mother, who had been raised in the strictest traditions of Shiite Moslem womanhood, assented without a murmur when told that she was to be the next wife of the great prince who was Aghajun's employer and whom she had never seen. Nevertheless, we all knew from my mother's stories of those days that it had been very hard for her. She had been only twelve years old.

Khanom was dark-browed and comely, with exquisitely smooth olive skin that always smelled of rosewater. Being very devout, she parted her thick, waist-length black hair straight down the middle, winding it tightly in a plain, heavy bun at her neck, and never set foot in public without her chador. But she had an endearing smile and a keen sense of humor, and in the dark, beautiful eyes that were her most expressive feature, the strong inner feelings she preferred to hide from the world gleamed like golden carp flashing across the surface of a pool. People said of her admiringly, "Massumeh-Khanom always talks to you with her eyes." Everyone in the compound loved my mother's kindness, her wit, and her unfailing generosity.

Her existence was one of unremitting toil. There were no telephones or electricity in the compound, except in Shazdeh's house, and no hot water or central heating. Cooking, cleaning, the sewing of our clothes and the servants' and the laying up of winter stores required Khanom, our six or seven nannies, and our stepmothers and their womenservants to work from morning prayers until bedtime each day. In addition to supervising her large household she had to manage the compound dairy, of which my father, who valued her extraordinary managerial skills, had put her in charge. As she had been apprenticed to a seamstress before marrying my father, she also had to sew all Shazdeh's underclothing and his pajamas, as well as go every morning to his house to shave him or give him a haircut. Like nearly every other Iranian woman of childbearing age, when she was not nursing one child she was usually pregnant with another, and by the time I was sixteen and she was about thirty-nine, she had not only me and Jaby, but my brothers Farough, Ghaffar, and Rashid, and my sisters Homy, Sory, and Khorshid, so that together with our eldest brother, Sabbar, who was studying in Paris, there were nine of us in all.

Khanom was always beset by two consuming worries. One of them was cash. Since 1921 Shazdeh had lost much of his great fortune. Several of his younger sons who had been born before or at the time of the coup were studying in Europe like my brother Sabbar, partly to acquire the European education considered essential for a Persian nobleman but also to keep them out of Reza Shah's hands, for they might well have served as hostages. My father had gradually sold off much of his land to pay for the older ones' schooling in Paris and London and for the compound's upkeep, and could not afford to send their younger brothers to Europe. Nor could he maintain the rest of us in anything like the luxurious surroundings for which the Persian aristocracy had been famous for three thousand years, and in which he himself, though he dressed and ate simply as a soldier should, had always lived. Hence, although our homes were comfortable and entirely adequate for our needs, they were Spartan by comparison to Shazdeh's, or the homes of Ezzatdoleh's royal sons next door. Furthermore, my father was an expert at finding ways to economize on the maintenance of his younger families.

Khanom, who regarded Shazdeh's fine residence as no more than his due, would have been the first to admit that in general his system was both practical and fair. My father insisted that harmony rule in our compound, and the method by which he achieved this remarkable feat was never to play favorites among his four families there. He gave each of his wives and their children presents that were almost identical and of equal value. All of us inhabited homes built and furnished exactly like the others: large, simple, thick-walled, two-story houses that faced south, in the ancient Persian style, to capture the warmth of the winter sun. These he filled not with gold plate, jewels, and Russian furniture but with whatever plain wooden beds, tables, and chests old Usa-Ibrahim, the compound carpenter, was capable of hammering together.

But in spite of his fundamental fairness, my father's stinginess drove our mothers crazy. They were just as responsible for the welfare of the numerous servants who depended on their bread and salt as he was for the whole compound's.

My mother's frequent complaints about how Shazdeh deprived her of cash made me feel torn and disloyal. I could hardly bear hearing her and my stepmothers describe him as a miser, yet I also hated her having to beg for money all the time. As all children do, I tried hard not to hear what made me unhappy, and to shut out their criticisms I would always concentrate completely on my sewing or embroidery, or whatever small task was at hand. I never liked to show I was hurt. Nevertheless, I felt that it would be agony to have to beg, and that I would never beg anyone for anything so long as I lived.

Khanom's financial woes, however, were nothing compared to her worries over Shazdeh's safety. Her anxiety on this subject was the bane of her existence and ours. Though she often read to Shazdeh from the newspapers and liked to read them herself, we were never allowed to discuss politics or current events, or to mention the ruler's name even in passing when servants were near. Our mothers had given Reza Shah the code name "My Cousin," so that they could remind us to shut up without the servants' knowing what they meant. My mother knew that not all servants were reliable. "If you are not careful," Khanom would say warningly when someone spoke out of turn, "I will tell my cousin what you just said." She especially distrusted one of Shazdeh's valets, a skinny, cold-eyed man named Ismail. One Wednesday night when she was alone with Shazdeh—in accordance with our father's strategy of not playing favorites, each of our mothers had "her" night in the big house at the head of the garden; Khanom's night was Wednesday—my father had told her that he was sure this man was a police informer, but that if he, Shazdeh, fired the fellow he might avenge himself by going to the police with some made-up story, and another would only take his place.

"Shazdeh is wise," my mother would say with feigned, nervous confidence. "This way he can take precautions, and the man can do us no harm. Let's give thanks to God and the Prophet if we have only enemies whose faces we know." We learned before we were old enough to go to school what careless words or malicious gossip could do. I myself knew that if anyone ever betrayed my trust, I would turn my back on that person immediately. The way to behave to those who injured you, I felt, was to ignore them utterly, forgetting their very existence; doing this proved they were of no importance to you. But we all knew that we must never speak foolishly—or, worse yet, behave greedily—for that could mean disaster for Shazdeh and a thousand people. "Never trust anyone outside your own family," both my mother and Mashti, my laleh, would say, "and never accept money or gifts from anyone but your parents." Self-discipline in Khanom's household was learned early in life.

Naturally, the necessity of making sure that nobody ever said the wrong thing was a constant strain on my mother's temper, which was normally frayed anyway. So intense was her anxiety that if I happened to stumble while we were on our way somewhere, she would swoop down on me, grab my wrist, yank me back with a jerk, and slap me across the bottom so hard that I had to set my jaw to stifle my shriek.

"May God the Merciful give me patience, you little hoyden," she would cry. "Why do you always go your own way? Shazdeh will never find a husband for a stubborn, self-willed little girl like you!" She must have reasoned that if we could not control our feet, perhaps we could not control our tongues, either, and though I quickly forgot the pain of falling down, I did not forget the pain of her spankings.

For this reason I learned not to reveal my heart in my speech. As I am the sort of person to whom action always seems more to the point than words, and as I thought that I should not have to explain myself to those who loved me, I did not find words useful for this purpose anyway. By the time I was ten, therefore, I had become accustomed to shutting away my feelings, not only from most of the servants but even from Khanom herself. Her fear of betrayal and her other cares threw a dark shadow across our existence, like a snake always coiled to strike. I felt that we had to protect my mother from harm, and not burden her more than necessary. I could not bear to see anyone suffering, and my father was old and not in the best of health. What would happen to all of us if she got sick from her work and worries, or were suddenly no longer there to look after us?

Thus I would have done nearly anything to relieve her of her many cares, and I am sure that I never once took her cuffs, spankings, and bursts of anger to heart, or imagined for a moment that she did not love me. Her sudden flares of temper were about equally distributed among all her children; even our mild, white-bearded old grandfather, Aghajun, had to put up with them. Like me, my mother could only show what was important to her through her actions, but I knew well how devoted she was to all of us. It was for our sake that she slaved so hard, plotted ways to coax money out of Shazdeh, and had scarcely a moment's peace from sunrise to sunset. When she did have it, she was a different person—kind, funny, affectionate, and a wonderful storyteller.

On the icy evenings of the Tehran winters, when a glittering frost lay on the window casements and it was too cold to work her Singer,

Khanom would send the servants away and we would all snuggle down together against the bolsters and cushions to warm ourselves under the *kursi*, a quilt blanket heated by a charcoal brazier beneath a small table. Then my mother, gathering her newest infant close, would hold us spellbound with tales of Shazdeh's life and hers during the long-ago, turbulent time in Iran's history when she and my stepmother Batul lived in the royal andarun of Ezzatdoleh, who had been daughter, sister, and aunt to three different kings of Iran. And if I not infrequently got a slap or a spanking I didn't deserve, I also knew that the new pencil or the apple or the small vial of rosewater my mother sometimes produced unexpectedly from the folds of her chador was her way of telling me that she was sorry.

Every morning in the cool waking time just before dawn, before Khanom stirred at morning prayers in her room, before Robab the cook began rattling the coal pan downstairs to get the samovar hot, or laughter and splashing noises from the pool outside told us that Nargess and our other nannies were up, the first pale light that washed the high walls of my room brought only quiet. In that moment, all would be still.

In those days there was no motor traffic in Tehran, and apart from the nightingales that trilled in the plum trees of our garden court below—an enclosed garden such as the ancient Persians called a *pairidaeza*, from which the English word "paradise" comes—there was little to disturb the silence. I would listen intently for sounds outside the compound. From my room over the enclosed courtyard I could not hear the calls to prayer from any of the city's mosques. But frequently, to my pleasure, the stillness would be grazed by the deep, slow, sonorous bonging of camel bells—the sound of a caravan swaying off toward the empty desert plain from one of the city gates not far to the north of the compound.

I had often seen this remarkable sight myself on trips outside, when we neared the bazaar or the northern gate of the city. Thirty, forty, or even a hundred beasts, guided by a single man holding the reins of the first animal, would roll forth from a caravanserai bearing merchants' cargo eastward along the legendary Khorasan Road, across the barren wilderness to the sacred city of Mashad. From afar, the bells' clangor had a distant, peaceful sound, steady and reassuring, like the church bells in the American missionaries' compound on Sundays. Lying in my low wooden bed, suspended between the quietude of dawn and the imminent commotion of breakfast, I would feel restlessly certain that one day I would escape the loving shelter of home and find out what lay beyond the walls of Shazdeh's compound.

On Saturday, the first day of the week, and on every other morning except Friday, I would hear my laleh's big voice bellowing from our gatehouse as I sat on the dining room carpet gulping down my boiled milk. "Come on, Satti-Khanom, you're late! Come on, Farough Mirza, hurry up—everyone is waiting!"

I and my next younger brother, Farough—despite our father's orders to the contrary, the servants all called him "Farough Mirza," or "Prince Farough"—would choke down the rest of our food and my mother would yell out the window, "Just a minute, Mashti, I'm fixing their snack." Then she would hastily roll some cheese into a bit of soft bread or tie a few handfuls of nuts and raisins into our hankerchiefs. As soon as she shoved them into our pockets we would scuttle down the staircase and out the path to the gatehouse where Mashti would be waiting, along with Batul-Khanom's son Abol, Fatimeh-Khanom's sons Ali-Naghi and Ali-Dad, and his own daughter Leila and some of the other servants' youngsters, to march us all off to Tarbiat Elementary School, which was down the street.

Mashti had come into my father's service at about the time I was born, and now served my mother as gatehouse watchman, baby-sitter, and general errand boy. He was also our escort and bodyguard whenever we needed to leave home to go to school, the bazaar, or a relative's house. Mashti was the strongest man in the entire compound and could lift furniture and carpets that no one else could budge. His hands, jutting like spades from the sleeves of his blue cotton tunic, were long-fingered and muscular, and his broad face and shiny, nearly bald head were as brown as walnut juice from the sun. He only called me "Satti-Khanom," Lady Satti, when my mother was in earshot. The rest of the time I was just "Satti."

I loved Mashti! I was tremendously proud of his strapping shoulders and brawny, sunburnt forearms, his big mustache and large kind eyes and flashing smile. We had been companions since I was old enough to walk. On weekdays he inhabited the gatehouse, where he had a tiny private room that held his bedding, clothes, and a small wooden chest for things like tobacco and matches. In cold weather we would often sit together for hours in the antechamber of the gatehouse, talking like two old chums and warming our hands and feet at his charcoal brazier. While I was still small enough, he used to hoist me onto his back or put me into the long wrought-iron shoulder basket he took to market when he shopped for my mother's groceries, and I would swing along beside him, wild with delight, he grinning at my ecstasy. Often, when we were at the market, seeing me gaze wistfully at the sticky, fly-covered candies at the confectioner's stall (both my mother and Shazdeh had expressly forbidden us these vermin-specked treats), he would hand the stall's proprietor one or two of his own hard-earned pennies to buy me a few, whispering in my ear, "Don't tell Khanom, or she'll eat my bald head for supper." Although I loved Shazdeh passionately, I felt with equal conviction that I was Mashti's daughter as well, though in a different way. When I visited the little house across from the compound where Mashti lived with his pretty wife Korsum and their three children, or rode to school on his shoulders or walked beside him to the market, I could imagine what it must be like to belong to a family of ordinary people and have a man live at home with us, someone whom I could hug and talk to and call "Father." I yearned to call Shazdeh "Father" instead of "Ghorban," to throw my arms around his waist and bury my face in his tummy, as I had seen Mashti's daughter Leila do with my laleh.

Unfortunately, even though my mother was very fond of Mashti, she also considered him a sort of emissary from heaven—one whom God had sent to add to her burdens and thus teach her the virtue of patience. Not only did Mashti, in her view, let me and my brothers run wild in the biruni, but he also let us drink filthy street water and fed me the confectioner's dirty candies. The fact that Shazdeh might get word that she had let him do these things was at least as significant to Khanom as the distinct possibility that we might catch typhoid, dysentery, or roundworm. But worst of all, my laleh was a terrible shopper.

Mashti invariably lugged home in his iron basket the very worst fruits and vegetables the vendors could palm off on him. Agriculture in Iran was poor like everything else, and the grocers, to make their wares go farther, cheated their customers shamelessly. Frequently, a perfectly fresh bunch of onions or a sound apple or a healthy radish would disappear behind the stallkeeper's scales to be weighed, bagged, and presented to the customer with a hundred polite Persian exclamations of gratitude and indebtedness, only to turn up in my mother's courtyard kitchen as a wormy apple, a black radish, or a rotten handful of onions.

Needless to say, my mother did not have money to waste on inferior or spoiled food. She would have been glad to send someone besides Mashti, who was too simple and trusting to spot a trick coming. But there was no one else to send. So, every day when he went off to shop, she would say, "Mashti, when you go to the market today, make sure that the fruit dealer gives you his best goods. For heaven's sake, try to *notice* what he's giving you—don't use just two eyes, use four!"

But Mashti's open, unsuspecting nature completely nullified whatever protection four eyes might have given him. Every day he came home with soft cucumbers or spoiled turnips, and every day my mother would storm across the courtyard to the gatehouse to bawl him out through the curtain that screened the andarun from the gatekeeper's view, shouting as loudly as her strict modesty permitted, "Mashti, I send you to buy a watermelon and you come back with something that is not red inside but white, like a cabbage! You know the children can't eat this thing! How can you waste our money this way? Do you think Shazdeh is going to give me more just because Mashti is such a fool that he doesn't know a good watermelon from a bad one?"

"Khanom," Mashti would plead, "it's not my fault—the man swore to me it was a good one. Some *jinni*—"

"Spirits have no influence over watermelons," snapped my mother, more irritated than ever. Superstition was another thing Shazdeh had forbidden.

"But, Khanom," Mashti protested humbly, "how was I to know it was bad? I was not *inside* the watermelon."

"God be praised forever and give me patience," my mother would exclaim. "If Mashti did not go to the bazaar, all the rotten fruit dealers in Iran would be out of business."

"There is no justice, Satti," Mashti would say glumly when we were alone, shaking his head and puffing on one of the cigarettes I liked to roll for him. "Your mother, a saintly and generous woman, is pleased to think that I carelessly brought home a bad watermelon. All I know is, it was good when I picked it out. Well, by God's will it turned out to be a bad one after all. Either I was cheated, or the watermelon was good when I bought it and bad when it came home. It was not my fault, it was fate. Who can argue with that?"

Mashti and all the servants and my mother as well believed that everything was in the hand of heaven. If you sat under a pomegranate tree and a piece of fruit fell into your lap, it fell not because of some force called gravity but because God had willed that the fruit should fall at that particular moment. And if something good or bad fell into your lap, that too was ordained. Scarcely a day passed in which Mashti and fate did not have an encounter of this kind, which Mashti usually lost.

Fortunately, my laleh could never be angry for long, and soon he would cheer up. "God the Compassionate and Merciful sees everything," he would tell me soberly, "and always punishes the wicked.

Nothing on earth gets past God, who is everywhere, and who made the cow that causes earthquakes by shaking her head and tossing the earth between her horns. If you do something bad, not even hiding in the privy can protect you, because God is everywhere and sees everything. But God protects the victims of injustice. He is the avenger of wrongs. Wait and see—I will pray for that fruit dealer to be punished, and God will have him eaten by a desert ghoul."

I was always upset and angry at the daily vexations the stallkeepers' frauds caused Mashti and my mother, and would gladly have marched off to the market alone—not that anyone would have permitted me to do so—to give them a good tongue-lashing. But I was old enough to know better than to place any faith in a desert ghoul, who in the case of my laleh would have too much work to do. The trouble was, I thought, that Mashti simply couldn't tell a good watermelon from a bad one, which my mother and my grandfather Aghajun somehow could, and for this reason the vendors were always able to fool him. Once or twice I told him to go to Aghajun and find out how to see what the watermelon was like on the inside by looking at the outside. I certainly wouldn't waste my time sitting around waiting for some imaginary creature to come along and help me, I said; what one had to do in such a case was educate oneself and find a solution for the problem.

But Mashti never went to Aghajun, for like all Iranians he hated to admit that he had made a mistake, and feared to show his ignorance by asking for advice. I was impatient with his refusal to make this small effort, which could so easily have eliminated his and my mother's daily battles. Nevertheless, sometimes I sensed, without knowing how, that Mashti's fecklessness came not from laziness—for Mashti was a very hard worker—but from insecurity.

It was an insecurity that nearly everybody felt, and it went so deep that they didn't even think about it—it was just there, like the sky or the desert. In Iran, everybody depended on somebody higher for survival, some benefactor who was richer or more powerful than they were and who could take care of them. Just as we and my mother depended on Shazdeh, Mashti depended on Khanom. He feared that if he lost my mother's favor by admitting ignorance or a fault, she might fire him, and then he and his family would have to beg or starve. Even I, I reflected, was careful not to let my mother find out that I had been climbing on the bathhouse roof or leading my brothers on a foray to Shazdeh's pantry to wheedle some of his custom-baked Yazdi cookies, which were stamped with the Farman-Farma crest. And though Mashti was always telling me, "The liar is the enemy of

God," he had a lot more to lose than I did, and he would come up with the most ridiculous lies and excuses to avoid taking responsibility for his actions when someone higher was angry with him.

Of course, I knew perfectly well that my mother loved Mashti almost as much as I did, and that she never would have fired him. Mashti must have known it, too. But he couldn't be sure of it. I knew that playing safe, not getting caught in a mistake, and letting God take care of the rest were simply the things everyone felt they had to do. It was their way of trying to have security, so they could survive. In the compound, Mashti was somebody, honored and respected by everyone. But outside our walls, where he did not have us to protect him and his family, he, like all ordinary people, was nobody—a human being without influence or connections, anonymous and helpless against misfortune. And Iran has always been a country where misfortune finds those who have no say in their own destiny, and no protector against fate.

2

STORIES FROM MY MOTHER'S CARPET

The worst calamity that can befall a nation is disunity.

—Ahmad Kasravi, twentieth-century Iranian historian

*F*ROM KHANOM'S STORIES ON WINTER EVENINGS AND FROM HER conversations with my stepmothers Batul and Fatimeh during their afternoon tea-and-sewing breaks in our family room, I learned of the terrible turmoil the country had endured for fifteen years before Reza Shah's coup, and the troubles she herself had gone through in the early days of her marriage to my father.

Often Jaby and I felt such sympathy for her that, as we sat on the carpet cloth listening to our mothers and doing our embroidery, tears would come to our eyes. As the afternoon sunlight played upon the brilliant red and indigo maze of the carpet around us, until its flowing pattern became an ocean of irises and roses that we rode as on a white raft, her stories about Shazdeh, herself, and our family seemed so vivid that I felt as though both I and my sister were being woven into the warp and weft of something very ancient, and that all of us in Shazdeh's compound, which was my whole world, were merely small threads in the endless, interlocking angles and twisted arabesques of our nation's past. And through these tales of our family's history and Khanom's, I

26

first began to understand what it means when a nation and its people have no choice about their fate.

My country is a kingdom of fire, a carpet of sand and stone that millions of feet have trodden. Iran, a vast and arid plateau lying between Asia and Europe, is guarded by immense mountains. But it is also vulnerable to floods, earthquakes, and the designs of foreign powers—a harsh country of austere and hazardous beauty, scattered with poor, parched, tiny villages that are no more than so many mud-colored blinks in an infinite expanse of light-blasted, lion-hued, waterless desert. Time and again, this land has been scorched by violent upheaval and foreign conquest.

I should explain, perhaps, that Iranians are not "Arabs," as Westerners always used to assume of anyone from the Middle East, any more than Turks are "Arabs." The original Iranians were of Aryan stock: "Iran" means "Land of the Aryans," a group of various tribal peoples, of whom some settled in what is now northern Iran. However, it was from the ancient southwestern province of Fars, or Pars, that Iran received the old name by which Westerners know it: Persia.

We Iranians have lived on our inhospitable land bridge between East and West for much longer than our three thousand years of recorded history, and for many centuries Persian civilization, with its arts and architecture, its poetry and its highly cultivated way of life, was regarded as the greatest civilization of the Near East. But by the time a great-great-granduncle of mine, an ambitious member of the Turkoman Qajar tribe named Agha Mohammed Khan, overthrew the previous dynasty and proclaimed himself king in the late eighteenth century, Iran had become a poor, backward nation. The glorious achievements of the ancient kings were merely a proud memory, and Iranians had been forced to absorb and adapt themselves to centuries of foreign conquest. After the great age of the Persian Empire, Iran had fallen prey to devastating invasions: the Greek armies of Alexander the Great, followed by the Arab legions of Prophet Mohammed, Turkic tribes, and finally the Mongol hordes, all of whom passed across the Iranian plateau with fire and sword, wreaking death and destruction.

Condemned by geographical circumstance to be the victims of many successive conquests, we became a mixture of many peoples. But we always retained our identity as Iranians, for every fresh barbarian who came to conquer was invariably seduced into admiring and embracing the ancient and more civilized Persian way of life. In turn, Iranians, compelled to adjust to so many new masters, became experts at the

art of survival—clinging to the sustaining memory of our great past
and learning, first and foremost, the ancient wisdom of the Middle
East: never trust anybody but your own family.

Being too weak to stand against the howling winds of political
change, war, and natural disaster, Iranians learned to bend with them
in order not to be destroyed, and to make the best of each new situation
that came along. Taught from childhood to be quick-witted and alert
to others' moods that they might know better who was a friend and who
an enemy, many Persians learned to admire those who were wily and
good at dissembling, since cleverness and disguising one's true feelings
often seemed the only way to survive against a stronger force. We became a people famous for the love of jokes, poetry, dancing, and other
fleeting escapes from the sadness and uncertainty of life—a people fatalistic, generous, skeptical, and forgiving of the weaknesses of human
nature. To Iranians it was nonsense to plan for what the next month,
next year, or next century would bring. One could never be certain of
the future and good fortune never lasted; by next week we might all be
dead or ruined. Human beings did not need to seek out change—that
would come soon enough. "You just worry about today," my mother
would say firmly, "and let God take care of tomorrow."

Khanom's own troubles had descended upon her as a result of an
agonizing period of upheaval for the country that had gone on for
fifteen terrible years before Reza Khan's coup in 1921.

Ironically, this national ordeal was the outcome of a truly glorious
event: the first democratic revolution in the Middle East. This almost
bloodless revolution took place in 1906, when Iranian liberal nationalists, many of whom were members of the Qajar aristocracy itself and
had admired and studied the democratic governments of Europe, led
the common people to demand that the Qajar ruler, Mozaffar al-Din
Shah, permit a constitutional monarchy and a national assembly,
called the Majlis.

Although the Iranian monarchy had been absolute for three thousand years, Mozaffar al-Din Shah was a pious man who knew that a
Moslem prince is required to bow to his subjects' will, and he agreed
to permit the form of government they desired, allowing ordinary
citizens to have a voice in their nation's affairs. But Mozaffar al-Din
Shah died shortly after fulfilling his promise, and in 1908, when my
mother was about nine, civil war broke out because the old shah's
impious and reactionary successor, Mohammed Ali Shah, tried to
repudiate what his father had done. In 1909 the liberal nationalists
who supported the new constitution triumphed over the forces of Mo-

hammed Ali Shah, and in 1910, in accordance with the new doctrine that the king, as the phrase goes, would "reign but not rule" over Iran, they named his ten-year-old son, Ahmad, the new shah. For a brief time it had seemed that Iran's troubles must now end. It was also at about this moment in our national affairs that my father's marriage to my mother took place—the consequence of a regrettable falling-out between Shazdeh and his first wife, the royal princess Ezzatdoleh, after more than twenty years of marriage.

I am sure that for a long time my father's first marriage went smoothly. He and Ezzatdoleh were wed about 1888, when he was close to thirty.* On both sides, the union was a brilliant match. Shazdeh's bride was the daughter of Mozaffar al-Din Shah (at the time he had still been the crown prince) and a great beauty. She had the white, moon-shaped face and dark brows that Persians consider the height of beauty, and she was exquisitely short: a dainty hummingbird, or a figure from a Persian miniature. The marriage was also propitious because my father and Ezzatdoleh were both descended from the second Qajar king, Fath Ali Shah, and were therefore distant cousins.

When he married Ezzatdoleh, my handsome, wealthy father was among the most promising of the younger men of the royal family (which was enormous, since Fath Ali Shah, Shazdeh's great grandfather and Ezzatdoleh's great-great grandfather, had taken pains to ensure the survival of his dynasty by marrying around two hundred wives and having more than one hundred seventy sons and daughters). On his father's side Shazdeh was a grandson of a gifted, energetic, and enlightened crown prince named Abbas Mirza, who would have succeeded Fath Ali Shah to the throne had he not died of an illness after campaigning against the Afghanis in 1833, and who had been the first Persian prince to try to import modern, Western-style military technology, science, and secular learning to Iran.

From boyhood my father, who inherited both Abbas Mirza's energy and his progressive temperament, had shown great ability. After growing up in an enormous household of his own on his father's huge family estate in the Shah's Garden, surrounded by attendants and tutors whose sole task in life was to groom him in swordsmanship, poetry, hunting, riding, calligraphy, ceremonial etiquette, and other subjects necessary to a great Persian nobleman, he received an education at

---

*Before Reza Shah, no one in Iran had ever thought of registering people's birth dates, although I believe that my father was born about 1858 and my mother around 1899. But I cannot be certain of this—indeed, I have never known the true date of my own birth.

the Austrian Military Academy in Tehran, a military school for the sons of the aristocracy with French-speaking Austrian instructors. Thereafter, he distinguished himself as a fine soldier and strategist who was also an enthusiastic builder of bridges and roads, and as a young man with a keen interest in the new Western sciences and in social improvements. His mentor was a powerful emir called Nezam Garoussi, for even a prince needed good connections, both to advance himself and for protection in case he fell out of favor with the king or made an enemy of some prince stronger than he was. This emir arranged to get him a command in the crown prince's household guard and then for him to marry Ezzatdoleh. As was the custom of the aristocracy, she and each of the six sons she subsequently bore him were all lodged in separate establishments on Shazdeh's family estate.

Even a royal princess like Ezzatdoleh had no choice about whom to marry, and at the time of their wedding she was probably no more than thirteen—in traditional Moslem societies, girls are considered marriageable the moment they reach puberty, and are often married as young as nine or ten. Nevertheless, my father was determined to be a good husband. He filled Ezzatdoleh's mansion on his estate with antique silk carpets, Gobelin tapestries from Paris, furniture from St. Petersburg, and jewel-studded plates of gold and silver. More important, he educated her.

Normally, no one bothered to teach women any skills at all, except those needed for housekeeping, husbandry, and weaving. In Iran, women are considered *zaifeh*, the weak sex, as frail in mind as in body, incapable of making important decisions. It was held to be futile and even dangerous to teach a girl more than she needed to be a pious, virtuous wife. To the consternation of Ezzatdoleh's relatives, however, my father immediately had his child bride taught to read and write, and even made her learn French and the ancient feminine art of gold-thread embroidery, so that she would possess some means of filling the empty hours after the last of their sons was sent away to school in Europe. Furthermore, Shazdeh had my stepmother—who, like all royal harem women, had never been taught anything of modern health practices, or even to bathe regularly—instructed in modern hygiene and child care by his own physician, Hadji Doktur Khan. Moreover, it was said in the astonished royal family that he refused to consummate the marriage until he felt that Ezzatdoleh was ready. And finally, out of respect for her father and for her high rank, for more than two decades he took no other wife.

Unfortunately, my father frequently had to be absent from the royal court, often for many months at a time. For thousands of years, the real job of governing Iran, a far-flung desert realm three times the size of France and full of quarreling local landlords, water feuds, tribal wars, and bandits, had fallen to the king's wealthy, powerful male relatives. Iran, in common with most Middle Eastern states at that time, had no true national army. Instead, aristocrats like my father had to act as administrators and provincial military governors, paying for the upkeep of these provinces out of their own pockets and maintaining their own private armies—my father's army was called "The Victorious"—to enforce the ruler's authority and prevent the country from collapsing into anarchy.

Thus, by the time Shazdeh and Ezzatdoleh had been married for twenty-two years, my father had served as commander-in-chief of the army in Persian Azerbaijan, governor of Kerman, governor of Kurdistan, governor of Kerman a second time, governor of the District of Tehran, minister of war, governor of Fars, governor of Kermanshah, and governor of Azerbaijan. After the civil war ended in 1909, Shazdeh, who believed that the people's will must be respected and had sided with the constitutionalists, served the new government in Tehran as minister of justice and as war minister, and became a leader of a party of conservative moderates.

I can truthfully say that he was an excellent public servant—energetic, compassionate, a great builder of public works, and deeply concerned about education, health, and justice. In Shiraz, the capital of Fars, he founded one of Iran's first secular schools for girls, and as minister of justice he introduced the Western custom of court trials into the Persian legal system. Like many enlightened Iranian aristocrats, he wanted to see our nation emerge from its backwardness and become an advanced society again, as it had been in ancient times.

His long career and numerous absences, however, had been hard on Ezzatdoleh. She had been a loyal wife: once, when a cabinet intrigue brought her father's wrath down on Shazdeh and he had to flee to Iraq for fear that Mozaffar al-Din Shah would let him be murdered by his enemies, Ezzatdoleh voluntarily went with him into exile and remained at his side for five years, until finally she was able to persuade the king to let them return to Iran and to take Shazdeh back into his favor. But her husband's extended absences on assignment were difficult to bear. After their sons were old enough to be sent to schools in Europe, she had little to do besides feel neglected and listen to malicious harem gossip. Ezzatdoleh was as used to having her own way as Shazdeh was, and to punish him for his neglect she began refusing him admittance to her rooms when he was at home. She and my father grew apart, with Ezzatdoleh more and more unhappy and Shazdeh unable to please her any longer.

A year or so after the death of her father in 1906 and the ascendancy of her ill-famed brother, the shah Mohammed Ali who plunged us into a civil war to destroy Iran's infant democracy, Ezzatdoleh was mortified to learn that my father, who had been dispatched to Tabriz in Persian Azerbaijan to make peace between warring Kurdish and Turkish tribes, had married a Kurdish mountain chieftain's daughter to seal a pact, and that a baby, my half sister Bodagh, had been born as a result of this union. The young Kurdish bride had actually been sent back to her tribe—where, sadly, she died only a few years later—and Shazdeh tactfully gave the baby to a favorite niece in Tabriz, asking her to be good to the little girl: in Iran, a child is considered to belong wholly to its father's family, and if a husband divorces his wife or sends her away, she has no rights at all regarding their children. But although Shazdeh's kindly niece raised my sister just as though she were her own child, Ezzatdoleh was still furious over the marriage, which she regarded as a slight to her prestige.

Her displeasure was all the greater because, more or less around this same time, Shazdeh, evidently without consulting my stepmother, had arranged for their handsome, brilliant eldest son, Nosratdoleh, to marry a niece of his, the daughter of his favorite sister. This sister, Najmeh-Saltaneh, was as strong-minded and forceful as Shazdeh himself, and they were devoted to each other. Ezzatdoleh, however, regarded the marriage as insufficiently lofty for Nosratdoleh, who was the apple of her eye. While Shazdeh was away on one of his assignments, she campaigned to make Nosratdoleh, who was only about seventeen, divorce his young cousin. As Iranian sons revere their mothers, after a year or so the youth became worn down by Ezzatdoleh's ceaseless hostility to his wife, and divorced her. Then, as was customary, he sent the poor girl, who loved him deeply and had just borne him a son, a boy named Mozaffar, back to her own family without her baby. Shazdeh took the infant under his protection and raised him as his own. But Najmeh-Saltaneh held him responsible for the divorce and her daughter's suffering and disgrace and never forgave him. Shazdeh, in turn, never forgave the meddling that had caused this rupture with his beloved sister. He and Ezzatdoleh became completely estranged.

Around 1911, however, Ezzatdoleh, who was by now in her middle thirties and thus of a rather advanced age for a Persian woman, fell ill with an ailment necessitating an operation, and Hadji Doktur Khan told her that any future resumption of physical relations with her husband would be medically undesirable.

Evidently this made my stepmother think. Perhaps she ought to try to mend the rift with Shazdeh. Though past fifty, he was still healthy, with a vigorous interest in what well-bred Iranians politely call "getting close." She herself could no longer bear children or offer him his conjugal rights even if she wanted to, and he would thus be morally as well as legally justified in taking a new wife. Furthermore, since Shazdeh was a pious Moslem and believed strongly that marriage was the proper context for sexual relations, he would probably do just that. It would be better if the new wife were someone Ezzatdoleh liked, and who would be in her debt—someone not highborn, so that she could not rival Ezzatdoleh in prestige. Moreover, she would have to be intelligent. My stepmother, who was quite an intelligent woman herself, knew that Shazdeh would never marry a fool.

One day, as the princess was being fitted for a dress by her seamstress, she noticed a young girl the seamstress had brought along. The girl, who was one of the dressmaker's apprentices, had warm, alert brown eyes and an endearing smile. Her appearance was pleasing rather than beautiful—an advantage, as far as my stepmother was concerned. Ezzatdoleh began questioning her and found that she liked her, for the child was devout, humble, and had a generous heart. At the same time she was observant, witty, and industrious.

The princess learned that her name was Massumeh and that she was twelve years old, had been apprenticed by her mother so that she would know how to put up a hem and do quilting when she was married, and though she could not read or write, had a little religious education, having been taught to recognize the Arabic words of Holy Koran. By a happy coincidence, Massumeh was also the eldest of the three daughters of the honest and devoted man who was Shazdeh's steward. Ezzatdoleh gave her dressmaker to understand that it would please her to see this lovely young girl the next time she summoned the woman to her home.

The princess became quite fond of my mother, and at last she approached Shazdeh. "Listen," she said, "if you want another wife, I've found a good one for you. She is extremely bright and I like her very much. If you want to marry her, you won't have any trouble from me."

My father, who knew a good offer when he heard one, was inclined to accept. He wanted harmony in the family again, and he also liked the notion of showing his affection for my grandfather. He sent a go-between to Aghajun. After the usual elaborate ceremonial compliments, which we Iranians call *ta'arof*, they got down to the real business at hand. At first, Aghajun did not want his daughter to marry Shazdeh. He venerated his employer, but princes were hardly famous for their fidelity or their respect for a woman's feelings. He bowed to the go-between and explained with much self-deprecation that he and his family were not worthy of this immense honor. He preferred to marry his daughter to someone of her own station.

"Look," said the go-between, "you've worked for this prince for a long time. He's an honorable man, not one of these shazdehs who just takes a virgin for one night and then abandons her, so that she has to become a prostitute to support herself and her baby. Farman Farma will always protect and care for your daughter, her children, and everyone else in her family—you can count on that."

Aghajun mulled this over for a while. Finally he went to my mother and gently asked her if she would consent to such a marriage. Divining that it was her father's wish that she do so, she at once bowed her head and said yes.

After that, harmony might have been restored to Shazdeh's first family but for the anger of two of Ezzatdoleh's six sons, who felt that Shazdeh was slighting both their mother and them by marrying again. One evening these sons visited Shazdeh in his mansion on the old family estate and delivered an ultimatum: if, after all this time, their father wished to remarry and beget a fresh mob of infants to diminish their inheritance and sweeten his old age—to "put bells on his coffin," as we say in Persian—he would have to do it someplace else. They didn't want the voices of this girl's children, and perhaps other women's later on, spilling over the walls of their villas and their mother's.

To these words, Khanom said, Shazdeh replied only with a cold and furious silence. Then, in a momentous decision, he turned disdainfully on his heel, cried "Ho!" to summon his servants, and strode out of the room. Commanding his valet to pack a bag, he sent for his carriage. When it arrived, he flung on his long cloak, marched out into the night, and drove away to another residence he owned—thereby bequeathing his great estate, with its many villas, its great garden, its priceless silk carpets, artworks, and jeweled plate, to the sole possession of Ezzatdoleh and her sons.

My twelve-year-old mother, newly married, soon found herself a far more powerless victim of her circumstances than Ezzatdoleh had been. My father had installed her in a summer cottage on a small piece of wooded land he owned in the Shah's Garden, and she quickly became pregnant. She knew nothing about this condition and had not a single competent adult woman to advise her, for she had not been married long before her mother died in a cholera epidemic that ravaged Tehran. Despite her anguished pleading, Shazdeh—who, to be fair, may have wished to keep his young wife from getting the disease—had arbitrarily refused to allow her to go and see her mother on her deathbed. (To the end of her days, Khanom never forgave my father for this.) Aghajun, helpless with shock and despair at his wife's death, had brought his eldest daughter her six- and nine-year-old sisters for her to raise. Then, suddenly, as she sat alone in her new household, pregnant, surrounded by strangers, and with two small sisters to care for, Shazdeh departed on a military assignment, for the country was disintegrating.

Despite the new, democratic form of government established in 1906, our country was still very much a feudalistic society, politically primitive and extremely unstable. Many of its important men were unused to considering the welfare of an abstract thing called a "nation," and, as we Persians say, thought only of themselves and the future of their families. No sooner had the liberal revolutionaries established the constitution as the fundamental law of the land in 1909 than the Majlis—our national assembly—and the new parliamentary cabinet fell to quarreling and dissension.

Meanwhile, the economy was in disarray from the civil war and years of mismanagement. By 1911, when my parents married, riots and street fighting had become common in Iran's cities, while in the countryside, where the cash-poor, armyless central government lacked any real means of keeping order, many of the country's fierce, powerful nomadic tribes were seizing the opportunity to take control of the provinces or to engage in unrestrained banditry. As if these things were not bad enough, that same year Russia and Britain, who had long been competing to dominate our impoverished but strategically important nation and the Persian Gulf, both seemed ready now to divide our tormented country between them. A brother of the deposed Mohammed Ali Shah, seeing a chance to make trouble, enlisted the Russians' help in fomenting a secession in Iran's western provinces, where the armies of the Ottoman Empire also loomed, a constant threat. The cabinet therefore appointed Shazdeh governor of these provinces and packed him off to raise an army and crush the rebellion, which was threatening to tear our already bleeding nation apart.

His young wife, who had just suffered the loss of a dearly loved parent and had only the dimmest idea of what was happening in the world outside her own small garden and in her changing body, was terrified at being without Shazdeh's protection and guidance. Three times, when she was growing up during the civil war, soldiers, ragged and hungry, had broken into their andarun and taken at gunpoint the rug she and her mother had been sitting on and the cups they had been drinking from. Now she knew nothing of the streets beyond her walls except that they were unsafe. Food was scarce and dear, and the small allowance Shazdeh's representative brought her every month was insufficient for her, her sisters, and Aghajun. The servants Shazdeh had sent her, eyeing her growing belly, constantly tried to blackmail her by threatening to leave if she did not give them more food and clothing. Every night she cried for her mother. When the baby, a boy, was born—Shazdeh sent word to call him "Sabbar"—she thought she was going to die.

After she had lived in this misery for a year, help arrived from an unexpected quarter: Ezzatdoleh, who had heard of the baby's birth and the plight of its mother, generously invited her and her small family to come and live in her own sumptuous quarters on Shazdeh's family estate. Now my mother no longer had to worry about food for herself and the children. But although she was better off, she was very lonely. She rarely saw her noble benefactress and had no one to confide her troubles in. Although the servants called her "Massumeh-Khanom," *Lady* Massumeh, they were cool to their mistress's supplanter. She had to take care not to let them or any partisans of Ezzatdoleh see how lonely and frightened she was. She had always been told that you should never trust people who weren't your relatives, and now she saw why: many of these highborn Persians and their servants, she discovered, pretended to feel what they did not feel. They often acted as though they liked you, or they promised to help you, but they didn't mean it at all. Their protestations were only ta'arof—false, insincere courtesies. On the other hand, when she, my devout, serious mother, promised that she would do something for someone, she always carried out her promise, for the liar is the enemy of God.

In 1915, when my mother was about sixteen and had been living in Ezzatdoleh's andarun for three years, Shazdeh, having quelled the secession in the west, returned to Tehran to take up a cabinet post again. Because the European war and the upheavals caused by the British and Russian occupations made his future plans uncertain, he thought it better for my mother and her family to continue on at Ezzatdoleh's; he could send for her when he wanted her company. But she was grateful just to have him back. And while he was away, Shazdeh had found her a present. He had taken another new wife, named Batul (as with the Kurdish bride, the marriage was to seal a political pact). Now he sent her to live at Ezzatdoleh's, too.

My mother was overjoyed. The new wife was a beautiful, statuesque girl only a couple of years older than herself. Batul-Khanom had already borne Shazdeh two enchantingly pretty little daughters, Maryam and Mehri, with whom my mother at once fell in love. Here at last was someone who was close to her own age, and in the same situation.

She quickly found that she had never known anyone even remotely like her new companion. Batul was from a modern, educated family in Kermanshah, a border city open to cosmopolitan influences. Not only could she read and write, but she even had a scrapbook with a collection of poems she liked. My mother, however, was disconcerted to find that there were things about the new wife that startled and shocked her. Khanom, as a proper Moslem, thought that above everything a woman had to be pious, serious, self-controlled, and reserved, whereas Batul-Khanom was by nature impulsive, openhearted, fun-loving, and volatile. Furthermore, she was as frivolous as a heathen—she absolutely refused to wear a chador—and spoiled her daughters shamelessly. What upset my mother most, however, was that the new wife made jokes about clergymen (or mullahs, as they are called in our country) and never said her prayers. To my mother, jokes about mullahs were the same as joking about religion itself, and she knew that Batul would go to hell for it. She could only hope that, as Islam taught that God sometimes forgave sinners if they repented and changed their ways, the Merciful and Compassionate would listen to the prayers she sent up every day and not take her new friend to hell before she realized her wickedness—not take her away at all, in fact.

For the first time in her serious, anxiety-ridden life, my mother had a companion her own age. She did not want to lose her. With Batul-Khanom there was someone with whom to sew, visit the baths, and enjoy the jokes, games, and clowning with which women entertained themselves in a big, fancy andarun like Ezzatdoleh's. My mother was too strict a Moslem to clown, but she enjoyed watching the others' horseplay, especially one of Ezzatdoleh's maids, who could paint her naked buttocks to look like two eyes and, dancing with them to the onlookers, would roll them so that the two eyes crossed. This made my mother, her little sisters, Batul and her daughters, and all the other women laugh until their sides ached. Above all, Batul's jokes and lightheartedness, so long as they were not about sacred things, could always make my earnest mother smile. With another young girl like herself to talk to, even her worries about money became less tormenting because there was someone to share them with.

My mother was equally good for Batul, who had her own problems. Above all, Batul-Khanom was extremely emotional. Women from modern middle-class families like hers were raised with somewhat more freedom than girls like my mother, and while my mother readily accepted the restricted life of an aristocratic woman, which was scarcely more confined than the way she herself had been raised, to Batul it was torture. Shazdeh would not let his young wives leave the andarun at all, not even to visit relatives. This did not much disturb my mother, who would have been appalled at the idea of going out into dangerous streets filled with strange men, but her soft heart was wrung by sympathy for Batul, whose wretchedness over her lost freedom expressed itself in tears and migraines that lasted for days. "I can't bear it," my stepmother would sob from the bed she always took to. "Why is Shazdeh so old-fashioned and cruel?"

When this happened, my mother would sit at her friend's side for hours, rinsing cold towels to lay on her brow, rubbing her forehead, and telling her that what happened to them must be God's way of teaching them to bear suffering with fortitude and patience, so that they could be better Moslems. Such advice always made Batul grumble, "Oh, you sound exactly like a mullah!" But whether it was the depth of my mother's rocklike religious faith or simply her profound compassion for anyone else's unhappiness, something about her always had a calming effect on Batul, as it did on everyone. Thus, despite their differences, they sustained each other, and amid the false, empty courtesies of Ezzatdoleh's andarun and the frightening prospect of losing Shazdeh again to some new assignment, the bond between them set like steel.

Shazdeh remained in Tehran for over a year, serving first as war minister and then as prime minister. All he could really do in this office at such a time was try to keep the country from falling apart until the situation somehow improved; however, during his tenure as Iran's premier he did manage to establish an Iranian ministry of health and gave land to create the Pasteur Institute of Iran, a public health institute whose first action was to introduce the smallpox vaccine, an effort that eventually saved the lives of millions of children. After three months he resigned from the premiership and in 1916 left Tehran again, this time for Shiraz and his second appointment as governor-general of Fars Province, which was near the Persian Gulf.

This area was in chaos, not only because of the central government's helplessness but because Fars was close to something of supreme importance to the Europeans and their war: oil. In 1901, backed by the British government, a canny Australian financier named William Knox D'Arcy had persuaded the Persian government to let him drill for oil in the southwest of Iran. Seven years later he made a strike, and the Anglo-Persian Oil Company was established.

The British company grew rapidly, and when war broke out in Europe in 1914, the British government realized that it was vital to ensure military control of the southwest of Iran and the oil supply— especially of wild Khuzistan, a province adjacent to Fars, where the English oil refineries and pipelines were located. The Germans, however, also understood the new importance of oil and were smuggling arms to the fierce coastal nomads to stir them up and make trouble for the British, while other tribesmen were preying on the caravan trade routes between Bushire on the Gulf and the cities of Shiraz and Isfahan.

To protect the pipelines, the British government had invested Shiraz with troops and had English officers train a force of Iranian recruits called the South Persia Rifles, led by General Percy Sykes, the British commander in the south. The British occupation had aroused anger and unrest in the province, while a famine had begun in the countryside. The Iranian government hoped that Shazdeh, whom the leading men of Shiraz remembered as a good and able governor from his first appointment, would be able to calm the resentful citizenry and somehow deal with the famine and the marauding tribes.

My father's most urgent task in Shiraz was to prevent the spread of the famine. He invited the town's leading citizens to the governor's palace, and in a magnificent speech suggested that they help him and his men pool the food supply and organize its distribution to the destitute to save the province from starvation. The idea of a community's organizing in such a way to save itself from disaster was a revolutionary concept in Iran, where help only came by chance to people in trouble, either through alms or the kindness of some rich protector. My father's speech galvanized the landlords, merchants, and leading mullahs of Shiraz, and in a short time they organized Iran's first agricultural cooperative and averted the famine.

To ensure his acceptance by the Shirazis, my father also took a wife from one of the leading families and raised an all-Iranian regiment to patrol the roads and oil pipelines on condition that the British, as was customary, reimburse and pay him for the protection. This, he knew, would take the teeth out of some of the opposition to the occupying forces, while his marriage would encourage the citizenry to trust their new governor. For his valuable military assistance General Sykes, in his famous *History of Persia*, refers to Shazdeh as "my friend," praises his great diplomatic skills, and calls him "one of the ablest men in Iran." Shazdeh's cooperation, however, wasn't an act of sympathy, merely a good example of how Iranians had survived for centuries— by remaining flexible and driving the best bargain possible with fate. Although my father was a well-known Anglophile, he had no more invited the British to occupy our country in the south than he had the Russians in the north. He wanted to keep order, and to spare his province as much suffering as possible. As for the postwar plans of the British for Iran and its oil, my father knew quite well that the only choice fate would give Iranians would be to guess which of the powerful victors would be the best ally for our war-ravaged nation when the fighting was over, and he preferred English foxes to German boars or Russian wolves.

Before his departure for Shiraz my mother had given birth to my older sister Jaby, while Batul had borne her first son, Manucher. My father therefore did not send for them until the war's end. Even in 1919, travel was still extremely dangerous, since the three hundred miles of desert road between Tehran and Shiraz were infested with bandits and nomads lurking in wait for poorly defended caravans. When the two women set out for Shiraz under the close supervision of Shazdeh's chamberlain with their children and my grandfather Aghajun, mounted on horses and donkeys and accompanied by nearly fifty porters, tent bearers, and armed cavalrymen, they were terrified.

Luckily, they reached Shiraz safely and there began making the acquaintance of my father's new wife. Fatimeh-Khanom was neither as lively and amusing as Batul nor as perceptive as my mother; instead she was quiet, timid, and plain, a follower rather than a leader. However, my mother and stepmother discovered that she always jogged along amiably with anything the two of them wanted to do, and my mother was cheered to find that Fatimeh-Khanom was a daughter of one of the town's wealthy mullahs, and therefore just as old-fashioned and devout as she. Now she had an ally—even if not a very brave one—whenever she felt constrained to gently chide Batul for one of her irreligious jokes.

My mother wondered if life might finally be taking a turn for the better. She humbly thanked the Merciful and Compassionate for safely reuniting them with Shazdeh and sending her and Batul their new friend. Batul, who could read the newspapers, pointed out that because of the war and all the other disruptions, the national government in Tehran was nearly out of money and was paying the civil servants with bricks from the rubble of old buildings. But my mother felt that she had to trust in God's will and hope for the best. Maybe, now that the foreigners' war was over, the *englis-ha* and *russ-ha* would tell their soldiers to leave Iran, and some way could be found to pull our country together. Then, perhaps, Shazdeh would take his harem back to Tehran and build them a real home there, and she and Batul and Fatimeh could settle down and raise their children together in peace. If all this turmoil were over, the roads might even become safe enough for her and Fatimeh to make a pilgrimage to the holy shrines at Qom or Mashad, if Shazdeh let them. She longed for security at last, for herself and the country. She wanted to stop wondering what new troubles God was going to send her next.

Early in 1921, when my father had resided in Shiraz for four years, he received a wire ordering him back to Tehran, where a new post awaited him. He decided to go on ahead and buy some land and houses on Sepah Avenue, next to the old family estate where Ezzat-doleh and their sons lived, so that his new families would finally have quarters of their own when they returned. He would live with them in the new compound whenever he was not on an assignment. Fortunately, his replacement was not only a nephew, the only son of his sister Najmeh-Saltaneh, but was also a close friend of Shazdeh's; his name was Dr. Mohammed Mossadegh. Shazdeh waited until the new governor arrived. Then, leaving his harem under Dr. Mossadegh's protection, about the beginning of February he set off for Tehran.

Suddenly, one morning late in February, an alarming telegram arrived at the governor's palace, asking that Fatimeh be sent to the safety of her father's home at once and that my father's chamberlain assemble a caravan to bring my mother, Batul, and their families as soon as possible to Tehran, where my father felt he could protect them better. There had been a coup d'état in the capital, led by a man to whom Shazdeh himself had given his start.

I suppose one could say that the Pahlavi dynasty, which finally brought real order to Iran, might never have existed if my father hadn't needed someone big and strong to carry his machine gun. Around 1907 or 1908, he had acquired a new German Maxim for use against the Ottoman Turks. Since it was heavy, he recalled a huge, illiterate sergeant by the name of Reza Khan, who had been serving in his household guard. Reza Khan (the name means simply "Master Reza")

was a scowling, iron-jawed man from a northern mountain village called Alasht. He was withdrawn and held himself aloof from the other men. But he was a brave soldier and others admired his bluntness and great courage. He was also six feet three inches tall, and Iranians fear and respect anything big. Shazdeh made him an officer and gave him the machine gun. After that, the giant northerner was known in my father's army as "Reza Khan-i-Maximi": Machine-Gun Reza.

Over the next thirteen or fourteen years, Reza Khan advanced slowly but steadily as a field commander under my father and as an officer in the royal Persian Cossacks, the palace guard, Iran's only national regiment. Men feared him but followed him into battle. As an officer he distinguished himself both for his bravery and for dealing out severe, humiliating punishments for cowardice or dishonesty. He was a shrewd strategist but an icy, suspicious, saturnine man with a savage temper. He had no real friends or confidants. No one knew what he was thinking, or realized yet that the desire to make Iran a strong, respected nation again, a nation that foreign invaders like the British and Russians could not bully, had seized his imagination just as the desire for education and social progress had seized my father and other enlightened men of the aristocracy. Reza Khan was on fire with ambition for himself and Iran.

Late in 1920, with the provinces still in disorder and the influence of the new Soviet Union appearing to be gaining in the north, the British government decided that it must act immediately to elbow out the Russians and ensure England a firm hold on our country. Aware that an army was the only real guarantee of power in Iran, London dispatched General Edmund Ironside, a famous soldier who had fought recently against the Bolsheviks to find a promising candidate for the role of puppet military dictator. Canvassing the ranks of the Persian Cossacks, Ironside noticed how Reza Khan, by now a colonel, towered over his short fellow officers. The story goes that General Ironside immediately pointed to Reza and said to his aide, "That's the man I want."

So it was that Reza Khan, elevated to the rank of general for the occasion, rode into Tehran with three thousand men in the small hours of February 21, 1921. Meeting with no resistance, he arrested the entire cabinet, forced the frightened young Ahmad Shah to appoint him commander of the armed forces, and installed as prime minister an opportunistic but liberal journalist named Sayyid Ziya Tabatabai, a man who had been pro-royalist during the civil war, pro-German during the European war, and was presently pro-British.

I don't think that Shazdeh, when he heard the news, worried much about Reza Khan, who had no reason to hate him. Sayyid Ziya, however, was another matter. The new premier had once printed a series of scurrilous articles about my father, and Shazdeh, who was normally unusually tolerant of press criticism, had been convinced that Sayyid Ziya only wanted to extort hush money from him. He had threatened the journalist with a flogging and imprisonment and then had him thrown bodily out of the house (my father was never one for half measures).

Now that Sayyid Ziya was prime minister, on the lofty pretext of purging the government of corruption he was arresting every Qajar noble against whom he had a grudge. He at once detained Shazdeh's first son, Nosratdoleh, who had recently served as Iran's foreign minister, and also his second son, Salar-Lashgar, a wealthy and important general, and locked them both up in the prison of Qaser-e-Qajar.

Shazdeh, having sent his wire to Shiraz, decided to go to Reza Khan's headquarters and plead for his sons' release. When my father was announced, Reza Khan jumped to his feet and told the guard to admit his old commander at once. But Sayyid Ziya was there as well, and he immediately ordered my father arrested. Shazdeh was sent to the Qaser-e-Qajar to join his sons. Having imprisoned more than sixty members of the government, Sayyid Ziya then set his agents to hunt down other men of the Qajar family. Shazdeh learned that his third son, Mohammed Vali Mirza, was also in danger of capture. But there was nothing he could do.

By now I had made my appearance in the world, probably a month or two before Shazdeh left Shiraz for Tehran. My mother said that I was colicky and screamed for all of the nearly three weeks it took our caravan to reach the first resting place, Isfahan, a hundred and fifty miles north of Shiraz. There, one of my father's cousins, a prince named Saremdoleh, installed us in lodgings on his estate and, after giving us several days to recover from the exhausting journey, broke the news to my mother and Batul that Shazdeh and his sons Nosrat-doleh and Salar-Lashgar were in prison.

My mother and stepmother were distraught. Sayyid Ziya had wired the Isfahan constabulary to confiscate all the private papers and valuables carried by the chamberlain who had escorted us to Isfahan, and we were now stranded. Thanks to Saremdoleh's kindness we had food and the basic necessities of life, but no means of support. If Shazdeh and his sons remained in prison for years, our mothers and ten others— I, my eldest brother Sabbar, and my four-year-old sister Jaby; my mother's two sisters and Aghajun; Batul's daughters Maryam and

Mehri, her son Manucher, and her new little son Aziz, who had been born ten days after me—would have to depend indefinitely on the charity of Saremdoleh. But their worst fears were for Shazdeh himself. Our mothers all loved Shazdeh deeply. He was the wisest man they had ever known, and the most just. They were in anguish at the thought of his suffering. "He's an old man," my mother would groan. "How can they treat him this way? Suppose he gets sick in a cold cell and dies?" Batul beat her breast, wailing and lamenting the disrespect and cruelty of Reza Khan and Sayyid Ziya to their aged and distinguished husband. In later years, whenever she talked to us of these three months, my mother's voice would always choke with tears.

All during this time, I had been driving her crazy with my constant squalling. As the dreadful weeks dragged on and her anxiety over Shazdeh's fate mounted, her milk dried up. Batul, who was as frightened as my mother was, had fallen ill with a high fever, but she had plenty of milk. Khanom would bring me to her room and lay me on the quilt beside my stepmother, and I would suck greedily at one of her breasts while my brother Aziz tugged at the other.

My mother would watch this, then sigh with all the weight of her accumulated woes. "Look at her," she would exclaim. "This one's not like my quiet Jaby—she does nothing but cry! That's not the way a girl should be, always yelling and putting herself forward. Believe me, this one's going to give me trouble."

After all the sad and frightening experiences she had been through, and in the terrible uncertainty of the future, my refusal to be silent battered my mother's nerves and entangled itself even with her prayers. Her favorite proverb had always been "He who gave you teeth will give you bread." She believed and trusted in God completely, and this thought had always steadied her before. But my mother, strong though she was, had had to cope with too many changes in her young life. Now, before the awful possibility that Shazdeh might die, she felt close to breaking at last, and my incessant howling must have seemed the final straw. I, this headstrong, willful female child, had unwisely made my arrival in a time of what Iranians call *harj-o-marj*.

There is no English equivalent for this word. It is a very Persian word, and suggests the worst thing that can happen to a nation. It expresses the condition of a country that falls into anarchy because its leaders cannot unite and no strong hand holds it together, or because foreign conquerors have come; the time when it slides into the abyss of lawlessness and rapine, looting, and slaughter reign. I was the yelling embodiment of chaos, the bawling distillation of my mother's anxiety and pain. In my howling she must have heard not only the helpless egotism of infant hunger, but a cry reminding her of all that she and millions of other ordinary Iranians had suffered for the past fifteen years: powerlessness, terror, and the constant, all-consuming fear that comes when people cannot be certain that a month or a year from now they will still be alive.

Meanwhile, in his prison room in Tehran, my father, who for perhaps the first time in more than sixty years was feeling as helpless as his wives, wondered desperately how to warn his third son to hide. No one could enter or leave the grounds without being searched down to his undergarments, and in any case, Shazdeh's contacts were limited to his jailers and to the illiterate youths who hung about the prison, hoping for work doing chores for prisoners with some money, like Shazdeh. However, he had become friendly with a burly, sweet-tempered country boy of about nineteen named Mashad-Hossein—"Mashti" for short. Shazdeh was paying Mashti, who lived with relatives outside the prison, a few pennies a day to bring him tea and sweep out his chamber. Mashti was simple but he was shrewd, honest, and industrious, and Shazdeh had taken a liking to him.

Now, seeing no other way, Shazdeh decided to trust Mashti. He asked him to smuggle out an important written message—whose contents Mashti, of course, was unable to read—and deliver it to Shazdeh's chief of staff in Tehran. One day, Shazdeh promised, he would reward Mashti for this service. Mashti, overwhelmed by the confidence this great and famous prince was reposing in a nobody like himself, promised to try.

This took courage, for he and Shazdeh both knew that he would be executed if he were caught. But Mashti was resourceful as well as simple. He took the piece of paper Shazdeh gave him and tied it around his private parts with some string. It passed through the inspection unnoticed and was in the hands of Shazdeh's chief of staff that evening. My father's third son was warned of his danger and went into hiding in time.

By May, however, Reza Khan had decided that he could dispense with Sayyid Ziya. It seemed that the journalist had annoyed him and horrified the British by arresting too many highly placed Qajars, without whose help Reza Khan, who knew little about government, could not expect to run the country or bring it under control. Besides, Reza, who had struggled to teach himself to read and write after his first promotion under my father, appeared not to trust men like Sayyid Ziya, who used a lot of fancy words. Reza Khan made the weak young Shah appoint him war minister and, one hundred days after the coup,

Sayyid Ziya, having been "invited" by Reza Khan to resign, went off to live in British Palestine. Shortly after that, Reza Khan had Shazdeh, Nosratdoleh, and Salar-Lashgar released from the Qaser-e-Qajar.

My father at once sent for the boy whose courage had saved his third son from prison, and made Mashti a servant in his household. He also began arranging to send my eldest brother, Sabbar, who was now old enough to go abroad, to school in Paris, where he would be safe. Although it was months before Shazdeh was able to complete the new compound he had begun organizing before his arrest, finally he had us all brought to Tehran, and established us in our new home. When everyone had settled in, he hired a teacher to give classes in reading and writing to my mother, Fatimeh, and the womenservants in the garden of my mother's new house, and sent Mashti (for whom he picked out a pretty young wife, Korsum, a niece of one of his old cavalrymen) to guard our gatehouse and be my laleh.

My father now had plenty of leisure to contemplate the significance of this abrupt new turn in our country's history, especially its significance for him and his children. Iran's new leader had placed him under permanent house arrest—for the remainder of his life, he would require police permission merely to visit his own country house in the nearby Shemiran hills. Reza Khan had let him off lightly because he needed the cooperation of Shazdeh and men like Nosratdoleh and Salar-Lashgar. But Shazdeh did not think that the ambitious soldier would stop with being war minister. At some point he would be able to do as he pleased, and then he would no longer need the help of the haughty, educated, fine-spoken men of the Qajar nobility, men he did not trust. Furthermore, Iran's new de facto ruler had made do with soldier's pay for years, and my father must have been fairly certain that like any strongman Reza Khan would view power as a license to help himself to other people's wealth—in fact he had already begun, confiscating the Rolls-Royce in which Nosratdoleh had been riding when he was arrested.

Shazdeh's fears gradually proved correct. In 1923, Ahmad Shah Qajar, at the request of the Majlis, appointed Reza prime minister and left the country for France, never to return. Two years later, the Majlis proposed a bill to end the Qajar dynasty and give the former gunnery officer dictatorial powers. Only five deputies dared protest that to give the prime minister supreme power would undermine Iran's young parliamentary democracy and, for all practical purposes, return the country to despotism. The arguments of these brave deputies, whose spokesman was Shazdeh's nephew Dr. Mossadegh, had no effect. Reza Khan, having taken the surname of "Pahlavi" from an old Persian word, crowned himself Reza Shah in the spring of 1926 and took his seat on the Peacock Throne. Beside him at the coronation stood his six-year-old son, Shapour Mohammed Reza, the first crown prince of the Pahlavi dynasty, and at the four corners of the base of the throne platform, in symbolic subjection, stood the leading men of the Qajar nobility, including Nosratdoleh. One hundred forty-seven years of Qajar rule were officially at an end.

I am sure that Shazdeh took this with philosophical resignation. Persian princes generally did, and in any case Shazdeh wasn't the sort of man to sit around and waste time hoping that somebody bigger than Reza Shah would come along and turn back the Qajars' clock for them. The carpet pattern of Persian history has many such sharp, twisting corners, and for all of those three thousand years, no fallen dynasty has ever returned to the throne.

Almost immediately, Shazdeh received a message from the new monarch, requesting that he join several other Qajar noblemen in "donating" his family estate to the crown in order that Reza Shah might build a royal palace and garden for himself on their property. Although Ezzatdoleh, Nosratdoleh, Salar-Lashgar, and Shazdeh's other adult sons still had their homes on the old estate, my father knew better than to protest. It would be all too easy for anyone, including an avaricious servant, to go to the police and say that my father and his sons were plotting to overthrow the new ruler. Shazdeh at once turned over his land with its great homes and superb gardens to Reza Shah and moved the bereft, hysterical Ezzatdoleh with as many of her servants and possessions as he could into a much smaller house. It was next door to ours, just on the other side of the compound wall.

Shazdeh was now almost seventy, and afflicted with gout, arthritis, and insomnia. He had spent his entire life in his country's service. Almost overnight, he had been shorn of his rank, much of his wealth, and his freedom. But he was above all a practical man, whose mind was always on how to solve a problem and make the best of a situation. What was past was past, and he always looked forward. Countless people depended on him for survival, and now he had to think about his younger children's education.

He decided that he didn't want his younger sons going into politics, like Nosratdoleh and his other older boys. Politics was no longer safe for the Qajars. Besides, Shazdeh had seen that a new order was dawning. Whether people liked it or not, Reza Shah Pahlavi was showing that he intended by any means to wrench Iran out of its sleep of centuries and into the modern world. The country was going to need Western-style professionals and industrialists to carry it into the new era: doctors, engineers, architects, economists, builders. That was what Shazdeh's younger sons would be, Persian gentlemen and at the same time men who need not depend on how the political winds blew. And his daughters would all have the kind of education that would make them good, capable wives for men just like their brothers.

With education, we, his younger children, might all be able to weather the storms that would surely come to Iran after he was gone, as they had always come. He had to teach us not to dwell on the past, but to look beyond it, to rely on ourselves and not on who our father was. Hope, his and ours and the nation's, lay in progress and in the education of human beings, and Shazdeh set his face toward that.

As far as I know, he never looked back.

3

THE AMERICAN SCHOOL

The king [of Iran] may do what he pleases; his word is law.
—Lord Curzon, *Persia and the Persian Question*, 1892

*I*N THE FALL OF 1933, WHEN I WAS TWELVE AND ABOUT TO BEGIN high school, "My Cousin" closed Tarbiat, the elementary school to which Mashti had escorted me and Farough and our half brothers every day, and which I had loved.

Tarbiat, which was run by the Bahais, offered an education emphasizing the Bahai faith's practices of tolerance and kindness to others. Shazdeh, who had nothing whatever against the Bahais, had sent us to Tarbiat because it was close to the compound. However, although several Moslem gentlemen, friends of my father's, also had children there, Tarbiat was an unconventional choice of school for a nobleman of his standing (not that this bothered Shazdeh, who was above such considerations). All the servants, even Mashti, whose daughter Leila had attended Tarbiat with us, approved of the Shah's closing the school. Normally, Iranians are a forbearing people, becoming intolerant only when someone manages to persuade them that their beloved Islam is in danger. But to our servants, being a Bahai was even worse than being an unbeliever, for the mullahs said that the Bahais, whose founder had originally been a Persian Moslem, were heretics who had abandoned Islam and rejected religion; sometimes they even incited ordinary people like servants to assault or murder Bahais. Nargess, my thin, plain nursemaid, who had been with me since I was a baby and whom I loved dearly, muttered that the king must have closed my school because the noise the Bahais made when they prayed offended even *his* wicked ears.

I, on the other hand, had heard that the Shah had shut it down because one day he noticed that Tarbiat, which was not far from his new Marble Palace—built on the other side of Kakh Avenue on the Qajar estates he had confiscated from my father and others in 1926— was closed for a Bahai holiday. The Shah, who was a demon for work, never took a day off, and since no one was allowed to take a holiday unless he did, too, he had decided to give the offenders a permanent holiday. I accepted this reason as the true one. For one thing, it sounded just like Reza Shah. For another, the prayers we said every day at school were so beautiful that I didn't see how anyone could hate them. But I knew enough not to tell Nargess and our other servants how much I liked the Bahais' prayers.

I had also loved Tarbiat partly because it was so different from Khanom's pious household. Where women were concerned, our religion was extremely strict. For instance, because my mother didn't want to encourage the display of female flesh, the only dresses she sewed for us were ugly, tight-fitting, long-sleeved frocks that were terribly hot in summer—I always gazed enviously at the lace collars and three-quarter-length muttonchop sleeves of the pretty dresses that Batul-Khanom, who loved the latest fashion in anything, sewed for her daughter Mehri, but my mother thought that Mehri's short sleeves were wicked because they revealed her naked forearms. My mother was quite the opposite of cruel; she was always giving food, money, and clothing to the servants' poor relatives and to destitute beggars, who would have starved without the charity of devout people like her. As both she and my father taught us, the great purpose of Islam (which in Iran is represented mainly by the Shi'a, the Moslems who owe spiritual allegiance to the martyrs Imam Ali and Imam Hossein, Prophet Mohammed's son-in-law and grandson, and whom Western-ers have lately learned to call "Shiites") was to help the poor and weak. But she was so severe with her daughters that we could not dance, sing, or even laugh aloud, lest our voices be heard by men outside in the biruni. If I giggled in her presence, she would say sharply, "Stop that—you're a girl! Do you want Mashti to hear that shameless noise?" At Tarbiat, on the other hand, girls had not only been permitted to dance and sing, but even to pray aloud, just as men did. I had reveled in doing things that my mother, had I been so indiscreet as to tell her about them, would have considered immodest enough to rate a sound beating.

Of course, even though the servants approved of Tarbiat's closing, everyone in the compound hated Reza Shah because of his injustices to Shazdeh. Often when it was too hot to work or play, one of our lalehs would sit down under the trees with a crowd of children and servants around him and chant stirring, hypnotic couplets from our Persian national epic, Ferdowsi's *Book of Kings*—about how the giant hero Rostam battled Iran's foreign oppressors, or how the blacksmith Kaveh, an ordinary Iranian, led his fellow citizens to rebel against the monstrous tyrant Zahak, who had tormented the people with many unjust acts. I would listen raptly. Reza Shah had imprisoned Shazdeh and his sons and seized his estate, and now he had closed my school. The longing for justice is inborn in Persians, who have suffered from so many foreign conquerors and homegrown tyrants; Imam Hossein himself, the Prophet's young grandson, was martyred, so we learned, because he had risen to fight a great injustice done to him and his family by a tyrant. Though I knew better than to say so aloud, I yearned to do the same.

Actually, Reza Shah hadn't closed Tarbiat because the Bahais had taken the day off, nor even, probably, because he particularly disliked the Bahais. The king was simply hell-bent on remaking Iran in the image of an advanced nation, and part of his notion of how to do this was to reduce the influence of religion in our country—*all* religion. Hell, in fact, was precisely where the servants and my mother knew Reza Shah was headed, for he was systematically eroding the power and prestige of Iran's mullahs.

In the years since the coup, Reza had moved gradually but ruthlessly to bring the country to order. Realizing that his power depended on a strong military, he had established and organized Iran's first standing army and used it to bring both the rebellious tribes and the Majlis under his control. To encourage a spirit of cooperation with the central government, he ordered a famous rebel's head placed on exhibit in Tehran. The troops he sent to the provinces crushed revolts, mutinies, and uprisings, killed bandits, slaughtered Kurds and Lurs, Qashqa'is and Baluchis. Reza Shah took the tribes' guns away, forbade them to migrate, drafted their young men into his army, confiscated their chieftains' lands, spread dissension among them, and had several of their leaders murdered. His soldiers also "supervised" the national elections so that only deputies hand-picked by Reza Shah and his cabinet ministers, whom the king himself selected, could be sent to parliament. Thus the Majlis gradually became no more than a rubber stamp for the measures the Shah wanted passed. Little by little he destroyed Iran's fledgling political parties, abolished independent newspapers, and banned trade unions. His generals reported directly to him—naturally Reza Shah had made himself the supreme commander of the Iranian military—and these men bowed before his ferocious temper in fear and trembling.

Having made considerable headway toward establishing his government's claim to authority, Reza began laying the foundations for enforcing it. He ordered all citizens to take last names and be registered with a new national registry office. He passed a law compelling every young Iranian male to enlist for two years of military service. At least in theory, all Iranian children, male and female, were now required to go to school, so that they could hear about the glories of the vanished Persian Empire and learn to be loyal, patriotic citizens of the equally glorious new Pahlavi state. (Reza Shah tried to emulate rulers who thought as he did, such as Mussolini.) In the provinces the Shah built roads, telegraph lines, and, with the help of German engineers, a splendidly ambitious trans-Iranian railway linking the capital with remote towns and provinces. For the first time in Iran's history, the central government was becoming physically able to exert real power over the vast and wild rural areas of Iran, and merchants, pilgrims, and others who traveled on the roads discovered that under Reza Shah the roads were safer than they had ever been. People agreed that although the new ruler had a heavy hand, he had accomplished something no one else had: he had converted anarchy into order.

Reza Shah was eager to reclaim Iran's lost greatness. Unfortunately, it was obvious from a walk through any neighborhood in the capital, including the Shah's Garden, that we had a long way to go before he did. Tehran was really just an overgrown version of the remote, disease-ridden village it had been in the eighteenth century, when the first Qajar shah decided to make it his dynasty's capital. By the 1930s, when I was growing up, it had nearly a quarter of a million people— this in a land of tiny villages of forty or a hundred families, and with a population so thinly scattered that a city of thirty thousand was like a metropolis. Yet despite its size, most of Tehran was still a sprawling mud-brick town of mazy, crooked streets too narrow for any traffic but wagons, mules, and camels. In the alleys, children splashed and played in the deep running gutters or *jubes*, which served the common people equally as wash troughs, toilets, and drinking fountains. The air was dazed with smoke from the thousands of dung fires over which the poor of the districts south and east of the old bazaar cooked their small daily portions of rice. The stench of urine and excrement was ever present.

And always, too, there was the age-old smell of waterless dust, as if the azure heaven and thirsty earth of Persia were there to remind everyone how unreliable life was, and that in Iran, no day was ever certain but the desert's. Peddlers selling hairpins or pistachios or charms for a penny roamed the filthy streets, along with itinerant hucksters in cone-shaped hats, patchwork cloaks, and long matted hair who called themselves Dervishes and offered to recite a poem or cure baldness for a few rials. Professional beggars, both men and women, crouched by the walls or on the steps of public buildings, emaciated, disfigured, and diseased, to dun passersby for alms. Ordinary working people, too, lived precariously, concerning themselves like the beggars and the hucksters only with their family's next meal and with wrenching from each uncertain day whatever small advantage or pleasure could be extorted from it.

Reza Shah, however, was determined to change this image of a shiftless, fatalistic nation in which the sons of Darius the Great, their age of glory forgotten, wallowed in medieval superstition, indolence, and poverty, letting the Russians and British treat them with contempt. The king wanted progress, and to him, progress meant a secular, Western-style society furnished with solid accomplishments that you could see and touch and measure: buildings, paved roads, railways, schools, and tourist hotels—the sorts of things you found in the West. Instead of ragged beggars sitting before the gates of picturesque mosques, Iran must have automobiles, paved avenues, and marble buildings that would rival the capitals of Europe. Even before his coronation, Reza had torn down the Tehran city walls, as if removing these backward-looking old sentinels would allow progress to come crashing through Persia like a wild boar tearing up a thicket. Laborers, supply wagons, the thudding of sledgehammers, and the ringing of pickaxes were everywhere in the Shah's Garden and the other fashionable parts of the city.

The king was quite prepared to send Iranians to drink from the well of Western-style progress at gunpoint, if necessary, and to do that he had, among other things, set out to break religion's hold over the common people, as Atatürk was doing next door in Turkey. This meant reducing the power of our loosely organized Shiite clergy. In Iran, clerics did not usually become directly involved in politics, but they had always wielded enormous influence, not only among the rich merchants and tradesmen of the bazaar but over all ordinary people. Every neighborhood, rich or poor, had its mosque, however grand or tiny, and every mosque had a mullah sitting in it. Mullahs, whether they were unlettered rustics or lofty ayatollahs (this meant "Sign of God," and was the highest degree of religious learning to which a Shiite cleric could aspire), presided over every important aspect of life, from births and marriages to funerals and memorial services. They even decided everyday questions of civil and criminal justice, dispensing their rulings according to Islamic law. Many Iranians made jokes about mullahs, but in times of injustice the people regarded them as their spokesmen.

Reza Shah knew, as did everyone, that if enough popular mullahs got really angry and preached against the government from their Friday pulpits, they could ignite demonstrations, general strikes, and even riots in the bazaar. The constitutional revolution of 1906 itself had started in the Tehran bazaar, triggered by events following the arrest of a fiery mullah who had denounced the government's tyranny.

The Shah, therefore, had begun moving to weaken the clergy as soon as he had become king. He had infuriated the mullahs by passing new legislation that took control of civil justice away from them and Islamic law, and placed it under a modern, secular legal code and in the hands of the ministry of justice. He enraged them still further by confiscating the lands of many wealthy religious foundations. His gendarmes and soldiers ignored the ancient custom of allowing criminals and escaped rebels to take sanctuary in the courtyards of the great shrines. He also banned long-standing religious traditions which, in his view, made us look barbarous and ignorant, such as especially pious men's custom of slashing their heads with razor-sharp swords and knives during the emotional flagellation processions for the Ashura festival in the Moslem month of Moharram, when all Shi'a mourned the martyrdom of Imam Hossein. This act had outraged the bazaaris as well as the mullahs, because such activities were very important to the devout men of the bazaar.

The Shah had even forbidden Iranian men to appear in public without a new type of headgear, which he called the "Pahlavi cap." This was a rimless cap that my father had originally designed, probably when he was war minister, and which had been known as "the Farman-Farma cap." Reza Shah stuck a visor on it, which some people insisted was to prevent men from touching their foreheads to the ground as required during prayers, so that they couldn't pray in public. This, religious people believed, was just one more proof that the Shah's real goal was to trample on religion and keep the mullahs from opposing him.

Now, my father was always careful to show respect to clerics, especially learned and enlightened ones, whose conversation he enjoyed. As an experienced politician, he knew very well the prestige the clergy enjoyed among the powerful and orthodox bazaar merchants, and the mullahs' influence over ordinary people in general. Besides, as a sensible man he knew there was no point in getting on God's bad side. My mother, on the other hand, venerated mullahs, though the way Shazdeh limited our mothers' movements gave her scant opportunity to meet many. She was horrified by Reza Shah's attacks on men who were God's spokesmen and the representatives of religion. She always bowed low to the portly, bearded, dignified Ashekh-Javad (this means "Reverend Javad") who was in charge of the mosque that Shazdeh's mother had built and endowed, and who often came to Shazdeh's house to dine with my father and discuss mosque business. Whenever Shazdeh asked her to send over some special dish because Ashekh-Javad was there for lunch, she always put more meat and butter on the rice than she did at any other time. We children had to be absolutely silent in Ashekh-Javad's presence, and I could tell that my mother, who always wore her black chador when she went to the mosque to hear him preach, was in awe of him. Like every sheltered, pious Shiite woman, she believed that all mullahs were highly spiritual men of stainless purity, sternly aloof from worldly matters and immune to sin. She was always saying to my stepmothers when there were no servants about that this godless Shah would be punished for what he was doing to religion.

"You must admit," Batul-Khanom would reply mischievously, "that Reza Shah, bad as he is, has at least made it safe for you to travel on pilgrimage to Qom or Mashad if you want. By the way," she would continue, with a wicked gleam in her eye that always made me look forward to what was coming next, "don't you think that Ashekh-Javad is looking very well lately? He must have eaten up all of Shazdeh's Yazdi cookies at lunch last week."

Everyone, even religious Iranians, poked fun at the greed and the voracious appetites of many mullahs, and I think my mother knew pretty well that Ashekh-Javad was a glutton. But although she had a delightful sense of humor, nothing could have induced her to encourage flippant gossip about a man of religion, especially in front of her children. She glanced down at her sewing in silence. "Do you know," my stepmother would continue, her face deadpan, "how to cause the death of a mullah? Have three different rich men invite him to lunch on the same day."

"Batul-Khanom," Fatimeh-Khanom would say warningly, "God will be angry with you."

"Fearing God and saying your prayers, Batul-Khanom," my mother would answer with dignity, "would do you more good than telling hoary old jokes. Or better still, come with the rest of us to the mosque at Ramazan and hear Ashekh-Javad's sermon."

At this it would be my volatile stepmother's turn to plunk down her tea glass and get angry. "Oh, I can't stand it!" she would explode. "Can't you see that those men only care about stuffing themselves at the tables of people like Shazdeh and gobbling up poor families' funeral mites? Go away, go away—you and your mullahs!"

In September of 1933, Mashti began escorting me to the new school Shazdeh had picked out for me: the American School for Girls in the Presbyterian missionary compound, two or three miles from our home on Sepah Avenue.

Like Tarbiat, the American School was not the most obvious place for a prominent nobleman to send his daughter. Nobody, including my father, really knew anything about America, and Jaby, Batul's daughters Maryam and Mehri, and Fatimeh's daughter Mahssy had all attended the French lycée. As usual, however, my father hadn't consulted anyone about his decision. I guessed that he had decided to send me to the American school because of his great affection for Doctors MacDowell and Blair, the directors of the American Mission Hospital in Tehran, which the Presbyterian mission had started to serve the poor, and because of the excellent reputation of the American school, which was run by Dr. Samuel M. Jordan, the Presbyterian mission's educational director.

In those days there were no more than a few dozen Americans in Tehran, mostly missionaries like Dr. Jordan and his medical colleagues. These people and the small American embassy and consular staffs were vastly outnumbered by Russians, Englishmen, Germans, and other Europeans, and their remote country was so far away that Iranians usually referred to it as *yengeh donya*, "the land at the end of the earth." Nevertheless, Americans were regarded with nearly universal affection and admiration by enlightened men like my father. The American contribution to the improvement and, it was felt, the dignity of our impoverished, strife-torn country had gone far beyond their small numbers.

In 1911, for example, a young American financial expert named W. Morgan Shuster had come to Iran at the request of the Iranian government to try to bring our country's economic chaos under control.

Knowing nothing of Iran but moved by the plight of the poor, illiterate people he saw, Shuster had tried to dictate various financial reforms, and when the Russians, whose interests he threatened, drove him out by invading northern Iranian cities and massacring civilians there, he went home and wrote an impassioned memoir about England's and Russia's ruthless behavior toward Iran; it was called *The Strangling of Persia*, and became an international classic in the history of the Middle East. Then, eight years after Shuster left, an American president made himself an Iranian national hero. In 1919, before the Paris Peace Conference at Versailles, Iran had tried to claim war damages on account of the British and Russian occupation, but the English had prevented this by arguing that Iran, as a neutral nation, had not been an official participant in the war and was therefore not entitled to war damages. President Woodrow Wilson, who indignantly protested this hypocrisy, had been the only member of the conference to take Iran's part.

But it was Presbyterian missionaries like Dr. MacDowell, Dr. Blair, and Dr. Jordan who made the greatest impression on us. Without attempting to force their way of life on people or convert us to their religion, they had learned Persian and started schools, hospitals, and medical dispensaries all over Iran. Dr. MacDowell's and Dr. Blair's hospital, which was free to the poor, offered the best medical care in Iran, while Dr. Jordan's school for boys, Alborz College, was unsurpassed in the country. My father and many other men in high society were generous donors to the hospital, where my father always sent us to be treated when we got sick, and Dr. Jordan, Dr. MacDowell, and Dr. Blair were often his luncheon guests.

Thus, when my father realized that he could not afford to send Farough and our brothers Abol, Ali-Naghi, and Ali-Dad to France and England, as he had my brother Sabbar and Batul-Khanom's older sons, Manucher and Aziz, he decided to send them to Dr. Jordan's school. Meanwhile, Mademoiselle Dupuiche, my older sisters' governess, had almost finished instructing them in the fine points of French culture and was becoming too expensive a luxury to keep on. Dr. Jordan's school for girls offered the best education available to women in Iran, and as I was not going to have a French governess anyway, evidently Shazdeh concluded that I might as well go and study with the Americans instead of the French.

I don't know exactly what my mother thought of Shazdeh's decision to send me and my younger brother to this foreign school, any more than I know exactly what she thought of his sending me to Tarbiat. I'm sure she had no reservations on account of the missionaries' being

Christians—Christians and Jews all believed in God's prophets, just like Moslems, and anyway we knew so little about Americans that she had no idea what religion they might be. Moreover, she liked Dr. Blair and Dr. MacDowell, to whom Shazdeh sent all our mothers as well as his children. (Although normally it would have been utterly disrespectful to his wives for a Persian gentleman to force them to meet male acquaintances from outside the family, my father assured my mother that there was nothing sinful in her being medically examined by foreign men who were physicians, any more than there was in her being seen by Hadji Doktur Khan.)

She soon learned, however, that the American school was much more unconventional than the French—much more than my mother considered either proper or advisable, especially for me. Khanom thought that I already showed a shocking tendency to argue. For Moslems, disagreeing with a parent, or indeed any family elder, is among the worst of all sins, and its punishment is everlasting hellfire. At twelve, I was approaching the age when women friends and relatives who visited our house would begin eyeing me as a potential daughter-in-law, and I knew that my mother wanted to be certain that I was a desirable marriage prospect. Gaining a reputation for contradicting my elders wouldn't put me in that category. Yet I couldn't seem to stop looking at many things differently from traditional ways—which, with the sole exception of what my father declared acceptable, were the only ways my mother approved of.

So I am sure that she did not at all like hearing that Dr. Jordan and Miss Doolittle, the school principal, allowed girls at the American School to gallivant about with their women teachers on school picnics and hikes in the mountains in summer, or that Dr. Jordan took the older classes to eat in public restaurants on very special occasions. It was bad enough that I had grown up in the biruni like a boy, but these were things that Persian schools did not allow even boys to do. My mother guessed that such unheard-of practices would only encourage my willfulness, and she felt little confidence that my studies there would help to inculcate in me the softness and pliancy Persians admire in a wife and daughter-in-law. But however perplexed she felt, she would not have dreamed of questioning Shazdeh's wisdom about something like our education. She accepted his choice and, whatever her real feelings were, she kept them to herself.

I loved my new school from the first day that I set foot in its leafy, poplar-shaded old garden. Everything about it was exciting, starting with the long walk Mashti and I had to take every morning to get there. At last Shazdeh was sending me to learn something about the world outside the walls of our compound!

The school, which more Moslem girls had also begun attending in recent years, was a magnet for the daughters of well-off minority families from all over Iran, and I now found myself sitting side by side not only with Moslems and several of my classmates from Tarbiat, but with Iranians who were also Armenian Christians or Zoroastrians or Jews, with Kurds and Azeris and Bakhtiari chieftains' daughters. Many were girls I would never have met otherwise because they were the daughters of middle-class factory owners or pharmacists or grocers, and, as they were not related to us, weren't part of our social set. I loved having so many kinds of people around me, and was very curious about all the different kinds of homes, backgrounds, and beliefs I encountered at school.

I also made friends with several American classmates whose fathers taught at the boys' school. I was fascinated by the home lives of new friends like Ruth Elder, the daughter of Dr. John Elder, the mission's minister. Sometimes, if I stopped by their homes in the mission compound to pick them up on the way to morning assembly, I would catch a tantalizing glimpse of the exotic way they lived. I knew that the missionary men lived in the same part of the house as their women and children not because they were poor, like Mashti and his wife Korsum, but by choice. Nevertheless, I always drew a sharp breath of amazement at seeing a missionary like Dr. Elder helping his wife and servants get their small blond children ready for kindergarten, with everyone acting as though it were the most natural thing on earth for a father to be right there in the andarun, doing women's work! Enviously, I tried to imagine these fair-haired, blue-eyed fathers coming home in the evening to have supper with their wives—or rather, wife—and children. But even though Ruth and my other American classmates insisted that they did, I could not picture this. It was all too strange and barbaric.

The freedom the mission school gave us was extraordinary. One of my strongest memories is of morning assemblies in the auditorium. There, after prayers, and after one of the older Persian students had read a psalm from the Persian Bible the Presbyterians had translated, Miss Jane Doolittle, a bespectacled, authoritative lady of whom everyone stood in awe, would play the piano and we would sing a Christian hymn, also in Persian. Moslems were not required to participate in the prayers or hymn-singing, but I joined in lustily as soon as I picked up the words and soon knew all the hymns by heart. On one side of the blackboard in the auditorium, some words in Latin letters had been scribbled in chalk. I could not yet read the letters (English was taught only in the two last years), but I knew that they had been put there by Nasser al-Din Shah, Ezzatdoleh's grandfather. During his long reign this Qajar monarch had allowed secular, European-style schools for Iranian men to be established and had brought a number of other advances to Iran, and when he visited the American School with his courtiers in 1890, he had written on the missionaries' blackboard to signify that he approved of the Americans' efforts to educate Persian women. The school had proudly framed his handwriting and kept it as a prized memorial.

In such an encouraging and liberal atmosphere I could not help but do well in my studies. I especially loved the novelty of organized team sports like volleyball and basketball, to which the American school introduced us. Even better, not long after I began at the school, an American who visited Reza Shah's new ministry of education, a gentleman named Mr. Thomas Gibson, explained to the king that advanced nations created loyal citizens through an activity called "scouting." So, once a week, I marched happily around the grounds of the American School in a hot green Girl Scout uniform with shiny brass badges that my mother had sewn for me on the Singer, waving an Iranian flag and singing patriotic songs—which, since the missionaries had to be careful to adhere strictly to the education ministry's policies or risk having their school closed as Tarbiat had been, were mostly about the wonderful things Reza Shah was doing for Iran.

All this was great fun. Naturally, I knew that Shazdeh had sent me to the American school to work hard so that I would learn how to serve our country when I grew up, like his eldest sons and my father himself. I was still hazy as to exactly how this would come about, but it seemed to me that somehow it would be the inevitable result of my leaving the andarun and our compound and going out into the world— a project which, I felt, was now well and truly launched. I did not doubt that one day, a very interesting life was going to happen to me.

Every June, Shazdeh had us all pack up—wives, children, nannies, Mashti and another laleh or two and their families, along with a few of our tutors—and sent us to spend the three months of our summer vacation at his big country estate, Reswanieh. Reswanieh, about ten miles north of the compound, was next to the village of Tajrish in the cool and pleasant Shemiran hills.

I cherished these vacations at Reswanieh, the heart of which was a lush, overgrown old garden with one large and several smaller summer cottages. Life here was much freer and less regimented than in the city. Shemiran was fruitful countryside, where plots of wheat, corn, and cucumber separated scattered villages, and willow trees shaded rocky glens where small streams gathered in pools to water the hard, dry soil of nearby fields and orchards. Accustomed as we were to hot, dirty Tehran, these mountain lowlands, though stony and thinly forested by European standards, seemed delightfully sylvan and bucolic to us.

These informal months at Reswanieh were additionally happy because we saw much more of my father, who managed our physical education in person. At a big irrigation pond deliciously overrun with green algae, frogs, and small wriggling water snakes, Shazdeh, sitting on a stool and exhorting everyone to be brave, would have the lalehs tie ropes around our waists, heave us into the green water, and keep us afloat until we discovered for ourselves how to dog-paddle. Best of all, whenever his gouty foot permitted, my father himself would lead us on a hike up into the mountains. Sometimes black clouds would gather without warning, blotting out the sun; the air would grow chill and a hailstorm would begin, forcing us to seek cover. Once, when I was perhaps eight years old, one of these freak storms caught us far up on the trail, the hail slashing at us and the wind whipping our faces so that everything became a gray blur and it seemed that we could go neither forward nor back. In horror I suddenly understood that we were lost and I opened my mouth to scream. Just at that moment, Shazdeh's voice floated back on the wind from the head of our line—not loud, but firm, clear, and confident: "Forward, children, march! Keep going. This is a splendid lesson for you. Remember, when you get caught in a storm, always move straight forward. Don't stop; always move ahead. Never falter in a storm!"

Now, when I look back at these memories, what amazes me above all is that my father taught his daughters to ride, swim, and face down tempests. I am absolutely certain that no other Persian nobleman at that time had ever thought of such a thing. But Shazdeh wished all of us, not just his sons, to be self-sufficient, physically as well as mentally, and to have the courage not to stop when some problem confronted us. I am sure that this showed how desperately he wished to infuse every one of us with the strength he feared we would need when he was gone.

And I am also amazed that we let ourselves be tossed into the water like that—not because we feared his anger, but because we knew that he loved us. He loved each of us, individually as well as all together.

When we stood for Friday inspection, he called each of us by name, chiding and rewarding us as individuals. And because we never doubted his love and wisdom, we knew that the water would sustain and support us, just as he did. In this way Shazdeh, sitting beside the green pond— a sick, white-haired old man who lived in constant fear of informers— bestowed on us all, sons and daughters alike, the greatest gifts he had to confer: self-reliance, and the knowledge that in a storm, we must always move forward.

Our mothers, too, had more rest from their chores and cares at Reswanieh, and even Khanom's irritability softened there. Like all upper-class Persian women, our father's wives were unused to exercise and could not accompany us on our hikes. However, they enjoyed ambling along the gentle slopes of the hills, and with Mashti and another laleh carrying food, the samovar, and carpets to sit on, we, our mothers, and Mashti's wife Korsum would often climb the footpaths that ran beside the streams, looking for a willow grove to picnic in.

Shemiran also afforded our mothers the opportunity to do something else they greatly enjoyed: getting around Shazdeh. My mother and stepmothers loved to go on the small excursions that constituted the local entertainments. One of them was a shrine in the village of Tajrish. My mother and Fatimeh-Khanom would gladly have visited the shrine every day, but my father considered shrines primarily an arrangement for fleecing the credulous. If my mother and Fatimeh so much as whispered together in his presence of visiting the shrine, his deafness would suddenly vanish and he would make everyone jump by drawing his eyebrows together and loudly growling, "No!"* However, as business demanded his presence in Tehran and he needed police permission to travel even to Tajrish, it was not convenient for him to be at Reswanieh all the time, and on the days he was gone his wives could sneak off somewhere without telling him.

---

*Before I was a teenager, our mothers had already ascertained the variability of Shazdeh's deafness. Some years earlier, my technology-loving father, having had his own home—but no one else's— wired for electricity, decided to show off an electric bullhorn that had somehow drifted into his possession. Proudly summoning all his wives to his front door, he commanded them to convey this modern miracle to Batul-Khanom's porch next door and speak to him through it from there.

When they arrived at my stepmother's, my mother placed her lips to the mouthpiece. "Ghorban," she thundered, the words booming through the poplar trees for the whole neighborhood to hear, "our kids have no shoes!"

My father was furious. "So this is how you women treat your husband now!" he roared, and, stomping back into his house, slammed the door behind him. This incident had buoyed our mothers' spirits through many subsequent bouts of deafness.

At that time Tajrish, which is now a suburb of Tehran, was a large hamlet consisting mainly of a few hundred mud houses, a bathhouse, a post office, and a mosque. Its chief attractions were the shops where villagers and vacationers could purchase necessities, and its big shrine, which stood in a square in the middle of the long, straggling bazaar that began not far from our compound gate just across the main road from Tehran. This shrine, where the bones of a holy Imam's son were said to lie, was visited by pilgrims from all over the region.

I had mixed feelings about these excursions to the Tajrish shrine. I loved any excuse to leave the compound and see what went on in the world, and I was always delighted by the milling activity and the colorful sight of the many poor families who camped in the courtyard, together with all their bedrolls, samovars, and water pipes, filling the time between prayers by napping, gossiping, and snacking on watermelon seeds. But the mullahs' stories of the cruel tortures of the martyred Imam Hossein and his family, to which devout women loved to listen, always left me ill and shaken. Nevertheless, whenever Shazdeh wasn't around and my mother realized that it was safe to steal off, she would collect Fatimeh-Khanom or one or two of her daughters, and Mashti would escort us through the long, dark, din-filled bazaar, pushing around jostling farmers, braying donkeys, trinket vendors, and housewives in chadors, threading past tiny shops that sold tea and watermelons and tobacco until we came to the square where the shrine was.

The streets before the courtyard were always full of beggars with the most heartrending afflictions, people who plainly had no means of surviving other than the vacationers and pilgrims who flocked to the shrine. My mother would give something to everyone who approached her, and when we reached the entrance of the sanctuary itself, would buy a candle from the scowling, black-robed mullah who sat there and pray and kiss the decorated silver cage that protected the sacred sarcophagus before paying another mullah a few coins to recite the stories of the holy martyrs.

One hot day in my thirteenth summer, my mother and Mashti and I were making our way to the gate of the shrine courtyard when a young woman in a black chador approached us. Five or six thin, dirty urchins clung to the folds of her dark veil. Her uncovered face was pretty but streaked with dirt, and her eyes were red, as though she had been weeping. She salaamed to my mother, bowing deeply. "Khanom," she murmured, glancing down as though ashamed to look my mother in the face, "may heaven grant your children health. In the name of the Merciful and Compassionate, let me show you what misfortune has done to a mother of so many, and a Moslem woman like yourself."

Turning her back to Mashti and still clutching the black chador, she moved close to my mother and me. "Look, Khanom," she whispered loudly. "See? I have no clothes."

Swiftly she opened the chador. Beneath its batlike wings was what no Persian child is ever supposed to see: a naked adult body.

I gaped as though struck by a magician's rod. Horrified and fascinated, I could not take my eyes away. I wanted not to look, especially at the pallid triangle of her shaven pubes, a part of the body we were not supposed to uncover or gaze upon even in the bath. But she loomed over me, her children swarming about her. The cave of her chador, black but with small white dots like stars, was like the sky arching over the garden of Reswanieh at night. In its shadow her thin body looked pale, like the early morning desert, and her ribs, which stuck out under her skin, reminded me of bones bleaching in the sun. Her breasts hung like exhausted fruits and her small brown belly looked like an empty water sack. She was obscene and at the same time terribly sad, like some lost creature howling in the wilderness.

Instantly she covered herself again. "See, Khanom," she whimpered, "what I must do to survive? I had to sell my clothes to feed my children. As you love religion, Khanom, show compassion to a pious man's daughter."

I looked at my mother. In spite of the heat, her face was drained of color. The sight of a decent Moslem woman reduced to such shame was more than her piety and kindness could endure. "Wait," she gasped to the woman. She turned to me, her eyes full of horror. "Hurry," she told me urgently, not as though I were a child but as if I were an adult her own age; "we must go back and get clothes for her!"

Without a moment's thought for the fierce heat, she turned around and hurried off in the direction of our compound, which was more than a mile away. Covered with shame and confusion, I followed her, Mashti stumbling along beside me. Soon her face was scarlet and pouring with sweat. It seemed to take forever to cover the distance home. When we got there, she hurried to the storeroom in the main cottage where she kept all our spare clothes. I stood by anxiously while she began ransacking a storage chest. Nargess and the other nannies crowded into the room behind us, watching in amazement as my mother, distraught and almost in tears, handed clothes to us, all the while crying, "Alas, a woman and her children are going naked and look at all we have here—I'm ashamed to call myself a Moslem!"

When she had assembled all we could possibly carry, we wrapped it in a big square cloth and, with Mashti lugging it behind us on his back and his wife Korsum hurriedly enlisted to help, we started back on the long, hot walk through the bazaar, my mother leading the way.

The beggarwoman was in the street where we had left her. There was a dark, urine-drenched passageway nearby where men went to relieve themselves, and while Mashti and I waited outside, he to guard the entrance and dress the ragged children and I to hand in clothes, my mother and Korsum escorted the beggarwoman into this stinking hole and, being careful to keep their eyes averted, helped her to cover herself.

I was glad not to go in with them. I knew instinctively that for the first time in my life I had seen someone bereft of dignity, devoid of even the most fundamental self-respect. Nor was I comforted when the beggarwoman emerged from the passage with my mother and Korsum, kissing her benefactress's hands and calling down a thousand blessings on her and her children.

But my mother, though trembling with emotion and the exhaustion of so much haste in the burning heat, was radiant with relief and joy. When she had pressed money into the beggarwoman's hands, we resumed our interrupted journey to the shrine. There she humbly gave thanks to heaven for vouchsafing her a charitable act so pleasing to God. Then we returned home and she went to rest, worn out with emotion and her exertions.

I suppose I don't need to tell you that the next day, as we were on our way to buy something in that part of the bazaar, we heard a woman crying out to us, "Oh, come, please come and help—this woman has no clothes!" Sure enough, there was the very same beggar, bobbing up and down like the needle on my mother's sewing machine and murmuring "Please, Khanom, help a wretched mother" to a pair of horrified ladies and their menservants, and no more altered from the day before than the Golden Dome of Rey.

All my shame and anxiety of the previous afternoon turned into blistering indignation. Even I, a child of thirteen, could see now that the woman was a professional cheat. It was bad enough that she had taken advantage of us and defrauded us of our clothing, which my mother had to sew for us with her own hands. But what outraged me most was that Khanom, who had sweated like a carpet bearer to help her and who I had feared would be overcome by heatstroke, was now being humiliated for her pains.

I waited for my clever mother, who stood as if rooted to the spot, to advance on the beggarwoman and upbraid her, or warn these new victims. But instead of speaking, she only drew her chador tighter across her face, turned on her heel, and strode back up the street. Mashti and I blundered after her.

I forgot myself completely. "Wait, Khanom," I cried. "The woman is a thief!"

"Khanom, let me go back," said Mashti through his teeth, "and I swear I'll give her a piece of my mind, or better yet a good beating."

My mother stopped and faced us. "No," she said evenly. Her calm astonished me. "God is great. It is not for us to punish her, but for Him. Let us pray instead that He makes her repent, so that He may forgive her."

Mashti was about to protest. Then he saw, as I had, that my mother's eyes were blazing, and swallowed what he was going to say. We walked home through the noisy bazaar, my mother livid but closemouthed, I in hot, confused silence, Mashti reviling the beggarwoman under his breath. "Curse her shamelessness," he muttered. "Your mother is a holy saint, and that woman's father was a burnt dog! 'God will make her repent!' I hope that God—may He and the Prophet be glorified forever—has her eaten by scorpions."

When we got home, he called everyone to gather round and launched into an account of the great wrong done to my mother. The servants were all furious, but Khanom said nothing except to murmur, "God is great. God will forgive or punish as He sees fit."

Finally I could stand it no longer. "Khanom," I burst out, "why don't we summon the gendarmes?" This was tantamount to questioning her judgment and I knew that I should never have said such a thing. But I could not help it.

My mother looked at me in sidelong exasperation; her eyes said, "Shut up." Aloud she said, in a level voice, "That will not be necessary, Satti. We must not burden my cousin with such a trivial matter." Then she stalked off to Batul-Khanom's cottage to vent her wrath. Several cups of tea, her co-wives' sympathy, and a bath calmed her down, and by the time she had a chance to complain of her wrongs to Jaby, she was herself once more.

I was sorry now for my impudence, and half-expected a beating. For once, however, Khanom, who had seen how upset I was, did not even scold me. Instead, after supper when everyone was sitting on the veranda in the dusk and Mashti and the other servants had gone to their own quarters, she took me off to a corner of the porch to explain why she had not sent Mashti for the gendarmes.

"I know as well as you do, Satti, that that woman cheated us," she said. "Don't you think that if I believed the gendarmes were our friends and would help us, I would have summoned them?"

"But Khanom," I protested, "the woman is a swindler. She ought to be stopped!"

"Indeed," said my mother dryly. "And what do you think the gendarmes would say if we invited them here? 'Lo, here is the wife of rich Prince Farman-Farma, who has given a beggar a few rials' worth of clothes, and now the prince's wife wants the woman flogged on the soles of her feet.'"

"Well," I said uncomfortably, "maybe they wouldn't flog her, but just tell her to stop cheating people and making fools of them."

"I'll tell you exactly what they would do," said my mother with an ironic smile that made me sure I wouldn't much like what was coming next. "First, they would go back to this woman, who would deny that she ever saw me or had any clothes or money from me. Then they would come back here and say, 'Well, there are two sides to every story, and heaven alone must judge the truth of the matter.' Meaning that I must give them a bribe. And if I refused to give them a bribe, or if they were not satisfied with the amount, the story would soon go like this: 'The shazdeh's wife had two coats and gave one to a poor woman; now she has changed her mind and wants it back again.' Then there would be a nice scandal and everyone would talk about what an injustice rich old Farman-Farma did to a poor beggarwoman. And how fast do you think an informer like that valet of Shazdeh's would rush to line his pockets? Don't you think Ismail would love to give the secret police a nice little story to pass on to Reza Shah? Next time they come to get Shazdeh, they will kill him."

She paused for the answer I was wise enough not to make. My mother knew the value of a well-timed pause. "And *that*, my hot-headed Satti, is the reason the wife of Farman-Farma is not going to call out the gendarmes." Then her tone softened. "Shazdeh always says that God punishes evildoers here and now, before He punishes them in the afterlife. But don't make your actions the mirror of your heart, Satti-*jun*—those who open their hearts in this world do not survive in it for long. Fear God and put your trust in Him, not in people outside your family, who do not care about what happens to you, but only to themselves."

This silenced me. But I felt soiled, both by what the beggarwoman had done to us and by what Khanom had just told me. Was this, I thought wretchedly, what the world outside Shazdeh's compound was like—treacherous, spiteful, and mean? I knew that my mother was right about the gendarmes, but I hated the disgraceful necessity of always choking back my feelings and accepting whatever the wind blew us. In our compound, anyone could go to Shazdeh with a complaint and he would settle the dispute in a way that seemed fair to both parties. Why, outside our compound, could people not expect justice from anybody except God?

Shabby though the beggarwoman's trick had been, however, it prodded ideas I had never had before. I tried to banish her from my thoughts as an ungrateful, deceitful person, but her presence continued to haunt me. I knew that Koran commanded Moslems to care for the poor. Why, then, did our country have so many beggars? I felt that I myself would prefer to die rather than beg for my living. It seemed to me that everyone should be protected from misfortune, as Shazdeh protected us, and not have to depend on chance for help, or on mean tricks.

But I could not get satisfactory answers to questions like these. The womenservants all said that beggars and gendarmes alike were part of God's plan, while Mashti just shrugged. "That's how life is, Satti," he said affably. "Some are poor like me, and some are rich. If God makes the crow black, can Mashti make him white?"

That was no answer at all, I thought in exasperation. If we could alter nothing by our own efforts, why did Shazdeh order our mothers to boil our milk to prevent tuberculosis, or command Hadji Doktur Khan to dispense pills to protect everyone against stomach worm? If catching malaria or diarrhea was part of an unchangeable design, why did my mother give us willow-bark and sour-cherry tea to cure them? Every adult I talked to thought that people's destinies were written on their foreheads from birth, yet my father told us every Friday that our futures depended entirely on how hard we studied and what we made of ourselves. I was sure that Shazdeh could have explained, but I never talked to him alone, and even if I could have, I would not have dared to engage my lofty, distinguished father in such intimate discourse. I would just have to wait. Maybe at school I would find the answers to these baffling riddles.

In spite of my anger and confusion, however, I understood that my mother was right to avoid attracting attention to us. We could not count on the benevolence of fate any more than the beggarwoman could. We and Shazdeh were as much its dependents as the supplicants and old pensioners in the compound were my father's, and as time passed we wondered increasingly what the unpredictable and ruthless power that guided Iran's destiny had in store for us.

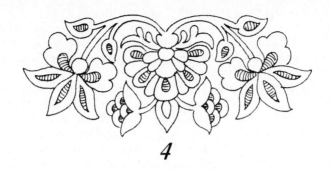

4

ZAIFEH

In the deep places of the heart, two forces, fire and water,
struggle together.
—Ferdowsi, *The Book of Kings*

SINCE 1930, REZA SHAH'S APPETITE FOR OTHER PEOPLE'S REAL ES-
tate had grown steadily. Having established his national army
and come far toward subduing the tribes, he was moving rapidly toward
the point Shazdeh had foreseen—the complete consolidation of his
power—and was building not only roads but other construction projects, such as schools and small factories, or hotels and gambling casinos
to bring in tourism. Some of these endeavors he was financing with
taxes on staples like tea and sugar. These taxes hurt poor people the
most, but they were still not enough to pay for all his projects, much
less for the salaries and sinecures with which he rewarded the officials,
military officers, and courtiers who served him, or for the palaces he
was building for himself.

On one pretext or another, therefore, he was now confiscating for
his own purposes not just the property of Qajar families and religious
foundations but the estates, farmlands, villages, and jewels of wealthy
merchants, rich mullahs, tribal chieftains, and other big landowners.
He even ruined poor farmers by diverting their water to his own holdings. On some of these confiscated lands he was building roads and

"public" buildings, like the Marble Palace he had constructed on Shazdeh's old estate, but in effect these lands and villages became the Pahlavis' personal property.

Thanks to the power that the military, the new central bureaucracy, and his control of court patronage gave him, Reza Shah had also become secure enough to begin dispensing with the services of members of the old nobility, especially with men he considered clever enough to become a threat to him. Thus, in 1930 something had happened to make Shazdeh much more concerned for the safety of our family, especially of my half brother, his and Ezzatdoleh's eldest son, Nosratdoleh.

Nosratdoleh, who was in his forties, was the most important person in our family next to Shazdeh. His real name was Firuz, but, as was customary with great noblemen, nearly everyone except Shazdeh and Ezzatdoleh addressed him by the deeply respectful hereditary title of Nosratdoleh, which means "Illumination of the State." We knew that when Shazdeh died, our brother himself would be our new "Shazdeh," the patriarch of the clan of Farman Farmaian.

Nosratdoleh was one of Iran's most famous statesmen. He was also controversial, having helped, when he was foreign minister in 1919, to bring about an agreement with the English foreign secretary, Lord Curzon, that would have made Iran virtually a British protectorate in return for a large and desperately needed loan. At the war's end we had been on the verge of bankruptcy, and Nosratdoleh, a strong Anglophile, had seen this drastic expedient as the only way to keep Iran from financial ruin.

I am sure that Nosratdoleh sincerely believed that Iran's sole hope of advancement in the postwar era was to attach itself to some great foreign ally, and of the two that were in the running, England and the new Soviet Union, both he and my father regarded England as distinctly the lesser evil. To my brother's way of thinking, and to many other educated, sophisticated people in Persian high circles, small, weak nations needed powerful helpers and protectors just as small, weak people did. However, as everyone quickly realized, even Reza Khan hated the arrogance with which the British had always interfered in Iran's affairs, and instead of doing London's bidding as Lord Curzon and General Ironside had expected, when they took power he and Sayyid Ziya concluded a pact of friendship with the Soviets, while the Majlis angrily repudiated the Anglo-Persian Agreement.

Even after the Qajars' overthrow, Nosratdoleh—who had not been the only minister involved in the negotiations—had remained unpopular in some quarters. Indeed, I have even heard that Lord Curzon himself was so angry at Nosratdoleh because the accord was not ratified after Iran had already accepted the British loan that some years later he wrote Percy Lorraine, the British Minister to Tehran, that the English should "have Nosratdoleh's head bashed against the stone," which is the Persian expression for doing away with someone. However, Nosratdoleh was so clever, experienced, and well connected that when he, Shazdeh, and Shazdeh's second son, Salar-Lashgar, were released from prison, Reza Khan had allowed him to return at once to public life, and for nine years he served as a member of parliament, provincial governor, minister of justice, and finance minister.

We worshiped Nosratdoleh, who was all that a great Persian prince should be—dashing, immensely wealthy, generous, arrogant, extravagant, and spoiled. My father had drummed into us that it would be silly for us to think of ourselves as "princes" and "princesses." We were an ordinary family, living in a rather simple old house with plain wooden furniture, sitting on the floor eating goat cheese and drinking boiled milk for breakfast. But our brother never wore anything but white gloves, a striped cutaway with a vest, shirts like the snows of Mount Demavand, and patent leather shoes polished like glass—of which, his housekeeper once told my awed mother, he had twenty pairs. In his Sulka cravats a diamond stickpin always glittered. Nosratdoleh believed in these things. He was, as Americans would say, the genuine article. He was *real* royalty.

His mere presence dominated any room, so that both men and women, even those who did not know who he was, rose to their feet when he entered, mesmerized by sheer personality. His charm captivated everyone, and a large part of it was his extravagance. His mother and brothers, who idolized him, gladly sold their own lands to raise the cash—Nosratdoleh was frequently short of cash—to help him pay for his lavish dinners, his hunting parties, his polo ponies, his rare book collection. On family occasions he invariably arrived with a servant laden with marvelous presents for everyone. These he ordered from Europe, where he carried on correspondences with famous literary figures like André Gide and Jean Cocteau as well as Sir Edward G. Browne, the great authority on Persian literature and history who taught at Cambridge. Some people even stated that Nosratdoleh, who had a doctorate, had helped Professor Browne with his volumes about Persia, though this may be untrue. Once, I remember, my brother gave me a little gilded walnut. When I opened it, a tiny bottle of French perfume tumbled out. Such presents drew us for a brief moment into the glamorous world of wealth, power, and influence in which Nosratdoleh had moved with ease all his life.

Nosratdoleh had worked loyally for Reza Shah. But in June of 1930, while he was finance minister, the Shah had had him arrested on a charge of accepting a bribe in the amount of five hundred tomans. Of course this was only a pretext to disgrace Nosratdoleh and get rid of him. Five hundred tomans was equivalent to about a hundred dollars, an amount so trifling to a man who lived the way Nosratdoleh did that even his accusers scarcely pretended to take the charge seriously. When it was read at his trial, my brother threw back his head and laughed. "Five hundred tomans?" he said. "That is what Nosratdoleh pays for a toilet can." He was jailed for a month, then released, as Shazdeh had been, to permanent house arrest.

Shazdeh was deeply alarmed by this episode, and warned Nosratdoleh that he must try to curb his famous extravagance. Shazdeh's love for his brilliant first son knew no bounds. Much as he cherished us all, we knew that his love for Nosratdoleh went beyond everything. Nosratdoleh was *the* child, *the* son. "My nightingale," our father would say to him tenderly. A "nightingale" is what Iranians call someone with a silver tongue—one perfect in flowery eloquence and rhetoric, which in the Middle East is considered among the most admirable virtues of a statesman. To Shazdeh, Nosratdoleh was not merely silver-tongued, but made entirely of gold.

And Nosratdoleh returned Shazdeh's devotion. When he came to dine with our father, instead of kissing Shazdeh's hand he would always kneel and kiss his slippers, which was the ancient way for Persian sons to express the greatest possible feelings of filial love, reverence, and obedience. Shazdeh, in turn, would raise our brother up, kiss his forehead, and, no matter how distinguished or important his other guests were, would seat Nosratdoleh on his right hand, the supreme place of honor, which was always saved for him.

But Shazdeh's warnings went unheeded. With as much aplomb as though the ruin of his career meant no more to him than a change of his patent leather shoes, Nosratdoleh settled down to an apparently enjoyable existence of playing polo, hunting ibex and gazelle in Shemiran, expanding his internationally famous rare book and manuscript collection, and inviting old friends and members of the foreign diplomatic corps to parties that featured quails' eggs and peacocks' tongues. He also kept up his correspondence with Professor Browne in England, and with Cocteau and his other literary friends in Paris.

My father fretted constantly over his son's free-spending excesses. If anyone needed reminding of Reza Shah's acquisitiveness, he only needed to glance at the Marble Palace, just east of Shazdeh's and Nosratdoleh's compounds on Kakh Avenue: its garden had once been

Shazdeh's. Moreover, Reza Shah was deeply distrustful of smooth-talking, clever men who could speak foreign languages and socialized with foreign nationals—to the suspicious monarch, any "foreign nationals," however innocent they appeared, might be "foreign agents." Nosratdoleh spoke five languages, and his oratory in Persian and Arabic was so famous among connoisseurs of both that when Professor Browne was invited by Reza Shah to speak at the opening ceremonies of Tehran University, the great scholar sent back the reply, "Why, in a country that possesses Nosratdoleh, do you need me?" Shazdeh was afraid that sooner or later, his son would turn out to be not a nightingale but a lightning rod to draw down the Shah's ever-present suspicions. But Nosratdoleh ignored Shazdeh's hints.

Reza Shah's hatred of foreigners and his ambitious plans to restore Iran's luster in the world's eyes were prompting him to adopt a brand of nationalism similar in some ways to that of the new German chancellor, Hitler, with whose approach to governing his own had much in common. The Shah, who refused to seek international loans because of the power such loans had always given foreign countries over our affairs, always feared that foreigners were laughing at him and that they despised him. However, he was an enthusiastic admirer of the goose-stepping new German state, and in 1935 he decreed that our country, previously called "Persia" by the West, would henceforth be known exclusively as "Iran," a name evoking the ancient splendors of the Aryan race. At about the same time, he also directed all foreign schools to take Iranian names. Dr. Jordan and Miss Doolittle, who were painfully aware that the American mission school could function only so long as the Shah believed it served the interests of his new nationalism, chose the name "Nurbaksh," which meant, "Light-Spreading."

Without ever discussing the matter, I and my Persian classmates all knew how it hurt Dr. Jordan, Miss Doolittle, and the other missionaries, who loved Iran, to see what Reza Shah's methods had done to our young democracy and to Persian freedom of expression. Indeed, a whole generation of educated Iranians now growing up felt that "Amrika" was the only Western country that was sincere and selfless, and that had truly supported our aspirations to be strong and respected by the rest of the world. People like Dr. Jordan, Miss Doolittle, and our missionary teachers were using their advanced knowledge to bring our nation help and hope.

I and all my classmates knew that Dr. Jordan, a tall, twinkling-eyed man with a cherubic face and a small, comical beard who had come to Iran with his wife before the constitutional revolution and now looked upon our country as his own home, was as eager as any Persian for Iran to become strong and self-sufficient. He was dedicated to turning all his charges into enlightened citizens who could guide Iran wisely and unselfishly in the new era. He especially wanted us to be able to stand up to foreign interference, of which he had seen enough during his more than thirty years among us. If Farough or someone else got roughhoused by an older, larger student and ran to Dr. Jordan, the mission school's director would give him a pep talk, and it wasn't about turning the other cheek. "Always look a problem straight in the eye," he would exhort my brothers, "and don't go running off to find somebody bigger, like me, to protect you. That just gives the other fellow the idea that he can push you around. If you men show everyone that you can take care of yourselves, the cowards and bullies of this world will keep off you."

The point of Dr. Jordan's muscular Christianity was not lost on his Iranian pupils. Young Iranians like Jaby and Batul's daughter Mehri, who were old enough to be studying English, proudly insisted that they were learning "American," not the language of the British. We even knew that the American president, Mr. Woodrow Wilson, had once said, in a speech widely quoted by Iranians, that America "stood for the sovereignty of self-governing people." It was quite clear that America wanted to help us instead of exploiting us. America's friendship was not just "ta'arof," empty words and promises that meant nothing. "The land at the end of the earth" had a special place in our hearts.

Apart from the Americans' hymns and their exotic living habits, however, I wasn't learning much about the land at the end of the earth. For one thing, the ministry of education wanted us taught about nothing but the past triumphs of the Persian Empire and the present triumphs of the Pahlavi dynasty. For another, nobody, not even the missionaries, saw any reason for Iranians to learn about the history or geography of the United States. No Iranian thought of going to "yenqeh donya." America was too remote for us to visit, too distant to trade with, and too far away to invade us. Hence, though I knew where the countries of Europe were, I never saw a map of the United States. I knew only that it was on the North American continent and was reached by going to Europe and sailing west. Nor was I learning anything from visiting my American classmates' homes, because I dared not set foot in them for fear of meeting their fathers or brothers. In Iran, men and women who are not related are not even supposed to look at each other's faces, and a decent Moslem girl, especially an

upper-class one, never spoke to males who were not her relatives—
strange men and women must never come together; who knew what
might happen if they did? (I myself hadn't the slightest idea.) I was
sure that had I ever thought of doing anything so scandalous as entering
Dr. Elder's house, Shazdeh would know about it instantly, by tele-
pathy.

Still, in spite of learning nothing whatever about the United States
at school, I did acquire one interesting bit of information on my own
when I was about fourteen. One day I noticed an imposing advertisement in a French fashion magazine that Jaby and Fatimeh-Khanom's
daughter Mahssy had been poring over. It had a drawing of an ocean
liner, and looming gigantically above the ship was a statue of a woman
holding a torch, while behind the ship and the statue rose a splendid
city that glittered magically in the sun. On the promenade of the
harbor, dwarfed by buildings so tall I could not believe they would
not topple over, strolled small, stylish figures: women in furs and men
in Western suits—elegant men, like Nosratdoleh. There was some
Latin writing at the bottom. I asked what the picture was, and Jaby
dutifully informed me that the advertisement depicted the entrance to
America, which was reached by taking the train to Paris and then
sailing west on a ship like this. The statue was a monument whose
name in English meant *azadi*, freedom.

I was enthralled. The only statues I had ever seen were of Reza
Shah. The word "azadi," on the other hand, conveyed nothing to me
except the opposite of being under house arrest or in jail. I asked my
sister what the statue was for.

"It symbolizes the American people," explained Jaby patiently. "The
Americans put it there to represent themselves and their nation."

This impressed me. What kind of people, I wondered, had put up
this monument? What was in their minds when they decided to do
so, and what had they gone through in their history to make them
want to? The statue, the tall buildings, and the people on the promenade lodged themselves like a question mark in my mind and became,
like the beggarwoman's trickery and Mashti's silly lies about the watermelon, yet another curious, interesting problem for me to think
about.

I might have thought of asking my American classmates about the
statue, had not an exciting family event during the school year of

1934–35 pushed the magazine picture out of my consciousness: the engagement and marriage of my sixteen-year-old sister Mahssy. This was especially thrilling; Mahssy wasn't much older than I was!

By this time, all told, my father had well over thirty children, of whom about a third were girls. As we got older, he would gradually begin introducing both boys and girls to Tehran high society. His practice was to have his chauffeur drive him and his butler around to the homes of friends and relatives nearly every afternoon in his big navy blue Essex sedan and spend a few minutes drinking tea, chatting, and garnering the latest political news and rumor before moving on to the next place—in a dictatorship, gossip and rumors were the only way one could get real news, since the press, as my father complained to Khanom, who read to him from the papers when his pain and worries kept him awake at night, printed nothing but pap to flatter Reza Shah. Often, when he went driving, he would take along one of our brothers, and once in a while, to our great excitement, he would round up a wife or a couple of his older girls and take us to visit his sister Najmeh-Saltaneh or another woman relative. This way, he could remind everybody that Prince Farman-Farma had daughters to marry off as well as sons.

One Friday afternoon Shazdeh sent his servant Owssein—being a eunuch, this man could enter the andaruns, so he was always the one to carry Shazdeh's messages—to tell me and Jaby to put on our chadors and join Mahssy and a couple of Fatimeh-Khanom's sons for a spin in the Essex with him. When we were all in the car, he ordered us driven first to the compound of a wealthy family he knew. There he sent his butler inside to announce us, and a moment later, to my surprise, a handsome army major of about thirty came out with his tunic unbuttoned and his sleeves turned up. He bowed deeply to my father. Then, seeing veiled women through the rolled-down window, he blushed, hastily adjusted his tunic, and modestly lowered his gaze to avoid laying eyes on my father's harem. After only a few minutes Shazdeh bid him adieu and, with a satisfied expression on his face, told the chauffeur to drive to the fashionable shopping street, the Avenue Lalezar, so that his butler could buy everybody candy.

Soon after, Mahssy came rushing over to our house in breathless excitement. "Satti, guess what, I have a suitor," she cried. "Neggar-Saltaneh"—this strong-willed woman, I knew, was the major's older sister; in all but name, she was the head of the family whose house we had driven to—"has come to see Shazdeh about me for her brother. Imagine, he's only thirty-three, and those people are *much* richer than

Shazdeh—I'll have diamonds, and my own apartments in their mansion, and my own droshky and horses! Oh," my sister wailed, "if I can't marry him, I'll die! Neggar-Saltaneh is so clever that it will take ages for her and Shazdeh to come to an agreement, and what if Shazdeh decides to look in his Koran at the last minute and tell her that God is against the match, the way he always does when he wants to get out of something?"

If I was the tomboy of our family, Mahssy was the butterfly. She was irresistibly plump and pretty, but hopelessly spoiled by her timid mother. Books and the lycée bored her, and she was frankly eager for Shazdeh to let her leave school and marry a rich, handsome man so that she could embark on the life of a modern young wife of our class: dinner parties, long, lazy, gossip-filled days at the baths, and shopping for clothes on the Avenue Lalezar. Evidently my father had decided not to fight nature any longer.

Having so many females on his hands made Shazdeh extremely nervous. Once he had taken Batul's beautiful daughters Maryam and Mehri out in the Essex. What two giggling teenage girls could have done to a man who had fought the Ottoman Turks and run whole provinces I cannot imagine, but when they all got home Shazdeh was chuckling and wiping his brow and growling to Batul-Khanom, "Hurry, take them, these girls are like glass—they will break!" The mullahs taught that women, being *zaifeh*, or the weak sex, were fragile and ruled by almost ungovernable passions, which was why they had to be protected by fathers, brothers, and husbands—not only from strange men, but from themselves. Shazdeh didn't believe everything that mullahs said, but I'm sure he believed this, and as far as he was concerned, the sooner we were safely married, the better for his mental health.

The weakness of women's minds and wills was also the reason that my mother behaved as though the proper condition of females were one of near-invisibility. Even when I was still in elementary school, if she caught me running through the courtyard on my return home she would say quickly, "Satti, you are running—women cannot do that. And go and comb your hair. It's a mess, as usual."

I had been running with my brothers for as long as I could remember, and had been a woman for about the same length of time. "But Khanom," I would ask in astonishment, "why can't I run?"

"Because you are a *woman*!" my mother would repeat in exasperation, adding that it was high time I started behaving like somebody for whom Shazdeh, one of these days, might want to find a husband.

Finally, after months of haggling over the terms of Mahssy's marriage settlement with Neggar-Saltaneh and her family, my father decided that the courtship interview could take place. Accordingly, Neggar-Saltaneh visited Fatimeh-Khanom's. There she ascertained that my sister, freshly scrubbed and glowing from the bath, was neither blind, bald from ringworm, too skinny, nor a stutterer, and she spent much time boasting to Fatimeh, my mother, and Batul of the major's generous and indulgent nature, his excellent monthly income, the strong likelihood that Reza Shah would soon promote him to a colonelcy, and the valuable jewels and magnificently furnished apartments that would be provided for Mahssy and her husband in his family's compound. My sister was ecstatic. The elaborate engagement celebrations took place at once. It was decided that the wedding ritual, or *aghd*, would be held late the following spring or early summer, when Mahssy's school year ended.

I realized, without ever having given much thought to its significance, that marriage was as much my destiny as my sisters'. Marriage was God's law, and we were constantly being told that its attainment was what gave a woman value, standing, and respect—or rather, marriage and the bearing of children. The old saying "The earth itself trembles beneath the feet of the unmarried" applied to men, too. But there was no question that the ground rumbled more ominously for women. A woman by herself was nothing, a nonentity, a creature who without a father, brother, husband, or son to guide her was incapable of making important decisions, looking after herself properly, or even leading a moral life. Besides, she had to be married in order to have the happiness—prestige and jewels—that a husband conferred.

Just when Jaby or I would enter this blessed state was entirely up to God and Shazdeh, though about such an important matter Shazdeh would certainly consult our mother, who had a right to give her opinion of any candidate. But when we graduated from school at nineteen, or at the very latest soon after that, our futures would be sealed.

Naturally, I had no way of looking for a husband myself. Western-style courtship was unknown; a girl sat in the andarun and waited until her father or brother or cousin found her someone, and if they couldn't, she was out of luck and had to spend the rest of her life being looked after by her brothers or other male relatives. She certainly couldn't survive on her own. In our society, women who lived apart from their families were outcasts. They were automatically considered lost to religion, and members of a profession so bad that our servants would not have spoken of it in the hearing of a pious woman like my mother.

Sometimes I felt a little anxious about whether Shazdeh would be able to find me a husband. Jaby was indisputably beautiful, but the pains my mother took to keep us from thinking ourselves attractive to men had convinced me that I, with my plain clothes and perpetually messy hair, was as boring-looking as a mule rug, especially by comparison to the pretty girls I saw at school whose fathers gave them jewels instead of books and whose mothers had their dresses imported from Paris.

Mahssy's wedding took place the following summer, in June of 1935, but because her new husband, who was now a colonel, was leaving Tehran immediately on a military assignment, the wedding night and the important festivity that went with it, the feast Iranians call the *arusi*, had to be postponed until the fall. Mahssy would stay with all of us at Reswanieh until then. However, her new, wifely status cast a glow over that whole summer. Although they were not living together, legally and in the eyes of religion my sister and the colonel were now man and wife. The colonel, looking extremely dashing in his uniform, came on leave every weekend to visit her, bringing with him a white horse for his bride. "My husband has come to take me riding," my sister would announce triumphantly, and in the English riding suit the colonel's tailor had made for her, she looked as pretty and buxom as though she had just stepped from the pages of Paris *Vogue*. Naturally, a manservant of Shazdeh's always rode with them as decency required, but when they reached their destination in the Shemiran hills, the colonel would give him some money and tell him to go back to the Tajrish bazaar and buy them some fruit, keeping the change for himself, and the fellow would know enough to spend a couple of hours looking for just the right fruit back in Tajrish.

I was therefore able to observe that summer that marriage was extremely romantic. Although Mahssy coyly refused to be explicit when she returned, flushed and slightly disheveled, from her jaunts with her husband, I gathered that a lot of hugging and squeezing went on under the willows while the manservant was searching for fruit. I had no notion at all what else could have taken place. Though I understood that married couples might stay together at night instead of retiring separately to the men's and women's quarters, no one had ever explained to me why this was. I attributed the fact that my mother and stepmothers took turns staying with Shazdeh at his house to their obligation to read him his newspaper when he couldn't sleep and act as his nurses when he was unwell.

Of course, I knew that marriage was for getting children, and I dimly divined that there must be some connection between our mothers' nights at Shazdeh's and the frequent appearance of new babies in our compound, but I could not imagine what it was. I knew only that every eighteen months, as regularly as clockwork, the old midwife would be sent for and somebody's children would be packed off to a stepmother's to stay out of the way until the danger and travail had passed. Why this happened was a mystery to me. So far, I had learned nothing at school to enlighten me, and somehow I knew better than to ask my mother to explain. Eavesdropping on my older sisters hadn't helped, either; no matter how hard I pressed my ear against the keyhole outside their room, I couldn't make out what they were giggling and whispering about. However, I loved hugging and squeezing my little brothers and sisters. Marriage sounded perfectly delightful. I envied my sister wholeheartedly.

When September came, Mahssy, escorted by her weeping mother and her old nursemaid, went to live in the colonel's and Neggar-Saltaneh's family compound. The rest of us went there as well, for the wedding festivities, Shazdeh and my older brothers to the men's feast and I with my mother, stepmothers, sisters, and smaller brothers to the women's.

This was especially exciting because Mahssy's new in-laws lived far more richly than we did, or even than Shazdeh. Oriental vases and French tapestries and paintings filled their huge mansion, as did the magnificent carpets for which their compound was famous. A vast feast of minted chicken, lamb kabobs, and the sweet saffron rice that is served at weddings had been laid out on cloths on the floor of the dining room where hundreds of women relatives, friends, and relatives-of-friends were celebrating and making an earsplitting din while de-vouring all that their plates could hold. I wandered about, happily wolfing down the delicious food with my mouth and eating up every-thing else with my eyes, until Jaby found me and hauled me back to our group with the news that Neggar-Saltaneh was going to show us Mahssy's and the colonel's new quarters.

This Neggar-Saltaneh was an extraordinary woman, and anything but "zaifeh." She was as domineering and confident as the legendary Iranian queen Turandot. The widow of a wealthy landowner, she managed her inherited property herself—unlike widows in the West, Iranian women have always been able to inherit their husband's prop-erty—and supervised her bailiffs by traveling on horseback through rugged and dangerous country to distant farm villages. A tall, bony woman of about fifty who concealed her gray hair with an elegant black rinse tinged with henna, Neggar-Saltaneh talked loudly, told off-color jokes, and if she was at a party of her women friends, she would simply get up and start dancing, singing and snapping her fingers to accompany herself, to show how good she felt. Furthermore, she was a great coquette and pretended to flirt outrageously with everyone, including my father. Far from making her unpopular, her earthy behavior made her a great favorite in our stiff and formal Persian high society. Shazdeh was mad about her, and loved it when she called him not "Ghorban" but "Shazdeh darling." (I, on the other hand, nearly fainted the first time I heard her say this.) Even my mother thought her a wonderful character.

Neggar-Saltaneh led us down some corridors to a large, handsome bedroom in dove gray, whose floor was covered with a superb blue Kerman carpet and which was furnished with Russian antiques. A beautiful set of hairbrushes with silver filigree handles was already laid out on the dresser for the couple's use that night. It was a tranquil, hospitable room which, I thought, would surely please the newlyweds.

But the most impressive thing about it was the gigantic, king-sized four-poster bed that stood in the middle, covered with a beautiful silk bedspread. I had never seen or imagined a bed so large. Not even Shazdeh's big wooden bed, which I saw every Friday when we visited his room, was the size of this monster. I wondered how even two people together could possibly find a use for such a vast expanse of bed.

Just as I was thinking this, Neggar-Saltaneh flounced gaily over to the bed, hiked up her skirts, and with a shriek of laughter jumped smack into the middle of the mattress, where she bounced gently for a second. "Look," she cried, "it has springs!" Then, throwing herself back and closing her eyes, she bent her skinny knees, spread her long legs apart, and began writhing with comical voluptuousness. "Come, my darling," she moaned, "don't be bashful. See, I am crawling with a thousand ants, here, and here, and here—come and take away the itching that has tormented me ever since I saw your face in the mirror!"

Jaby was staring openmouthed at our hostess. My mother and Batul-Khanom were giggling—I had never before heard my mother giggle like that. Her face was scarlet. Batul, who normally appreciated even the most unusual jokes, was looking desperately for something to fix her eyes on.

Bewildered, I edged closer to see if proximity would help me figure out what everyone but I had understood. By "mirror," Neggar-Saltaneh meant the mirror in which the bride was allowed to see her husband for the first time during the wedding ceremony, when he entered the room from a door behind her. Obviously, Neggar-Saltaneh was pretending to be Mahssy. But what did the rest mean?

Already, however, our hostess was getting up off the bed and ushering us toward the chamber that would be Mahssy's private sitting room. I was left to flounder alone in my ignorance, thoroughly frustrated and crazy with curiosity. It drove me wild when other people knew a lot and I knew nothing.

That evening we bid Mahssy a tearful farewell and she, weeping, hugged and kissed us over and over again. As we drove home in the carriage, Fatimeh sobbed, inconsolable. She had spoken the traditional words of mother to daughter: "You are leaving in a white dress—come home in a white dress." This meant that Mahssy must never come home to us again except in her shroud, because to do otherwise would mean that her husband had divorced her, as Nosratdoleh had divorced the daughter of Shazdeh's sister Najmeh-Saltaneh.

I had never had to say goodbye to anyone in my family before, and the next morning I moped about disconsolately, until finally Khanom, watching me sitting idle and depressed, said gently, "Satti, I have work to do and cannot visit your stepmother this morning. Get up and pick some flowers and take them to her." Without enthusiasm, I trudged across the compound to my stepmother's house carrying a bouquet of autumn roses from our garden. I found Fatimeh-Khanom in her kitchen in the courtyard, red-eyed and miserable as she dragged herself about her chores.

"Fatimeh-Khanom," I greeted her awkwardly, "I hope you don't miss Mahssy too much. I've brought you some flowers to comfort you."

My stepmother looked at the roses and at me, and a rare smile of pleasure suddenly illuminated her pinched, morose face. She invited me to come into the house and sit down. Pouring some tea, she gave me a cookie, then began reminiscing about the wedding feast and the magnificence of Mahssy's new home. Suddenly I realized that Fatimeh-Khanom was desperately lonely. She had lost the only daughter she would ever have, while her sons would all leave her for the world of men. From now on, for the rest of her life, except for her servants and women visitors and my mother and Batul, who would make sure that she had company, she would be all alone in her andarun.

I went back to my mother's house, surprised to find that the effort to cheer up my stepmother had made me feel better, too. How lucky we all were, I thought gratefully, to live in Shazdeh's compound and be able to love and care for one another. I promised myself that I would always look after my stepmother and help my mother and Batul-Khanom see that she did not become too lonely. I felt that I could not have endured living out the rest of my life locked up in an andarun—not if someone were to offer me five big diamond rings.

By the end of 1935 Shazdeh had come to consider Nosratdoleh's style of living to have grown extremely dangerous. Reza Shah had become much more tyrannical and unpredictable than in the past. Many people believed that this was because, two years before, he and Iran had both suffered a humiliating defeat at the hands of the British over the matter of our oil—a defeat that brought home to Iranians as nothing had done before how impotent we were to control our own affairs and our nation's destiny.

All Iranians, including Reza Shah, detested the agreement with the Anglo-Persian Oil Company, drawn up before the oil was actually discovered and before anyone realized how important petroleum would become to the world. Many of the exact terms of the oil concession were secret, but Iranians knew about and deeply resented its main point: the English company, in return for a small annual tax, would keep all but sixteen percent of the annual net profits. The concession, which was valid for sixty years, further stipulated that while the Iranian government might inspect and supervise the English company's facilities and production, and while Iranians could be employed as laborers and engineers, no Iranian would be allowed to examine its books— which meant that we simply had to rely on the English managers' word that Iran was getting what it had been promised. During the First World War, great numbers of Iranians had come to realize the injustice of this agreement. Iran desperately needed an income if it were to advance. Thanks to the concession agreement, our income from the one and only major resource we possessed was negligible.

Ever since coming to power, Reza Shah had been trying to reduce the influence of foreign powers in Iran. In November of 1932, the Shah decided that he was going to get a fairer oil agreement from the British. He suddenly canceled the 1901 concession and demanded that Iran be granted a much larger share of the profits. Iranians were so jubilant at this decree that there were celebrations and fireworks everywhere. At last our country was standing up to the British!

Perhaps I should explain that we Iranians didn't exactly hate the British—or rather, we hated and admired them at the same time. Actually, my father liked them. Unlike the Russians, who were just simple brigands and plunderers, the British were very smart. They had made a great nation of their little European island, and he had enormous admiration for their ability as world leaders, as well as immense respect for their deviousness, which was universally acknowledged to be unlimited, surpassing even that of Iranians. He considered them fine soldiers, masterly diplomats, and crafty politicians—a breed with which my father felt sympathetic, having once been exactly that kind of politician himself. He didn't think they were evil, just looking out for their own interests like anybody else.

Mashti and all the servants, on the other hand, believed that the *englis-ha* were so diabolical that they could even cause floods, droughts, and earthquakes. And it was true that to Iranians, the British seemed almost supernaturally clever. They took nearly all the money from Iran's oil while we stayed poor. They had informers and agents in their pay at court, the Majlis, the government, the bazaar, the mosques, and anywhere else they could find Persians—and among us there were always many such people—who thought only of themselves and the future of their families. Through their spies in the Anglo-Persian Oil Company, the British manipulated our affairs so adroitly that everyone believed that even Reza Shah, who hated them, still had to ask their permission for anything he wanted to do. "This morning," people would say sarcastically (but only in the safety of their own families), "Iran's prime minister visited the British Embassy again to get his orders," and, "The British ambassador spits into his telephone and the Shah's ear sticks to the receiver." The British made us feel like nobodies in our own country—a small, weak people, eternally pushed around by outside interests that only cared about oil money and power over the Middle East.

The Shah's effort to get Iran its fair share of the oil money was soon outflanked by geopolitical reality. London threatened to confiscate Iran's foreign assets and English gunboats sailed into the Persian Gulf. Reza Shah had to back down. A year later, it was settled that the oil company would give Iran twenty percent of the profits instead of sixteen. Twenty percent was a pittance by comparison to what the British got and what Reza had aimed for. To add to the Shah's mortification, the original concession was extended by an additional thirty years, until 1991!

The 1933 concession agreement was a terrible loss of face for the Shah. The British had shown that they were Iran's real masters. Iranians, bitterly disappointed, blamed the king for the nation's weakness and called him a British stooge. As far as public opinion in Iran was concerned, the new national army, the Shah's proud refusal to take foreign loans, and his ambitious efforts to make us look more like a modern, Western nation—by now he had even forbidden the use of camels for commercial transport—meant nothing if foreigners could still do with us as they pleased.

From this time onward, the Shah's savage and distrustful moods seemed to increase. No one had ever enjoyed giving Reza Shah bad news, or telling him what they thought he wouldn't like hearing, but now he began to surround himself with military officers and courtiers who sought to promote themselves by servile flattery and by fanning his easily roused suspicions and jealousies of other men. Late in 1933 a brilliant, progressive, charismatic politician named Hossein Teymourtash, who had long served the Shah as minister of court, had been arrested on trumped-up charges of corruption, just as Nosratdoleh had been. A few months later, he died mysteriously in his jail cell. Teymourtash had been Nosratdoleh's best friend, and after that my father trembled for his son.

One morning a frightening incident occurred in our compound. A fire started in a chimney at Shazdeh's and spread rapidly to the other rooms in the wing. Seeing the black smoke rising, we, my mother, and the maidservants all rushed out to the biruni and stood watching with the other families and the womenservants from the safety of the fountain, about thirty feet from Shazdeh's mansion. My father was standing in front, shouting orders at the menservants and secretaries who were trying to put out the blaze with buckets of water from the fountain; beside him stood Nosratdoleh and his young son, who had rushed over to Shazdeh's when they saw the smoke.

Suddenly some figures strode into the compound through the narrow east door from Kakh Avenue: a huge man in a brown general's uniform and a long blue cloak, flanked by two uniformed guards. Everyone froze with astonishment and shock. I felt that even without the whispers around me I would have known instinctively that this was Reza Shah.

We all bowed low, astounded and fearful. The shah of Iran did not simply stroll out the door of his palace to call on a neighbor, and no one knew what this extraordinary visit might portend. Everyone was very quiet. I could tell that my mother thought the end had come.

But Reza Shah merely gazed at the flames with curiosity and interest. Then he turned to his old general and clapped him heavily on the shoulder. "Well, Shazdeh," he said affably, "old houses burn easily." I think he was trying to make my father feel better.

Shazdeh bowed again and thanked the monarch for his magnanimous condescension and concern. The king stayed for a few more minutes, watching with my father and Nosratdoleh as flames engulfed Shazdeh's guest quarters. We all sighed with relief when, like a sinister apparition, Reza Shah and his guards vanished through the Kakh

Avenue door again. But a shudder seemed to pass through the entire compound, and for a long time the tension in my mother's house was greater than usual. No one knew what Reza Shah might do. At school I was hearing dreadful, whispered stories of friends with male relatives who had been imprisoned and whose lands had been confiscated. A rumor circulated that since 1933 the Shah had become an opium addict. My mother and Mashti constantly warned us, "Don't ever talk about politics at school. Never trust anyone except your family."

Shazdeh now felt that it was urgent to get Nosratdoleh to curb his extravagance, but he could not warn him to his face. This would have been an unpardonable breach of etiquette, especially between a father and a grown son of Nosratdoleh's standing. Because Iranians are terribly touchy about admitting that they are in the wrong, even within the family, polite people are always careful never to criticize directly, but always to find some roundabout way of making their point. A courteous Persian never says bluntly, "You are mistaken," but, "Perhaps I should explain this to you, because I see that you have not yet been correctly informed." Among well-bred Iranians, there was no such thing as "constructive criticism," only criticism, and if there was a problem in the family, you had to choose someone to intercede for you. For instance, if I didn't like the color of a dress my mother was sewing for me, I never went to her myself, but would send Jaby to explain how I felt, thus avoiding the sin of disrespect to a parent.

For this reason my father composed a strong letter addressed to Salar-Lashgar (my father's second son's real name was Abbas, but he held the title Salar-Lashgar, "Commander of the Army," because he had been the chief general of my father's troops). The letter said that Nosratdoleh would endanger himself if he did not curb his extravagance and lead a less ostentatious life. Shazdeh asked Salar-Lashgar to go to Nosratdoleh and read him the letter, which Salar-Lashgar did. But although Nosratdoleh knew that Shazdeh really intended the letter for him and not Salar-Lashgar, its warning did no good. To Nosratdoleh's way of thinking, there was no point in being a prince if he couldn't live like one. That was an article of faith, like his diamond stickpins.

Aside from Mahssy's courtship under the willow trees, the chief excitement for my own family in 1935 was a reunion. For the first time I laid eyes on my own eldest brother, Sabbar, who was twenty-three and studying medicine in Paris.

I had only the dimmest notion of who he was. All through my childhood, Khanom had talked about our *dadash*, or "eldest brother." Shazdeh had sent Dadash to Paris in 1923, when he was eleven, to live with a French family named Rustant. He had not been back to Iran since then, for fear that Reza Shah's police would not allow him to return to France.

My grandfather Aghajun had helped my mother raise her first child during the long, lonely times of Shazdeh's absences on his assignments as military governor. He had been as much a second father to Dadash as Mashti had been to me, and every time the letter carrier knocked at our gatehouse, my grandfather, who could not read anything except the Arabic letters of the Koran, would appear and inquire in his mild, grave, ceremonial way whether there was anything from "Prince Sabbar in Paris." If there was, Aghajun would joyfully give the man a big tip, kiss the letter many times, and take it to my mother to read aloud to them both.

The effect that these letters had on my mother was astounding. Instead of slaps, after one of Dadash's letters my misdeeds would be greeted with laughter, kisses, and candy. Everyone's transgressions were instantly forgiven and forgotten, and my mother would talk with delight and pride of nothing but Dadash—of how, when he was six, he had inscribed one thousand poems in his copybook and had been able to recite them perfectly to Shazdeh, who had given him a coin for each one (my mother still kept his copybook hidden on a shelf next to her Koran), and of how Shazdeh had wanted him to go to military school and Dadash had written dryly and humorously from Paris, "Ghorban, I don't like military hats; I want to be a doctor."

Who, I wondered, was this mysterious saint whose letters had the power to make Khanom forget all her troubles and become a laughing, happy young woman? When we learned at Reswanieh that Shazdeh had at last decided to take a chance and bring Dadash home for six weeks at the end of the summer along with our fourteen-year-old brother Aziz, Batul's son, who was just my age and whose milk I had shared, we were all rapturous. Aghajun talked of nothing else, while Khanom and the servants plunged into a happy frenzy of cleaning, baking cookies, and sewing new clothes for everyone. My mother beamed at everybody and grew prettier daily, her eyes bright and her cheeks rosy with life and excitement.

One hot day in August of 1935, the Essex rolled majestically through the gates of Reswanieh and Dadash stepped into our garden. With tears streaming down their faces, my mother and Aghajun rushed to embrace him. Then the rest of us were introduced to him. I was wide-eyed at the novelty of seeing a young man enter our andarun for the first time in my life, and bursting with pride that this was my eldest brother, my mother's firstborn. Dadash had a long, kindly face, humorous, observant eyes, and a grave and serious manner just like Aghajun's. He looked like a doctor already, I thought. How full of knowledge he must be, of information I couldn't even begin to imagine!

The six weeks went like the wind. It was thrilling to hear the servants call Dadash "Doktur Sabbar Mirza" and to have Dadash, between rounds of visits to influential people in the city with Shazdeh, take us rock climbing in the mountains on weekends. Dadash had learned the proper, scientific way to climb in the French Alps, and I was eager to partake of his store of modern knowledge. Aziz, too, impressed me. Aziz was a swimmer. He had turned into a handsome boy, with very strong arms. Watching him swim in the pond, I saw that he did not dog-paddle, as I did, but ploughed through the water with powerful, graceful strokes. He had learned the right way to swim, he said, at his school, the lycée Jansen in Paris, which Nosratdoleh and Dadash had also attended.

I began to give this some serious thought. Aziz was exactly my age—we had nursed together. But he could swim correctly and I could not. He and Dadash conversed as easily in French as they did in Persian, sprinkling French expressions all over their talk like cinnamon, while I would not even begin learning French or English for another two years. They had traveled in Europe and Russia, while I had never been farther from home than the mountain passes above Reswanieh.

Suddenly it dawned on me: I was backward. I needed more education, and I wasn't going to get it by staying home. I knew that Dr. Jordan's school was good, but it was quite evident that the education Dadash and Aziz had received was brilliant. By comparison to them, I felt like an ignorant, untraveled yokel. Shazdeh wasn't even giving me a governess to teach me etiquette! I was certainly as smart as Aziz—I was the best of any of Shazdeh's children now in school. I should have the same advantages as he, my contemporary and equal. How was I going to get anywhere if I didn't have the best education?

I didn't stop to think that no other Iranian girl I had ever heard of had studied in Europe. My brothers, before high school had separated us and we had still played together every day in the biruni, had never thought of me as a girl—"girls" were dainty, passive creatures who sat uselessly in the andarun playing with dolls, but I could climb trees! I was one of them, and they and I both knew that I was an exception to the usual rules for girls. Shazdeh, I thought, should be doing as much for me as he had for my older sisters. He wasn't giving me a governess, so he could afford to send me abroad to study with Aziz.

I decided not to deliver my request through Jaby. This was too unusual a matter, and too urgent. In less than a week, Dadash and Aziz would board the train that would take them back to Europe. I would approach my mother directly, so that she could speak to Shazdeh at once. She might, of course, just snap as usual, "You can't do that, you're a woman." But this, I assured myself, was a different matter entirely. This concerned my education. With Dadash here, my mother was in wonderful spirits. If she said no, that would be that. But I decided to try anyway.

The only way to speak with my mother, who was always busy, was to catch her on the wing. Finally, two or three days before my brothers were to leave, I waylaid her as she was supervising the morning dusting and sweeping and announced firmly that I wished to go back to Europe with Dadash and Aziz.

She gazed at me calmly, blinking a little but showing no other sign of surprise. "Why do you want to do that?" she said.

"Khanom, I want to study abroad, too, like them. I want more education."

My mother looked at me in silence for a few moments more. She only looked a little confused. I had no idea what she was thinking. Finally she asked, "And where do you imagine you would live, a young girl like you?"

"I will live with Dadash and the Rustants, or with Aziz or someone else. It would not be very expensive," I persisted daringly. "I don't need much to eat, or a lot of fancy things. Nargess can just pack my summer clothes and I'll take those along. Shazdeh isn't giving me a governess and he isn't sending any other boys to Europe, so that's a double saving. He could afford to send me."

I tried to read an expression in her brown eyes, but they were impenetrable. She looked at me, thoughtful and a little troubled, for a couple of seconds more. Finally she said, "I will ask Shazdeh." I waited, surprised, for her to tell me that she did not like the idea, but evidently she had no objection. I went away relieved and excited: the first hurdle had been overcome. My mother deferred to my father in all matters. It remained only for him to agree, and my request was certainly reasonable enough. He might say yes.

Shazdeh was staying at Reswanieh for the few days that remained of my brothers' visit. My father loved to sit surrounded by as many of his children as possible, and that evening before supper, he summoned us to his room in the main cottage—my mother, Batul, Fatimeh,

Dadash, Jaby, Aziz, myself and some of the other children—and sat in his armchair, leaning on his cane for comfort, while the rest of us lounged crosslegged at his feet or reclined on cushions on the carpet.

I waited, apprehensive but eager, for my mother to mention my request. I knew it was chancy—but the worst that could happen, I thought with a mental shrug, was that he would be in a bad mood and say no. It couldn't hurt to try.

At last my mother said casually, "Ghorban: Satti says that she wishes to study abroad." I held my breath. For a split second, there was a hush.

Then somebody laughed.

Shazdeh's eyes narrowed. His white eyebrows drew together. Leaning forward on his cane, he look at me quizzically, then at my mother. Then, with finality, he sat back. Resting one hand on the cane, he flicked the other dismissively in the air. "It would be a waste of money," he said. "She is a woman. A woman will be nothing."

I sat there as stunned as though he had struck me. Several of my brothers and sisters smiled at me good-naturedly. To them it was as if I had suggested becoming an acrobat in the Russian circus. But my mother did not laugh. She said nothing at all. Her face was as closed to everyone in the room as the volume of Hafez's poetry that lay on a table nearby.

I could have sunk through the floor with shame. That he might refuse I had known, but that he would refuse because he thought me stupid and not worth spending money on was something I had never imagined for an instant. Didn't I bring home the highest grades in my class? I was blind with humiliation and anger. Mortifying tears choked my throat. With a supreme effort, I forced them back—everybody had laughed at me enough for one evening.

My distress, however, must have been obvious, for afterward at supper no one teased me. Dadash and Jaby were far too kind to embarrass me further by dwelling on my folly, and my mother seemed, blessedly, to have forgotten the whole matter. I wondered why she had agreed so easily to convey my request. Perhaps it was just because she was so happy that Dadash was still here. Or maybe, I thought bitterly, she knew that Shazdeh thought I was stupid and would say no, so she could save herself the trouble of an argument with me.

That night, I lay awake racked with shame, disappointment, and chagrin. I knew I could never discuss today with anyone. I was dizzy with resentment at Shazdeh's arbitrariness. Since I was old enough to stand on my two feet, not a single Friday had passed that he did not tell us—all of us, boys and girls alike—how important education was.

In fact, it had never occurred to me that Shazdeh's enlightened ideas went only as far as thinking women capable of learning to be good wives and mothers. I had never even had a conversation alone with my father, much less asked him what he and other educated men thought a woman's brain capable of. His views on women were essentially no different from any other Persian's, man or woman: not only he and my mother but also my stepmother Batul-Khanom and even Neggar-Saltaneh would have agreed that a "zaifeh" was incapable of living without her family to protect her, because no Iranian woman had ever done so—at least not of her own free will, and certainly no one of our own class. There had been nothing personal in his remark about me, but I didn't know that.

I lay awake, glaring through the mosquito netting at the stars in an agony of shame and resentment. How could Shazdeh say that I would come to nothing? How dare he? I could see for myself that women like my mother and Neggar-Saltaneh were as intelligent and capable as men. Furthermore, Miss Doolittle and the other women missionaries who taught at Nurbaksh lived by themselves, without any help from men at all. *They* were not "nothing."

Through this fog of pain and anger, I did feel a pang of gratitude to my mother for her restraint during the whole affair. Now I realized that she must have considered it the height of immorality to suggest that a young girl go off to study in an unknown, unclean land, far from the love and protection of her family. But if Shazdeh had agreed that leaving a Moslem country to go to school among foreigners and barbarians would be best for me, she would have bowed to his will. She must have had to summon every bit of her own strong will and self-discipline to convey such a shocking request. I was sure that she could do so only because Shazdeh had truly convinced her of the importance of our education. This, however, was scant comfort, as I myself had no choice but to accept Shazdeh's decision. I would just have to make the most of whatever education I could get. I longed for school to start again, so that I could bury the humiliating memory of this evening in hard work.

Someday, I vowed, I'll show them all—women are not nothing! If he doesn't marry me off first, I'm going to do something with my life. Just let them watch! One day I'm going to prove that a woman can be somebody, too.

5

THE END
OF CHILDHOOD

*Avoid the service of rulers, for though the benefits of a sea
voyage are many, safety lies on shore.*

—Sa'adi

A YEAR AFTER MAHSSY'S WEDDING, IN THE FALL OF 1936, WE CEL-
ebrated another wedding. This time it was our beloved Jaby—
at twenty, she was the last of the older girls in the compound to marry.

Shazdeh was marrying her to just the sort of man he liked to find
for his daughters. Abbas Parkhideh was a petroleum engineer with the
newly renamed Anglo-Iranian Oil Company, the AIOC. Because the
AIOC's British managers had agreed in 1933 for the first time to train
and promote Iranians to management positions, Abbas, who was
bright, honest, and extremely conscientious, had been sent to the
University of Birmingham for advanced training and had a good future
ahead of him. As he came from a clerical family, he was a little old-
fashioned, with a low opinion of women. Shazdeh, however, probably
felt that Jaby would have no problem with her husband's traditional
views, since she, like our mother, was very devout. I hoped that Abbas
would value our lovely Jaby as she deserved. She had been the kindest
of older sisters, helping me with my homework, tactfully getting me

to comb my hair and soften my boisterous ways, hugging and comforting me when I had to bear the brunt of Khanom's temper. She
was gentle, generous, an excellent manager, and artistically talented
as well. I naturally considered that Abbas was getting the best of the
bargain. But I was happy and relieved for my sister, too: after twenty,
an unmarried Persian girl was considered an old maid.

Jaby's marrying was also momentous for me because, with Dadash
and all the older boys away at school in Europe, I would be the eldest
child, not only in my mother's household but in the compound. This
was a solemn responsibility that I took very seriously. I was determined
to set a good example. My mother still had plenty of us at home: in
addition to Farough and me, there were my brothers Ghaffar and
Rashid and my sisters Homy and Sory. But Khanom was sad and
depressed at Jaby's leaving. The newlyweds had to depart immediately
for torrid Abadan, the city the AIOC had built around its huge oil
refinery on the Persian Gulf. Abbas's assignment would keep them
there for several years. This time it would be Khanom who had to
pronounce the melancholy injunction, "You leave in a white dress,
come home in a white dress." It hurt me to see her sadness, which I
shared. We all hated to lose Jaby.

But when everyone crowded into my mother's salon for the wedding
and Jaby blushed to see Abbas behind her in the mirror as she sat in
her white Western-style wedding gown on a divan across from Ashekh-
Javad, we were all filled with a deep emotion for which we had no
words. A kind of electric murmur seemed to move beneath the sobs
of the women that wove this new thread into the interlocking web of
clan. We Iranians, who value the family above all else and spend our
whole lives within its hot, protective walls, know that from it we derive
our very being, our deepest and most meaningful sense of self. Through
it we define who we are, to the world and to ourselves. As long as the
family is intact, secure, and complete, we know that we are somebody
instead of nobody.

I am sure that on that day this was what Shazdeh felt, too, because
during the reception in Khanom's garden, he was in great spirits. After
the photographer had taken dozens of pictures of him and Jaby and
Abbas and scores of our other relations, Shazdeh, not yet tired, called
for his oldest son and Batul-Khanom's little boy, Abdol Ali, his youngest son. My father was now close to eighty, but at that moment, as
he sat with Nosratdoleh beside him on his right and the four-year-old
Abdol Ali at his knee, he looked as sharp-eyed and proud of the little
kingdom he had made as one of the stone kings at Pasargadae. He had
begotten us, educated us, taught us the meaning of duty and justice.

We were his masterpiece, his poem, the great work of his life. On that day, I am sure, Shazdeh was happy.

It was the last time that we were able to say so.

Two weeks after Jaby and Abbas left for Abadan, Tehran's police chief, a man named Mokhtari, went to Nosratdoleh's home and arrested him. My brother, who had been working in his library, did not protest or resist. He telephoned Shazdeh and asked him to inform Ezzatdoleh and to watch over his children. Then he left with the police.

No formal charges were brought. However, Reza Shah had lately been much occupied by the idea that the French were laughing at him, and my anguished father was certain this was the reason for Nosratdoleh's arrest. My brother still kept up his literary correspondences in Paris and had many friends in the French diplomatic corps in Tehran, among them the French attaché and his wife, and it may have been around this time that a certain famous cartoon appeared in the French press that mocked Reza Shah's well-known appetite for land by showing a ferocious black cat devouring a map of Iran, with a caption that read, *"Le chat de Pers":* "The Persian Cat." To be compared to an animal is very insulting to Moslems, and since *chat,* "cat," is pronounced the same way as "shah," Reza couldn't very well miss the point, and he threatened to break off diplomatic relations with France.

Anyway, whether this cartoon was the reason or not, the Shah undoubtedly distrusted the fact that Nosratdoleh had so many French connections, and he apparently concluded that my brother's inviting Frenchmen to dine with him and writing letters to others the king had never heard of was as good as plotting against him with the French government.

Ezzatdoleh wrote a letter to Reza Shah imploring him to forgive Nosratdoleh. Over the years she and Shazdeh had already suffered the loss of two younger sons, Nezam and Jaffar, and in 1935 Salar-Lashgar had died of cancer. But the Shah refused her plea. Nosratdoleh was locked up in a prison in Tehran. He was not uncomfortable: the Shah permitted him to send not only for many of his books but also for his valet and his dog, Coty. But Shazdeh was not permitted to see him and he was allowed no visitors except his youngest son, who was twelve. Two months later, in January of 1937, he was transferred to a guarded house in Semnon, a village about eighty miles east of the capital, where he was held incommunicado. My mother now went every day to Ezzatdoleh to try to comfort her and give her hope.

By this time my mother hated Reza Shah more than ever before.

Two years earlier, the Shah had done something that Khanom, along with millions of other devout Iranian women, knew they could never forgive.

Strange though it might seem, Reza Shah was anxious to emancipate women—or rather, to create the appearance of emancipation. Starting around 1934 he had begun opening higher education and professions like nursing and schoolteaching to women, and forcing cinemas, restaurants, and hotels, on pain of heavy fines, to admit both sexes. As he did not give women the right to vote, run for political office, divorce their husbands, have custody of their own children, or even get a passport without their husbands' permission, and as women applicants found it extremely difficult to get admitted to the few areas of study open to them at the University, these improvements, while significant, were less meaningful than they appeared to foreign observers. The Shah, however, was universally praised in the West for his enlightened "Western" views on women's rights.

The climax of this campaign had come in February of 1935: suddenly, the Shah had outlawed the veil. With his usual incisiveness, he let it be known that the heads of old society families like ours risked his serious displeasure if they did not show their wives in public, and in Western garb.

When my mother had learned that she was to lose the age-old modesty of her veil, she was beside herself. She and all traditional people regarded Reza's order as the worst thing he had yet done— worse than his attacking the rights of the clergy; worse even than his confiscations and murders. Shazdeh, however, realized that he did not dare disobey.

I am sure that this was not an easy decision for him. For a Persian aristocrat to allow strange men to gape at his wives in public was shameful in the extreme. Having made up his mind to comply, however, my father resolved that for the sake of his family's safety, his wives would be the very first of the old aristocracy to appear formally in Western dress. He sent to the Avenue Lalezar for hats for all his wives in the compound and told them that the next day they were to put them on and ride with him in the open droshky. To my mother, it was exactly as if he had insisted that she parade naked in the street. Only her respect for his wisdom and her fears for his safety could have enabled her to submit to such degradation.

The next day, weeping with rage and humiliation, she sequestered herself in her bedroom with Batul-Khanom to put on the hat. "First Reza Shah attacks the clergy," my mother sobbed, "and now this. He's trying to destroy religion. He doesn't fear God, this evil Shah—may

God curse him for it!" As she wept she struggled futilely to hide her beautiful masses of waist-length black hair under the inadequate protection of a small French cloche. There was nothing my stepmother could say to console her.

In April of 1937, my father received word that Nosratdoleh was dead and that he must come personally to collect his son's body.

Chief Mokhtari told my father that Nosratdoleh was to be buried without any ceremonies. Reza Shah did not intend to give the murdered man's family and friends the opportunity to channel their sorrow into opposition. At the same time Shazdeh was called, Nosratdoleh's twelve-year-old son received a letter his father had written the night before his death, a letter whose words made it clear that our brother knew the end was only hours away. Years later it became public knowledge that Nosratdoleh had been killed in his room by strangulation under the supervision of a doctor named Ahmadi.

No announcement appeared in the press of the death of one of the country's most famous men. The terrible blow of this tragedy to Shazdeh and Ezzatdoleh was greatly compounded by Reza's order not to hold a funeral or the usual mourning rites. In Iran and all Moslem countries, the death of a family member is always followed by more than a month of intensive mourning, during which all one's relatives and friends are invited to visit, break bread with the family of the deceased, and share in their grief, until on the fortieth day after the death the mourning process formally concludes with a final memorial rite. These forty days of mourning are of tremendous psychological importance to the bereaved, because the rituals of crying and suffering help the family to release its grief, after which it can pick up the broken pieces of its life and go on. But Reza Shah was making us keep our pain inside our hearts.

Shazdeh took Nosratdoleh and buried him at the Shrine of Shah Abdol Azim, south of the city, where Nasser al-Din Shah, whom my father admired as the most progressive of the Qajar shahs, also lay buried. Wishing to be reunited someday with Nosratdoleh, he also ordered a plain white tomb to be built there for himself.

"Be sure not to cry at school," my mother said. "Don't talk or answer any questions about Nosratdoleh's death. You know what might happen to Shazdeh if Reza Shah heard." Even at home we scarcely trusted ourselves to open our lips. We all felt that we could only speak to curse the king. Ezzatdoleh was prostrate. My mother went every day to see her, but there was nothing that she could do.

As for Shazdeh, I can hardly express how he suffered. In the space of weeks, he became truly old. His hair and mustache, which had still had some gray in them, went chalk-white. He lost all his vigor and vitality. My mother, who went to stay with him every night, said that he talked to himself now, like an old, old man. On our Friday visits, he seemed not to see us at all, and we were hushed and quiet, as if in the presence of someone very ill—even the smallest children behaved themselves, trying not to startle or annoy him as he struggled to bear a burden so heavy it made his eyebrows droop down over his eyes like white willow trees. I felt his suffering so keenly that his pain seemed my own.

School offered scant relief from the terrible leaden ball of unreleased grief and anger inside my chest that seemed at times to swell until I thought that if I could not curse and scream at Reza Shah's cruelty, the metal ball would swell up into my throat and choke me. In class my Persian and American teachers, seeing that I was unusually quiet and lost my place when called on to recite, gave me sympathetic glances. Farough, Abol, Ali-Naghi, and Ali-Dad told me that Dr. Jordan had called them into his office at the boys' school and told them, in his humorous way, to be extremely careful. "He said," Farough added, "that all walls have mice, and the mice have ears—so even when you think nobody is in the room with you, watch out." I listened to this advice with my lips pressed tightly together so as not to let any words break forth.

Not long after Nosratdoleh's death, Reza Shah seized his compound, forcing his family to seek refuge with Ezzatdoleh while Shazdeh found another home for them. Shazdeh also had to sell off a great deal of land to scrape up money to pay off Reza Shah, who was suddenly claiming that years before, Nosratdoleh had received twenty-eight thousand English pounds sterling from the British government as a bribe for negotiating the Anglo-Persian Agreement, and the Shah was demanding that his widow remit this sum to the government.

I thought of Shazdeh and Khanom telling us that God punished evil deeds on earth as well as in the hereafter. But how could God punish Reza Shah and his henchmen for making us miserable? The Shah was so big and strong that I feared that not even God could touch him. He had taken away our rights, stopped our mouths, suppressed our constitution and our parliament, stolen people's property, and ruined, imprisoned, and killed men with impunity—not only my brother and his friend Teymourtash, the minister of court, but many others: Sardar Assad, the chief of the Bakhtiari; Solatdoleh, the chief of the Qashqa'i; Samuel Haim, the Jewish community's representative to the Majlis; Eshqi the poet; Modarres the mullah, who, along with

Shazdeh's nephew, Mohammed Mossadegh, had been one of the few members of parliament to protest his being given dictatorial powers. And these were only the most prominent. I was terrified. It seemed merely a matter of time before he sent the policeman Mokhtari to take Shazdeh away, too.

However, more weeks went by and nothing happened to Shazdeh. Slowly things began to take on the barest semblance of normal life again. After six weeks or so, as if by an effort of his splendid will, my father recovered enough to begin attending to everyday affairs. My mother, who had become pregnant before Nosratdoleh's imprisonment, had her ninth and last child, my youngest sister: a sweet little girl whom Shazdeh named Khorshid. And I discovered that not even tragedy could keep me from enjoying school and my studies for long.

Then, one afternoon at the end of May, Mashti picked me up early at Nurbaksh with the news that Reza Shah's men were at the compound.

When the two of us got home, the whole place was in an uproar. People were crying and lamenting as though Imam Hossein had just been murdered a second time. Frightened, I went automatically to the dining room where I usually gave my younger brothers and sisters their afternoon snack, and found Khanom already there. Her eyes were red. "Drink up your milk quickly, children," she said to my six-year-old sister Sory and our youngest brother Rashid, who was four. "I must go."

"Khanom," I said fearfully, "what's wrong?"

"Surveyors came to Shazdeh this morning. They brought equipment with them." Her voice quavered and my fear grew. "They drew a line down the middle of the compound, from the front gate to Shazdeh's. Reza Shah is taking everything on the other side of the line—the whole compound from there to Kakh Avenue. Shazdeh's home, your stepmothers', everything except this house will be torn down."

I struggled to take in what she was saying. Reza Shah in our compound, I thought; it wasn't possible. I tried to thrust away what I already knew to be a certainty. "Khanom," I stammered, "what will happen to us?"

"I don't know," she said wearily, "but Shazdeh says we can't stay here. Everything will be gone—the bathhouse, the kitchens, the storehouses, the servants' quarters. There will be no one to buy food or bring supplies and the biruni will be full of workmen. The big wall around the compound will go, so the whole street will be able to look into this andarun. We have to move to Reswanieh. Shazdeh has a thousand people to find homes for."

The world seemed a blank, filled with nothing, a thick gray blur, the way it had been the day we went hiking with Shazdeh in the mountains and got lost in the hailstorm. I realized that I was trembling. "How long before they come, Khanom?"

"They have already begun on Batul-Khanom's wall and gatehouse. We must pack everything and leave right away." She pulled her pretty household chador over her hair wearily, as though it were made of lead. "I must go and help Batul-Khanom, Satti," she said, rising. "Make sure the little ones finish their snack."

Suddenly, the tears began to pour down her cheeks. "Pray!" she gasped. The word burst out as if she could not contain it any longer. "Pray to the Merciful and Compassionate, Satti, and to Imam Hossein and his family who protect the victims of injustice—pray to them to curse this evil Shah!"

I remembered that I was sixteen now, and the eldest, and could not give way to my own feelings. My mother had Khorshid to worry about. Farough and Ghaffar and my sister Homy were old enough to know what losing our home meant, and someone would have to take care of Sory and Rashid, who were too young to understand what was happening. All these years Khanom had worn herself out to give us a good home. I must not think of my own sorrow now, only of helping her and the children. My words of anger would have to stay inside me, where they belonged.

So began the destruction of our world. The next few days are a blur in my memory, but I know that they were terrible. Reza Shah never wasted time. The next morning, Sepah Avenue was swarming with laborers carrying shovels, pickaxes, and sledgehammers. Soon the part of the compound wall that hid our own andarun crumbled as though a giant hand had smashed it, and our house and my mother's garden and the places in it where I had played as a small child lay open to public view, exposing us to the street and leaving us frightened and ashamed of our nakedness.

Ever since I could recall, I had been hearing what were supposed to be noises of modernization, of progress. Now they became sounds of lawless despoilment. The laborers set to work on Shazdeh's house, and for the few days that it took us to prepare to move to Reswanieh I watched them attacking it like red ants tearing the flesh of a dead beast in the desert. Soon dust was rising from the antechamber where we had waited for Shazdeh to receive us, from the room where he had chided us, hugged us, exasperated our mothers with his deafness, exhorted us to serve our country. The dust covered everything—our clothes, our books, my little brothers' and sisters' toys.

Reza Shah, I felt, was tearing apart not just our physical home, but our very selves. It was us he was despoiling and trampling on, as if a thousand human beings were just maggots to be plucked from a carcass he was dismembering. We had no rights, no justice, no power to defend ourselves against the violation being visited on us and on those who needed us.

I no longer cared if my curses were heard. What kind of a king, I cried to Mashti, ordered a thousand people thrown out into the street? What kind of country was it when you could not fight an injustice or even say that it was wrong?

But Mashti just shrugged sadly. His and Korsum's little house across the street was being torn down along with the wall. Only Khanom and my father stood between them and destitution. This, Mashti said, was just how things had always been. There was nothing to do about it. Outside your family, nothing was safe.

At last Khanom collected all of us and loaded us into the Essex, which would take us to Reswanieh. Mashti, Korsum, Nargess, and our maidservants were to follow in the droshky with our belongings. Ever since Reza Shah had forbidden the black chador, my mother had refrained from leaving the compound even for one of her rare trips to the bazaar. Now, unable to bring herself to appear completely uncovered in public, she wrapped herself in a length of cotton cloth to make the dismal journey. Tears rolled down her swollen cheeks, which she kept wiping away with her improvised veil. I had never seen her so hopeless.

Sitting beside her and trying to keep the little ones from crying as the Essex pulled out of the compound, I looked for one last time on the places of my childhood: the reflecting pool; the flower beds where my father had sat with his cane, entertaining his guests; the sycamore trees I had climbed; the shady groves where we had listened to the chanting of the stories of Rostam, Kaveh, and Zahak. I remembered all the happiness we had had, and all the people in the compound. It seemed to me that we had lost our happiness forever. The wall around us had vanished and the single harmonious family it had contained would never exist again. Reza Shah had granted my wish to go out into the world. It was the end of childhood.

My father wasted no time on lamentations. Somehow, despite the shock, his infirmities, and the lacerating grief of Nosratdoleh's death, he was still indomitable. He rallied his strength and set about relocating everyone. My mother braced herself and followed his example, carrying out his orders, looking resolutely forward and showing that she expected all of us to do the same.

Shazdeh moved my family to cottages at Reswanieh for the summer; we could return to our own house in about a year, when the Shah's road was finished and our wall had been rebuilt. Batul and her children and servants were settled in a large house in the northern part of the city; he built Fatimeh-Khanom and Hamdam-Khanom and their families new houses at Reswanieh. He himself moved with Delrobah and his other personal servants into the main cottage there, while his clerks, secretaries, and other staff set up office quarters in another small house he owned in the city. There were still hundreds of other servants, staff, and military pensioners to take care of, and for all of them he built modest homes. As a result, not a single one of our old servants or staff was made homeless or destitute. My mother moved Mashti and Korsum and their children into a house not far from where their old one had been. Now that the compound and gatehouse were gone and there was nobody to bring rice, cloth, and other supplies to our house, Mashti would have to take my mother to the bazaar so that she could do her own shopping. She needed him more than ever.

In the fall I and one of our younger sisters, Batul's daughter Lili, went to live in the student dormitory at Nurbaksh, and Farough went with Abol, Ali-Naghi, and Ali-Dad to the dormitory at Alborz College. I saw my brothers only when the Essex arrived on Thursday afternoons to take them and me to Reswanieh for the one-day weekend, and I badly missed them, my mother, and everyone else. However, living away from home was a great adventure—and in only a year, I told myself, we would all be together again. I could not allow emotion to distract me from my tasks. I was now a junior at Nurbaksh, and nearly seventeen, and must set a good example. Besides, the best way to cheer up Shazdeh would be to work harder than ever, so that he would be proud of me.

Happy, as I always am, to drown my troubles in hard work, I threw myself into school with renewed energy. I was especially good at math and geometry because they were so logical. However, we had now reached the level where a smattering of English and French was taught, and I found languages difficult. Persian is an Indo-European language like English, and many words are similar (for example, "pedar" in Persian is "father" in English, "madar" is "mother," and so on). But the sounds, alphabet, and left-to-right writing style of English are maddeningly difficult for a Persian, and in my efforts to master the strange Latin script I spent hours every week copying and recopying my lessons, struggling against lifelong patterns of hand-eye movement that were based on the flowing right-to-left script of Persian. However, I was cheered by the knowledge that speaking a little English would bring me closer to the missionaries and their families. Above all, I knew that Shazdeh would be pleased to hear that I was applying myself.

Not until we returned home just before my senior year in September of 1938 was I forced to recognize fully the enormity of the loss from which school and sheer hard work had successfully distracted me. Instead of being a part of a vital, self-sustaining universe, our house now stood all alone behind its wall on Sepah Avenue. Mashti's gatehouse had vanished, as had half of our front garden.

And where the great green biruni had lain, there ran a bleak, twelve-meter-wide stretch of road. The gardens and trees and flowers were gone; the fountains and pools, the lovely, airy space were gone. But worst of all, the people were gone. Disoriented and confused, at first my brothers and sisters and I felt as though our arms and legs had been cut off, and could hardly function in this lonely, isolated home. I saw the road the Shah had built, which was called "Accounting Street" because it connected his palace with his accounting offices, as if it were still engaged in its work of destruction: a wave of asphalt rolling over the spot where the studded entrance gate had been, crashing through the middle of the garden, toppling trees and crushing flower beds until it reached Shazdeh's house, smashing his staircase and portico and laying his spacious rooms open to the sky, sending the inhabitants of our little universe scurrying in terror for safety. Nothing of what had once been there was visible—the laborious activity, the bonds of bread and salt we had shared, the hardships and pleasures, the lives.

Reza Shah's stony testimony to his own power to shatter mere human happiness had obliterated everything. I saw now why Shazdeh had taught us never to depend on the winds of politics, or on anyone but ourselves. By destroying our world, the Shah had taught me a great lesson in self-reliance.

Our isolated home was additionally lonely because my older sisters and half-sisters were no longer around. Jaby was still in Abadan, while Mahssy was off in the north of Iran, where her husband was on a military assignment. I felt that if I didn't find something to keep me from thinking about all the distressing things I had on my mind, I would shrivel up like a dead grasshopper.

Fortunately, that same fall I found another escape. The school's service club sent seniors to help out for an hour or two every week at a medical dispensary that served the sprawling neighborhoods south of the old bazaar. The dispensary was an outpost opened by the American Mission Hospital in a small former warehouse. Poor women and children came there to get aspirin, eyedrops for trachoma, and salve for *katchali*, a ringworm of the scalp common in the Middle East. European-trained physicians were desperately scarce, and a doctor could only come once every couple of weeks, so the few untrained orderlies the hospital could pay were supervised by Mrs. MacDowell, the hospital director's wife, and by Mrs. Elder, the minister's wife. I and the other volunteers rode to the dispensary, five miles south of Nurbaksh, once a week with Mrs. Elder or Mrs. MacDowell in a droshky.

South Tehran was most of Tehran, but girls like me never went there and never saw the way vast numbers of Iranians lived. Here were none of the Shah's large, imposing, European-style buildings, good stone streets, or wide, paved avenues with pretty, fashionable orange-and-white awnings like the Lalezar's. While the walls of the twisting byways around the bazaar did hide many solid brick homes belonging to merchants, pharmacists, teachers, or other middle-class people, most of the city was a sea of poverty, squalor, and disease, a stunted maze of crooked streets and crumbling mud hovels that went on and on.

As we drove southward from school I would watch the streets grow narrower and dirtier and see houses of one- or two-room homes behind tottering walls where eight or nine children lived with parents, grandparents, babies, and unmarried aunts. In South Tehran there were no clean water, no electricity, and nothing green in view except the standing water of the clay jubes, which stank like cesspools because they carried all the filth and garbage from the north. The rutted dirt streets were so packed with sickly, scrawny children who had no place to play that there was hardly room to walk. Skinny women bent over their washing in the jubes and filthy, half-naked children, watched by older sisters who were themselves hardly more than toddlers, splashed and played in them. Beggars were everywhere.

All this was a searing revelation to me. Of course, not only street beggars were poor—so were our servants, not to mention Shazdeh's sick old pensioners and hungry farmers, or the servants' relatives who came to our mothers' doors to receive food and clothing. But before,

I had seen only a few poor people at a time—beggars outside a shrine, or servants' relatives, whom my father and mother made sure were taken care of. Not until now had I encountered so many sickly, shabby, needy human beings at once, people for whom constant, unrelieved poverty was their whole life, and who had no one to care for them. Every day, even before the missionaries' small dispensary opened, a hundred women and children would line up outside, then sit patiently for hours on the floor of the waiting room. I was overwhelmed, horrified. Was this how common people lived in our country? It was as if the whole world beyond the Shah's Garden were awash in dirt and disease. How could something like this, I wondered, exist only a few minutes from my house?

I was filled with admiration for the Americans' little dispensary. Here, I marveled, were people who tried to do something about the problems they saw—not like us Persians, who just sat down like Mashti with his watermelon and waited for somebody else to fix the problem! Glad and grateful to have something to keep me from thinking too much, at home I praised Mrs. MacDowell's and Mrs. Elder's efforts to the skies. "You and your Americans," my mother would say impatiently, though I could see that she liked the idea of my helping the poor. But I was careful not to tell her what South Tehran was like. I knew that if she ever learned that such a place existed, she would forbid me to go there.

In my senior year, relations between us were often strained. With all that Shazdeh had been through recently, I was now terrified that we might lose Khanom. At school in biology class I was learning important things about health and hygiene, and I nagged my mother incessantly. For instance, I had noticed that her gums bled easily, and I told her that people must not rinse their mouths in the courtyard pool, where the laundry was done, because dirty water was infectious. At this, my mother would bristle. "I am rinsing my teeth the way God says, praise be to Him," she snapped, "and I don't need your Americans to tell me what is right."

I was still more persistent about trying to persuade her not to have any more children. Nearly all Persians, but especially women, who bore a child nearly every year, were worn out and toothless by early middle age, and my mother was almost forty. It frightened me to think that she could become like one of the aged crones who brought their children to the missionary dispensary, many of whom I knew to be scarcely more than thirty.

For a long time I had felt a deep, inexplicable shame at school over the fact that new babies always seemed to be appearing in our compound. Finally I had realized from my classmates' conversations that matters were no different in most other families where there was more than one wife, but my feelings distressed me so much that I refused to think about them even in private. Recently, however, over several days of excruciating embarrassment for our biology class, I had at last found out, in a general way, why our mothers' babies kept on arriving.

"Khanom," I would say to my mother, "perhaps you should not have so many babies. Mrs. Payne, our hygiene teacher, says you lose something from yourself every time you do."

"Oho, is that what Mrs. Payne says," my mother would reply with an ironic lift of her eyebrow. "So now, according to your Americans, women are not supposed to bring children into the world. Well, God decides if a woman has a baby, not Mrs. Payne."

I had no idea how my mother could keep from having more children. My classmates and I had been ashamed even to look at the drawings of various human organs Mrs. Payne had sketched in chalk on the blackboard, and rather to my relief, she hadn't gone into the subject of how not to have babies.

"Sometimes," my mother would say, "I think you are learning nothing from your education but to go against everything that is decent. How do I know you even say your noon prayers?" Khanom was especially shocked and angry that whenever she pointed out to me that women were weak and that there were many things only men could do for them, I would persist in contradicting her.

"Khanom," I would say earnestly during these painful discussions, trying to keep my tone deferential, "you surely do not believe that a person like Miss Jane Doolittle, a teacher and the principal of a school that is famous all over Iran, is 'zaifeh'? Mashti is a man, but he can't even read and write. Surely if we compare Miss Doolittle and Mashti, it is Miss Doolittle who is strong and Mashti who is weak."

"Just because a woman can read," my mother would answer sharply, "doesn't mean she has the mind of a man. The proof is that women can't live alone—did you ever see a woman do that? Even someone like Neggar-Saltaneh knows that she needs her family to care for her and protect her."

"Miss Doolittle and our American teachers all live alone," I replied. It upset me that my mother, even though she did not say it in so many words, thought that women were nobody and could achieve nothing by themselves. The sympathy of the American women at school after the destruction of our home had been a great comfort to me, and I admired my teachers' independence more than ever. But my opinions only distressed Khanom, who I am sure was privately beginning to doubt even Shazdeh's wisdom in sending me to Nurbaksh.

The mission school was where I felt most at home now. I had come to associate "Amrika" with my own youthful Iranian yearning for justice. One morning the school's favorite male professor, a celebrated scholar of Persian literature and a passionate liberal nationalist named Dr. S. R. Shafaq, told us the story of the American who had made the deepest impression of all on Iranians who thought of that distant, unknown country as our moral ally.

During our civil war more than thirty years before, Dr. Shafaq said, when he himself was only a seventeen-year-old student at the American Mission School in the Azerbaijani city of Tabriz, one of his teachers, Mr. Howard Baskerville, had believed so strongly in Iranian democracy and Persia's democratic revolution that he had organized a brigade of students to fight the Russian troops who were supporting Mohammed Ali Shah. Dr. Shafaq's young teacher, who had been only twenty-four, was shot in the first skirmish and had died in Dr. Shafaq's arms. The whole city of Tabriz, Dr. Shafaq said, mourned Mr. Baskerville, a foreigner who had given his life for Iranian democracy, and thousands of Persians, even women, had followed his bier through the streets of Tabriz to the American churchyard.

By the time our teacher finished, my face and my classmates' were streaming with tears. We never discussed civics or politics in school— Reza Shah was such a dictator that teachers didn't even dare to describe how our own government worked, for fear that something they said might be taken as criticism and reported. But everyone understood that by telling us this, Dr. Shafaq was expressing his own longing for Iran to return to democracy and the rule of our constitution.

The story of the young American's unselfish sacrifice made a deep impression on me. I spent much time in my senior year thinking about self-sacrifice, democracy, and justice. Reza Shah had trampled on my family's rights and denied us justice. But even if we could not speak our minds openly, it was deeply consoling for me to realize that others shared the tormenting feelings I was experiencing. If I, I thought, ever had a chance to fight for our democracy, like Mr. Howard Baskerville, I would do just as he had done, and show the world that a woman could do something for her country, too!

Although Shazdeh had confronted the emergency of the confiscation so resolutely, over the year that had passed since then, the ordeal of this loss and Nosratdoleh's death had told greatly on him. He could no longer walk without his cane and an arm to lean on. Despite physical afflictions and heartsickness, however, he was once again standing as erectly as before.

He still took a powerful interest in world affairs. As the eldest, I now went often on weekends to Shemiran to attend him. When my mother and stepmothers were not around, it became my task to sit in his room and read to him of international events, or tenderly wave a fan as he slept to drive the flies from his face. Though our conversations were never about anything more personal than my schoolwork, I was happy just to be near him. Sometimes, while he was asleep, I would stop fanning and surreptitiously touch the fingernails of the hand closest to me. Lightly brushing each ridged, yellow surface with the tip of my finger, I would test to see if he felt the sensation. If he didn't stir, I would take courage and touch the next fingernail, then the next, until I had touched all the five fingers of his hand. In this way I stole the chance to know how it felt to touch my father in the normal, intimate way of other children.

I did not pretend to understand much of what I read to him, but I listened to the comments he made with the feeling that I was being favored with great new insights into the world. The news that autumn filled Shazdeh with gloom. Though Iran was officially neutral in the gathering storm, Reza Shah's government was employing hundreds of German technicians, teachers, and advisers. Resentment of the British and Russians was so great that many Iranians, on the old Middle Eastern principle that "the enemy of my enemy is my friend," hoped that war would break out and Hitler would vanquish the British and the Russians. But Shazdeh knew that this was foolish: if the world plunged into chaos again, sooner or later Iranians, as always, would suffer to serve the plans and interests of others. Although he had great faith in England, he was furious at Mr. Neville Chamberlain, whose vacillation and lack of resolve he considered unworthy of a British statesman.

"Chamberlain, that woman!" he would say to me, glaring with disgust, "that *fess-fess*." (A fess-fess is a slowpoke.) "Why does he wait to attack Hitler? Hitler is a bully like Reza Shah. You can't deal with an enemy like that by letting him grab what he wants and hoping that he won't grab more—the only way to stop him is by seizing the offensive."

The Munich Pact of September 1938 sickened him. "Now Hitler has Czechoslovakia, and he will go after Poland. *Then* England will have to get involved, and the Russians, too." The name for Warsaw in Persian is Varshaw, which also happens to be the word for a pewter alloy made of tin and silver. "Chamberlain," my father would joke bitterly, "is giving Hitler the silver—and then only the tin of Warsaw will remain."

The deepening shadows in Europe and his ebbing strength were bringing home to Shazdeh more strongly than ever that his power to protect and provide for his family was waning. One sign of his anxiety was that he had lately begun to give earnest attention to the matter of finding me a husband.

Every time one of my cousins married or became engaged I wondered uneasily when, if ever, these desirable events were going to happen to me instead of to someone else. Occasionally a candidate would appear on the horizon and my mother would say to Batul or Fatimeh on one of their visits together, "Shazdeh told me that a representative from such-and-such a family came to him and asked for the hand of one of his daughters and he asked me, 'How about Satti?'"

But for one reason or another, none of these inquiries had come to anything. My mother was holding out for someone she thought would be right for me, and that someone wasn't easy to find. "I said no," she would report. "I told Shazdeh I didn't like that suitor, he was much too old," or, "I don't like the women in that family—they don't care about anything but money and fancy clothes. A girl like you wouldn't be happy among them." Such considerations were important, because after marriage a woman belonged not to her own family but entirely to her in-laws. I knew and was grateful that even though Khanom was anxious to see me safely wed, she wanted a match that would make me happy. Of course, if Shazdeh insisted, there would be nothing she could do.

I was not at all vague about the sort of man I wanted: someone with a good head on his shoulders, and who, preferably, looked just like my father had when he was young—handsome and strong, with a cleft chin and piercing eyes, and who was an educated, elegant gentleman like all my older brothers. I was no longer certain, however, just how I felt about marriage. I had begun to wonder whether raising a man's children, cooking food for his dinner parties, and exchanging social gossip in the baths were what I wanted of life. The prospect of having to figure out ways to wheedle money from a husband or get his permission to travel revolted me. Mrs. Elder, Mrs. MacDowell, and my American women teachers were urging me to continue in school, and working at the dispensary made me long to find out how to do something about the way common people lived. In 1935 the missionaries had opened a college for women called Sage College. It offered little more than an advanced high school education, but they wanted to make it a four-year college. Marriage would prevent my attending Sage College.

My fate, however, was not in my own hands. If a man swam into Shazdeh's net whom he and Khanom considered suitable, I would have no choice but to obey.

One warm Friday afternoon in the fall of my senior year, I was playing volleyball in the garden at Reswanieh with our brothers Abol and Ali-Naghi. Suddenly Delrobah, her ebony forehead gleaming with sweat against her white chador, appeared on the steps overlooking the clearing we used as a makeshift volleyball and soccer court. She was breathless from running. "Shazdeh wants you," she shouted.

I realized with annoyance that my father must have company. He often liked to honor guests whom he had invited to Reswanieh by showing us off. Hot and sticky and irritated at having my game interrupted, I kept on defiantly hitting the ball, ignoring her. "Satti!" shrieked Delrobah, who had a high, squeaky voice, "Shazdeh has summoned you—come along this minute! What are you doing?" Enjoying her fury, I continued to bat the ball over the net until finally I sensed that she would tolerate no more. "Well," I said impatiently, going over to her, "who is with Shazdeh?"

"He has guests. You must go to him immediately."

"Like this?" I looked down at the sweat-soaked trousers I was playing in. Shazdeh was at the other end of the garden, about a quarter of a mile away. "I'm not going to meet his guests smelling like a camel driver. Go back and tell him I'm not presentable. I want to finish my game."

"Give up, Deli," Abol laughed. "You know that Satti always does what she wants."

Glowering with disbelief, she turned and stalked back up the gravel path between the willows and poplars.

When evening came, I made my way up the overgrown path in the twilight to go to supper. To reach the main house I had to pass by the main gate, which looked out on the road and the village. There, on a stone bench overhung with tangled branches that made a shady little bower, my father often rested in the evenings, watching the people, the donkeys, and the occasional automobile that passed the open gate. I saw him sitting there now. He looked very old and frail. I tried to slink past behind him.

He turned and looked at me. "Come and sit down," he commanded.

I sat beside him. He said nothing. My bravado vanished. I felt dirty,

ill-dressed, and uncomfortable. Incredulously recalling my earlier de-
fiance and squirming a little, I said nothing. My father's silence continued. Finally, when he knew he had made his point, he looked at
me again. "Listen, when your father calls," he said slowly, "you come.
And then, when you come, you can tell your father that you don't
want to get married."

So the guest had been a suitor—one he was taking seriously, or he
wouldn't have summoned me. "Ghorban," I said, bowing my head.

"Deli came back and said, 'Your daughter does not want to come,'
so I dismissed my guests."

I said nothing.

"I will ask your mother to come from the city. She will tell you
about these guests. And the next time I call you, you will appear."

"Ghorban."

In the week following this exchange, which was the only intimate
conversation I ever had with my father, my mother came from Tehran
and explained that the man who wanted an alliance with the Farman
Farmaians was of a good family. He had come to boast to Shazdeh
of his son, whom he had brought with him.

"Your father has invited them to come again this week," she said,
pointedly ignoring the reason for the return visit. "So you will come
and serve the tea. Then you can see whether you like the looks of
them." This time I came as instructed, properly dressed and docile.
The son, a doctor who had just graduated from a European medical
school, was young, handsome, and agreeable, and I liked him. Soon
after the interview, however, Shazdeh, for reasons I never learned,
decided against the match. My mother was disappointed; she was
getting nervous. But Shazdeh had spoken.

At the end of March, 1939, a more immediate and exciting prospect
momentarily wiped the problem of marriage from my mind. The
school had announced that, following No Ruz on March 21, the senior
students would be taken on a two-week excursion to Isfahan, Shiraz,
and Persepolis.

Such excursions were unknown in my country, which was an extremely wild place. Some areas were still infested with bandits, and
travel was always dirty, difficult, and dangerous. The only city in the
Western sense was Tehran, and even large towns like Isfahan and
Shiraz were few and far between. There were few real hotels and in

many places there was nowhere for a woman to stay, so that she could visit only if she had relatives or family friends who could put her up for a few weeks. Intoxicated with the prospect of travel, I was afraid that Khanom would never consent to it.

However, the school assured her that the trip, with thirteen other girls, was being organized down to the minutest details. We would be watched every second by our female teachers, and a contingent of male missionaries would follow behind in a car. Doubtfully, Khanom said that she would consent if Shazdeh did. I held my breath for several days—except for the year at the dormitory, my father had never permitted his daughters so much as an overnight stay at an aunt's home, and since he himself was under house arrest, I would have to get a police permit to travel outside of Tehran. Moreover, his mood these days was increasingly dark. "Look at this Hitler," he would say to me. "Look at all these people he's killing—the socialists, the Communists, the Jews, everybody! He's a dictator like Reza Shah. Why don't the British attack him? Can't they see what he is?" Miraculously, however (was it his faith in Dr. Jordan, or another sign of his weakening hold on the reins?), he at last gave the trip his blessing.

I was overjoyed as my classmates and I clambered into the school's ancient bus in the missionary compound. For the first time I was leaving ugly, dirty Tehran to travel to places that all my life had been as distant and romantic as the legends in *The Book of Kings*. Several American teachers from Alborz College and their teenage sons were also traveling behind us in an old sedan that lurched sympathetically along in the white dust the bus churned up. A young bachelor in their party, a good-looking American archaeologist, was rumored have come along because he was interested in Miss Birch, our chemistry instructor, and this tailgate courtship became a subject of feverish whispering and giggling inside our bus. This was as near as I had ever come to a party of strange men, and it was very exciting. When the bus stopped for us to rest by the side of the road and an American boy of about fourteen politely took my hand to help me down from the step, my cheeks burned furiously. Except for my brothers and the servants' sons I had played with in the biruni years ago, I had never before touched a young man's hand.

The trip to Isfahan took eighteen hours, but I scarcely noticed the long ride or the bumpy roads. Outside the rattling windows, as my classmates and I chattered and joked and giggled together, a landscape of lion-yellow hills and dusty, buff-brown earth was unfolding around the bus. It was early spring, and the sparse little cultivated plots and orchards around the huddled villages south of the city were green with shoots and blossoms, the unwatered desert beyond them full of wild-flowers.

For the next two weeks the great world stretched itself before my eyes. We stopped for picnic lunches along the highway, stayed over-night in hotels, ate in public restaurants. The barren wastes between Qom and Isfahan, which contain nothing but the black tents of no-mads, ruined caravanserais, and a few wretched, thirsty hamlets, seemed charged and alive with my own excitement. Even the most desolate vista was a freshly unlocked mystery, the tiniest village a brand new sentence in the lengthening scroll of my knowledge. The jeweled city of Isfahan burst upon us out of the desert like a spring of turquoise, its blue-green domes sparkling in the sun as though set there only a moment before by the hand of Shah Abbas the Great. Shiraz, where I had been born, was jammed with cheerful crowds of spring visitors come for the New Year to picnic in the city's gardens of roses, pines, and orange trees. The tombs of Sa'adi and Hafez were like the homes of unseen but hospitable hosts whom I had known my whole life. All of this seemed somehow familiar, as if I had always carried these things in my heart without knowing they were there.

At Persepolis we wandered freely and in awe over the vast platform of desert stone with its massive columns, and at Pasargadae we climbed stairs that Cyrus and Alexander had trod thousands of years before. Suddenly, instead of being merely a word ringing in my father's Friday exhortations, "Iran" had become something I could see and touch and enjoy, and at the same time something that I recognized as part of my deepest self, locked in my soul since before I was born. I saw that I was not just myself, not just my family or clan, but an Iranian, that my own small existence was part of something grand and magnificent, and that everything I had known until now and thought familiar and permanent was the merest flourish in the long, complicated weave of the pattern of Persian history.

As the bus bounced and rattled over the long road back to Tehran, I struggled to understand the meaning of these dazzling sights and impressions. Once Iran had been great. But who had made it so? Shazdeh said that it was individuals, not conquest, that made a nation great. Through individuals, he said, a little island like England had become a great civilization. Now I thought that I understood what he meant. When the conquerors were gone, it was the contribution of individuals that remained—not only shahs and shazdehs and military governors, but ordinary people: merchants and pious women who endowed mosques and schools of learning, clerks and scribes and magistrates who kept laws and traditions intact, craftsmen and artisans and planners who conceived and built the splendid Persian past I had inherited. All these people were the reason my father believed that the life of everyone, from the king down to the poorest villager's child, had value in the eyes of God.

All at once I realized what I seemed to have known forever: that I must have more education, that whatever else happened to me, to serve Iran and its people was my destiny. Shazdeh had tended us like a gardener tending an orchard of prized apple trees so that we could make our people strong again. I must find out how to save us from the poverty and illiteracy that crushed and weakened us, and made us dependent on the advanced foreigners who had become great while we had become backward, ignorant, and poor.

The friendly sounding voices of Miss Birch and our other American teachers a few seats ahead floated back to me, and I made up my mind to try to get Shazdeh to let me go to Sage College next year. I was only eighteen, and Jaby hadn't married until she was twenty. Maybe he would be willing to put off finding me a husband until I had studied there for two years. After that, I would just have to see what happened. At least I knew that was what I was meant to do.

Suddenly for the first time in years I remembered the picture of the statue I had seen in Jaby's French magazine, the "azadi" statue. All at once it struck me that "freedom" could mean more than not being under arrest or in prison. It meant that you could go where you wanted, say what you thought, change what you didn't like about your country—all the things we weren't allowed to do under Reza Shah. And again I wondered about the people who had put up this statue as their symbol of themselves. Why had they done it? Maybe in America, I thought excitedly, they knew how I could help my country. Maybe I could even go there and study someday.

I knew that this excursion was a turning point in my life, and that these two weeks had in some mysterious way changed me forever. I could hardly wait to get home and tell my father about the sights I had seen. I was brimming with happiness at how pleased he would be to hear all that I had learned about Iran's past. When the bus was back at Nurbaksh again, I jumped out, ran to the school office, and telephoned Reswanieh to tell them to come and pick me up.

But instead of joy at my safe return, anxiety and anguish greeted my call. While I had been away, Shazdeh had suffered a stroke. I went to Reswanieh and stood at his bedside, looking down at him as he slept. Grief-stricken, I realized that now I might never be able to tell him what I had learned.

* * *

Shazdeh regained consciousness, but could not speak; the doctors did not yet know the extent of the damage. Then, as if his worry about his children's future had enabled him to triumph over his damaged brain by the sheer force of his will, he began to speak again. By July, he was able to walk short distances on the arm of a wife or servant, and though he was now almost totally deaf and spoke slurringly, his mind seemed as vigorous as ever. It was as if, unable to abandon his little kingdom, he had temporarily returned to us from the dead—an old lion whose spirit nothing could entirely break.

In June, I graduated at the head of my class. My mother agreed to my going to Sage College in the fall. Shazdeh, she said, had told her, "When I die, sell your clothes if you have to, but see that your children get an education."

That summer the turmoil in Europe brought an unexpected blessing: Dadash had finished his medical studies in France and Switzerland, and in July my father reluctantly consented to his returning home. In the summer of 1939, even Reza Shah seemed safer than Europe. Khanom and Aghajun were giddy with joy, and all of us felt an overwhelming sense of relief for my mother's sake at Dadash's return. Our brother Sabbar was strong and energetic, a physician, and a serious, well-traveled man of twenty-seven, with experience in worldly matters. Khanom trusted his judgment second only to Shazdeh's. With Dadash back, there would be someone she and we could lean on, someone to guide us and tell us what to do. We felt that he had been sent by God to help us.

As soon as Dadash arrived, Shazdeh told him to volunteer for his two years in the army; doing so immediately, Shazdeh felt, would demonstrate his son's loyalty. Secretly, however, he was ecstatic at the idea of Dadash's joining the army, and he fumed with impatience until August, when my brother was finally inducted and assigned to the military hospital in Tehran. When Dadash appeared at Reswanieh in uniform for the first time, my father was radiant. "Is this real?" he murmured in his slurred voice. "Are you truly a soldier now?"

On the first of September, 1939, the Nazis invaded Poland, and the great conflagration began just the way Shazdeh had predicted: England announced that it would go to the aid of its Polish ally. Dadash, hearing the news on the hospital's radio, hurried to Reswanieh to tell our father that the Europeans were at war with each other again. Shazdeh was bedridden with gout, arthritis, and other ailments, and to tell him, Dadash had to bend down and shout into his ear. "Ghorban," he said, "the war in Europe began today." Shazdeh lay for a long time without saying anything. Then he whispered thickly, "My son, England will win." He took Dadash's hand and, with a great effort, pressed it reassuringly. "You may be sure of it," he repeated in a stronger voice. "England will win."

One day in November when I was at school, my mother called me to say that Shazdeh had had another stroke, and that he was in a coma. I and my brothers and sisters and Batul-Khanom and her children went to stay at Reswanieh to be there at the end, and Dadash, who had been given compassionate leave, came to attend him along with my father's regular physicians—Hadji Doktur Khan had died several years earlier—and a nurse. My mother moved quietly and calmly about the house. Delrobah hovered about somewhere, weeping, while my fifteen-year-old brother Farough and my other brothers and sisters tiptoed around, silent and waiting. We had always known that one day Shazdeh must die, but we were unable to imagine life without him. Ezzatdoleh, a diminutive, wasted figure clad in black, also visited him, together with Nosratdoleh's widow. My stepmother and Shazdeh had remained on amiable terms, but her grief for Nosratdoleh had broken her. She sat for a few minutes looking at my father. "Shazdeh," she implored, stroking his hand, her tears falling onto it from beneath her spectacles, "it's me, your Ezzati." When he did not reply, she rose. "Farman-Farma is gone," she whispered. "Poor Farman-Farma."

I sat by his bed as long as Dadash would permit, memories from childhood flooding me of our hikes, of the swimming hole, of his Friday inspections. I remembered how sometimes when we came on Fridays, Delrobah would open the door, poke her head out, and hiss, "Don't come in yet, he's still saying his prayers." I would peek inside and see Shazdeh praying. Even when he was very sick, Shazdeh always left his bed to pray. He did this in his pajamas, with a cloak thrown over his shoulders to protect him from drafts and a cotton skullcap over his white hair to warm his head, but I felt that my father never looked more distinguished than when he prayed. He would lean forward and rest his forehead on a stool to recite the ritual Arabic prayers. Then came his personal prayer, which he said out loud, and in Persian. This was always an energetic prayer of thanksgiving, and it always began, "O God of Abdol Hossein."

Hearing my father speak to God as if they were intimate acquaintances never surprised me in the least. I took it for granted that they had a close personal relationship. Of course, my father talked to God very respectfully—as one general to a much higher general. "O God of Abdol Hossein," he would say, "be eternally glorified! I thank you for your many favors! I thank you for letting me live so long and for giving me all these children in my old age! I thank you for the safety of my family, and all of these people who depend on me!"

I knew from his tone that my father truly loved the great commander he was speaking to—perhaps even more than he loved us, his children, who were dearer to him than anything. And I treasured his conversations with God all the more for knowing what he dared not say aloud: that he wanted God to protect us from Reza Shah, and to let him live until we didn't need him anymore. I was sure that even now, from behind the high wall of unconsciousness, Shazdeh was trying not to let go of us, although his God wanted him to. But my father's face was chalk-white, and when I massaged his hands and feet, desperately hoping somehow to restore him this way so that he could stay and keep on taking care of us, his skin seemed as thin as paper.

After four or five days, early in the morning, he died. Soon the garden was filled with the men of our family and Shazdeh's staff. His third son, Mohammed Vali Mirza, was now "Shazdeh," and the head of our clan. He, our older brothers and brothers-in-law, and one of my father's nephews made the arrangements for the funeral procession and the service. As they bore his shrouded body away on the wooden bier, Batul-Khanom and I stood together in the chilly November air, watching him go. When he was carried down the path through the tangle of poplars and willows, my stepmother burst out wailing, beating the top of her head and crying over and over, "Look, look, they are taking him away from us!" My mother, preferring privacy, went to her room and shut herself up there to weep. I felt as if not only my childhood but my whole world were being borne away on that wooden plank. All our lives we had understood that without Shazdeh we were nothing. How could we get along without him? How could we protect ourselves from Reza Shah? What would happen to all of us now?

Soon, however, we became very busy. A tent was set up in the garden to feed the guests who came to offer condolences. Since everyone remembered that mourning for Nosratdoleh had been forbidden by the Shah and since Reza Shah seemed more unpredictable with each passing year, Khanom and Dadash thought that people would be afraid to come to the funeral, and I am sure that fear kept many away. Even so, hundreds did come: diplomats and foreign citizens, rich merchants, ordinary bazaaris, retired cavalrymen, villagers. My father was laid to rest in the plain tomb he had built not far from the grave of Nosratdoleh. When the will was read, we learned that he had left a third of his remaining wealth to Firuzabad Hospital for the poor in the south of Tehran, and in the months that followed, Mohammed

Vali Mirza and our other older brothers received many letters not only from men in Shiraz, Kerman, and the other places where my father had governed, but from men in Baghdad and everywhere else in the Middle East, praising his wisdom, humane leadership, and generosity to the common people.

I and my mother and stepmothers, being women, were not allowed to attend the funeral and the eulogy in my grandmother's mosque. But if I had been permitted to be there and praise his life and character, I would have said that he was a man who was able to change when he saw the need for change. He saw the necessity of a constitution. He respected the people's voice and willingly accepted the sacrifice of his dynasty's power for their sake.

At the time of his death he had thirty-two children still living, of whom twelve were girls and twenty were boys, all obedient, well educated, and healthy, males and females alike. In addition, he had adopted and raised many other children who lacked a father or mother, caring for them and bringing them up just as though they were his own.

His teachings to all his children consisted of good manners, respect for elders and teachers, and service to humanity and the nation. He taught us to obey those above us, aid those below us, and never to accept a bribe, nor to seek honors that we had not earned through hard work. From his example we learned to take pride in what we made of ourselves, not in who our father had been; to say our prayers; to have faith in God. From him I learned to live simply, to help the destitute, and, most important, never to betray a trust or repay kindness with ingratitude. Above all, he encouraged us to love one another, to feel that we were all equal in his sight. He taught us to live in harmony together, always thinking of the larger goal. And he taught us to love the common good more than our own individual interest.

Sometimes when I lie in bed at night and say my own prayers in the darkness, it is in my mind to pray, "O God of Sattareh Farman Farmaian." But I always say, "O God of Abdol Hossein."

6

THE FALL OF REZA SHAH

When a man prospers, people sing his praise.
When he falls, they trample his neck.

—Sa'adi

*A*STONISHINGLY, DESPITE THE FACT THAT MY FATHER'S ESTATE had to be divided among so many heirs, there were no fights over the inheritance. In part, this was because there wasn't much to fight over. Most of Shazdeh's lands had been confiscated or sold off bit by bit, and all that remained were the Reswanieh estate, his office in the city, and some farm villages and rural holdings in various parts of Iran—a wheat field here, an apple orchard there. But things also went smoothly because we knew what his real legacy was: cooperation. We divided up Reswanieh among ourselves. As many of the rural properties were small and remote, we agreed to pool the smallest parcels, sell them, and share the proceeds. Thus I acquired a few thousand dollars of my own. I also owned a Singer sewing machine on which I helped Khanom sew everybody's clothes, and a six-piece setting of china with the Farman-Farma crest, which Shazdeh had given all his daughters.

Dadash was a godsend, especially to Khanom. He was capable and decisive, someone she could lean on. He had also proven to be a wonderful eldest brother, open and affectionate, concerned not only about us but also about our stepmothers and their children and servants. He kept an eye on everyone's health, comforted us when we were afraid of the future, and to take our minds off our grief over Shazdeh, told us fascinating stories about his life in Europe.

Nevertheless, these months brought a deluge of troubles to my mother and stepmothers, who had to support not only us but all of Shazdeh's hundreds of dependents and pensioners. My mother was also going crazy over tortuous discussions of inheritance and property law with Shazdeh's three executors, Ashekh-Javad and two old and trusted friends of my father's. Until the estate was sold off, there was no cash available for immediate expenses. Dadash's salary was very small and despite all my years of schooling I was unqualified for a job even in the few professions open to women and therefore could not help my mother with her cash problems.

I had never seen her so nervous and distraught. "How will we live," she would groan, pressing her hands to her face as she worried about the lack of cash. "In a few weeks we won't even be able to buy meat." She had no jewels that she could sell because Shazdeh had never given us any, but I realized that she had sold a gold watch and chain he had once presented her with. Soon, rugs began to disappear from our floors as well.

All this would have been harrowing for any new widow, but it was doubly so for a traditional woman like my mother, who had lived since the age of twelve under Shazdeh's protection and guidance. Even though she had always been an excellent manager, she did not believe that a woman could understand legal matters or cope with all the problems Shazdeh's former employees, pensioners, and villagers now brought to her instead of to my father. I tried to help her any way I could and to avoid upsetting her. These days I longed for a rich husband to come so that I could save her from all this misery. Unfortunately, Dadash, who had to juggle our problems with his job at the military hospital, was far too busy to hunt one up for me. But Khanom refused to hear of my leaving school, which would have saved the fees for the spring term of 1940. Shazdeh, she insisted, wanted us to have an education.

School wouldn't be a problem much longer, however, thanks to Reza Shah's affinity for Hitler. No sooner had I begun at Sage in September of 1939 than the Shah, who had declared Iran officially neutral, ordered all foreign schools to close, whether they were German, British, French, or American. I'm sure the Allies found this gesture as unconvincing as his pretense that Iran was not pro-German. But whether they did or not, as of June, there would no longer be a Sage College for me to go to.

Then, around February, just as some money was coming in again and my mother, with Dadash's warm encouragement, was finally telling herself that perhaps a woman might be as good at managing her new affairs as her old ones, another shattering blow fell: Reza Shah sent word that he was confiscating our remaining property. He would leave us half our house—after he had torn it down to its foundations to build another road. Ashekh-Javad advised my mother to yield at once, lest the Shah be tempted to show his displeasure by arresting Dadash. This time, when the workers came, they did not wait for us to remove our own things but simply threw them out the windows. Beds, carpets, books, clothing, and toys lay strewn all over the ground in a jumble.

"Be calm, children," said Khanom when Mashti and the servants had picked up everything and we had climbed into a hired car for the long, dreary ride to Reswanieh. "Shazdeh always said that the evildoer is punished in this life, not the next. This Reza Shah is not greater than God."

By the end of the following September, most of my American teachers had left for the safety of their distant homeland. Only Miss Doolittle was staying on, starting a school for the poor in her own home. War or no war, after so many years she could not imagine a life that did not include teaching Persian children. Mrs. Elder and Mrs. Mac-Dowell, whose husbands were not connected with the schools, were keeping the dispensary open, and I now went several times a week as a volunteer to teach the Persian alphabet to dirty, malnourished, lice-infested little boys while their mothers waited for medicine.

The Shah's order had devastated Dr. Jordan. This devoted, whimsical educator had given fifty years to Iran. He had taught generations of boys to be patriotic, unselfish citizens, and counted some of the country's most notable men among his graduates. He had sent the Shah a plea in eloquent Persian begging him to rethink his decision: from education alone, he wrote, came a country's true greatness. Reza Shah had relented—he had given the schools a year to close instead of the two weeks he had first stipulated. Dr. Jordan knew that his life's work was over. In October of 1940 he departed, and with him faded a noble and unselfish American era in Iran. He and the other missionary teachers had embodied everything we loved about the United

States. Now he vanished with his wife into the mists of his far-off land, and became, with Mr. Howard Baskerville and President Woodrow Wilson, only an affectionate and honored memory.

Around February of 1941 we moved back into our rebuilt home. The confiscation had eaten our property down to a thin strip. There was no garden, only a small, forlorn, treeless courtyard. Because of the shape of the remaining foundation, Khanom had been forced to rebuild the house as a narrow chain of small rooms linked by a corridor, like a row of European train compartments. We dubbed it "the railroad house." I tried to remind myself how lucky we were that Reza Shah hadn't taken everything, but it was unspeakably depressing.

That summer Dadash finished his active military service and moved in with us; though enrolled in the reserves he was at last free to begin his medical career. However, he still had no time to look for a husband for me. There were so few trained physicians in our country that he had not only joined the government as a public health doctor but had also opened his own clinic in North Tehran, in a couple of rooms above a photography studio.

Jaby and her husband, Abbas, were also living with us now, in two small rooms at the far end of the house. Abbas had completed his assignment in Abadan and had returned to AIOC headquarters in Tehran, where he was awaiting reassignment. I had grown to like Abbas. He was a nice-looking, stocky man, a skillful bridge and tennis player, and extremely honest, intelligent, and straightforward. He had spent four years studying in Birmingham, England, where the oil company had sent him. Even though Abbas was from a clerical family, he, like Dadash, was modern enough not to think it indecent for a man to entertain good friends at home with the women of his family present, and with my mother's and Dadash's consent he often invited close associates from the oil company to play bridge with him.

Their conversation was always interesting for me because Abbas, as one of the few Iranian engineers who had advanced to a middle-level position in the British company, was well aware that as Iranians he and his friends would never be promoted to the policy-making level. He and they often complained of this injustice. "Reza Shah made them promise to train Iranians as managers," he would say, "but they'll never promote me over an Englishman even if I'm better qualified. They think we're mental defectives and can't run an oil industry. Certainly, they had to start it for us thirty years ago because we didn't have the technical knowledge, but I know as much about it now as any Englishman. God gave us that oil, it's part of Iran! The British make nine times the profit we do, and since we can't look at their books we aren't even sure they're paying us what they owe us."

What upset my brother-in-law and his friends most, however, was the British company's arrogance toward its engineers and workers in Abadan. "They treat Iran," Abbas would say angrily, "as if we were one of their colonies. London uses the AIOC to spy on us and keep us in line. In Abadan, Jaby and I have English friends, but Iranians can't join their sports club. Our laborers live packed into tin-roofed shacks, like animals, and there are signs on the water fountains saying Iranians can't drink from them. And now they've started importing Indian laborers and giving them jobs that poor Iranians could fill. In our own country, they act as if we were nobody!"

With Abbas and Jaby I also had my first experience of Western dancing. Reza Shah wanted to get men and women to mix with each other to show that we were becoming modern, and the AIOC therefore held monthly afternoon tea parties for its executives in a fashionable hotel. Many Europeans, Armenians, and other non-Moslems came to these, and Jaby and Abbas took me to several. Jaby could not dance because she was married, but I found it delightful to sit in my best dress and gloves, sipping tea with my sister while an orchestra played in the background for any couples who wanted to dance. Occasionally, with Abbas holding me at arm's length, I would dance with him, or with some trusted friend of his or another man from our family so that I could learn to waltz and fox-trot in the manner of the fashionable and elegantly dressed Europeans around us.

But despite these pleasures, I was bored and unhappy. Before, I had always been able to throw myself into hard work for relief and escape from my sorrows. Hard work had comforted me like a faithful retainer. Hard work had pleased my father, had told me that I was moving ahead, making progress as he wished us to do; had allowed me to ignore trouble, to shut anger, loneliness, and pain completely out of my mind. Now this obedient servant was gone.

Having neither school nor gainful employment, I felt that my existence was empty. I was spending as much time as I could at the dispensary, where, as at Nurbaksh, I felt at home. The women who came there were illiterate, ignorant, superstitious, and lived in misery and squalor. But they were simple, kind, and generous, with their own sort of dignity.

Occasionally my friends and I would attend the foreign cinema together, sitting in the women's and children's section while an attendant stood beside the small screen and called out what was being said.

The Western cinema was a popular form of fashionable entertainment—we had even heard of "Hollywood," though we didn't know what this word meant. Once, a friend and I went to *Gone With the Wind*. It was always strange to see women actresses, and I blushed when Rhett kissed Scarlett, although the attendant always held something up to cover the actors' faces so that the audience would not witness indecencies. But I was amazed at the magnificence of American native costume, which was utterly different from what the missionaries wore. It was abundantly clear that in America the young were beautiful and rich, the old were rich and distinguished-looking, and everyone was extremely well fed—to us, indisputable proof of what an advanced nation the Americans came from. Yet Mrs. MacDowell and Mrs. Elder, I told Dadash and my mother effusively, were completely unpretentious and friendly, and called everyone "Khanom"; unlike Persians, I said, they were always the first to say salaam to show that they weren't haughty! They never bragged or tried to impress anybody, as we did. And they were from an advanced and scientific nation! Why was it Americans and not we ourselves who did something for the women at the dispensary? "Oh, you and your Americans," sighed my mother.

I had, of course, plenty of friends and female relations with whom to socialize. Nearly all my friends who were my age had married as soon as they graduated from school; many now had babies, and when I visited them, I was chagrined when I realized that they had moved on while somehow I had been left behind, deprived of womanly honors and the reward that they had been lucky enough to obtain. Yet I knew now that I could never be happy depending on the favor of some man to be able to live. And if I didn't want to burden my mother and Dadash, I had to find a means of supporting myself.

But what was I going to do? I did not want to be a schoolteacher or nurse, or even a doctor like my brother. Medicine seemed too narrow. The women I saw at the dispensary needed more than just pills and injections. I wanted to—to—I didn't know what I wanted! I felt only that what I was looking for must exist somewhere, and that I wanted to help the common people, whose lives, like Mashti's and our other servants', seemed real to me in some way that I couldn't explain but which my heart seemed to understand. But although a few of our teachers at Sage had dropped hints that some of us might consider going to America to study if we didn't get married, I had never pursued the idea I had conceived on my senior excursion. I had not forgotten the magazine advertisement, with its drawing of glamorous promenaders and its curious monument to "azadi." But the war made travel impractical, and anyway I had heard that Reza Shah did not give Qajars exit visas to travel to foreign countries.

In the spring of 1941, the Europeans' war moved eastward, and in the fourth week of June the newspapers reported Germany's invasion of the Soviet Union. A few days later, Reza Shah reasserted our neutrality. Churchill and Stalin, however, didn't trust such "neutrality" to safeguard Allied oil supplies in the Middle East, or to guarantee that Russia's southern supply route through Iran wouldn't be cut off. In the predawn hours of August 25, 1941, the Allies invaded Iran from the north and south. The Iranian military was helpless against their superior power. Reza Shah's great new national army, on which he had lavished huge amounts of money, began to fall apart.

At the news of the invasion, panic seized Tehran. People started fleeing in whatever direction they thought would bring them to safety. On August 27 the cabinet resigned, and the beleaguered Shah, at its advice, named as the new prime minister a respected statesman named Mohammed Ali Forrughi, an elderly man whom the Shah had rewarded for much honorable service to our country with years of house arrest, to come to terms with the Allies who were once again occupying our soil.

Dadash and Abbas at once announced that they were rejoining the army. They put their affairs in order, and on the third morning of the invasion they were ready to depart (Abbas, like Dadash, was in the reserves). First, however, they had to buy new swords. A Persian officer could no more go off to war without his sword that he could go without his head.

I was furious over the invasion. It was maddening to be a woman and stand by helplessly while the same British and Russians who had always pushed us around took over our country again. Why should I sit idle, I thought, while men took action and marched into battle? I could defend our country's honor as well as anyone. I told Dadash and Abbas that I was going with them to join the army.

"Women can't be soldiers," my brother replied impatiently. Abbas merely stared in disbelief.

I answered that I didn't care; *I* was going to fight for my country, too. There must be some job I could do.

Dadash frowned heavily. "That's absurd. You'll stay home, where it's safe." Red-faced and walking as fast as their dignity permitted, they marched solemnly out the door. I followed, trailing just behind them and paying no attention to their glares and Dadash's frequent commands to return home.

There was a military supply shop about a mile and half away; our house on Sepah Avenue was not far from the military training grounds. Everywhere, I saw, uniformed Iranian soldiers were milling about. But there was something strange about them. Instead of looking purposeful and resolute, they looked bewildered, shamefaced, and scared. Many, I noticed in surprise, were without their guns and swords and seemed to be moving swiftly away from the barracks.

I caught up with Dadash and Abbas, who, not wanting me to fall behind in a crowd of soldiers, grudgingly slowed down to let me walk with them. When we reached the shop and Dadash said that we had come to purchase swords, the owner just laughed angrily and pointed to a radio that was playing on a shelf. An announcer was speaking.

"You hear that?" he said to my brother with bitter irony. "Dear gentlemen, it's all over. You have come just in time. After three days of fighting, the glorious Army of Iran has surrendered to the Allies, and the Shah has ordered our men not to offer further resistance."

Too shocked and amazed to speak, we drifted out of the shop again and made our way back along Sepah Avenue. Now I understood the expressions on the soldiers' faces: they were deserting. The thought of such ignominy—had it really taken only three days to defeat the whole Iranian army?—was more than I could bear.

A couple of frightened privates, mere boys, were hurrying toward us, their tunics flapping open. As they neared, I thrust myself in their way. "Stop," I pleaded. "Why don't you go and fight? Don't you want to defend your country?" They did not answer but rushed on, their eyes averted. "They're going back to their villages," said Dadash with great sadness. "The army has fallen to pieces."

When we arrived home, Khanom's living room was jammed with excited brothers and sisters, servants, women neighbors and cousins, and former clerks of Shazdeh's who had come to give my mother the news of the surrender. Jaby was stunned and weeping: in the Gulf, the British had wiped out the tiny Persian navy, killing its commander; he and his English wife had been close friends of my sister and her husband. The reports and rumors we heard were appalling. Not only common soldiers, said one man who had worked for my father, but even field commanders were deserting—running off to Isfahan and Shiraz in black chadors, disguised as women.

I was stricken with shame and disgust. "But when are they going to defend their country?" I cried. "They aren't," said someone dryly.

Over the few next days more friends and neighbors came, terrified and talking about getting out of the city before the Russians moved in. Village recruits had torn off their uniforms and were looking desperately for nonexistent transportation back to their families in the remote hamlets from which most of them had come. We heard that the military barracks had been plundered—not only by ordinary soldiers desperate for something with which to buy a ride home, but by officers, too. Scared, hungry deserters were knocking at the door of our courtyard, asking for food. Khanom, touched like everyone by their plight, fed a couple of them and gave money to a few more. I no longer blamed them. Unlike the cowards who had commanded them, these frightened boys were not at fault. They were just teenagers from the wilds of Sistan or Khorasan. They didn't think beyond their own families, villages, or tribes. Reza Shah had been not only a cruel ruler but, as it had turned out, a weak one, powerless to repel the foreign conqueror. An ordinary soldier's loyalty was to someone who could protect him, not to a lord who couldn't defend him and his family against invaders.

By now Tehran was in a state of chaos. Martial law was declared. Over the radio in Abbas and Jaby's room we heard Prime Minister Forrughi appealing for calm, assuring people that food was plentiful and that we must wait to see what the Allies had in mind. In the days that followed, frightening rumors made the rounds: The Allies were going to execute all of Reza Shah's pro-German generals; the Red Army was going to quarter its soldiers on Iranian families. Anyone with a car was fleeing southward toward Isfahan, where safety was said to lie. Someone suggested that we get out while the prime minister was still negotiating, before the Allies arrived. "But how can we?" asked my mother, spreading her hands helplessly. "How could I afford to buy a big house in Isfahan for all of us?" Besides, having already once experienced the hardships of being a refugee in a strange city, she dreaded exposing us to them. "Here, at least, we have the railroad house, and the cottage in Shemiran. We will just have to remain and see what happens. The Russians aren't here yet—let's worry about getting through today, and let God take care of tomorrow." So, despite the fact that we were as scared of the invaders as anyone, we stayed put.

Meanwhile, British employees of the AIOC in Abadan were joyously celebrating the Allied victory. The German Embassy in Tehran was closed down, and Reza Shah agreed to expel all German nationals. In September the humiliating news we had waited for became official:

Russian and English troops would shortly occupy Tehran to aid the Soviet Union's war effort against Germany. So far, however, Reza Shah still seemed to be king.

Then one evening, a voice speaking in Persian was heard on the BBC from London.

There was a voracious worm in Iran, this accusing voice said, who was swallowing all the villages and lands around the Caspian; who ground down the poor; who had secret police everywhere; who jailed his opponents and killed the country's intellectuals; who had stolen people's lands or forced their sale to him under threat of death; who was as bad and cruel and greedy a king as the tyrant Zahak.

Clustered around the radio in Abbas and Jaby's room, we listened, at first in disbelief and then in growing astonishment and exhilaration. "They're getting rid of him," said Abbas excitedly. "It's obvious. The British have decided to get rid of Reza Shah."

For several evenings running, the broadcasts continued—open denunciations excoriating the king, bluntly rehearsing his offenses against his people. Once Reza had been the choice of the English, this authoritative voice acknowledged, but he had become a dictator who favored the Germans, a devouring beast plundering the nation, and for Iran's sake, he must go.

We could hardly believe our ears. Suddenly Reza Shah, whom the British had imposed on us and whom some Westerners had not hesitated to call "Reza Shah the Great," had become what Nosratdoleh and so many others had been—expendable. "He doesn't suit them anymore," Abbas remarked. "They're just laying the ground for whatever they're planning to do in Iran anyway." None of us much cared, however, what English motives were; we were too jubilant. For two decades we and our nation had been under Reza's thumb. People had been robbed of their property, their rights, their dignity, their dear ones. Now the BBC was shouting openly to the whole country the truths we ourselves had not even dared to whisper.

Tehran seethed with expectancy and suppressed exultation. Members of the Majlis, realizing that the Shah's powerful backers no longer supported him, passed a resolution demanding political reform. The rumor mill went mad. One story was that the Shah had pulled a revolver on his chiefs of staff and threatened to shoot them but had relented because the British told him that if he did they would have the Russians send him to Siberia. It was said that the British wanted to bring back Sayyid Zia; they wanted to bring back the Qajars; they were going to abolish the Pahlavi dynasty and establish a republic; they had arranged with Mr. Forrughi for the twenty-two-year-old crown prince Shapour Mohammed Reza to become the next Shah on condition that Reza Shah abdicate.

This rumor turned out to be true.

On September 16, Reza Shah, realizing that he could not continue but desperate to ensure the survival of his dynasty, signed a letter to Premier Forrughi abdicating in favor of his son. He made a radio speech asking Iranians to support their new king, and the next thing we knew, he was gone. Within twenty-four hours, Mohammed Reza Shah was sworn in before the Majlis. The Allied forces rolled into North Tehran, where they took up quarters in barracks that only a day or two earlier had still belonged to Reza Shah's Army of Iran.

Nothing could have shown more clearly that the old king was gone for good. We were free. A kind of ironic miracle had happened, wrought by the Russian and English soldiers who now walked our streets, and it was as if a great dam, standing filled and motionless for many years, had finally burst. Suddenly people realized that they could say or write anything they wished. A torrent of outrage, vilification, and denunciation of the former ruler unleashed itself, as deputies and bureaucrats who for years had cravenly carried out the Shah's most irrational orders and trembled at his least frown now decried his greed and cruelty. Women who had felt humiliated by the Shah's dress code put on black chadors and flaunted them in the streets, reveling in the freedom to wear what they wished. Families whose fathers and sons had been murdered filed charges. Mullahs whom the king had deprived of their livings cursed him from their pulpits. Newspapermen, writers, and pamphleteers from the nationalist right to the communist left vied, often in obscenities, to outdo each other in denouncing his confiscations, tortures, and killings of innocent people.

Though we prudently confined our celebrations to the privacy of our own circle—the habits of caution my mother had drummed into us were not easily lost—we were as intoxicated with our newfound freedom as everyone else. Mohammed Reza Shah was anxious to show the Allies that he was cooperating and assure himself of more popularity than his father. He restored much of the control of political power to the Majlis, and even promised to return the confiscated lands his father had left him as his personal inheritance.

Qajars who had fallen afoul of Reza Shah began to emerge from house arrest or exile. In our family, one of Shazdeh's two living elder sons was appointed to the strategically important post of minister of roads. Dr. Mohammed Mossadegh, my father's sister's son, who had spent all of the 1930s living under house arrest for opposing the king's suppression of the constitution and had been imprisoned under barbarous conditions for six months in 1940, now found himself the idol of thousands of liberal nationalists for his long and unyielding resistance to tyranny. But our greatest happiness was that Dadash, whose arrest and imprisonment we had always dreaded, was no longer a potential hostage.

The new Shah made no effort to protect his father's henchmen. Immediately following the abdication, Nosratdoleh's eldest son, Mozaffar, whom Shazdeh had raised after the divorce from his niece, Dr. Mossadegh's sister, initiated legal proceedings against his father's murderers. Throughout the long months of trials of police officers and other government officials, we waited tensely with hundreds of other Iranians to see if justice would finally be done to our relatives' killers. It was a grim satisfaction when the judges ruled that Nosratdoleh had been murdered by the Shah, by the policeman Mokhtari, and by Ahmadi the physician, who had killed dozens of other prisoners as well. Though vengeance could not wipe out what so many had suffered, when the court condemned Mokhtari to a long prison term and the frightful Dr. Ahmadi to death by hanging, a great burden disappeared from our hearts.

Strangely, however, as time went on I found myself less and less able to rejoice over the country's new situation. I could not rid myself of the shameful recollection of the soldiers throwing down their guns and running through the streets. No one could realistically have expected that raw recruits would be able to stop an Allied invasion. But even the officers had fled when their leader proved weak. They had felt not only no sense of obligation to him, but to the nation. Moreover, divisiveness, not consensus, filled the air now. No one seemed interested in coming to an agreement on what to do about problems like the oil agreement or political reforms. Individuals and factions fought and bickered. Our precious new freedom of speech, I thought, was being used only to castigate one another and blacken the memory of Reza Shah.

By now it was impossible (for me, at any rate) not to feel a few small stirrings of pity for the fallen monarch. He had stolen and murdered and trampled on our rights, suppressed his people's voice, and deprived us of the chance to learn how to be a democracy. His overthrow was a blessing. Yet I knew that he had also done much good in Iran—he had restored order and constructed roads and factories, built a more modern state, and even attempted to get us our fair share of the oil money. Millions of Persians now had children in the schools he had built. But the moment he fell, all these efforts counted for nothing.

The Allies had made it painfully clear that they could abolish our government with a snap of the fingers, and now all we could see was that Reza Shah had been a tyrant who, in the end, had been not too strong but too weak. Not a soul had a good word to say about him, not even people who at this very moment were enjoying the benefits of his rule. I, too, was happy to see him go, but I was appalled to see how so many people could change their tune so fast. His departure, as the Persian phrase goes, had opened everyone's hand: people were now showing their true colors.

I once heard someone say of our politics, "The party all Iranians belong to is the party of the wind—we go where it blows us." Where Reza Shah himself had gone, no one seemed to know. Much later, we heard that the British had taken him to the island of Mauritius in the Indian Ocean. A year or so after that he was removed, in poor health, to Johannesburg, where he died in 1944. Later it became prudent to speak well of him again, and people said that he had died of heartbreak. Maybe, since he had good reason, it was true.

Our hopes of recovering at least my mother's property soon died. Reza Shah was said to have left his son a bank account of three million English pounds sterling and his confiscated lands came to more than three million acres, but Mohammed Reza Shah was returning only the villages his father had left him—city holdings, like those that had been stolen from our family, were not being returned. The railroad house was going to be a permanent affliction.

Life was becoming more uncomfortable for everyone. It was frightening to see Sepah Avenue and the other familiar streets of North Tehran filled with foreign soldiers. The Allies appropriated houses, offices, and most cars and trucks for their own use. A typhus epidemic had begun in the camps set up for war refugees from Eastern Europe and this had spread to the general population. Food shortages were becoming acute and the death rate among the poor from disease was appalling. Dadash and the city's other trained physicians were overwhelmed. At home, my mother had to scrimp on everything.

I now found it unbearable to know that she was sacrificing herself to feed an unmarried daughter of twenty-one. My friends were all assiduous—as in such circumstances Persian friends always are—in arranging meetings for me with their husbands' and brothers' friends, and when a female cousin I liked, a daughter of the Qajar crown prince, who now lived in France, proposed that I marry one of her brothers, I was sure Khanom would be pleased, and dutifully asked Dadash to broach the subject with her. To my surprise, however, she refused even to receive the go-betweens. "I've lived among the Qajars all my life," she said flatly, "and every one of those big, rich, spoiled shazdehs is just like your father, peace be upon him. They marry some new woman whenever they feel like it, and they don't care how much pain or inconvenience it causes. A girl like you would be miserable. I didn't take the trouble of raising you all those years just to see you go and marry a prince."

I was secretly relieved. Now that Qajars didn't have to worry any longer about Reza Shah's travel restrictions, I did not want to cut myself off from a wider existence than I could ever find in an andarun. My younger brothers would go abroad to study when the war was over, and there was even talk in families like ours of sending girls to school in Europe when it was safe again. Well, war or no war, I decided, I wasn't going to wait for my brothers to outstrip me yet again. I wanted to see this Statue of Liberty, and I wanted more education. In the spring of 1942 I went to Mrs. Elder and Mrs. MacDowell and asked them to help me find a school in America. They kindly agreed to send away for something called catalogues.

Dadash raised his eyebrows when I told him. He knew that it was a long step from ordering college catalogues—which would take months just to reach me—to what I wanted to do. But he didn't try to dissuade me. "Well," said Khanom tightly after my brother, at my request, had informed her of my plans, "we know by now that you do what you want. But you forget that we live in an occupied country. Anything can happen."

My mother was no longer the same woman she had been. Even though she still never left home unless covered in her chador, or in a long black dress and stockings and black kerchief that hid every strand of hair, since the destruction of the compound she had started going to the bazaar with Mashti and had become good at bargaining for cloth or rice. Moreover, since my father's death she had learned much besides that: to settle the disputes and problems in the villages where we still owned property, to supervise the running of our grandmother's mosque, to pay dozens of old servants their pensions every month and make sure their families were taken care of. She was far more broad-minded than most women of her generation, always insisting to her sisters, cousins, and nieces that women nowadays had to be educated, even if that meant that they married later. Nor did she fear or distrust foreigners; when I graduated from Nurbaksh she had warmly shaken hands with Dr. Jordan, whose funny little beard and comical jokes she had loved hearing about from Farough and the other boys at Alborz College.

Nevertheless, I knew that my idea horrified her. She would not have objected now if I had said that I wanted to study in Europe when the war was over, and live with some nice family in Paris or London. But what I was announcing went well beyond what was safe or proper. I was a fatherless, husbandless daughter who wanted to abandon all protection and go alone to the land at the end of the earth in the middle of a war. This was clearly something to which she could never consent. How could a mother watch over her daughter from so far? How could Dadash protect me or keep me from falling into the hands of unscrupulous men? How could she know that I would not become an apostate? Furthermore, as we both knew, her own most conservative relatives would reproach her to her face, asking her why she couldn't control her own daughter.

"Maybe, Khanom," I said meekly, "the war will be over by the time the American ladies find me a school. They say that it may take several years to make the arrangements."

She gave me an ironic look. "Years?" she retorted. "Years? How do you know what's going to happen tomorrow?"

She put down her sewing and paused. I understood how upset she was. None of us, including me (as she was perfectly well aware), knew anything about America. It was no more than a word to us, a white fog. "I am against it," she said finally. "Who knows what is in America? How would you live when you got there? It would be dangerous and unclean. And how would it look if your brother and I let you, an inexperienced young girl, place yourself in such a situation? No, I want you to stay here, with the people who care about what happens to you."

I said no more. I felt guilty at having made her so unhappy. And since she had explicitly told me that she disapproved, I could not carry out my plans without publicly shaming her. My only hope was that if enough time passed, she would grow more accustomed to the idea, and if she could not endorse it, would at least not oppose it.

In no time it was all over the family that Satti wanted to go to Yengeh Donya. "Darling, why are you talking about going there?" asked Batul in hurt, perplexed tones. "You cannot be all by yourself. We know nothing about America."

I explained that I wanted to learn how to help people with their problems. "But it is so *far*," my stepmother sighed. "No, no, I want you to stay here, where we can take care of you." However, as my departure was obviously not an imminent concern and everyone knew that my mother did not approve, nobody tried seriously to talk me out of the idea.

I guessed that even Dadash had mixed feelings. However, to my relief and gratitude, he was encouraging. Times were changing, he said, and we had to change with them. He loyally pleaded my cause to Khanom. "What are we going to do with her here?" he would ask. "She can't sit at home doing nothing—she might as well get an education." Sometimes, when we sat together at a meal or when I was sewing with her, I would mention the subject of America casually and then drop it again, hoping that she would grow used to the idea. "Well," my mother would say calmly, "it will be as God wills." I knew that I would just have to wait until the time came.

Most of our servants, who would have been disgusted at the idea of shaking hands with Dr. Jordan or any other strange foreigner, made their disapproval clear, but Mashti, when I told him that I wanted to go to school in Yengeh Donya, simply could not take it in. He merely shook his head uncomprehendingly, as though I had said that I was thinking of flying to the moon. "We will miss you," he said sadly.

Time had eaten like acid at the dearest friend of my childhood. Mashti was now about forty, or a little more than that, and very old. A life of laboring from sunrise to sunset six days a week and living in a country with virtually no medical care had taken its toll. My strong laleh had become stooped and wasted. His eyes and cheeks were sunken and hollow, his face as deeply lined as a European peasant's or an American farmer's at seventy. I had always worried especially about the fact that it was Mashti's job to shake out our dirty carpets; I had heard from the missionaries that breathing dust could make people very sick. But Mashti only replied that somebody had to help Khanom with all her work.

I noticed now that he breathed with difficulty and always seemed slightly feverish. Korsum came often to say that he wanted to rest in bed. My mother, unable to bear seeing him hanging around exhausted but still trying to help her, had finally hired a younger man, Mashreza, to take his place, and told Mashti to take his pension and give God thanks that he no longer need work. Soon, however, Korsum began reporting that he had a cough every morning and a fever at night. When Dadash heard this, he looked alarmed and said that Mashti must go to the public clinic and get cough medicine. There was nothing more to do. We had plenty of diseases in Iran, but few cures— the miraculous new medicines called antibiotics, which Mrs. MacDowell had told me about, were only just becoming available in the West—so everyone was always coughing or sick or feverish with something, all the more now because of the war and the thousands of refugees. Mashti's symptoms, Dadash said vaguely, could mean many things. We must just hope for the best.

For a while Mashti seemed to get better on my mother's herb medicines. His cough almost disappeared and he seemed stronger. Then, though the weather was getting hot, the coughing and sweating returned. One morning Korsum came to my mother in terror, saying that her husband was spewing bloody foam from his mouth and could not breathe. Terrified herself, my mother sent for Dadash, who came hurrying home from work. When he heard what Korsum had to say, he looked upset. But he spoke calmly. "He should not stay at home any more, Korsum. The next days or weeks will be too hard for you. He must go to the public hospital." The foul, overcrowded public hospital was where patients with infectious diseases were taken.

Korsum began to sob, and the rest of us were horrified. Dadash was pronouncing a death sentence: people only went to the public hospital when they were so far gone that their relatives could no longer care for them. But my mother quickly went to get some money. "This is for the droshky," she said softly to the weeping Korsum. "Have your son Mehdi take Mashti to the hospital. God is great and will protect you and your family."

When I said a day or two later that I wanted to visit him, my mother forbade me to go. Dadash said the typhus epidemic was now so bad that the orderlies at the hospital, to make beds available, were taking patients' corpses away and burying them the moment they saw that the person was dead. Besides, it was a men's hospital, and she couldn't spare Mashreza to escort me. However, the thought of Mashti lying there sick and alone among strangers was more than I could stand. I put on a kerchief and went by myself in a hired droshky.

The hospital was a big two-story building like a warehouse, with large windows open to let in both hot air and flies. The registrar was on the ground floor in an outpatient ward filled with the coughs and groans of feverish men waiting to be examined by a medical attendant. I felt dreadfully conspicuous. I wished that I had insisted that Mashreza come with me, and tugged nervously at the knot of my kerchief. I asked the registrar, who was careful not to look at my face, where I could find "Mashad-Hossein." He shrugged; it was a common name. Maybe if I looked around the medical ward on the second floor, he would turn up.

Acutely uncomfortable, I went upstairs to the medical ward, a long, high-ceilinged hall with twenty-five beds on each side. Each bed contained a scared, dying man. Moving along the aisle, I heard the moans of patients in the delirium of typhus. I felt more and more frightened. The stench of blood, urine, and excrement was overpowering. Two dirty orderlies went by, casually lugging a body wrapped in a sack as though taking a carpet to wash in a stream.

Seeing this, I forgot my embarrassment in my terror of the plague. I wanted only to turn and run. Fighting the impulse, I stopped one of the orderlies and described the person I was looking for. "Ah," said the orderly, "that fellow is down there with a couple of lung patients. Tuberculosis, the attendant says."

Mashti was in a bed at the end of the row. The covers, which looked as if they had not been washed in weeks, were smeared with blood and yellow sputum. His face was ashen, but he was awake, his big, dark eyes sunk deep in their sockets. They seemed glittering, unnaturally bright. "Satti-Khanom," he whispered when he saw me standing by the bed, and began struggling to sit up to show his respect.

Tears gripped my throat like a vise. I swallowed them down, knowing that I must not cry. I ordered him to lie back, then got a low stool and sat by the side of the bed. He must not think I've come because he is dying, I told myself. I have to find something to talk about. In a hoarse, rasping voice he asked how Khanom was. I saw that he could hardly breathe.

I gave him my mother's greetings and the greetings of Dadash and the younger children. My throat ached with the effort not to cry as I brought him news from home. It was clear that our conversation was robbing him of the little strength he had. After a short time, touching his hand, I murmured that I would come and see him again in a few days, and left.

Riding back to Sepah Avenue in the droshky, I cried uncontrollably. Mashti's wasted body and his eyes, bright with death, rode with me. Mashti had been our rock, our anchor; except for Dadash, he was the only man we had ever had at home. Once, in my longing for an ordinary father, I had told myself that I was Mashti's real daughter, his firstborn. Now he was lying in a filthy hospital, old and dying from his hard life, from breathing all the dirt and disease of our wretched country.

My mother, Farough, the other children, the cook, and all the maidservants were waiting anxiously for news. Mashti was part of us all. My eyes fell first on Khanom. Nearly out of my mind with grief and rage, I screamed, "I told you he was sick from the dust in the air! They told us that at school—the sickness comes from the dust that people spit in. If you hadn't made him shake all those filthy carpets he would be alive now!" Then I whirled on poor Dadash, who had just come home from work. "Why is the hospital so dirty? Why don't you doctors take care of people? Why don't you *do* something for human beings?"

Running to my room, I flung myself on the bed and wept for hours until I was sick and exhausted and had no tears left. In my agony, I had to blame someone. But I knew that Dadash and my mother, who was almost as racked by sorrow as I was, were not at fault. It was Iran's backwardness that was to blame for Mashti's dying, and the troubles of a country deprived of scientific knowledge, clean hospitals, and modern drugs, its people left to flounder in poverty and ignorance.

A few days later, Korsum was notified by a messenger that Mashti was dead and that someone must take the body away. She and her children went to the hospital, but Mashti was not in the bed where he had been. No one had any idea what had happened to him. Korsum returned home in hysterics. Without a body, we could not hold a funeral. Dadash telephoned the hospital's director and learned that Korsum must go to the hospital morgue. There, an attendant, after getting a description of Mashti, took her and her children to the paupers' field and showed them an unmarked grave. This, he told her, was Mashti. Whether he spoke the truth or not we had no way of knowing.

It was, I thought, as if he had never existed. We didn't even know where he was buried. He had been torn away from his wife and children, from me, from everyone who loved, respected, and cared about him. He had died alone, forgotten and nameless, outside the great embrace of family, without anyone to bury him and send him decently to God. He had died that way because no one in our country did anything to help people like him. In the end, he had been just another poor, ignorant, anonymous Iranian—a nobody. And the death of this nobody broke my heart.

My mother, who understood very well how I felt, never chided me for my outburst about Mashti, while Dadash tried to lighten my grief by joking or hugging me when he saw that I was moody. But as time passed, a boiling rage that I could barely control would roil in me for weeks together and then suddenly spill over into tears or bursts of fury at Farough, Homy, or one of the younger children. The afflictions of the women at the dispensary were now almost more than I could bear, and only admiration for the dignity with which they bore their troubles kept me going. Why didn't someone help these people? Why was I leading this useless, claustrophobic, intolerable life? Why did Mashti have to die that way?

Aghajun died, in his mid-eighties; he had always been there, and it was as if a piece of us had been broken off. Jaby and Abbas returned to Abadan, where Abbas had a new assignment. Nargess became very ill and went back to her village in Shemiran to live on a small pension my mother settled on her. I got news of her when someone came to collect the money. As with Mashti, no one could say what sickness my former nanny had. I saw her when I could get a ride to the village, which, because of the wartime lack of transportation, was not often.

Not long after Mashti's death, in the summer of 1942, Dadash was sent as district health administrator to Hamadan, an ancient Median town in the barren mountain country in the west of Iran. That fall, college catalogues began to arrive, along with dozens of forms which, with my American sponsors' patient help, I filled out and sent off. With the war on, I couldn't expect to hear anything until next summer at the earliest. I felt depressed and disheartened. Suppose I was doing the wrong thing, and making my mother suffer for nothing? Suppose I did go to America and failed in my purpose, or did something of which my family would have to be ashamed? For almost a year, time dragged unbearably, and I became scarcely fit for civilized company.

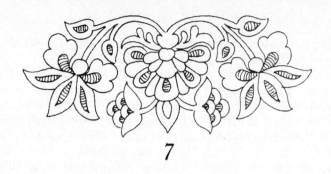

7

SETTING OUT

Strange, is it not, that of the myriads who
Before us passed the door of Darkness through,
*   Not one returns to tell us of the Road*
Which to discover we must travel too.

—Omar Khayyam

*D*URING THAT YEAR THE UNITED STATES HAD BEGUN SENDING engineering and transport troops to Iran under the Lend-Lease Act, so we were now seeing American soldiers on the Avenue Lalezar as well. Everyone reported that these new foreigners were polite, open-handed, and friendly. We had gradually grown used to the sight of the Russian and British soldiers, and the Americans, being unconnected with the humiliation of military defeat, aroused little more than the amiable curiosity Iranians usually feel at the sight of exotic visitors. I myself was surprised to see American men with young, unlined faces. The only American men I knew had been doctors and teachers, people who were old and wise.

At long last, in May of 1943, a letter arrived: I had been accepted at a small missionary school for women called Heidelberg College in Tiffin, Ohio. The worst of the waiting was over, and even though it would take many months more for a visa to be approved, for the first time I began to feel some excitement and purpose. Having obtained an Iranian passport, in July I applied for a visa at the American Consulate on Naderi Avenue.

The return of my own optimism was soon followed by widespread excitement that fall as preparations began for the Tehran Conference at the end of November. Among my friends, no one could talk of anything else. It was exciting to think of President Roosevelt and Churchill and Stalin sitting down together in Tehran. America was more popular and beloved than ever. The United States had been sending us food and financial assistance. Moreover, after Reza Shah's abdication, Prime Minister Forrughi had persuaded the Allies to sign a treaty agreeing to withdraw all their forces from Iranian soil not later than six months after the formal end of hostilities; now, as they reaffirmed that commitment, some people said that the United States government, stronger than either the British or the Russians, had made them agree to respect our sovereignty after the war. Perhaps the long-wished-for day of Iran's freedom from foreign control was not too distant.

In my own family that winter there was also much excited talk about the parliamentary elections. Dr. Mohammed Mossadegh was running for a seat in parliament, and had the support of a new party of moderate democrats and liberal intellectuals and professionals. Dadash, who had finished his assignment in Hamadan and was staying with us while awaiting reassignment, was a close friend of Dr. Mossadegh's younger son, Gholam, who was also a physician, and an enthusiastic supporter of our cousin's views. So was Abbas, who would return permanently to Tehran with Jaby the following summer. Dadash and Abbas both said that Dr. Mossadegh was the most incorruptible and principled man in Iran, and the country's greatest hope for real constitutional democracy and economic independence.

In February of 1944 the consulate notified me that my visa had been approved. I could leave as soon as I found a way to get to America.

I knew that the way people usually got to America was to travel to Cairo or Paris and then take a ship to New York, where they were met by the Statue of Liberty, now imprinted so indelibly on my mind. But the overland routes across Europe and North Africa were right in the line of the firestorm. I hadn't the slightest idea how I was going to solve this problem. Nevertheless, I decided to try to leave before the Persian New Year celebrations began in March, and I asked Dadash to tell Khanom that my visa was ready.

I felt as though I were asking him to deliver a blow. She no longer showed surprise or distress when I mentioned America, but I knew that this was because my departure had not been imminent. Now it was, and I did not know how it would affect her. My brother, however, approached his task like the skillful physician he was, giving her the news casually while she was engaged in some routine chore and then, after it had gently sunk in, reassuring her that all would be well and that my plan was the best one for me.

When I asked him what she had said, he replied that she now accepted my decision. For many days, however, she could not bring herself to speak to me, and each of us avoided the other's gaze. I understood what she was feeling. Her conviction that I must be happy was at war with her love for me. All around her, young Iranian women were getting educations, becoming teachers and nurses, growing interested in reading about and discussing politics and society. She sensed that all this was good for women and for the country, yet it seemed to fly in the face of the tradition she loved. The world she lived in was changing in ways she didn't understand and couldn't stop, and now I was setting out alone to America, to live there by myself. Her pain was not something she was angry at me for inflicting, but it was also not something she could bear to discuss with me.

The problem of transportation, however, occupied much of my thought. Somehow I had to get to a port and find a ship to take me to New York. Some people had been stranded in Cairo for five months before they had set sail, but I was hoping that if I could reach Cairo or maybe Casablanca, I might find something. I decided to ask at the American Consulate. There I learned that if one journeyed east instead of west, one could reach America by sailing across the Pacific. I was very pleased to hear this, although just where and how I would find passage was anybody's guess, as all ship movements were secret. However, Bombay was a likely possibility. If I took a train eastward toward Mashad and from there made my way south, along our eastern border with Afghanistan, I might get to India. I left the consulate in triumph and in more of a hurry to leave than ever. I would just head in the general direction of India and go from there to the entrance to America. Once I actually reached New York, surely it would be a comparatively simple matter to make my way to Tiffin, Ohio, which lay roughly in the middle of the country. I needed only enough cash for the journey and my school fees and initial living expenses in America—Mrs. MacDowell had told me that the visa stipulated that I could earn my living once I was there. The picture with the Statue of Liberty glowed before me, alluring, magical. Fate, I felt, was with me. I was as good as on my way!

I had a bit more than six thousand tomans in a bank account, or about two thousand dollars. This was a lot of money in those days, especially in Iran. If I could find someone in the family to buy my sewing machine and the china with our family crest—my dowry, in effect, which obviously I wasn't going to require—I would have a little more. However, I didn't know how I was going to sell them. Jaby, who had been writing me affectionate, encouraging letters from Abadan, wasn't around, and I couldn't ask my stepmothers, who looked doleful and stricken whenever they thought of my leaving, not only on my account but because of the public loss of face their best friend, my mother, would suffer. Not knowing what lay ahead myself, I could hardly reassure them.

Though I had been so cavalier about my transportation, accommodations were something I wasn't leaving to chance, and I made a careful list of family connections—which, thanks to our prolific Qajar forebears, we had in profusion in every corner of Iran; through one of my sisters-in-law, we even had connections in Bombay. This was extremely important, because outside of major towns like Mashad, where there were hotels women could stay in, I would have to rely entirely on relatives, friends, and relatives of friends. I wrote down all the names and addresses in a notebook, as well as those of all the American teachers who had gone back to the United States when Sage closed, even Dr. Jordan, whom I barely knew. Of course, except for "New York" and "Tiffin, Ohio," no place in America had the slightest meaning for me—I had no idea where any of them were, and didn't think I would need them. But the names of American cities sounded exotic and romantic, and writing them down made me feel that I was making progress.

With the cessation of the winter rains at the beginning of March, I asked Dadash if he would consult with Khanom about how I might dispose of my things. Though she was still quiet and withdrawn, her mood was lighter now, and I sensed that he was succeeding in convincing her that what I was doing was for the best. A day or two later, he took me aside. Khanom herself, he told me, would buy my sewing machine and give it to Homy, who was sixteen and could put it to good use. She had also written to Jaby to say that she was buying my china in case Jaby needed an extra set for dinner parties. She would give me a check for two thousand tomans, or about seven hundred dollars, and he would take me to the bank and help me change some of the money into Cook's traveler's checks.

After this my mother became much more cheerful, and I realized that the arrangement appealed to her practical nature: she could benefit my sisters, while at the same time what she had done would help to ensure that I wouldn't become stranded or starve to death in Yengeh Donya.

In spite of our lifelong differences, I thought, Khanom and I were exactly alike. Neither of us could talk about our feelings or show our emotions openly. But I knew what my mother was saying to me, and I vowed that if I had to kill myself in America, one day I was going to come back and give her reason to be proud of me. With all the sacrifices she had made for us, never had she shown herself greater or more generous than now.

Next morning, Dadash escorted me to the Maidan, Tehran's main square, where we converted most of my money into dollar traveler's checks for use when I arrived in the United States. The crisp notes felt like destiny. Dadash, smiling broadly at my happiness and nearly as happy as I, insisted on taking me to a French café he liked, to celebrate. I had never been inside a café. A little nervously, I walked beside him to the Lalezar, where the orange-and-white scalloped awnings of fashionable shops fluttered in a light breeze. Straight to the north, the peaks of the Alborz with their kerchiefs of winter snow seemed to spring right up from the end of the street, like giants towering above a frivolous little flower bed. For a moment I felt a pang: when would I see these splendid mountains again?

The café smelled pleasantly of coffee, pastry, and cigarettes. But when we walked in, I shrank back in shock. There was not one other woman in the room. Pretending not to notice my blushes and downcast eyes, Dadash found us an obscure table in a far corner where I would feel less conspicuous. He ordered café au lait and a selection of cakes, but I couldn't touch the food. I sat covered with shame, my eyes down.

My brother watched me sympathetically for a few minutes. Finally he said, "Satti, going to America is a great thing for you. I have encouraged it and I am happy for you and proud of your bravery. You will get the education you wanted so much and then you'll come back and do great things. But you cannot be a shy girl from an andarun in the Shah's Garden any more. Soon you will have to eat in public and talk to strangers. When I was studying in Paris, I often saw women eating by themselves in the cafés there. If we want to move among people, we have to get over our shyness. And if you do this, you can no longer be like other Iranian women."

I saw that he had brought me here for more than café au lait, and I felt that once he, too, must have been shy.

"Sometimes it will be lonely," he added quietly.

I remembered the heartrendingly lonely letters our mothers had all received from their oldest sons when we were children, and realized that Dadash must written such letters to my mother and Aghajun. Knowing that he had already walked the road I was setting out on calmed me, and I managed to eat and drink a little. When he saw that I felt better, Dadash's spirits picked up, too. Calling for the bill and leaving an absurdly generous tip, he proposed that we go to a photographer's studio to commemorate this important occasion.

I still have the photograph we took together that day. Dadash, with his long Persian gentleman's face and his kind, intelligent eyes, looks very proper but pleased in spite of himself, while I am smiling as gaily as though I hadn't a care on earth. My brother could see a great deal more of the future than I. But when you are young, you think you are there to do all the things no one else can do. Going to America was my destiny. I was sure that luck would be with me.

That same afternoon I went to the American Consulate to get the visa stamped into my passport. I spent the remainder of the time before my departure visiting all our relatives and my own friends to say farewell, beginning with Mohammed Vali Mirza, our new "Shazdeh," then everyone else, according to age. Everyone wept and wished me well. I said goodbye to Batul-Khanom and Fatimeh-Khanom last. They cried and hugged and kissed me twenty times apiece and said they prayed for God to protect me wherever I went but they would miss me nonetheless.

I was to leave on Thursday afternoon—March 14, 1944—but my mother had been commuting frequently to Reswanieh to supervise some renovations to a house there, and she announced that she would be going there the day before I left. I understood that she didn't want to have to go to the train station to see me off. On Tuesday evening she admired my new suitcase and cheerfully offered to help me pack. She would miss me, she said, but she was glad that I was going to go to school. "Be in God's protection," she said tenderly, "and whenever you are in trouble, always pray to God for help."

Dadash and I said our goodbyes on the morning of my departure, before he left for work. It would be a long time before we could be sure of communicating again, for my family would have nowhere to write to me before I sent them an address in America, while because of the war my letters might not even reach them. As I wept, he laughed and hugged me and patted my back and said that I would come back with my head full of ideas and they would all be proud of me.

The train was to depart at four o'clock. I put on the dark, long-sleeved dress, thick stockings, and kerchief I would travel in, and around three Mashreza loaded my suitcase into a droshky outside where my brothers and sisters were waiting and I said goodbye to our womenservants, who were lined up at the door of the courtyard looking as if they were going to a funeral. They and Mashreza looked upon my project as they would a murder. Didn't they know of countless stories from their villages at home of girls alone who had been kidnapped, or had run off to the city and ended in circumstances too dreadful to speak of? When I had hugged and kissed them all, the eldest servant held the Holy Koran over my head and I stepped through the door and out to the street. "Be in God's care and protection," she wept, "and may you come back someday to us who love you." Then she sprinkled the dust around the threshold with a little water to ensure my safe return and closed the gate of the courtyard behind me.

The railroad station was jammed with Allied soldiers and pilgrims going to the Shrine of Imam Reza in the holy city of Mashad, for the Khorasan Road, as the ancient route that connects Tehran and Mashad is called, is the Persian equivalent of the road to Canterbury. The platform was a sea of laughing and crying families. Ghaffar, who was now sixteen, and Rashid, who was eleven, were trying to be brave, but Homy and Sory, my young sisters, were sobbing, and our baby, Khorshid, who was nine, whimpered softly; Mashreza and the nurse-maid were crying and lamenting in open horror. I hugged them and kissed and squeezed all my little brothers and sisters one last time. Only my nineteen-year-old brother Farough did not look sad; he was going to be the next one to go to America, he said—I was just going to blaze a trail for him.

Finally, at the last possible moment, I got on the train alone. Desperately shoving my way through the crowded aisle in search of a compartment, I found one with an empty seat, went to the window, and pressed my face against the dirty glass. Afraid to let go of my suitcase even for a second, I seized it with both hands and, heaving it in front of me, clumsily waved it from side to side at everyone.

The train began to move, their faces to slide backward as though pulled by a giant invisible string. All at once I, too, was filled with horror. I must have been mad! I could never exist without my mother, Dadash, my brothers and sisters and my stepmothers, everyone I loved and who loved me. For a second of blind panic I wanted to turn around, run out of the compartment, and jump out of the moving train. But already we were going too fast. Collapsing into my seat and hiding my face in my handkerchief, I cried helplessly, berating myself for the folly and stupidity of what I had just done.

After a while my storm of weeping ebbed. We were passing through South Tehran, not far from where the dispensary was. The sight of its dreary mud hovels steadied me; this, after all, was why I was going.

The compartment was full of the belongings of the pilgrim family that occupied the other five seats. I sank back and watched the scenery pass. The train was speeding along through the Varamin countryside, where my mother had often taken us, Mashti, and Korsum to buy fruits and visit the nearby mosques and shrines. One of these, which we now passed, was the beautiful Shrine of Abdol Azim, where Shazdeh and Nosratdoleh lay buried.

Seeing its golden dome rising above the ripples of green gardens that appeared behind the walls of the nearby village of Rey, I suddenly missed Shazdeh with a choking intensity I had not felt since his death. Not for the first time, I wished I had had a father to discuss all my recent decisions with. Sometimes the audacity of my plan had frightened even me. "O God of Abdol Hossein," I had prayed in bed at night, "please forgive me for hurting my mother, and do not condemn me to a life of eternal misery for disobeying her advice. I only want to fulfill my duty and help our country."

Over the last several years I had often reminded myself of a poem by Sa'adi that I had memorized for Shazdeh as a child. It went, "Although love of country is required by the Prophet,/ one should not live in misery/merely because one was born in a certain land." Seven hundred years ago, I told myself, Sa'adi had said that I must not tie myself to one place—that I must find something wider and more interesting than just marriage and the andarun. Sa'adi, I felt, had been someone like me: he needed to leave the confinement of home and see the world (once, I knew, he had walked all the way from Egypt to Turkey). I always imagined that in this poem he was giving me his blessing. But was Shazdeh?

I imagined my father drawing his white eyebrows together in disapproval. He had never needed words to tell me that I was disobeying his wishes. Was I doing that now? I wasn't sure; I did not know. All I knew for certain was that I had shoved my future into motion, and I had to go on. But I felt that if he had seen the occupation, and Mashti's death, he would have understood why I had to leave, to learn what the world beyond Persia had to teach me. I would just have to see what happened to me next.

A tired, elderly tea vendor came by, sold me a glass, and paused gratefully to chat. He had worked for the railroad, he told me, since

Reza Shah had constructed it ten years ago. The old king had meant the line to run all the way to Mashad, but only got about eighty miles, to Semnon, before the foreigners threw him out. Semnon, I thought sleepily; that was where Nosratdoleh was killed. I half-listened, sipping the hot tea and hardly able to keep my eyes open. After a few minutes, worn out with emotion, I fell asleep. Two hours later I awoke abruptly. It was dark, the train had stopped, and everyone was getting off.

Hauling my suitcase behind me, I too clambered down from the train, looking around in bewilderment. It was pitch-dark. Then the significance of the tea vendor's words dawned on me: this was the end of the line. Except for a single dim light burning in the stationmaster's room, there was nothing around but thick darkness. We were in roughly the middle of nowhere. Trying not to panic, I reasoned that if all the pilgrims were on this train, they must expect to be able to get to Mashad. In the one-room train station, I learned that in the morning I would have to look for a car to hire. Afraid to leave, I sat all night guarding my suitcase, sleepless. At dawn a broken-down taxi took me to a garage milling with pilgrims also trying to get rides to Mashad. A car was leaving soon, going by way of Shahrud, seventy-five miles away. We had cousins in Shahrud with whom I could stay the night. Feeling pleased with myself for having survived my first brush with danger, I got some bread and tea in an old teahouse. Other travelers were eating there, too, and after some curious glances, I saw with relief that no one bothered about me; they simply assumed that I was a married woman traveling alone, perhaps to meet her husband or her brother. Moving about in the world alone, I thought, was not so very difficult after all. I was sure now that I was going to be lucky.

The car going to Mashad was an ancient, battered Chevrolet that smelled like an old camel. With a great sense of adventure, I got into the back with two women in chadors. We drove all day along the fawn-colored foothills of the Alborz and arrived in Shahrud after dark. My cousins were away, but the caretaker and his wife welcomed me and gave me a bed. I fell asleep the instant I lay down.

The next morning we started again, leaving the fertile foothills for the northern edge of the Great Salt Desert. The hills grew smooth and pale and seemed to fold in among themselves. Salt boulders glared white in the sun. This fiery, barren wilderness was the very heart of Iran, pitiless and immense. Sometimes the empty landscape was punctuated by the stone ruins of a caravanserai, its crumbling bricks inhabited only by wasps and vipers, or by a herd of wild donkeys, or by one of the small, ancient towers built for protection from the Turkoman raiders who had once caused the Khorasan Road to be called "the

Stages of Terror." I listened absorbed as the driver told us proudly that this was where Marco Polo had traveled the Silk Road to Samarkand, and where the Mongol hordes had poured into Persia from the east. As we passed Nishapur, the home of the eleventh-century astronomer, mathematician, and poet Omar Khayyam, the driver, relishing his knowledge, said that the Mongols had left not even a dog or a cat alive in the city. I thought about all the foreign conquerors who had ravaged our land, and how we Iranians had adapted ourselves to them and then absorbed and outlasted them all, surviving with our families on this unforgiving soil when they had become part of its dust.

Toward sunset we arrived at the sacred city of Mashad. It was full of pilgrims, for the next day was No Ruz, our joyous Persian New Year, which is a holiday as happy as Christmas. In my cold-water hotel room, still aching from the shock of my departure, I felt lonely, but Jaby had an old friend here whose husband was a son of Hossein Teymourtash, the court minister and friend of Nosratdoleh who had died a few years before our brother while imprisoned by Reza Shah. When I called her, she invited me to spend No Ruz with them. After the arrival of the new year, my hostess and I went to pray at the great shrine, and for the first time since my departure I felt peaceful and free of doubts, as if, for the moment, I had shed a skin that was too tight to wear any longer.

I was unable to leave Mashad for many days because of the holiday, and began to be afraid that I would have to start using the traveler's checks I was saving for America. However, I finally learned that a large lorry owned by a British transport company shipping supplies and weapons to the British and Russians would leave soon for Zahedan, a desolate frontier town three hundred miles to the south in Persian Baluchistan, on the border with India. I was seated in the lorry's front cab with two laborers and a White Russian driver.

The trip, which took three and a half days, was one of the worst I have ever experienced. We drove almost straight through, stopping only to sleep for a night at Birjand, the one large town on the way, and eating nothing but hard-boiled eggs, tea, bread, and dried fruit as hard as rocks, which were all that the inhabitants of the domed desert villages had to sell. From time to time in the empty, stony landscape of low, reddish hills, groups of fierce-looking nomads in black robes would appear on horseback, reminding us that there were still bandits in the region. I wondered how the desert dwellers survived here in the summer, when the flat red hills radiated their heat like a living thing. I was stiff from sitting for hours without moving, and my clothes stank;

I was bleary-eyed with fatigue and wished the journey were over. Yet I was also excited to be seeing all this, proud that this stupendous landscape and these tough, tenacious, independent people were Persians, like me. They belonged to me and I to them.

At last we reached Zahedan, whose chief claims to being a "town" were a bazaar and one paved street. From here, however, I could get the twice-weekly train to Bombay, if it wasn't held up by Indian rebels who had been sabotaging the Northwest Indian Railway lines. I found lodgings in the guest quarters of an admirable Indian physician and his wife, who ran a small but clean and efficient hospital for the Indians, Baluchis, Afghans, and Persians who lived in the border area. The British government of India had sent the kindly Dr. Satralkar to care for them, and for the first time, it occurred to me that the British might be capable of benevolence in a country they ran.

Four days after my arrival, I got on the train to Bombay. If all went well, I should reach Bombay in about forty-eight hours. There were eight people on the benches in the compartment, and several more had made themselves at home on the overhead baggage racks. I watched with excitement as we wound slowly up the steep mountainsides. After several hours we descended and the landscape became the low, hilly countryside of northwest India. Even from the train window, the dirt and poverty were more startling than anything I had ever seen at home.

Late that afternoon the train suddenly screeched to a halt and a large contingent of Indian Army soldiers got on. As the train started again, they moved from one compartment to another, brandishing their rifles and barking orders in English, evidently looking for something. A little scared, I asked another passenger in English what they were doing. He shrugged and said that they were looking for saboteurs. At the next town, which was Quetta, they ordered everyone out of the train. Clutching my suitcase tightly, I got out and stood on the platform to watch the train start up again and disappear down the tracks.

I waited in the confused, milling crowd, looking around and feeling worried. I had no idea where we were, and knew no one in Quetta. After a while most people began to drift away to look for shelter, while others simply sat down on their baggage to spend the night on the platform or went to buy dinner at a nearby market. No one had any idea when another train would arrive—perhaps today, more probably tomorrow, maybe not for several days. By this time I was really alarmed and thought that my luck might have deserted me after all. I had the choice of spending the next few days on top of my suitcase or finding somewhere to stay but perhaps missing the next train. Not knowing what else to do, I stood right where I was, facing the tracks and hoping that perhaps this would help the next train materialize sooner.

All at once I noticed that a dark, middle-aged man in a suit and tie had broken away from a group of men standing and talking near the marketplace, and that he was walking toward me. As I wondered nervously what he wanted, he came up and bowed politely. "Salaam, Khanom," he said in southern-accented Persian. "I see that you have come from Iran on the train that was sabotaged by Gandhi's followers, and I wonder if I might assist you? My name is Bushiri; I am an Iranian merchant, and a resident of Quetta. May I have the honor of knowing your name?"

A little uneasy despite his polite manners, I told him. He looked at me astounded. "Are you, then, a daughter of Prince Abdol Hossein Farman-Farma?" he asked.

When I answered in surprise that I was, he bowed again. "Then, Khanom, God is great! Many years ago in Fars, at the time that His Highness was our governor and saved us from the famine, I was a young merchant, and during the war, when I had to get a caravan to Shiraz, your father had his men escort me. Without his protection I would have been ruined. Since he gave me second life, ever since then I regarded him as my second father, and I now give thanks to God for granting me the opportunity of at last repaying this great debt. I beg you to stay with me and my wife in our home until the next train arrives, which won't be for another two days."

That night I went to bed in Mr. and Mrs. Bushiri's guest room, feeling that the God of Abdol Hossein must finally have decided to approve of my plan.

Two days later, with many thanks to my rescuer, I resumed my journey. Mr. Bushiri and his wife had showered me with generosity and kindness, taking me driving in Quetta and answering my curious questions about India. When he learned that I was unmarried and traveling to America alone, Mr. Bushiri begged me to remain in Quetta, where he would consider it a privilege to find me a husband among the men of his family. I politely declined this generous offer, but said that I would be grateful to know more about the Indian independence movement. Mr. Bushiri replied that the followers of Gandhi were trying to drive out the British by disrupting their institutions, not by violence, and he thought that they would succeed. I listened with mingled admiration, envy, and disbelief. I could scarcely imagine that scrawny, starved-looking peasants like those I had seen from the train could go unarmed against the might of the British.

The train was so crowded that men were even riding outside, clinging to the tops of the cars like caterpillars to a rose leaf. I managed to get a window seat, which was fortunate, since more than a dozen people crammed themselves into the compartment with me. The smell was nearly intolerable even with the window open, and from time to time someone would lean across me to spit a mouthful of red betel juice out the window. Squeezing as close to the window as I could, I closed my eyes and tried to sleep.

The next morning when the train was standing still, a large white object suddenly thrust itself through the open window and onto the floor. I gasped. A young Indian, swathed in thin white cotton, his head wrapped in a flowing shawl of the same cheap cloth, sat down on the bench across from me, which someone had just vacated, and tried to catch his breath. A hempen sack filled with books and pamphlets swung from his shoulders.

I stared. Nobody said a word. He looked around at the faces in the compartment, evidently examining us to see who, if anyone, appeared likely to turn him in to one of the armed guards patrolling the train. Then he smiled genially at no one in particular. "Did I scare you?" he demanded in English, speaking to everybody. "Are you surprised? No harm will come to you. We are fighting for your freedom from the British."

There was a resentful silence. Two women with infants looked frightened. One or two people went to sleep. Somebody got up angrily and left the compartment. The rest ignored him as though he had not spoken.

"*I* was surprised," I said breathlessly, in my halting English. I was burning up with curiosity.

Realizing that a foreign woman was going to be his only audience, he smiled at me. "I am a soldier of Mahatma Gandhi," he said. I saw that he was just a skinny boy, dirty and poor, with a gentle, pleasant face. I waited, dying to hear more. "What is your religion?" he asked. When I said that I was a Moslem, he reached into his sack and pulled out a small, thin book with a green cover. "This is an English translation of the *Bhagavad Gita*," he said, handing it to me. "It contains the entire philosophy of Gandhi-ji, and therefore of our struggle for independence. Gandhi-ji," he went on fervently, "wants Hindu and Moslem to live and work together, and because of his wisdom and the simplicity with which he lives, our whole country is behind him. He wants Indians to be self-sufficient, and urges the hand-spinning and weaving of textiles at home to make us independent of British cloth."

He pointed proudly to his clothes. "This was spun and woven by an Indian woman in her own home, as Gandhi-ji has instructed us."

He gave me a fold of his shawl to take in my fingers and I examined it carefully and admiringly, wondering if his mother was the woman who had woven it, and whether she and his brothers and sisters knew of the brave, dangerous thing he was doing and were worried about him. They must, I thought with a sudden stab of pain, wish they knew where he was now.

We reached Lahore, the capital of the Punjab; some people left the compartment and others took their place. Fascinated by the young revolutionary's intensity and courage, I listened with complete absorption as he talked for hours about Gandhi's philosophy. I had never met anyone who was so committed, and I was deeply impressed by Gandhi's teaching that a country, like a person, should learn to be self-reliant. I thought of how Dr. Jordan used to tell my brothers at Alborz College that we Iranians had to learn to be self-reliant and depend on ourselves.

Toward dusk, his book still on my lap, I fell into a light doze. I awoke again a few minutes later, just in time to see the young rebel, his face covered with his shawl and his robes clutched tightly about him, swinging himself out of the compartment again. Fearing for his safety, I leaned out the window and looked back in the fading light, but saw nothing. I had no idea whether he had gone back to the roof or jumped, or whether he had escaped unharmed. I sat back with my heart pounding and my thoughts on fire. Why couldn't we produce brave people like him in Iran, who wanted to fight for their country and for social justice? This skinny, ardent youth, from a country even poorer than mine, had no guns—all he had was a bagful of pamphlets, his cheap cotton clothes, and his courage. I would have given anything to be able to fight like him.

I spent the rest of the trip to Bombay immersed in the *Bhagavad Gita*. We reached Bombay the next day. I went to a small English pension whose name I had obtained at the railroad station, and which appeared to cater to business travelers, the wives of low-ranking British officials, and junior military attachés. It was clean but very dreary. However, some merchant cousins of my sister-in-law, a family called Nemazi, welcomed me with open arms. The war had cut off communications with Tehran and, delighted at my unheralded arrival and news of their cousin, they insisted on showing me around Bombay and giving me all my meals. One of the Nemazi sons, Yahyah, an elegant young man in impeccable summer whites, drove me to the harbor dispatch office in his roadster so that I could ask about ships going to America. I was told that I must be prepared to sail on as little as five hours' notice, and on whatever was available. There was a long waiting list, and the schedules were all classified because Japanese submarines lurked off Bombay waiting to torpedo any vessels attempting to sail. But, I reasoned, the ocean must be big enough that submarines couldn't be everywhere at once, and I didn't care if they sent me to America in a motorboat. I was excited to be so close to the final stage of my trip.

The Nemazis, who knew everyone in Persian diplomatic and cultural circles, introduced me to dozens of people and went to endless trouble to entertain me. I found the great Indian city half lovely dream, half nightmare. The jewels and shimmering saris in the luxury stores and the freedom, undreamed of in my country, of Indian women to move about in public and even to work seemed to exist on a different plane from the swarming poor trapped in their hideous poverty. Yet three hundred and fifty million of these hungry, wretched people, I thought, were standing up to the British Empire as we never had; someday, perhaps, Indians of all faiths would live in harmony and be able to feed and clothe themselves, while we might still be under the English thumb, too disunited and concerned with our own individual interests to stand up and demand a fair share of the oil money so that we could cure our problems. Yet I was even more baffled and confused by the handsome buildings, splendid public parks, and hospitals the British had built. How could a nation be benevolent in one country and coldly exploitive in another? The world was evidently a more complicated place than I had imagined when I was still in Tehran.

Gradually, however, my fascination began to give way to uneasiness and despondency. Reaching Bombay had taken over six weeks and all that time I had thought of little else, but now that I had nothing to distract me I became homesick. Writing long letters home in the pension's gloomy little Victorian parlor was some relief, but I had no idea when or if these letters would reach Tehran. At first I had been confident that I would shortly be on my way, but two weeks passed and no call came from the harbor. I began to wonder if I would ever get a ship. I scarcely dared unpack my suitcase for fear that I would not be able to leave quickly enough. I was afraid I would run out of cash, or be permanently stranded and cast upon the charity of the Nemazis until after the war. I became afraid to leave the telephone.

On the afternoon of May fifteenth, a call came: a ship had room if I could come immediately. Yahyah rushed me to the harbor, presenting me with a farewell gift: a Koran in an English translation. The ship was a small, grimy passenger freighter with a French crew of six and twenty small cabins, but I gleefully paid my fare at the dispatch office, bade Yahyah a warm farewell, and went on board. No one I spoke to at dinner had any idea what route we would follow, only that our destination was America and we would not leave until midnight, under cover of darkness. The first full day out of port passed monotonously, broken only by lifeboat drills. Next morning at about four-thirty, however, I was jolted awake by a soft thud. Suddenly alarm bells began to clang. Irritated at being awakened so early for another drill, I put my things in my suitcase, hurried to the lifeboats, and was ordered to get in. We had been torpedoed.

Terrified, I huddled in the darkness with the other passengers as the lifeboat was lowered, not daring to move or speak and thinking that now the luck I had enjoyed so far had run out. We sat in total darkness as the lifeboat wobbled and pitched on the waves. For the first time, I fully understood how rash I had been to leave in wartime, and realized with something close to hysteria that I might never see Khanom, Dadash, and my brothers and sisters again. When the sky lightened and dawn broke, we saw that the French ship was gone, sunk. Then someone gasped and pointed to a dot on the horizon. The dot grew larger and broke in half, and we saw two ships steaming toward us; we had been sighted by a pair of British destroyers. Within twenty-four hours I was back in my dreary lodging house, thankful but still trembling.

My ordeal on the face of the void was such a shock that I was now convinced I would be trapped in Bombay forever: my money would run out and the kind Nemazis would have to take me in and feed me until the war was over. I was so depressed at this thought that only the still more unbearable one of returning home in defeat goaded me to keep on calling the harbor every two days. Two weeks later, when the news came that another ship could take me, I could barely rouse myself to pack my suitcase and telephone poor Yahyah to take me down to the port again. When I filled out the forms and saw that the boat was American and would have a military escort, I felt a little better, but not much.

Once more I thanked Yahyah and said goodbye, then went out to the pier to board, looking for another boat like the French freighter. However, I saw only a massive gray wall of metal ahead of me. Then, with a shock, I realized that this wall, which was at least five stories high, *was* the ship. I looked up and up. Rows of portholes stared down. This boat was so large that I didn't see how it could float.

Openmouthed, I slowly made my way up the gangplank to the passenger deck, where I was too astonished even to be embarrassed when an American naval officer who stood there in a gold-braided white uniform smiled and took my hand, giving it a hearty shake. "Welcome, Ma'am," he said cordially, "to the U.S.S. *General Butler*." I, a twenty-three-year-old Iranian girl who wasn't supposed to talk to strange men, was standing on the deck of a U.S. Navy troopship escorted by three destroyers and bearing six thousand G.I.s back from the South Pacific. I was going to get to America after all.

Strangely, now that my goal seemed within my grasp, the sense of urgency that had propelled me gave way to a kind of lassitude. Borne along on this mountainous ship in the drifting monotony of a long wartime voyage I felt suspended, as if my will had been taken out of my hands. My dreams of education and my old images of the statue, the tall buildings, the glamorous promenaders and beautifully dressed people from *Gone With the Wind* that had beckoned so long still did so, but they seemed to have receded, smiling at me from a great distance. No one could say where the voyage had originated, what our route would be, or when we would arrive. Life was an aimless, rigid routine. Evening began at four or five in the afternoon, when a complete blackout was imposed, and we had to remain belowdecks. During the day I reread the *Bhagavad Gita* and Yahyah's English Koran. (Since I could not read classical Arabic and knew of no Persian translation, it was the first time I had ever known what our holy book actually said.) In spite of my bad English and shyness I managed to befriend a dedicated old American missionary couple from Madras and a pleasant, gregarious army major named Williams, who was retiring and going home to Missouri, a place he clearly believed to be the most delightful spot in America. But the endless days were broken only by enormous meals and constant torpedo drills.

One small incident, however, I remembered vividly in the years after. Walking the deck at the rear of the ship with Major Williams one afternoon, I saw two sailors throwing what looked like a stream of fish over the side. Curious, I asked the purpose of this activity, and was told that this was food we had not consumed at lunch. I gasped, horrified at the thought of wasted food, then ran toward the sailors, crying, "Stop!" Laughing, the major pulled me back. The sailors weren't doing anything wrong, he explained. That was how the United States Navy chose to dispose of its uneaten food.

That evening as I lay on my bunk, I thought about all I had seen on my journey. I remembered the tough, hungry Iranians in their desert settlements, whole families living off the milk from one goat and the eggs from one chicken; I thought of the emaciated Indians I had seen from the train and on the streets of Bombay. What the sailors had thrown overboard in fifteen minutes would have kept a whole Persian village alive for a week. If the Navy did not have hungry servants on its ships, why did it choose to supply us with so much more than we could possibly consume? In countries like mine, a policy that wasted food in this manner would be tantamount to murder. I felt that the nations of the earth were complex and contradictory, and that there was much I did not understand. The British, whom I had always thought of as evil exploiters, had sent a doctor to Zahedan, while the United States, so sincerely unselfish and benevolent, squandered a precious resource for no reason that I could see. Plainly, I would have to work hard to understand America.

At last, after thirty-two days at sea, the news went around that someone had spotted land. All my excitement returned in a flash. Running to look, I strained to make out the great city on the horizon. There was only a flat gray mass, but I remained determinedly by the rail, sure that I would soon see the small pointed shapes of skyscrapers.

For a long time the ship steamed closer. Finally a port appeared, edged with low, featureless buildings. By now I realized that something was wrong. This port was not even as large as the one at Bombay. The water was filled with refuse and was black with oil slick. There were no skyscrapers, no strolling couples, no glittering promenade. Above all, there was no statue.

I was aghast. We were not at the entrance to the United States. "Where are we?" I cried to Major Williams, who had joined me. "*This* isn't New York!"

"I believe we're putting in at Los Angeles," he said.

"But I want to go to New York," I wailed. "This is just a dirty old harbor. Where is the Statue of Liberty?"

For a moment he looked baffled. Then, with a face so straight it did his military training credit, he said, "New York is on the other side of the United States. You can't really get to it from here. This is Los Angeles, California."

My heart sank. All this way and no statue. The sight was to have been my glorious reward for having come so far, proof that I had reached my goal. For a few minutes I was bitterly disappointed, close to tears, and more exhausted than I had ever felt in my life. I had never heard of, and wasn't interested in, some place called "Los Angeles." I was ready to give up the whole business.

After a while everyone was ordered below while the ship was brought to dock. When a long time had passed, we were told that we were in port and could leave. I took my suitcase and glumly followed the other passengers up to the deck. All I wanted was to get this long journey over with. I felt so tired I could hardly walk.

Then, as I made my way down the gangplank, a little unsteady on my sea legs, I began to feel some of my optimism returning. Soldiers and sailors, not promenaders, were moving about on the pier before large, warehouselike buildings, but they had the same air of decisiveness and purpose I associated with the Americans I had known in Iran. Here and there were women in military uniform, the first I had ever seen. I had done it, I thought—I had arrived. All I had to do now was reach Tiffin, Ohio. Then I could start learning what America had to teach me.

PART TWO

YENGEH DONYA

8

THE LAND AT THE END
OF THE EARTH

*Do not give your heart to one mistress, nor your loyalty to a
single place, for countless are mistresses, and extensive are lands
and seas.*

—Sa'adi

*I*N THE IMMIGRATION AND CUSTOMS BUILDING IN THE TERMINAL
my passport was stamped with a Western date, meaningless to
me but exciting nonetheless, as it would always be the anniversary of
my arrival in America: July 4, 1944. Along with five or six other
passengers who had no one waiting for them, I was ushered to a Red
Cross station wagon that would take us to a hotel in the city until the
Red Cross could decide how to help us reach our destinations.

I stared from the window in fascination as we pulled out of the
harbor area. Soon we were driving through vast neighborhoods of wide
streets, skinny palm trees, and low, white shops and bungalows. I saw
the houses standing isolated and without walls, and wondered whether
the inhabitants could not afford to build any. Yet every home looked
prosperous, and after a while I began to realize in astonishment that
Americans built homes in this exposed, innocent, and trusting fashion
because they wanted to.

At a clean, pleasant hotel in the center of the city, the woman driver helped us register and then asked me where I was going. Haltingly, I told her my destination, asking how far Tiffin, Ohio, was from the city where I was now.

"This is California," she said. "Ohio is thousands of miles from California."

Fatigue overwhelmed me, and I felt as if every crisis I had survived already—the anxiety of being stranded in Semnon and Quetta, the discomfort of the awful truck journey to Zahedan, the terror of dying after being torpedoed—had caught up with me.

Seeing my distress, the Red Cross woman asked if I knew anyone in Los Angeles. Pulling myself together, I found my address book and handed it to her. She leafed through it. "Here's a Dr. Samuel M. Jordan in Pasadena," she said. "That's not far from here."

Not daring to believe that I had heard correctly, I stood beside her while she dialed the number at a row of telephones in the lobby. She handed me the receiver and I heard Dr. Jordan's familiar comically accented Persian. In a voice trembling with excitement, he asked what I was doing in Los Angeles. When I had explained, he commanded me to stay where I was until he could come and get me. The next morning he arrived at nine o'clock sharp, looking as glad to see me as though I were a small piece of his lost world fallen from the sky. Overwhelmed with happiness, I greeted my father's old friend like a long-lost relative. When I told Dr. Jordan that I had thought about my situation during the night and now planned to go on, he dismissed the idea as nonsense, saying that his own city had perfectly good schools right here. With that American decisiveness I so admired, within two hours he had driven me to a nearby university and persuaded a skeptical admissions director to let me register. Then, having deposited me at a residence hall for older women students and announced that he expected me to visit him at home every Sunday, he left me, stunned but relieved, to my new existence as the first Iranian ever to attend the University of Southern California.

Finally my American education had begun! Walking around the USC campus, I felt as though everything I saw had sprung up out of my own dreams: the abundance of trees and green grass; the handsome red brick buildings; the bustling activity in front of Doheny Library; the clean, healthy, well-fed appearance of Americans.

But in class I was close to tears. The Americans on the boat had spoken slowly because I was a foreigner, but here I could only sit helplessly, unable to catch the drift of the teacher's remarks or to write them down. And for the first time in my life I was sitting in a classroom with men. Terrified of doing anything that might disgrace my family and Shazdeh's memory, I could not even bring myself to look at them. In the dining room of the dormitory where Dr. Jordan had arranged for me to live, I ate in silence, not daring to speak to the pretty, well-dressed American women next to me lest their confident laughter turn on me. In the mirror in my second-floor cubicle, I saw someone who, in these surroundings, looked out of place here even to me: an olive-skinned Persian girl with a long nose and a knot of braided black hair, still wearing the same thick black woolen stockings and humble long-sleeved dresses in which she had left her mother's andarun. I was someone odd and foreign, whose own tongue was incomprehensible here. I felt as if, between Tehran and Los Angeles, I had somehow lost myself.

During registration that fall I was asked if I knew what I wanted to study. I said that I wanted to learn how to help my people, and was advised to study sociology. In my eagerness to know everything quickly, I decided to take seven courses a semester, and to study year round.

Slowly, I made a few friends at the dormitory, and although, with the new semester, more men appeared in class, I found that I was getting used to them. I often saw men and women sitting close together on the stone benches or holding hands on the grass under the magnolia trees in front of the library. In Iran this would have been shameless, and at first I averted my face. One day, however, I observed a woman professor passing by such a couple, and when I saw that a teacher paid no attention to them, I resolved that I was not going to think about it anymore, either. I knew from the women at the residence hall that this was called "romance," a Western form of courtship. After a while I began to find it pleasant to see courting couples sitting on the lawn and smiling at each other, like an illustration out of Hafez or Sa'adi. I reminded myself that it was good to see other people feeling happy, and soon it was as if they were not even there.

However, I was very lonely. Although I had written to my family as soon as I had an address, I had heard nothing from Tehran yet, and did not even know whether the many letters I had written had ever reached them. The weekends, when the dormitory was empty, were the worst. I would spend all of Saturday studying alone in the library, eat by myself at the student union, and then return to the silent building to pass the evening in my room. Sometimes, too depressed even to study, I lay on the bed listening to the mice that scuffled under the radiator, trying not to cry. Every Sunday I visited Dr. Jordan and his wife in Pasadena, where for a few hours their kindness, our common memories, and the brass lamps and Persian carpets that filled their home made me forget how far away Iran was.

Though I had thought that Americans would be as curious about Iran as I was about the United States, I quickly discovered that Dr. Jordan had been right, and that Americans knew perhaps even less about my country than I did about theirs. My new friends had heard of Persian cats and Persian carpets, but America's knowledge of the Middle East stopped at the film version of *The Arabian Nights*. Strangers would look me over curiously, their eyes running over my face and body as though I were from another planet. I soon got tired of explaining that I was "not an Arab." Their questions were naive and childlike: Did we have houses in Persia, or live in tents? Did we have cars, or travel on camels?

I learned that almost no one had ever heard of "Iran," and that nobody who had knew where it was. Once, a professor of sociology asked me if Iran was in China. I was coming to expect a good deal of geographical innocence from my fellow students, who had scarcely any idea where the cities of their own country were. But on hearing this, I was incredulous. If a university professor, I thought with horror, had so little knowledge of the world, how much more ignorant must illiterate people be, like the merchants and villagers?

I was asked about my religion. Almost nothing had been heard then in America of "Islam" or "Moslems," and I saw that out of politeness my friends did not care to ask too many questions about the subject.

Thanks to Hollywood, however, they had heard of harems, a topic of the greatest fascination to my fellow dormitory residents. They seemed disappointed when I explained that, although Moslem men were allowed four wives, few could afford more than one. Their curiosity about this made me very uncomfortable. I reminded myself that it was not my place to judge my new acquaintances but to enlighten them, and would take them to my room and show them pictures of my brothers and sisters, so that they could see that we were normal people who dressed like anyone else and did not live in tents. This, however, would provoke more curiosity about my father, mother, and stepmothers, and though I tried to be patient (there was so much, I told myself, that I didn't know about *their* country), all this prying made me angry. Knowing that it would have been rude to say this, I decided simply to ignore such offensive questions as if I had not heard and they hadn't asked. But while this strategy succeeded in letting them know how I felt—naturally, I preferred silence to quarreling with those in whose country I was a guest—it also made me feel lonelier and farther from home than ever.

America continued to amaze and confound me. I felt dwarfed by the immensity of Los Angeles, but loved the extravagant vegetation, the magnolias and azaleas and orange trees that I was told blossomed not in spring but in winter. I could not get over the extraordinary clothing people wore, especially the men—who, in their plaid sport shirts, looked like tropical birds. It was taken for granted that everyone, even venerable and aged persons, could dress in ways that to me were wholly against self-respect, and I couldn't get over hearing my friends refer to their fathers as "my old man."

The American way of life was as extravagant as the vegetation and the costumes. Never had I imagined such an abundance of food as I saw in the supermarkets of Los Angeles. But along with this limitless supply of food and goods came the same horrifying indifference to its value that I had seen aboard the *General Butler.* Americans would eat part of an apple or half a steak, then toss the rest into the garbage. My new friends would buy an inexpensive blouse or a pair of shoes, wear them for a month, then throw them away rather than wash or repair them. When I asked them why they threw things away instead of giving them to the poor, they replied that they didn't know any poor to give them to.

Perhaps, I told myself, this fault grew out of the generosity of Americans, a kind of defect in what was essentially noble. But nothing I saw in Los Angeles shocked me more than seeing people treat with such disdain the abundance they had been blessed with. America, I thought, must be a very wasteful nation.

Life became a continuing series of small shocks and great revelations. I was stunned, for example, by the freedom I found in the American classroom and everywhere in American life. Americans were allowed to criticize anything and everything, and it seemed to me that they went out of their way to do just that. Political cartoons in the Los Angeles *Times* took liberties with the president and other powerful officials that under the Pahlavis would normally earn the artist a jail term and shut down the newspaper. The first time I heard a student make a joke in class about President Roosevelt, I stiffened in fear: Mohammed Reza Shah was not frightening like his father, but jokes about him or anyone in Iran's government were still made only when no servants were present.

I soon learned, however, that in America even professors could be argued with or criticized with impunity, and that remarks that in a Persian school would have earned the student a flogging passed completely unnoticed here. I reveled in the debates that flew back and forth in the classrooms of the best of my teachers. My eyes would bulge with astonishment when a professor urged his students to find fault with his arguments. I was still far too shy and worried about my English to participate in such discussions, but I would follow along with parted lips, my heart pounding with excitement at what students and teacher were doing together. In America, I realized, people could say exactly what they thought. I was beginning to understand why they had put up their statue.

One day in a flash it dawned on me that there was a connection between this freedom and the decisiveness I loved so much in people like Dr. Jordan. If you could talk about things openly, I realized, you could discover what to do about a problem. Surely it was this that was at the heart of Americans' confidence, their boundless energy and faith in themselves: they were allowed to speak their minds, to criticize their government, to say exactly what they thought without fear of punishment. And was the opposite not also true? Did we in Iran not lack confidence in ourselves, and therefore the faith we needed to solve our problems, precisely because, in our mutual mistrust and suspicion of outsiders, we were afraid to say openly what we really thought and tell the truth about our problems?

I also observed Americans at home, for my teachers would ask me to dinner with other students, or sometimes someone would invite me for the weekend to her parents' home in one of the suburbs. An Allied victory in Europe was almost within grasp now, and I would listen with fascination to the talk around the dining table or in my friends' kitchens of the fathers, husbands, sons, and brothers who were overseas, of mothers, aunts, and even grandmothers working in the aircraft plants, of victory gardens and clothing drives and blood drives and paper drives. I was lost in admiration for the American ability, which I saw everywhere, to unite in the face of a common enemy, and to work together not only with persons who were not their relatives but with total strangers, people whose fathers they had never heard of.

But what impressed me above all was what Americans called "initiative." Again and again I observed that whenever people had a problem in their community or perceived that something needed doing, even if it was only calling the police to get a traffic light repaired, they didn't just sit there as we did, waiting for the bailiff or the landlord or somebody who was bigger and stronger to come along and do it for them. They found out how to get it done themselves.

Mashti, I reflected, worked hard all his life and would have done anything for my mother and Shazdeh, but not in a thousand years would he have thought of organizing the neighbors to dig a well so that everyone could have better water. In Iran, we always assumed that we weren't capable of changing anything, that we were too small and weak and impotent to alter our society. Yet surely, I told myself, if we had "initiative" and could learn to trust and work with one another as people did here, we could become a great, strong nation. And if we could learn to speak openly about our problems, as Americans did, we, too, would come to believe in ourselves.

At such moments of understanding, a shiver would go through me, for I was certain that I was beginning to find out what I had always longed to know. Though I had caused my mother pain, I had done the right thing in coming to Yengeh Donya. I was getting the education I had dreamed of.

Loneliness was making me work like someone pursued by demons, but still I heard nothing from home. Finally, in December, a letter came from Farough—not from Iran, but from Tarrytown, New York! My nineteen-year-old brother, having graduated from high school, had decided that he wasn't going to wait any longer to go to college in America, either. He had come to America by the same route I had, and was making up deficiencies at Tarrytown High School. He had passed through Los Angeles in December, he said, but as my first letter from Casa de Rosas had not reached Tehran until months after he left, no one had known until now where I was.

I was in agony. Farough, in Los Angeles—and I had missed him! I briefly considered telephoning. But in those days a phone call to New York cost far more than I could afford, and connections were always bad. We would have to wait. I was sure that Farough, who was the most gregarious of us, yearned for home as desperately as I did, and I now suffered for both of us. In spite of my American friends and teachers, I had never dreamed that it was possible to feel such loneliness as I felt now.

In my second semester, the spring of 1945, looking for a cheaper way to live than in a university residence, I moved in with a group of fifteen American and foreign women whose core was several former WAC nurses studying on the G.I. Bill, and who were interested in foreign people and customs. With other foreigners around me as well as a wider and more traveled circle of American friends, my loneliness diminished greatly. Furthermore, by the fall of 1945, with the war finally at an end, more students from India, Asia, and Middle Eastern countries, including Iran, were starting to appear. Despite its large international population, the university had no organization to help with the special problems foreigners faced. I wanted to try to make new students' lives easier than mine had been, and I thought it would be beneficial to our American hosts as well to know more about the diverse, complex world beyond America's borders. I spent much of the fall of 1945 and the spring of 1946—my second academic year— working with my roommates to organize an international students' club, which had its headquarters at the house we had rented.

Shortly after I had heard from Farough, letters finally began to trickle in from Iran. My mother and stepmothers were all well, and Dadash, whose dedicated work as a public health doctor was earning him an excellent reputation, now had a high position in the health ministry. My middle sisters Homy and Sory, who were now sixteen and thirteen, were still at home, but Dadash had sent our fifteen-year-old brother Ghaffar and also Rashid, who was eleven, to a progressive school in England. Jaby and Abbas were back in Tehran, where Abbas had become one of the AIOC's few senior Iranian technical managers. I pored over all the news until I had committed every word to memory and the soft yellow paper was tearing along the creases. Merely to touch the letters was comfort and reassurance itself.

I was still studying as hard as I could, and between running our club, various part-time jobs, cooking and household chores, and taking as many courses as the university permitted, I barely had time to think. I had not really found this schedule much more arduous than the one Shazdeh had set us, and was surprised when, at the beginning of February 1946, I received a notice from the registrar telling me that I would be able to graduate in June, the end of my sophomore year, with a bachelor's degree and a B-minus average. Knowing that I was the first Iranian graduate of USC, I felt that even my demanding father would have been proud of me.

Not long after graduation, I received, for the first time, a letter from Khanom herself. Having learned writing so late in life, my mother had never written letters easily and had relied on my sisters to convey her greetings to me. Now she congratulated me and enclosed a gift of money as a token of her pride. "I am very happy," she wrote in her uncertain script, "to hear that you are living in a safe place and are going to school and are healthy." Then, as if it were an afterthought, she added, "I have just come back from Mehrabad Airport, where I have put Homy and your niece Nahid on a plane to England. Homy will go to college there."

I was beside myself with joy. I knew that in telling me herself that Homy was going abroad to study, she was at last putting the seal of her blessing to my long struggle. She could not tell me how she felt— we were still alike in not speaking easily of our personal feelings— but now I was sure that she truly approved of what I had done. I felt repaid for every day, every hour of what I had been through since I first dreamed of coming to America. Not only had I overcome her fears but I had won Homy an education, too. I read the letter over and over. How I wished that I could hold Khanom in my arms and hug her, over and over again! For a euphoric week or two I felt complete again. My whole being was affirmed by knowing that I and my family were one and inseparable.

I had given much thought to my next step. Sociology offered theories about the causes of social problems but did not explain how to solve them. One woman professor who had befriended me, Dr. Mary Sinclair Crawford, who was active in the international women's rights movement, had urged me to study political science, but as I explained to her, in Iran women couldn't even vote, much less run for office. Fortunately, I had learned of a profession called social work, which, unlike sociology, not only studied the causes of social problems but tried to find practical ways of solving them. USC had an excellent professional school of social work, so I applied and was accepted for the fall of 1946.

By my second week there, I knew that I had found the weapon I needed to fight Iran's human miseries. Whereas in my country help came to the needy only through alms, for the first time I saw how social workers developed ways to address the problems that made people needy: well-regulated orphanages, licensed homes for the aged, the disabled, and the mentally ill. There were thousands of family service agencies, hospital clinics, and training programs in which social workers not only assisted human beings in emergencies but tried to give them ways of dealing themselves with broken families, sickness, physical disability, mental illness, old age, relocation, unemployment, alcoholism, and other problems—always with the goal of helping them to rely not on benefactors and protectors, but on themselves.

With a mounting sense of discovery I realized that this was what I wanted to start in my country—programs that would help people become stronger, improve their standard of living, and give them pride in their own self-reliance. In my classes and practice assignments I plunged into acquiring every scrap of knowledge or information I could find that would teach me about social programs and show me how to organize them.

I studied how to develop short-term and long-term programs for everything from disaster relief to job training, from mobile health clinics to the care of neglected children. I followed the progress of social legislation, and studied American social security laws, public policy covering children, the blind and disabled, the unemployed, the retired and the elderly. On my own, I wrote to dozens of states asking for information about their agencies and professional licensing standards, collecting every document or piece of literature I could lay my hands on about child welfare, services for adults, public assistance. I observed carefully how private agencies and professional associations operated, funded themselves, carried out research, implemented programs, and recruited and trained volunteers, while at professional conferences and at the different institutions where I was placed for student training, I watched with fascination how Americans planned and implemented ideas and decisions.

The social work faculty at USC was an especially noted one, and my teachers warmly encouraged me to learn all I could. The dean, Dr. Johnson, who had a national reputation in my new field, was a plump, energetic little woman of disciplined but unlimited compassion. Like Jane Addams and Dorothea Dix, Arlien Johnson had devoted every moment of her existence to fighting for social reform, and from her small, cluttered office—barely larger, as I often remarked to myself in amazement, than my father's old dining table—she had turned her school into one of the best in the United States. There was a wonderful spirit of cooperation and harmony at the USC School of Social Work that affected everyone connected with it. In those days our profession in America was still in a pioneering phase, and the teachers and the faculty who supervised our practice training, or fieldwork, had the gift of making us feel that we had been chosen, like physicians, to heal all the ills of society. With such dedicated mentors, my own ideas about what I wanted to do in Iran proliferated, and hardly a week passed that I did not learn something that fueled my thoughts about the future. By the end of my first year of graduate school, I at last understood my mission. One way or another, I must establish this profession in Iran.

My greatest happiness at the end of that year, which was the summer of 1947, was seeing Farough. He was now studying electrical engineering at the University of Illinois at Urbana, and we met in Chicago; Farough had a summer job on the lakefront, so I took courses in social work at the University of Chicago to be near him. He was now a tall, strikingly handsome young man, affable and smart and talkative. I was very proud of him, and we spent all our free time together, talking about the family, our own plans, and Iran.

Our country had just been through another crisis. After the occupation had ended in March 1946, the Soviet Union, to extort an oil concession in the north of Iran, had refused to withdraw its troops from Azerbaijan. Thanks largely to the adroit leadership of our premier at that time, Qavam al-Saltaneh, and the support of the United States in the United Nations, the Soviets had finally left, after nearly a year and much unrest in the northern provinces. Once again, we had had a frightening lesson in how easily the "superpowers," as they were called now, could trample on us when it pleased them to do so.

I was still very happy in my residence hall, whose rooms were always bustling with activity. The international student club was a smashing success. Many of our members were young men from prominent families in Mexico, South America, China, or India. A crowd of us often hiked together in the dusty mountains around Los Angeles, which was a great boon to me, for although I had gone on one or two dates at the urging of my American friends, I had never become comfortable with this custom, and I missed hiking and the masculine companionship of my brothers. There was even a sprinkling of Iranians at USC now, both men and women. Many of the men had joined our club, and as all of them, of course, knew who everyone else's father was, I was sometimes embarrassed when a new boy would come up to me and address me as Shazdeh-khanom, "Princess." I always asked him not to do this—for one thing, we were in a democratic country, but I also wanted to prevent malicious rumors from reaching Tehran that a Farman Farmaian was passing herself off as "royalty" to Americans, who wouldn't know a Qajar from a Pahlavi, and I had not mentioned my descent to any of my American friends. Once, indeed, I was rather chagrined when a housemate came home with the news that we "had a Persian princess at USC." But it only turned out that a young woman whose name I recognized as that of a distant Qajar cousin of ours (a great-grandmother, I remembered, had been one of Fath Ali Shah's many daughters) had moved into an undergraduate dormitory and affixed a calling card to her door announcing that she was "Princess So-and-So." I felt like saying that I hoped she would soon learn how to conduct herself like one.

A great many of the new students were Indians, both Hindu and Moslem. My memories of India were still powerful and stirring to me, and I often thought of my meeting with the young revolutionary on the train, for there were many heated discussions that year between Hindu and Moslem Indians in the lounge of our residence. The most eloquent speaker for the Moslem side was a youth of barely twenty named Zulfikar Ali Bhutto, who was from a prominent family in what was now called Pakistan. Zulfi, as we all called him, passionately supported the Moslem leader Jinnah, while the Hindus, who out-numbered the Moslems, argued with equal fervor for Jawaharlal Nehru. I listened to both sides in silence, saddened by the divisiveness that was undermining India's cause. The bloodshed between Hindus and Moslems that followed India's independence in August 1947 filled me with sorrow. I wondered why people could not learn to understand each other's point of view, and whether my friend from the train was still alive.

Among these Hindu students was a slim, gentle, dapper boy from Calcutta named Arun. He was studying cinematography, and spoke with veneration of his father, who, he said, was an important man in India's huge movie industry. Arun was full of grand dreams for when he went back to India, "America-returned," with a diploma from the best cinema school in the world, to direct films for his father. Like me, he came from a large family that he missed badly, and somehow he was always there when I was too busy with work to run out and buy a book or fetch myself something to eat. Soon Arun began ac-companying me to parties, and by sheer perseverance, he gradually established himself as my principal escort.

But I was not ready to let my close friendship with him or any of the other boys in the club become more than friendship. I had hundreds of ideas by now about what I wanted to do in Iran, and I needed additional experience, credentials that would cause my ideas to be heard by the men who ran my country. I expected to work in the United States for several years, then see if I could go to a Middle Eastern country where social work had already been started, so that I could gain experience in a land more like my own. I also felt that I must learn more about teaching: since Iranians are not naturally given to cooperation or mutual trust, I would have to learn the proper method of inculcating such values in them. "Romance," I felt, could only interfere with the exciting future I had laid out.

In June of 1948 I graduated, a full-fledged professional with a Master of Social Work degree, or M.S.W., and took a job at an East Los Angeles agency called the International Institute, an old settlement house for Asian and other immigrants, where I had done fieldwork.

By this time, however, my close circle of friends was breaking up. Zulfi and many others had already left to round out their educations at European or other American schools or had returned to their own countries, while all the women who had started with me and become my friends had either finished their degrees and moved away or had married. Again others were finding happiness, leaving me behind.

I began to feel alarmed. The only family I had in this big country, I thought, was vanishing around me. Soon I would be alone again, an unmarried woman in a land not her own. The house where we had all lived had come to seem cavernous instead of homelike, and though I flung myself heart and soul into work, I couldn't escape depression. Arun, who was one of the few people left from our tightly knit community, was as despondent as I. Finally, he proposed that we marry.

Wishing that I had had Dadash or someone else in my family to advise me, I tried to think objectively about his suggestion. Although "love" in the romantic Western sense was foreign to me, I reasoned, Arun and I cared for and respected each other. I had been in America for four years, and was twenty-seven. This was still young by American standards, but in my own society women my age were often grandmothers. Memories of the lonely weekends in the dormitory pulled at me like a black undertow. For the first time I felt a deep dread that the choices I was making for myself might rob me forever of the joy of a child, and that I would never know the life of a normal woman. I decided that I must anchor myself: marry and be happy, like every other woman.

I sat down and wrote to Dadash and Khanom that I was getting married. As the head of our family, Dadash had, of course, the right to forbid me, but I was certain that he would never do that, and surely Khanom would be pleased that I was marrying. It hurt me to deprive her of the ceremonies and celebrations that every Iranian mother dreams of for a daughter. But there were many Indians living in Iran, and perhaps, I thought, we could eventually go to my country and Arun could make films there. I told Khanom not to worry, that I would come back one day. She knew that I always did what I said I would.

Arun, of course, also wrote to Calcutta for his parents' permission. He was their eldest son, and bore responsibilities even heavier, if possible, than a Persian eldest son. Weeks passed before we had an answer, and when finally a letter came, it was brief and cold. Arun's family was deeply displeased with his decision to take as his wife an unknown woman, a foreigner, and a Moslem. Nevertheless, his parents did not actually withhold their consent, and we drove to City Hall to get a license. There the clerk on duty refused to issue one until Arun produced a passport to show that he was a foreign national and not, as the clerk suspected from his dark complexion, an American Negro trying to marry a white woman. Furious and shaken at this indignity, I had to force myself to remember that our happiness would not depend on how bigoted people judged our union.

Soon, however, I was contented again. My own family and friends sent gifts and congratulations. Arun was going on for a master's degree in cinema, and talked excitedly of getting apprentice work in one of the studios so that he could learn directing. Though he was unable to find any and had to settle for a part-time student job instead, I was perfectly happy to support us on my salary. Along with my job, I signed up for night courses and teacher training at USC, which would lead to a teaching certificate.

To my great happiness I also became pregnant. In the spring of 1949 I gave birth to a beautiful, healthy baby girl. Holding her in my arms, touching the exquisitely graceful baby limbs with brown skin softer than a lark's feathers, I decided to call her "Mitra," a name I had heard in Bombay when I had gone to see some Indian dancing, and which I connected with the beauty of the dance.

I was completely engrossed in caring for Mitra, in my job, and in practice teaching when, one day not long after her birth, I had a rude awakening. Arun's family, I learned, had asked the Indian Embassy in Washington to investigate their unknown daughter-in-law, and inquiries about me had been made. Evidently the embassy had been satisfied with what it could learn of me, but I felt degraded. If anyone desired to know who I and my family were, I thought, they could write and ask me directly; going behind my back was insulting and suggested that they did not regard me as a legitimate daughter-in-law. I was angry for a very long while. Then I decided to just put the whole annoying incident out of my mind. I didn't care to waste time and energy on devious people.

In June, Arun graduated with his master's degree, but to our surprise, could not get any studio work. As we soon learned, without capital or connections it was almost impossible to become even an apprentice director in Hollywood. Having come from so far and studied for so long, Arun was keenly disappointed. He began working part time for Kodak, but earned very little, and I knew that he was depressed because I was contributing more to our income than he was. Nevertheless, I urged him to keep trying. Perseverance and hard work, I assured him, would always be rewarded, and meanwhile, he should not let the matter of the money trouble him; we had all we needed with my salary, and *I* didn't mind supporting us. Privately, of course, I knew that if worse came to worst, we could always go to Iran, where my own family would gladly accept and help us.

While I was enjoying life in Los Angeles and rejoicing in Mitra's growth, however, the political situation in Iran, which I had been following avidly—not only through an Iranian newspaper and the little that the American press reported, but through my family's letters—had been growing steadily more turbulent. And at the eye of the storm was Shazdeh's nephew, Dr. Mohammed Mossadegh.

While I had been studying in Los Angeles, the political popularity of Dr. Mossadegh had been soaring. He had been elected to parliament in 1944 and had recently become the de facto head of a coalition party called the National Front. In my family we took great pride in our cousin's past refusal to compromise with dictatorship and his defense of Iran's democratic constitution. His steadfast opposition and refusal to support Reza Shah's tyranny had earned him the supreme accolade that Persians reserve for leaders who, like Kaveh the Blacksmith, stand for the people against injustice. He was called a "lion of God."

Now nearly seventy, Dr. Mossadegh was still fiercely independent, a populist aristocrat who believed that the government must serve the people, not the other way around. He was a tall, stooped, gangling man with shrewd, deep-set black eyes that glittered with energy and humor in his sallow face. He walked with difficulty, a disability said to be due to physical abuse during his imprisonment by Reza Shah in 1940. But despite his frailty he was an impassioned orator and a crafty politician who sometimes wept and even fainted (Iranian politicians are expected to show great emotion in public addresses) while arguing against foreign interference, dishonest elections, and the government's attempts to juggle the favor of the British and the Russians. Among other things, he and the National Front were advocating a neutral foreign policy, political reform, and freedom from our long economic dependence on foreign powers.

His concern for the general welfare was famous. His mother, my aunt Najmeh-Saltaneh, had endowed a free hospital for the poor before her death, and Dr. Mossadegh, his physician son Gholam, and his daughter Zia-Ashraf, who was a nurse and the hospital's administrator, were working to make it the best in Iran. Dr. Mossadegh's personal simplicity, his wit, and his warmth and love for common people were as endearing to Iranians as his dramatic style. He never betrayed a principle: in fifty years of public service not even his worst enemies had ever accused Mohammed Mossadegh of accepting a bribe or seeking to advance his own or his family's interests. Illiterate and educated Iranians alike knew that this wily, humorous, emotional old aristocrat truly cared about them and Iran's rights and dignity. I, too, felt that Dr. Mossadegh was the one person who had the courage and vision to lead our nation, as Gandhi and Nehru had led India, to becoming a self-supporting, democratic, truly independent country. But there were many obstacles in the way.

Iran, as Dr. Mossadegh had been pointing out for years, was supposed to be a constitutional monarchy, and the king was supposed to reign, not rule. For a long time Mohammed Reza Shah, who lacked his father's iron will, had appeared to be a tenative, uncertain young ruler with no wish to interfere in politics. However, after his accession he had quietly retained the royal position of commander-in-chief of the army, and like Reza Shah had been doing all he could to expand the military. More recently he had also been acquiring more and more power at the expense of the Majlis, rigging elections to pack parliament and the bureaucracy with royalists and conservative sympathizers.

This made him unpopular, and many were angry for another reason as well: like his father, he could not stand up to the British. Ever since the end of the occupation, Iranians had been demanding that the government assert Iran's rights in the matter of oil. We would never overcome our massive economic and social problems without more oil revenue. The AIOC was now one of the largest and richest concerns in the world, and its officials scornfully rejected the notion that Iran deserved a single pound sterling more than it was getting. Huge numbers of people felt that such a response was no longer acceptable. For years, Dr. Mossadegh had been calling for the nationalization of the Iranian oil industry, which would not only bring us a fair share of the profits but remove England's chief lever over our internal affairs. The struggle for nationalization, Dr. Mossadegh insisted, was not just over revenue—it was over who was to be master of Iran's destiny. The Shah, on the other hand, was afraid of jeopardizing relations with London, and people were murmuring that the king himself was merely a servant of the British and doing their bidding; his father, too, they complained, had been England's stooge.

In March of 1951, General Razmara, the prime minister the king had appointed to persuade parliament to ratify a new oil agreement to which the British had grudgingly agreed, was murdered by a right-wing religious assassin—an event greeted by public jubilation. In April, Dr. Mossadegh, as the leader of the tiny National Front deputation, introduced a bill calling for the nationalization of the Anglo-Iranian Oil Company. The eight National Front deputies were overwhelmingly outnumbered by conservatives and royalists. But the pro-British members of parliament had been terrified by the rejoicing over Razmara's assassination. The bill nationalizing the AIOC passed in parliament with an overwhelming majority, and late in April, the Shah, afraid of defying public opinion, offered Dr. Mossadegh the premiership, thus giving him the opportunity to form a progressive nationalist government. On May 2, 1951, as bonfires burned in celebration all over Iran, the new premier signed the nationalization bill into law. It was the beginning of a long, complex tragedy that would alter forever what I and other Iranians felt about America.

In Los Angeles, following these great events, I was euphoric. If Dr. Mossadegh could come to a settlement with the British soon, who knew what might not be accomplished? I was certain that America would be on our side in the coming crisis. When the Russians had refused to pull out in 1946, President Truman had demanded that they do so. The American government, I told Arun joyfully, believed in our right to self-determination. The most powerful democratic country in the world would not allow the British to use gunboat diplomacy as they had in 1932. Of course, a British invasion would also furnish the Soviet Union with an excuse to march back into Iran, and in 1951 everyone knew how frightened the Americans were of international communism. But the American government had long ago proven that it sincerely supported our sovereignty. The British Empire in Iran was over, I said—this was the age of America.

I also had a more personal reason for elation: in June, a letter from my sisters announced that the premier had placed Dadash in charge of the Iranian health ministry. Our brother was by now one of the most respected public health doctors in the Middle East, having developed a highly successful malaria control program. But his appointment was truly extraordinary because Dr. Mossadegh was famous (some in the family may have preferred "infamous") for refusing to give jobs to his relatives. My pride in Dadash knew no bounds.

Dr. Mossadegh did not have to wait long for a reaction to his nationalization of the largest and richest English company outside Great Britain. The English public was incensed. The British press was vitriolic, presenting Dr. Mossadegh as an impudent Oriental, a thief who had stolen a British company, a fanatical and probably insane extremist. English oil executives and technicians dismissed with bitter contempt the notion that Iranians could manage an oil industry. British paratroops were positioned on Cyprus and a British war cruiser sailed into the Persian Gulf off Abadan.

Even so, at first a solution seemed possible. Dr. Mossadegh was anxious to reach a reasonable settlement quickly. The United States insisted that the British negotiate, sending Averell Harriman and other high-level diplomats to Tehran and London that summer. But the talks failed. London and the AIOC insisted on keeping responsibility for the production and marketing of the oil in British hands, which was precisely what gave England so much control over our affairs and economy. Dr. Mossadegh could not consent to this—even if he had wanted to, public feeling against the British ran so high that he might well have paid for such a compromise with his life. Realizing that our premier would not agree, the AIOC angrily suspended negotiations. In September, Dr. Mossadegh ordered Iranian troops to the Abadan refinery to maintain order during the takeover, and more British gunboats materialized in the Gulf. London announced an embargo on Iranian oil, and sat down to wait for Persian incompetence and the damaging effects of the embargo to force Iran's "insane" premier to implore British personnel to return. But in Iran, an explosion of joy greeted the sending of Persian troops and administrators to Abadan. Mohammed Mossadegh had shown the world that a small, much-bullied people could stand up for their rights to one of the greatest nations on earth.

Naturally, everyone assumed that since the Americans would not let them invade us, London would try to undermine Dr. Mossadegh at home. The British method of meddling in the affairs of Middle Eastern nations always included boring from within, and in an unstable country like Iran it is never difficult for a foreign power's agents or anyone else to purchase street demonstrations and riots. Usually no one can be sure who is really behind these apparently spontaneous explosions of popular feeling.

Indeed, in my own family we had at least one notable example of this time-honored method of influencing the course of national events. According to my mother, Shazdeh, when he was prime minister in 1916 during the first Anglo-Russian occupation, had come under great pressure from the Russians to cede to them a peninsula on the Caspian. Shazdeh knew that if he refused, the Russians would take the peninsula by force, while if he weakly resigned in protest, they would take it anyway. My father's solution was to go in the dead of night to a wealthy, altruistic merchant named Amin Al Zarb, who was a man of great influence in the bazaar. Shazdeh explained to Amin Al Zarb—who was known to dislike him on account of an old property dispute—that he was going to announce the government's capitulation the next day. He wished this announcement to be followed by a strike in the bazaar and an outburst of demonstrations protesting it. This would "force" my father's resignation from office and perhaps intimidate the Russians into backing off. It was a drastic expedient, but the only one my father had, and as the merchant was his enemy, no one would suspect their collusion.

Amin Al Zarb, a public-spirited man, was so moved that he threw his arms around Shazdeh on the spot, swore that from this moment on they were friends, and, as a sign of his respect for my father's self-sacrifice, even insisted on paying for the riots himself. The next day the bazaar shut down and a yelling, outraged mob of hired ruffians and indignant shopkeepers, craftsmen, students, peddlers, mullahs, and assorted rifraff poured into the streets. My father promptly resigned, and the Russians dropped their demand.

Knowing, therefore, that one could always purchase this kind of aid for any cause, good or bad, every Iranian was well aware that London would have no difficulty finding agents and turncoats to carry out its aims. I only hoped that Dr. Mossadegh would be able to stay in office long enough to fulfill his political and economic reforms. But for the present, I and all Persians like me were far too happy to worry about British plots. Dr. Mossadegh had finally opened the door to progress, if only a crack. If God gave his old lion enough time, we could at last begin to be a modern nation, one that other nations would have to respect.

In the autumn of 1951, more happiness came my way: Abbas visited us in Los Angeles for several days. He was now the head of the new National Iranian Oil Company's sales commission, and was in the United States to convince American oil companies to help the NIOC sell and distribute our oil. When he had answered my countless questions about the family, Arun and I asked him what success he had had. I was dismayed when he somberly replied that the American "majors" were all afraid of nationalization's spreading to Saudi Arabia and other countries where they themselves had holdings, and few oil companies would even consider the idea of helping Dr. Mossadegh.

This was very bad news: because Dr. Mossadegh had wanted to come to any settlement he could reasonably and safely agree to, the Iranian government had not expected the failure of talks with the British. Iran's economy was not strong, and the boycott added to the strain. The premier, Abbas said, wanted Iran to sell the oil itself, but we didn't have the means to distribute it. Dr. Mossadegh was campaigning, with surprising success, to get Iranians to plant truck gardens so that the country could feed itself, but you couldn't pay civil servants with fruits and vegetables. If the embargo held, the result might be economic and governmental collapse—which was just what London hoped for.

Abbas's news worried me even more because all the American newspapers were taking the line of the British and the American majors. They constantly derided Dr. Mossadegh as an elderly, incompetent fanatic and a "Communist tool"—*Time* called him "old Mossy," although, as Arun pointed out, this was the level of writing one would expect of a magazine that referred to Jawaharlal Nehru as "a misty yogi." Although I was sure that a man like Harry Truman would never let the British overthrow an elected head of state, I was extremely upset that the strongest democratic leader we had ever had was being attacked by the one press in the world that should have been happy to give him a chance.

Then, in October of 1951, Dr. Mossadegh visited the United Nations in New York to rebut a British charge that he was a threat to world peace for taking over Abadan. He defended his actions at the U.N. with such fire, humor, and conviction that the Security Council voted against the British. Even in the United States, public opinion seemed to turn in our favor. I felt like dancing and singing. Mohammed Mossadegh had done what no Middle Eastern leader before him had dared—he had stepped on the tail of the British tiger and, thanks to his Persian wits and courage, had not been eaten!

He returned to Iran a greater hero than ever. After this, I told Arun, President Truman would never listen to those who wanted him to believe that Dr. Mossadegh was a stooge of Communism! It was natural for Americans to sympathize with the underdog. The United States would always side with international justice and the soverign rights of small, weak nations like mine.

Mitra was now a bright, healthy infant of two. She had enormous brown eyes and a long, tapering face that came from my mother's side of the family. She was contented and affectionate, and her sweetness endeared her to our friends, her nursery school teachers, and most of all her mother.

For a long time, however, my marriage had been under a strain. Though he had tried hard, Arun had not succeeded in getting film work. Having often shared hopes and plans with his Indian classmates and all our other friends, he was mortified at having failed so conspicuously. In the past year he had begun observing frequently that if he were in India, he could be working in his father's studio.

We had begun our marriage in mutual affection and regard, and I was unhappy at seeing him so wretched and discontented. I did not want to deprive Mitra of her father, but finally I proposed that he return to Calcutta to see what help his family could give him. I myself would not live with people who disliked me, but perhaps later he would be able to afford a separate home for us and we could join him. If not, he could always come back and live with us here.

At first Arun was reluctant, but after a year of these discussions, he too admitted that a visit home was the only solution. In my heart, I hoped guiltily that he would return without getting what he wanted. I admired India, but I certainly did not want to raise Mitra there, nor did I trust his family not to harm her. Iran, surely, needed film directors, and many Indians lived there. If all else failed, I would write him and suggest that we go to *my* homeland instead. Arun, however, was so happy that I tried to stifle this selfish wish. In March of 1952, he departed, full of hope.

It was not long before cheerful letters began to arrive, first from New York and then from Paris. After that, they stopped. At first I was unworried by the silence—in the early 1950s, even mail from Europe could take weeks, and from India, months. But by early summer I was waiting anxiously for news, and had grown lonely and depressed. Dr. Jordan had died about two years earlier, followed soon after by his wife, and with him had gone a precious link to Iran. I had been away for eight years, and again I had lost the family I had made for myself in America. I had many friends and former teachers like Arlien Johnson whom I cared about, but not a real home, full of life and people. Now I often thought of my mother's loneliness when she was first married, and tears of self-pity would come to my eyes. I fought them by reminding myself that at least I didn't have to depend on a husband for my income; unlike my mother, I could support myself and my child.

Finally I received a letter from Calcutta. Arun said that the work in his father's studio had not materialized, and although he was going to Bombay to see what he could do there, he was not optimistic. As I had a profession, he said, and as he knew that I was an excellent mother, I ought to do what was best for myself and Mitra. In India he could not offer us a life like the one we could enjoy in America, or with my family in Iran.

I was stunned at this totally unexpected blow. I had never seriously doubted Arun's chances of finding work at home. Nor had it ever occurred to me that he might not return even if he didn't find work—after all, he had a child to consider. Nevertheless, he was not coming back and clearly did not want us to come to India. It appeared that Mitra and I were in the situation of many women from my part of the world: we had been deserted.

As husband and wife, Arun and I had never quarreled, and I saw no point in launching into recriminations. I was angry, of course, and badly shaken. At the same time, I pitied him—I could not imagine giving up my own dreams so easily, after barely even trying. I only wrote back politely that Mitra and I were safe and well. I urged him to keep on looking, and concluded by saying that in the meantime I would make whatever plans I thought best for us. As yet, of course, I had no idea what these were, but I certainly was not going to suggest that we come to India. About some things I felt no uncertainty at all. Never would I ask someone to accept me who did not want me.

I spent the next weeks trying to overcome my shock, anger, and sadness and think clearly about what to do next. In Los Angeles I had many friends and a job I liked; most important, here it would be easy to give Mitra a good education. But nothing really bound us to Los Angeles. Shortly before Arun's letter I had received a letter from Julia Henderson, the director of the new United Nations Bureau of Social Affairs. At the suggestion of Arlien Johnson, she had written to say that she was looking for trained social workers for the U.N.'s Middle East projects, and that I was welcome to come to New York for an interview.

I was enormously flattered to have been approached by the United Nations, and political events at home were making me more and more anxious to return to the Middle East. London showed no interest in reaching a settlement—the longer the embargo continued, the more damage it would do the despised and hated Mossadegh. The 1952 American presidential campaign was under way, and if General Eisenhower, the conservative Republican candidate, won it, the AIOC would have reason to expect more sympathy for its cause. Dr. Mossadegh also had serious domestic problems. He and his allies were winning back for parliament many rights that the Shah had gradually been appropriating. However, broad cracks were forming in the National Front, a coalition representing many different views and interests: liberal intellectuals, socialists, right-wing nationalists, rabble-rousing religious leaders. In addition, I was worried by reports in the press of rising food prices and unemployment.

In mid-July, as I sat in Los Angeles debating what to do, Dr. Mossadegh attempted to wrench control of the chief pillar of power, the army, away from the Shah, and the smoldering political situation burst into flames. Parliamentary supporters of the Shah and the British tried to replace Dr. Mossadegh, who appealed to the Iranian public over the radio for support. Violent demonstrations in his favor broke out and were put down by the military and the police. In five days, more than two hundred and fifty people died or were seriously hurt. Dr. Mossadegh returned triumphantly to office, apparently stronger and more popular than ever. But the violence frightened me. If his government were overthrown, I did not know what might happen to Dadash, Abbas, and others who not only served him but were members of his family.

I decided to return home as soon as possible. I would go to New York with Mitra and see if the United Nations could offer me anything. I wanted to stop off in New York anyway to visit Batul-Khanom's son Manucher, who was living there at the moment, and Farough, who had married an American college classmate and was working in Philadelphia as an electrical engineer for Philco. Also, I could not return to Iran or travel in the Middle East with Mitra until I had her name entered into my passport. I wanted to do this in New York; the Iranian consul-general, Mahmoud Forrughi, a son of the premier who had presided over the Allied occupation, was a close friend of Dadash's. I took a month or two to settle my affairs, wind up matters at work, and say farewell to my American friends and teachers. I had heard nothing more from Arun, so before leaving I wrote him a brief, noncommittal letter informing him of my plans.

By the end of September, I was ready to depart. I felt sadness at the thought of leaving the United States. But I was relieved to have made a firm decision, and felt my optimism returning. I had always trusted my fate—and in any case there was nothing for me and Mitra to do but move ahead. I would just have to see what happened next.

9

THE FALL OF THE LION
OF GOD

*Just what is it that America stands for? If she stands for one
thing more than another, it is for the sovereignty of self-
governing people.*

—President Woodrow Wilson, January 29, 1916

I ARRIVED IN NEW YORK IN THE FIRST WEEK OF OCTOBER, 1952.
The presidential campaign was at its height, the sidewalks were
thronged with people, and the city's mood in the brisk autumn air was
electric. Since I did not know how long I would be there and didn't
want to impose on Manucher, I took Mitra to Philadelphia and settled
her with Farough and Jean, his American wife; they had two little
girls of their own. Then I went to the Iranian Consulate on Fifth
Avenue, where I learned that, as Arun was not an Iranian and the
marriage had not been registered with our embassy, my marriage was
not considered legal in Iran. Mitra was stateless.

I was outraged. What was I supposed to do, I upbraided the consular
staff—go home and abandon a three-year-old infant? Mr. Forrughi
was sympathetic but insisted he could not help. Under Iranian law, a
child could not inherit citizenship through its mother. As Mitra's father
was not there to provide her with an Indian passport, he suggested that

I take U.S. citizenship for her, which was granted automatically to children born in the United States. Mitra could then travel on an American passport. She would, of course, need a visa to come to Iran, the land of her mother's birth.

I returned to Manucher's apartment on East 94th Street distraught and beside myself with fury. It did not matter that I had studied and worked for years to be able to go back and devote my life to Iran, nor that I was going to raise Mitra to love and help our people and to take the same pride in her Persian heritage that I did. Iran said that my child's Persian descent came to her through a woman, and was therefore meaningless. I wanted to scream and curse the laws of our country which declared that women were nothing.

I vowed that I would not rest until I had made someone enter Mitra in my passport as an Iranian. I was sure there must be something the consulate could do, and went there every morning. But as I sat vainly in the small waiting room day after day to remonstrate with officials, sipping the tea that was served by the polite assistant at the reception desk, I began to see that these efforts were going to be futile. I had no choice but to get Mitra American citizenship, and I feared that I would be in New York for a very long time. I had barely enough money to pay for our return to Iran, much less for a hotel room or an apartment. Wondering what to do, at night I lay awake on Manucher's couch in a cold sweat of anxiety.

One morning at the consulate, having little else to distract me, I fell into conversation with a well-dressed American who was also waiting, and who said that he worked for Cities Service Oil. At hearing this, I became deeply interested. Cities Service was an independent oil company, one of the few Abbas had contacted on his visit a year ago that had shown any interest in selling and distributing our oil. Only last month, the Iranian press had been full of the news of a semisecret visit to Iran by its executives to see what might be done to help us resume oil production.

London had been indignant at the visit, but Tehran was delighted. The party's leader was W. Alton Jones, the company president and a self-made multimillionaire who was close to the State Department. Even more significant, so far as we were concerned, he was said to be one of General Eisenhower's most intimate personal friends. Iran's government was nearly bankrupt and there was unrest all over the provinces. Alton Jones's friendship with Eisenhower, who was expected to win the election, and his interest in helping us seemed to suggest that a Republican administration might prove sympathetic, and the visit had included secret talks between Jones and Dr. Mossadegh. Jaby, in one of her monthly letters to me, had written excitedly that Abbas himself had acted as interpreter for Dr. Mossadegh and Mr. Jones and had escorted the party on a motor tour to Abadan, so that they could see for themselves the wretched conditions in which our people lived and how unstable the situation was.

When I explained that I was Abbas Parkhideh's sister-in-law, the oil executive asked for my telephone number. The same afternoon I received an invitation to call on Mr. Jones. The next day, very excited at the prospect of hearing news of Jaby and Abbas, I took the subway to the Cities Service Building at 70 Pine Street.

Alton Jones was a handsome, forthright, immaculately dressed man of about sixty who, despite his gray hair, had an appealing youthfulness and energy. I was especially struck by his light gray eyes, which were shrewd, perceptive, and immensely kind. He at once began speaking with much warmth of the time he had spent with my brother-in-law and his family. What Abbas had shown him of our country, Mr. Jones said, had opened his eyes. He himself, he told me, came from a family of hardscrabble farmers, and he could see the miserable lives the children in Iran's villages were leading. Dr. Mossadegh wasn't a demagogue, a fanatic, or a Communist sympathizer. He was an unselfish, courageous leader who only wanted to get Iran its fair share—Abbas had told him how our premier had stood up to the Shah's father, who was a dictator. Mr. Jones also said that the sight of Iran's long northern border with the Soviet Union had "scared the heck out of him." If something wasn't done soon, Iran might have a Communist revolution, the way China had. Oil could help those children he had seen, he said. The British government ought to be trying to work with Mossadegh, as it had with Nehru. That was why he wanted to see what he could do to help sell our oil.

I could hardly believe my ears. I cautiously ventured that I didn't think the British would settle so long as Dr. Mossadegh was in power; they wanted revenge for what he had done. Mr. Jones replied that the premier had told him the same thing. Nevertheless, some Cities Service engineers were going to Abadan soon, and that was why the man I had met yesterday had been at the consulate. The British might sue, but, Mr. Jones said, he "wasn't going to lose any sleep about that." British policy was simply wrong.

Before I had time to digest this astounding speech, Mr. Jones asked me why I was in New York and how long I expected to be there. When I explained that I was returning to Iran but had been stranded because of my daughter's passport problem, he asked why I didn't come and work for him? Nobody at Cities Service, he said, knew anything about Iran. He needed somebody to answer questions and brief the men who were going. I could also cover the American and foreign press. I would be doing him a favor and at the same time be helping Dr. Mossadegh.

I was too flabbergasted to reply. "Just take the job for a few months," Mr. Jones urged. "Ike," he said, was committed to settling this problem. Once he was elected, the crisis would be resolved quickly. Then I could go home.

Overwhelmed, I stammered my thanks, but said that I must think about it over the weekend. On Friday I rushed off to Philadelphia to consult Farough, who advised me to accept my would-be rescuer's offer at once. At home, the National Front was breaking up into quarreling factions and Dr. Mossadegh had made bitter enemies by purging the military command of royalist and pro-British officers who wanted to unseat him. If I went back there, I could do nothing, while here I could help a wealthy, influential oilman get money flowing into our country again.

Realizing that he was right, and that in any case I really had no alternative, I returned to New York and told Mr. Jones that I would come to work for him. That was just great, Mr. Jones said, and asked me what sort of salary I had in mind. Hideously embarrassed, I replied that my last salary had been two hundred and six dollars a month, and he could pay me that. Mr. Jones looked shocked. "This is New York," he said. "You can't live on that. Just name a figure." I must have looked as though I wanted to fade into the wall. Finally he said that he would pay me five hundred fifty dollars a month. My eyes widened: in 1952, that was more money than I would have made after ten years as a social worker.

I found a one-bedroom apartment for us in Forest Hills, not far from a good nursery school and the subway, and began a daily voyage from Queens into the America I had seen rising behind the Statue of Liberty in the magazine all those years ago—not the America of university campuses or settlement houses, but the United States of Wall Street. Cities Service owned not only the huge skyscraper I worked in but another one across Pine Street, called 60 Wall Tower; they were joined together by a concrete bridge, like twin mountains held in place by a stone cloud. Every day I took one of the elevators from the beautiful red marble lobby to a large windowed room on the seventeenth floor, just down the hall from Alton Jones, and where, if I was too busy to go out to eat, I was brought lunch from the executive dining room on the sixty-third floor. From this luxurious eyrie, Los Angeles seemed almost as distant as Iran.

I set to work putting together a library on Iran for Mr. Jones, gathering books and making a scrapbook of everything published on Iran and Dr. Mossadegh in the international press and oil industry trade magazines, translating articles that appeared in Persian myself. I also composed a short history of the Persian oil industry for the Cities Service executives, struggling to present only objective facts, and not my subjective opinions, as I had learned in college.

The more I saw of my benefactor, the more I liked him—indeed, I felt that it would be impossible to dislike "Pete" Jones, as he was universally known, for he was as honest, friendly, and generous with everyone as he was with me, including the newsstand vendor, whom he tipped every day with a silver dollar. He had a great deal of behind-the-scenes information, often picking up news before it became public, not only from other oil executives but from his many contacts in the State Department and from frequent golf and hunting trips with General Eisenhower. Though I was used to American informality by now, I never ceased to feel startled when, instead of summoning me as an Iranian millionaire would have done, Mr. Jones would simply stop by the door of my office to pass on something he had heard concerning the Middle East, listening respectfully to any comments I made in reply.

I grew to be extremely fond of him, and naturally I was happy whenever he spoke of his personal admiration for Dr. Mossadegh. He was genuinely convinced that this was the leader Iran needed to move ahead and be a real democracy, and that the election of Eisenhower would mean an end to the stalemate, resulting in a warmer and closer relationship between our two countries. To my surprise, I found these sentiments echoed by a great many executives at Cities Service who had heard Iran's side of the story from Mr. Jones and the men who had gone with him. They all knew by now of the unfair treatment we had received for so many years from the British company. "I can't say I blame Mossadegh," one vice president told me. "If they tried to do here what they were getting away with in Iran all those years, they'd find a lot of their tea floating in Boston Harbor." I was moved by this fresh evidence of the sincerity of Americans. When you educated people to know both sides of the story, I saw, they behaved justly. Perhaps if the British government and press had not been so prejudiced, even the English people themselves, supposed to be famous for their sense of fairness, would understand why Iranians felt as they did. I wrote excitedly to Jaby and Abbas that if the goodwill I was encountering at Cities Service could be translated into selling oil, millions of our people might eventually have all the food, education, jobs, and social programs they needed.

Alton Jones was cheerful and energetic after the November election. At the same time, however, he was pressing me to write to Abbas and say that Dr. Mossadegh should be more flexible in his talks with American mediators. His men had found that Iranian engineers could run Abadan as well as the British—the place, said Mr. Jones, was in better shape now than when the British left a year ago. But the AIOC and the American majors were the only ones with the tanker capacity to get the oil out of Abadan. Somebody, he said, had to make Dr. Mossadegh understand that only tankers, not principles, could move oil. Cities Service was too small to provide all the ships that were needed, and he had told Dr. Mossadegh that.

I agreed that Dr. Mossadegh was being extremely stubborn. But I added that Iranian politics weren't the same as American politics. In my country, we slandered each other and thought only of our own interests, and didn't care that such destructiveness injured the entire nation. If Dr. Mossadegh compromised even slightly, his enemies could say that he was pro-British and bring down his government, or even have him assassinated. Mr. Jones, however, continued to point out that "you couldn't run an oil industry by not selling oil. Write to your brother-in-law again," he would say, "and ask him to tell Dr. Mossadegh that Pete Jones—and I advise this very strongly—urges him to make concessions."

"I do not think," I replied, "that the British have made it easier for him to compromise by plotting to overthrow him." In mid-October, Dr. Mossadegh had uncovered a conspiracy headed by General Fazlollah Zahedi, a disaffected former military man. During the Allied occupation the British and Russians had jailed Zahedi for collaborating with the Nazis, but Dr. Mossadegh had learned that the British were now backing Zahedi. The premier had broken off diplomatic relations with the British and closed their gigantic embassy in Tehran, which had always been the nerve center of British intrigue. Like most Iranians I was glad that he had taken this long-overdue step, but I was also sure it meant the British would have to try to enlist American help to get rid of him.

"Please," I implored Mr. Jones, "the next time you see Mr. Eisenhower, warn him that he must not listen to the British after he is president. I'm sure they will tell him that Dr. Mossadegh is clever and deceitful and a Communist. A military man like General Eisenhower cannot see how clever they are themselves, and that they will say many things to him that are not honest. You don't know them as we do in the Middle East."

Mr. Jones, who I am sure thought my mistrust of the British excessive, reassured me that "people at State" had a pretty fair idea of what went on, and that anyway Ike wouldn't be fooled. I was sure, however, that it was not I who was too suspicious, but the Americans who were naive. I still feared that the British would have much less trouble with the conservative Eisenhower than they had had with Truman, and for this reason I, too, felt that the premier was too inclined to put principle before practical matters. I wrote often to Abbas, imploring him to urge Dr. Mossadegh to be more flexible and find a compromise solution, emphasizing that this was the opinion of Mr. Jones, who was in the confidence of General Eisenhower and the State Department. Abbas always replied with studied neutrality, "I have given your message to your cousin and he sends you his very warm greetings." I had no trouble understanding that Iran's premier was not greatly interested in advice from his young female cousin in New York. Nevertheless, I was sure that my brother-in-law agreed with Mr. Jones's views. Time, which was not on our side, was slipping away.

Despite these worries, I was enjoying my new life. Mr. Jones introduced me to his family, and I socialized a good deal with people from the international community and the United Nations, as well as with our many Persian connections in New York and with the Iranian diplomats we knew in Washington. Once, at a dinner party, I met Julia Henderson, who had originally invited me to come to New York. I had not given up the possibility of approaching her when the oil crisis was resolved; Mr. Jones had obligingly arranged for the Cities Service attorney to help me get Mitra a U.S. passport. I was deeply relieved not to be in the appalling position of having to choose between my daughter and my homeland any longer.

At first I had been anxious about leaving Mitra alone at her new nursery school, but she seemed to accept being separated from me here just as she had when I was working in Los Angeles, calmly and without any fussing; I saw with slightly mixed feelings that behind a sweet, affectionate, and compliant disposition, Mitra was nursing her own brand of independence. I had written to Arun to let him know my address and my plans at present, and had received a carefully worded letter wishing me well and granting me power of attorney in case I wanted to dissolve our marriage. I guessed that his family had found him a more acceptable match and was waiting for him to arrange for a divorce. However, I didn't want to rush into something so important without a pressing reason, nor did I want Mitra to conclude one day that just because her father had not achieved his goal in India, I had divorced him after he had been gone for six months. I merely replied that I would think about his suggestion, and would let him know if I ever decided to pursue a divorce. Then I banished the matter from my mind.

By February of 1953, I was again preoccupied with events at home. Dr. Mossadegh had made real gains in several important social and economic programs, but the oil issue was becoming evermore urgent as unrest grew in the rural areas. The premier, knowing that a reminder of Shazdeh would help win support in Fars, had replaced Dadash as health minister and sent him to Shiraz as provincial governor. But nothing, it seemed, could overcome the impasse. A few months earlier the outgoing Truman administration had held out the possibility of a British-American oil consortium, but Dr. Mossadegh had recently rejected this proposal.

His domestic position grew steadily worse throughout that winter and spring. Prices and unemployment escalated. The premier, who had won back for parliament much of the power the Shah had been arrogating to himself but who still did not have control of the military, was relying heavily on radio appeals that always evoked mass demonstrations in his support. Unfortunately, some of this street-level enthusiasm depended on the on-again, off-again cooperation of the pro-Soviet Communist party of Iran, the Tudeh. Though he was struggling to rule according to the constitution, to maintain public order Dr. Mossadegh had used temporary emergency powers granted him by the Majlis to impose martial law. His enemies accused him of aspiring to dictatorship; many of his supporters, on the other hand, were convinced that he was not being dictatorial enough and that his democratic principles were making him too tolerant of extremists on both the right and left. Acts of violence and conspiracies were coming thick and fast, and in April of 1953, they culminated in the kidnapping, torture, and murder of Tehran's honest and conscientious police chief, General Afshartous, a loyal Mossadegh supporter. General Zahedi and a leader of a political party that had recently broken with the National Front were among those implicated.

I was very much distressed not only by these developments themselves but by the way they were reported in the United States. The American press was still echoing the views of the large American oil companies which feared the impact of nationalization in Iran on "their" countries. Paid-for riots, anti-government plots, and murders committed by Dr. Mossadegh's opponents with the avowed purpose of destabilizing his government somehow became, in the American press, further proof that our premier—who was neither a Communist nor personally sympathetic to the Tudeh—was a crazed radical and a Soviet tool who was allowing us to become "another China." To me and other Iranians I knew in New York, it seemed plain that the British government had designated General Zahedi as its chosen instrument and was working through its diplomats in Washington and its agents in Tehran to manipulate both the Eisenhower administration and American journalism. However, we knew that if we told our American friends this, they would only dismiss us as "paranoid."

What worried me most in the spring of 1953, however, was the profound change that had taken place in Mr. Jones. Before the inauguration he had been in high spirits. He despised the cynical press articles that mocked Dr. Mossadegh's dress, appearance, and mannerisms (*Time* derived much amusement from the fact that Dr. Mossadegh, who was often ill, wore lounging pajamas to receive reporters and diplomats, though the Luce magazines seemed to find it endearing when Churchill conducted meetings from bed), and I was aware that both before and after the election he had been actively striving to persuade the future president that "we had to work out a plan with Mossadegh." But in January, this energy and optimism had suddenly evaporated, and Mr. Jones began returning from his visits to Washington moody and depressed. His frequent comments about the friendship and goodwill between our countries had ceased abruptly. More ominous still, he was no longer exhilarated and talkative, nor did he make any response now to my naively persistent warnings about the British. Above all, I was disturbed by the new expression in his gray eyes, which had been so striking and vital when I met him. It was as if the light had gone out of them. I was convinced that this great change in my kind benefactor meant that the British had at last succeeded in winning over Eisenhower to let them do as they wished in Iran, and that Mr. Jones had ended up on the losing side.

That spring, Dr. Mossadegh rejected a joint British and American plan for compensation, and late in May, desperate over the deteriorating situation, he wrote a letter to President Eisenhower urging the new American president to increase economic aid to Iran, ending with dark hints about the political consequences to our country if it were not forthcoming. After a full month, Eisenhower replied with a chilly rebuff. This was a devasting blow to the morale of Dr. Mossadegh's supporters. Only a short time before, the new American ambassador, Loy Henderson, had met with the Shah, giving rise to frantic speculation in my circles in New York that the Americans would support the Shah and Zahedi if Mossadegh were replaced. Dr. Mossadegh's followers, fearing that he could not stay in power, were now deserting him and conspiring with his antagonists to unseat him by intrigue or by violence. Pro- and anti-government mobs, religious extremists, and the Tudeh battled the police and each other in the streets every day. Meanwhile, legislation in the Majlis, blocked by Mossadegh opponents, had ground to a standstill. Finally, in mid-July, Dr. Mossadegh announced that he was appealing directly to the electorate in a referendum that would force the reluctant Shah to dissolve the Majlis, thereby breaking the hold of the premier's opponents on it.

I was wretched over the course events were taking, not only out of fear for the safety of my family in Tehran but because the referendum was a clear departure from the document Dr. Mossadegh had defended with such devotion all his life. He felt a deep kinship with the Iranian masses and was convinced that their will and his were in harmony, and that a public expression of confidence in his policies was therefore justified. Even so, only the monarch was permitted to dissolve parliament, and the referendum was unconstitutional. Worse yet, the "Yes" and "No" voting boxes for the referendum were separated, so that the balloting was not secret. I knew that Dr. Mossadegh was resorting to these schemes only because the situation had grown so desperate that otherwise he could not continue in office long enough to carry out his reforms. Nevertheless, I found it ironic and painful to see such a democratic leader resorting to antidemocratic strategems of the kind practiced by his opponents.

However, he won the referendum, and the Majlis was dissolved. Then, in mid-August, just as everyone was wondering whether our old Lion of God would survive, the situation suddenly seemed to reverse itself in his favor. On Sunday, the sixteenth of August, Mohammed Reza Shah fled Iran.

On Monday morning I arrived at work to read with amazement of the Shah's flight. The papers were full of the tangled story. Since the previous Wednesday, the *New York Times* reported, Tudeh newspapers had been predicting an attempted overthrow of Dr. Mossadegh by royalists and General Zahedi's supporters. On Saturday night, an army colonel named Nematollah Nassiri had gone to Dr. Mossadegh's residence on Kakh Avenue with an order of dismissal bearing the Shah's signature, with the intention of installing General Zahedi as premier.

But Dr. Mossadegh's supporters had been forewarned. Colonel Nassiri, who found the premier's house surrounded by tanks and loyal army troops, was himself arrested. The Shah, at his summer palace on the Caspian Sea, evidently became frightened for his own safety. The next day, accompanied by Queen Soraya, he left for Baghdad in his private plane, and was now in Rome. Zahedi, from a hideout somewhere in the hills, was proclaiming himself the rightful premier and arguing that Dr. Mossadegh was guilty of an illegal coup for resisting the dismissal order. Fortunately, the papers said that the army appeared to be on Dr. Mossadegh's side.

My first and overwhelming feeling was one of profound shock that the Shah would leave his country in such a crisis—this, I thought, was not the act of a king. But also, his flight simply didn't make sense. Dr. Mossadegh had never questioned the Shah's right to be king, only to rule in disregard of parliament and our constitution. An aristocrat himself, as premier he had repeatedly declared his loyalty to a constitutional monarchy and would never have attempted to overthrow or harm the monarch, an act that he knew would have brought on a civil war. Even so, I was relieved at the way things had turned out. Perhaps now, I thought, Dr. Mossadegh could govern more easily for a while. No doubt when things calmed down a little the Shah would see how badly his actions reflected on him and return to Iran.

The next day, however, my optimism gave way to alarm. In the wake of the Shah's flight, a mob, described by the *Times* as "Tudeh partisans and extreme nationalists," suddenly materialized and toppled statues of the Shah and his father. There were reports of Communist-led attacks on American property and of rioters fighting with police. Dr. Mossadegh had no choice but to restore order. On Tuesday he called out the Tehran army garrison, and I was horrified to read that soldiers had hurled tear gas and smashed the heads of left-wing and pro-government rioters with their rifle butts.

I felt shaken, bewildered, and frightened. Only forty-eight hours ago, the government had appeared to be in control. Now suddenly a mob had appeared out of nowhere and rioted, forcing Dr. Mossadegh to use the army against civilians and his own leftist allies. I went home Wednesday evening praying that everyone at home was safe. After many telephone conversations with Iranian friends in New York, who were all as worried about their families as I was, I went to bed.

On Thursday morning, August 20, as I was fixing Mitra's breakfast, I turned on the radio. What I heard seemed to plunge the room into darkness. The government of Iran had been overthrown. A gigantic mob screaming "Death to Mossadegh" and calling for the Shah to come back had attacked and destroyed the premier's home. Dr. Mossadegh had fled and was in hiding.

Trying not to let Mitra see how panicky I was, I finished dressing her and walked with her to the nursery school a few blocks away. At the subway I bought a *Times*. The headline on the front page said that hundreds had died in the fighting. As I sat on the subway, trying to concentrate on what I was reading, my mind seemed to be racing faster than the train. I was certain that no matter how divided his supporters were, it was simply inconceivable that Mohammed Mossadegh, who was still the personal idol of vast numbers of Iranians, could suddenly have lost so much popularity, whereas the Shah *was* unpopular, a king perceived as weak and unable to confront the British. His headlong flight in a time of crisis could not possibly have made ordinary people long for him so much that they would spontaneously riot and call for the downfall of a premier as beloved as Mohammed Mossadegh. Someone had arranged this—the British, I was sure, and Zahedi's backers.

As soon as I reached my office I rushed to telephone Mahmoud Forrughi. The whole floor was in a tense, hushed mood; everyone anxiously murmured their sympathy and glanced at me with worried faces. When I finally got through to the consulate, I was told that Mr. Forrughi was still waiting to find out what had happened to Dr. Mossadegh and other members of the government. The consular staff was completely occupied with trying to determine who in Dr. Mossadegh's family and immediate circle had been killed or injured and who was in charge of the government. They had no idea when they would be able to give me any information about members of my own family.

Someone had thoughtfully placed all the morning papers on my desk. Spreading them out, I tried to read carefully. That morning a huge "pro-Shah" demonstration had suddenly begun pouring into the streets from South Tehran and the bazaar. Simultaneously an armored tank unit from a garrison in the foothills where Zahedi had been hiding had appeared and joined the mob. Together, the truckloads of soldiers, the tanks, and the screaming, slogan-shouting rioters had rolled north from Parliament Square toward the Mossadegh residence on Kakh Avenue, a few blocks from my mother's house. There, after a nine-hour battle with those inside, the tanks had destroyed the walls of the premier's home. The mob had rushed in, but Dr. Mossadegh had managed to escape through the garden. His bodyguard was dead. The *Times* said that the man who had warned him of the midnight attempt to depose him, a loyal army colonel named Ezatollah Mumtaz, had been found and torn to pieces. Dr. Mossadegh's state papers, locked in his safe, were looted and burned, his home pillaged, and its modest furnishings thrown into the street, where the attackers contemptuously auctioned them off to passersby.

Elsewhere, other mobs had captured the telegraph office, several government buildings, and the state radio, while army soldiers were evidently attacking any civilian they decided was a member of the parties that supported Mossadegh. A curfew had been imposed. The whole neighborhood around my mother's house, I realized, must be in a state of siege. In agony I wondered whether Abbas had been killed, whether the fighting had spread to Shiraz where Dadash was, whether the country was falling into civil war.

I searched frantically among the different reports for more information. In Rome, the Shah had received the news of the premier's overthrow while lunching with Queen Soraya and had said that "everyone who was not a Communist" had always been for him. A small article in the *Times* said that according to the British government, the coup had come about "because Communism did not appeal to large segments of the Iranian population." I wanted to shriek in protest at these smug, self-serving lies, at the British government's hypocrisy, at the gullibility of the American press. For a moment I stared at the black newsprint, ready to tear the page to shreds. Hundreds of thousands of Iranians would have risen to support Mossadegh. Why was he not calling for help on the radio? Then, thinking of the half-lame premier fleeing for his life—an old man who had served his country uncompromisingly for more than fifty years, now searching for someone to hide him from those who were betraying him to Zahedi and the British—I put my face in my hands and wept.

At ten o'clock Mr. Jones arrived and came straight to my office. I saw from his expression that he had already heard about the coup—whether from the papers or from the State Department itself I did not know. "You told me," I almost screamed at him, "that it would be all right! You said, 'Don't worry, Eisenhower will not let them hurt Mossadegh and Iran.' The *Times* says that three hundred people are dead! Call Eisenhower and tell him to make them stop killing people—tell him they must not kill Dr. Mossadegh!"

Mr. Jones looked angry and sorrowful. He didn't know why this was happening, he said. His voice, I noticed, was embarrassed, apologetic. He has lost face, I thought grimly, because his friend listened to the British and not to him. "You must call Mr. Eisenhower," I repeated, trying now to keep my voice steady. "You know that Dr. Mossadegh is not a Communist. You have told me many times that you love him, that you are a friend of Iran. Call Mr. Eisenhower and say they must not kill him!"

Mr. Jones answered soothingly that he didn't think there was much we could do at the moment. In terrible frustration I saw that he was more interested in calming me down than in telephoning Eisenhower. He asked if I had any news of my family. Crying, I said that I knew nothing about what was happening to Jaby, Abbas, or anyone else and was petrified because the fighting had been in our neighborhood. Mr. Jones said that if he learned anything at all from the State Department or his friends at other companies he would pass it on immediately. A radio was brought in for me and I spent the rest of the day listening to it, rereading the same reports over and over as I waited for the afternoon papers. Almost the whole company, even Mr. Jones's German chef, Kurt, came by to console me and say that things were "going to be fine." Early in the afternoon I called the consulate again, but they had no more information than before. I knew that everyone with a family in Tehran was in the same situation, and that I must restrain myself from calling too often.

From time to time Mr. Jones himself, drawn and unhappy, would appear at the door to ask what I was hearing on the news. He was not, I saw, going to call Eisenhower. Despairingly, I realized that this generous and well-intentioned American was as helpless as I was. He couldn't call Eisenhower, or turn his own system on its head. His goodwill had done nothing to stop the British from deciding the fate of my country again. He might as well have been some nobody—or an Iranian, like me.

That same evening, as we learned on Friday, Dr. Mossadegh surrendered to General Zahedi, who took control of the military and rounded up Dr. Mossadegh's advisers and cabinet. Tanks and soldiers were forestalling any National Front or Tudeh demonstrations against the new military regime. I had no idea what was happening to Dadash or Abbas. The consulate said that it would take ten days or more before a wire could reach me, and I would just have to be patient.

Two days after the overthrow, Mohammed Reza Shah Pahlavi returned to Iran.

It was a week before I learned that no member of my family had been killed or injured during the fighting near our home. A couple of weeks later I received a letter from Jaby letting me know that Abbas and Dadash were both safe; they were staying at home until the dust settled. As Abbas had been employed only by the National Iranian Oil Company and had not held any political office, she thought that after a while he would be able to go back to work. Dadash, however, would have to look for a position in international public health. For any relative of Mossadegh who had served in a high political post, a government career now was out of the question.

The Shah and Zahedi quickly set about eliminating their opponents. Foreign Minister Fatemi, Dr. Mossadegh's closest associate, was executed, his minister of justice murdered, and other important National Front members sent to prison. Communist leaders—those the government was able to hunt down before they fled the country—were imprisoned, tortured, and executed.

As far as Dr. Mossadegh himself was concerned, Zahedi and the Shah were in a quandry. Killing the old hero was as risky as freeing him. On the other hand, imprisoning him indefinitely would make him a living martyr. At last, in November, the government tried him in a military barracks outside Tehran, on the grounds that he had resisted the dismissal order. This, it hoped, would limit public attendance. However, the makeshift courtroom was packed to the walls with the old premier's supporters. Dr. Mossadegh defended himself and his actions with undiminished wit and passion. The trial made the government look ridiculous, for his followers repeated his speeches every night to all their relatives and friends, and by this means everyone in Tehran, and soon people all over the country, knew what he had said even though not a word of his defense was reported in the now-censored Iranian press. In Persian bazaars and mosques, in cafés and teahouses, in baths and gymnasiums, the final ordeal being inflicted on our frail old Lion of God became the last verse in his legend.

For me, however, who sat in New York and read only what the American and Iranian newspapers chose to report, the trial was an excruciating form of mental torture. The American newsmagazines had a field day. A derisive series of photographs in *Life* magazine became world famous. Everything about Dr. Mossadegh that had made us love him was ridiculed—his age; his infirmity; his passion, humor, and stubborn, fiery commitment. There were pictures of him dozing on his attorney's shoulder, beating a table with his slipper, laughing at his own jokes. With its last word on the subject, the American press was reducing the most benevolent and democratic leader we had ever had to a foolish, half-mad old man making an indecent spectacle of himself in public.

But Mohammed Mossadegh, I knew, had lost neither his sanity nor his dignity, and it was the American press that was indecent. He had represented a true mobilization of our national will. His twenty-eight months in office had been one of the few times Persians had ever cooperated and achieved something together. He had been obstinate, made many mistakes, and once even resorted to unconstitutional trickery. But he had not failed because of the way he looked, or because of his eccentricities and mannerisms. He had failed because he had struggled too hard and too uncompromisingly against a superpower. He was suffering now because he had never wavered in trying to make us masters of our own fate. Whatever his sins and shortcomings, he was a patriot who believed in democracy and our constitution. Mohammed Mossadegh had been punished for being what he was—an Iranian who had held fast to his principles.

Dr. Mossadegh was found guilty and sentenced to three years in prison. In view of the alternatives, this was lenient. After his elimination, the oil negotiations made solid progress. It was announced that the Zahedi government would receive forty-five million dollars in aid from the United States, a vast increase. A consortium proposal, the same one that Dr. Mossadegh had turned down, was under discussion. Iran would receive fifty percent of the profits. The Anglo-Iranian Oil Company—now renamed British Petroleum—would have a forty percent share in the consortium, and the five largest American companies were rewarded for supporting the British embargo with a forty percent share of their own. A Dutch and a French company would get what remained. Once again our affairs and our oil would be in somebody else's hands—only now the hands would be American as well as British.

I followed these events in the most profound depression and heaviness of heart. I saw now how foolish I had been to believe that Mr. Jones's good intentions would prevail over the combined persuasiveness of British diplomats and the large American oil companies. Staying at Cities Service, I thought, had lost any point it had ever had. I ought to be doing something useful at home. But I could no longer return home to work. For one thing, I was disgusted by the thought of working under the Zahedi regime. But also, even if social work had not been an unknown profession in Iran, finding a position in the government— a difficult enough task for a woman under normal circumstances— would now be impossible because I was a relative of Dr. Mossadegh.

By Christmas, however, I knew that I had to make some concrete plans. I was sure that Mr. Jones would be happy to keep me on in some capacity, and Mitra and I could have a comfortable life in New York. But I wanted urgently to be near my family again, and after the disillusionment of the past months I greatly desired to return to my real work. I went to see Julia Henderson at the United Nations and was offered a two-year renewable position with UNESCO as a social welfare consultant to the government of Iraq, working with officials of King Faisal to develop a social welfare system and going to the desert to settle nomadic Arab tribes. As a United Nations expert, I would also participate in social work projects and teaching at schools all over the Middle East. However, for much of the first year I would be living in the rugged and almost empty desert of southern Iraq, training settlers and Bedouin nomads in hygiene, nutrition, and vocational skills. Since Mitra was an American citizen, she could attend the American Community School in Baghdad, while she and I would have long home leaves in Tehran together during the summer, but the Iraqi desert was no place for a five-year-old girl. When I went there, I would either have to arrange for her to live with my family in Iran or send her to a boarding school in Europe.

This was a difficult prospect, but I decided to accept the United Nations offer, which meant that I would at last have a chance to practice my profession among peoples whose cultures and style of life were similiar to mine. If I left in the late spring, we could have a month in Tehran before going on to Baghdad in the summer. When I told Alton Jones that I was accepting a post with the United Nations and would be leaving Cities Service, he was surprised and disappointed. I explained, however, that there was nothing more for me to do in his company. I had come to him, I said, because I had thought that he and his people were in a position to do something for mine. Now I understood that it was not in his power to help us. Laughing a little to take the edge off my sharpness, I added, "I don't want you to waste any more of your money on me."

I added, however, that I would be grateful for the advice of his company attorney. After settling in New York I had received one additional letter from Arun, repeating what he had said in his previous letters. By this time I was really more disappointed at his lack of spirit than angry. For whatever reason, he was not demanding that I hand over Mitra, and for that I would always be grateful to him. With the help of the Cities Service attorney I obtained a divorce decree from a New York court on the grounds of desertion. The judge also ordered Arun to pay child support, but I only sent him the divorce papers and ignored the support order. I wanted us to end without bickering— Mitra and I, I thought, didn't need to ask for assistance from someone who had deserted us. I myself would give her everything she needed, and I was certain that my family would make sure that she was loved. Only one question gnawed me—would Mitra spend the rest of her life wondering why her father had abandoned her? Maybe all of us together, I thought sadly, would be able to make it up to her.

Late in the spring I was ready to leave. On my last day at Cities Service, I went in to say goodbye to Mr. Jones. We talked for several minutes and I thanked him with deep emotion for all his kindness. When we said goodbye, my voice choked with tears. I knew that I would miss him, as I would all my frank, generous, sincere American friends.

But I had finally come to understand that I had been wrong to depend on America. We, I and the other educated Iranians of my generation who had thought like me, had all been wrong. Now I knew that we could not depend on powerful protectors and benefactors, only on ourselves. We had, I thought, learned just the same lesson from Dr. Mossadegh that my brothers had learned from Dr. Jordan—don't rely on someone stronger, only on yourself. Outside the shattered compound of my childhood, there were no Shazdehs.

The plane I took in June of 1954, in those pre-jet days, seemed to fly and fly and never arrive. Over Europe, the sky was overcast, but as we neared Turkey, it cleared. Craning constantly from the window, I saw the earth turn from forested green to craggy, stone-gray desert, ancient and unchanging. Then it turned reddish brown and in the far distance I sighted the twisted ramparts of the Alborz, enclosing my country like a wall around a garden. Rare and precious, a few rivers, trickling down from the mountain snows, made thin traces of green in the arid wastes. How gifted the Persian poets were, I thought, who created for us a world of trees and blossoms in the wilderness of Iran!

Then, suddenly, after the endless flight, I was there. My whole family was out in force, shouting greetings from the barrier. I plunged into a bedlam of cries, shouts, embraces, and floods of tears, including my own. I had been gone for ten years and three months. I prayed that I would never have to leave my family again.

After we had gone to my mother's house for the homecoming celebration and the first, overwhelming flood of our emotion had passed a little, we all began trying to catch up on the years of separation. By this time most of my younger brothers and sisters and our other brothers and sisters had been to college in Europe or America. Most of Shazdeh's younger sons had businesses or professions, and many had advanced degrees and had become engineers, architects, economists, and professors. Both men and women had married and started families, and with everyone together, including our mothers, there were already nearly a hundred Farman Farmaians in the world.

Dadash was going to work for the World Health Organization. He had built a large, lovely home with a magnificent rose garden at Tajrish (which was now almost a suburb of the city), just inside the entrance of Reswanieh, and Mitra and I stayed with him. My daughter's sweetness and beauty at once endeared her to Dadash and Khanom, as it did to all my brothers and sisters and the rest of the family. In the United States, Farough had taken the place of Mitra's father; here my next-youngest brother, Ghaffar, seemed to be assuming this role, while I could see that Dadash, whose gentle personality was very like our grandfather's, was going to be her Aghajun. And now it was my daughter who, together with all her cousins, sat spellbound while Khanom told stories of the old days and her life with Batul-Khanom in Ezzatdoleh's andarun.

Ezzatdoleh had died while I had been gone, but my mother and other stepmothers still saw each other all the time. Khanom was now in her middle fifties. She seemed smaller and frailer than of old, but she also seemed more relaxed and laughed more easily—though still not at jokes about mullahs. Tehran itself was noisier and more crowded than ever, and I was astonished at the number of vehicles. At Mehrabad Airport, the major airlines now took people back and forth every day between countries of which Iranians of Khanom's generation had never heard when they were young. In North Tehran, buildings were going up and taxis, Western movie theaters, and restaurants were proliferating. But vendors and scribes still lined the steps of the post office and small white donkeys still trotted through the streets—occasionally one even saw a camel caravan. Indeed, somehow the city, like Khanom, seemed smaller than I had remembered it. In some surprise I realized that I was over thirty, and no longer the young girl who had set out to embrace the world ten years before.

Often I would sit with my mother, Dadash, Jaby, Abbas, and others in my family and talk about Dr. Mossadegh. Only now did I learn what had transpired during the trial. Dr. Mossadegh had claimed that the Shah's original dismissal order was a forgery and argued that a military court did not have the authority to try a civilian premier. He had testified in open court that a day or two before the coup, he and his government had learned that huge amounts of American dollars were being converted into Iranian rials at the Central Bank of Iran, and his advisers had realized that a conspiracy was afoot. However, when the mob attacked his house, he had preferred the risk of being lynched to issuing a call for resistance that might have plunged the country into a second civil war. Needless to say, none of this had appeared in the Iranian or foreign press.

Thus, like fish converging in a river to spawn, rumors and stories and information had flowed together to point Persians to the truth. Even before the trial, common laborers and bazaar ruffians had gone about boasting that they had been paid ten days' wages to pull down the Shah's statue or to shout "Death to Mossadegh." Thanks to this and to the courtroom revelations, Abbas told me angrily, everybody in Iran now realized that the overthrow had been financed by dollars from the American Central Intelligence Agency. As always, there had been Iranians willing to sell out their country, and as always, the British had arranged for the sale. But this time, the United States had been the paymaster.

I was stunned. At first I simply did not want to believe that the same nation that had produced my cherished American friends and teachers, people like Dr. Jordan and Arlien Johnson, could have done such a thing. Then I remembered how Mr. Jones had suddenly become so old and weary-looking after the inauguration. Perhaps he already knew what Eisenhower and the CIA had decided to do. Maybe that was why he had sounded so apologetic when I shouted at him to call Eisenhower.

America, I thought bitterly in my room that night, was truly a wasteful nation. It had thrown away our affection exactly the way it threw away food it did not want. Thinking only of its fear of communism and of the interest of American oil companies, it had used its great power to stifle our nation's aspirations to independence and dignity. The way we felt about the United States would never be the same again.

Since the beginning of the twentieth century, I reflected, every time we had begun to achieve a sense of national purpose, of dynamism, foreign powers had stepped in to abort it. When we adopted a constitution, the Russians started a civil war and the British imposed Reza Shah on us. When Reza Shah was gone, we became a country occupied by three foreign armies. When the occupation was over and we thought our land was our own again, the Soviets seized Azerbaijan. Now America, the nation so many of us had loved and trusted, sat in the seat of the British. No wonder we were suspicious of everyone and everything. No wonder foreigners thought Iranians "paranoid" to the point where we sometimes saw foreign poison in every bottle and foreign treachery behind every tree. Once again, our dream of controlling our own destiny had come to nothing. Yet we could not give up, I thought, merely because we and the foreigners had disenfranchised ourselves. We had to go on, and tackle as best we could the job of becoming a modern nation.

Sometimes I wondered whether Mr. Jones had known all along what the CIA was planning. But as the time for my departure for Baghdad drew upon me, I saw that I must repudiate disillusionment and distrust. They could only thwart my hopes and plans.

I knew now that, like us, other nations saw the rest of the world and its peoples only through the narrow lens of their own experience, their own pride, their own interests. Lamenting failed hopes was impractical, and reviling those who did not deserve our trust was a waste of time. Better to thrust from your mind someone who wounded and betrayed you, and get on with the job. Someday I was going to return to Iran, and when I did, I didn't want to be part of the suspicion, mistrust, and sense of impotence that crippled us. I wanted to teach Iranians to believe in something—to give them the knowledge that we could solve our problems ourselves. I felt that I had learned what America had to teach me.

PART THREE

KHANOM

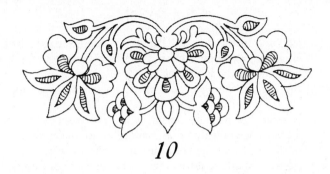

10

TWENTY PEOPLE WHO BELIEVE IN SOMETHING

Human beings are like parts of a body,
created from the same essence.
When one part is hurt and in pain,
the others cannot remain in peace and be quiet.

—From the motto of the Tehran School
of Social Work, 1958–1979

*A*N EARLY NOVEMBER BREEZE, UNEXPECTEDLY WARM, DRIFTED IN from the garden outside and filled my office in what had once been somebody's living room with an odor of decaying roses, tinged with the smells of dust and traffic fumes. From beyond the garden wall came distant sounds of construction work and honking cars, now fixtures of life in Iran's capital. Half a decade after Mossadegh's downfall, North Tehran was looking more like the West every year.

I had returned the previous spring, in April of 1958, and late in August, with government backing, I had opened a private two-year professional school to train young Iranians to be social workers. Except for my summer leaves, I had been away over fourteen years, first with the United Nations among the Bedouin and afterward for another two years in the Iraqi capital. I had performed welfare work, training, and research among the reed-hut slums of Baghdad, the mud dwellings of

Nile farmers, and in the dreadful Palestinian refugee camps in Lebanon. With all this experience behind me it was strange to think that after teaching the methods of social work to so many others, I was teaching the average young people of my own country for the first time.

My U.N. years had been deeply satisfying. The progress UNESCO made might have been measured in inches, but we made some nonetheless, and the fact that the countries and cultures in my own part of the world were as different from each other as those of Europe had fascinated me. After New York and the despair I had felt at Mossadegh's overthrow, four years of hard work among ordinary people who had problems I could do something about had been like a long, invigorating course of physical and mental therapy.

I had been able to keep Mitra with me for a year in Baghdad. But before going to the desert, I—like many Persian parents before me— had arrived at the painful decision to send her abroad, so that she could receive the best possible education. I had chosen the Dartington Hall school in Devonshire, England, the institution that my brothers Ghaffar and Rashid had attended. Ghaffar had at once assigned himself the role of "father" to my five-year-old daughter in all matters concerning her schooling. To make our wrenching separation easier, he had arranged for Mitra to stay on weekends and holidays with a Devonshire family who also had children at the school.

Mitra suffered as any child would, and I missed her terribly. I visited her in London whenever she had a long vacation, and I lived for our summers together in Tehran. However, I had always sensed a streak of my own independence in her, and when I returned to Tehran in 1958 and Mitra joined me that summer, I discovered that I had not been wrong. At the age of nine, my sweet, affectionate daughter took a look at the American Community School and announced firmly that she wanted to go back to her English family and friends at Dartington Hall. A little sadly, I sent her back. I wanted her to have the education I had longed for as a girl. But I told myself that one day, when that was finished, she would come home to Iran, and then I would have her with me forever.

During these four years, I had watched and waited to see how the political situation at home developed. The unrest of the Mossadegh era was now a thing of the past. Zahedi and the Shah had stifled the National Front and crushed the Tudeh. The old premier who had tried to wrest control of the military from the throne had been released before the end of his prison term but lived virtually in solitary confinement on his estates in the village of Ahmadabad, ninety miles northwest of Tehran. Dr. Mossadegh was allowed no correspondence with anyone and was visited only by his wife and children, who could see him for just a few minutes each week. There was no hope that his banishment—especially cruel for a man who loved people and who was now nearly eighty and in constant pain from stomach ulcers and other afflictions—would ever be rescinded. The Shah, it was said, bore an unrelenting hatred for the old statesman who had come so close to making him a monarch who would reign but not rule.

Mohammed Reza Shah, however, no longer had any real opposition to fear. The Majlis was again a rubber stamp, the national elections rigged, and every member of parliament selected by the king personally. Persian newspapers and the state-owned radio and television stations were forbidden to discuss anything the imperial court or the Pahlavi family did not want discussed—nor, as the Shah was deeply grateful for America's assistance, could the press criticize the United States without the imperial court's approval. Worst of all, a dread new secret police called SAVAK, said to have been trained by the CIA and the Israeli MOSSAD, watched the trade unions to prevent strikes and imprisoned left-wing activists or hounded them out of the country. To judge from his public speeches, the king sincerely believed that God and divine providence were responsible for his restoration and his present absolute power. But many people could read the international press and exchanged information and rumors to inform themselves, and everyone understood the role America now played in the maintenance of his power. Since the signing of the oil consortium agreement in 1954, the Shah had been spending a great deal of our new income on the armed forces and the officer corps, and accepting large amounts of American technical and military aid.

The slender, tentative young monarch depicted in photographs and newsreels in the days of the Allies' occupation had given way to official portraits of a stiff, aloof-looking ruler of forty. Like Reza Shah, Mohammed Reza Shah never appeared in public except in uniform, as though he were reviewing an endless military parade. However, he had turned out to be a far subtler politician than his father. He not only allowed men who had been his opponents to reenter public life, rewarding them with sinecures and numerous perquisites, but he even accepted former Mossadegh followers and Communists into the fold— on condition that they never utter the slightest criticism of his policies. He was taking pains to stay on good terms with the clergy, whose influence and support in tradition-minded economic sectors like the bazaar he evidently appreciated more than Reza Shah had. Moreover, when Zahedi's oppressiveness and corruption made the general a political liability, the Shah ousted him from the premiership.

I had watched this enforced stability developing with divided feelings. Reza Shah had robbed us of the chance to develop into a politically mature, stable society, and now his son was doing the same thing. Yet I did not want to remain in semiexile forever, and the Shah, like his father—whose memory he revered—was ambitious to modernize Iran. He had recently activated a government agency called the Plan Organization and entrusted it with supervising our economic and technical development. The government was always boasting in the press of the great new Iran to come under the guidance of Mohammed Reza Shah, "the Light of the Aryans," "the Source of All Blessings," "the Father of the Nation," but it was also talking, though doing no more than that, about improving the conditions of ordinary people's lives.

These had changed little since my days at the missionary dispensary. South Tehran was still the filthy, teeming slum it had been when I left. The few public facilities that existed to serve the poor had no trained staffs besides the overworked doctors and nurses in our overcrowded hospitals. In the rural areas seventy percent of the total population of Iran still lived in over sixty-two thousand scattered villages without schools, medical care, electricity, running water, or rudimentary sanitation. We had no social security or unemployment insurance, no employment agencies, vocational schools, or retirement programs—none of the things that people in the industrialized West took for granted. In a country like ours, human beings lived lives that were devoid not only of help but of prospects and possibilities. Nevertheless, I believed that if I could start small programs to help individuals and their families improve their standard of living, as the United Nations was helping governments do elsewhere in the Middle East, I could not only give people a chance to change their lives, but might eventually be able to persuade the national government to see the value of modern, organized social programs on a large scale.

However, I could not take social work to Iran without turning to the regime for help, because in Iran there were no private foundations to give me start-up money. No undertaking could succeed without the support of the Shah or someone close to him, and I was still uneasy about approaching the government. Even with Zahedi gone I didn't want to work within the confines of the Shah's stifling political system, which was growing stronger each year. I had spent one of my home leaves helping a distinguished American social worker, Arthur Altmeyer, conduct a U.N. study for the Iranian labor ministry on the welfare needs of factory workers, and the cynical, cowardly toadying I saw among our politicians and officials nauseated me. Politics in my country after Mossadegh, I thought in disgust, was only for the party of the wind. Furthermore, even though I was only a woman, and therefore presumably harmless, the Shah was known to distrust Qajars, especially those closely related to Dr. Mossadegh.

In the end, however, I had realized that so long as I remained in my self-imposed exile, I would accomplish nothing. Having witnessed my own and Alton Jones's helplessness as the CIA, the British, and Zahedi went ahead and destroyed Mossadegh, I had realized how futile idealism was when one was nobody, someone without influence or the ability to bring about changes in the things one cared about. Despite the Shah's rumored distrust of Qajars, in Iran the Farman Farmaians had influence, for my family possessed many excellent connections. Everywhere in the Middle East, getting something done always depended on such alliances—the people whom one knew, or to whom one was related, nearest the source of true power, which in my country was now the throne and nothing else. If I went home, and if I could stay clear of politics, I might be able to avoid the bureaucracy and achieve the independence I needed to attack our social problems. And if I could do that, I might finally be able to start fulfilling my dream of helping our people achieve a better living standard. I was in my middle thirties now. I longed to return to my family at last and begin my real work, even if that meant keeping quiet and waiting for better times.

In December of 1957, at a dinner party in Baghdad, I was introduced to Abol Hassan Ebtehaj, the honest and forceful economist-banker whom the Shah had recently appointed director of the Plan Organization. Ebtehaj, who loved empty small talk no better than I did, had instantly demanded to know why I was not working in our homeland, for which I liked him immediately. Encouraged by his insistence that I was needed in Iran, I told Julia Henderson that I would not renew my U.N. contract that spring, but would go home to try to introduce my profession to my own country. As for democracy, I could only hope that the years to come would bring more of it. I could do nothing about the lack of freedom and political participation in our country— as a woman, I wasn't even allowed to vote. But perhaps, I thought, once the Shah felt completely secure he would allow more political freedom—if not because he cared for his people's progress, then at least to please his American benefactors.

The following spring I returned to Tehran and, having moved in with Dadash until I could settle down in a house of my own, I began looking around for the right connections to help me. Dadash and several of our brothers agreed that my best chance of success lay in approaching a relative of ours named Hossein Ala—Ala was the minister of court, the official who acted as the king's personal representative.

Luckily, he was also a man I greatly admired. Well over seventy, he was known for his loyalty to the Shah, but he was also a hero to Iranians like me because, as our ambassador to the United Nations at the time the Russians had refused to withdraw from Azerbaijan, he had represented us with dignity and courage. There was a family story that after the aborted attempt to serve Dr. Mossadegh the notice of his removal from office in 1953, this loyal servant of the Crown, at the urging of Dr. Mossadegh himself, had bravely gone to the king and begged him on the premier's behalf and his own not to take the selfish and disgraceful step of fleeing the country and thus abandoning his government and his nation in a crisis. Hossein Ala's daughter, Iran, was married to our nephew Eskander, a son of one of Shazdeh's two remaining elder sons; in addition, Mr. Ala himself had been a close friend of Shazdeh's.

To my joy, I found that I had knocked at an open door. The court minister gave me his undivided attention and sponsored me before the council that supervised Iran's social welfare agencies, a council whose chairman he was. I was authorized to start a training school, the Tehran School of Social Work. It would be independent of the government and the university system but accredited by the ministry of higher education. I was given an eminent board of trustees made up of some of the most important ministers and officials. Whoever was court minister would be the board's chairman, and I would be responsible to him and the trustees alone.

I was jubilant. As the director of an independent professional school, I could run my institution as I liked, while my board would give me the influence I needed to get things done without depending on politics, the imperial court, or a government bureaucracy in which jealousy and timidity always smothered new ideas at birth. At last, after all these years, I had what I needed to begin!

I was starting, however, with little more than the government's good wishes and a small monthly stipend. There wasn't even a Persian word for "social worker," so I invented one, coining the term *madadkar*, meaning "one who helps."

The task facing the "madadkar" was virtually unlimited. Iran's future social workers would have to deal with all kinds of immediate and urgent problems—find ways to teach job skills and literacy to men and women; help the sick and disabled to get the health care and medicines they needed; show people how to clean their streets; teach women to care properly for their infants, budget their meager incomes, and manage the size of their families; and even locate experts to travel to distant communities to teach villagers modern methods of irrigation and agriculture. But these and a hundred other tasks, to which our government had barely begun to pay attention or had never thought of doing, would be only the starting point. I myself didn't know all the things that families and communities would need from us, because there were no textbooks to tell me or my students what Iranians required from a profession that had never existed among us. I did know, however, that if we were to have the slightest chance of success, I must begin by finding the right people to train.

The old house I had rented on Takhteh-Jamshid Avenue in North Tehran contained only a living room with my office—a small alcove overlooking the garden—a dining room, a basement with laundry and shower facilities and a kitchen for cooking the students' lunches, and a couple of upstairs bedrooms. The last, with the help of donations from my family and a married friend named Forouq, who was assisting me as a volunteer office manager, I had converted into two classrooms that would hold scarcely more than twenty students.

Since I was offering two years of free higher education and a guaranteed, salaried position with the respected status of a professional if they graduated with our diploma, I had to be careful to pick men and women who would not be attracted merely by these inducements alone—which, in a poor country like mine, were considerable. A madadkar had to be a person whom I could teach to believe in something more than just himself and the future of his family, and I could not afford to squander our resources on anyone uncommitted or opportunistic. However, I was sure that if I just convinced my recruits that I myself was sincere and determined, by following my example they would learn to trust themselves and each other, and to stick to the job we had to do. Besides, I knew that not many fence-sitters or cynics would want the job I was offering. Social work in Iran wasn't going to be for anyone looking for a soft life.

I had organized a demanding curriculum for my apprentices. Upon completing a six-week orientation period, they had to attend classes and field practice six days a week for two years, with more fieldwork during the summer. I was requiring them to study numerous subjects: planning a family's diet, hygiene, first aid, human physical development and reproduction, family finances, and social and individual psychology. (There were no courses in psychotherapy, a subject of exceedingly limited use to social workers in the developing nations of the world, whose inhabitants are mainly concerned with surviving from one day to the next.)

I also believed that learning the principle of responsibility to the community was as important a part of a madadkar's training as professional skills. Iranian public schools, which Reza Shah had established not to produce discerning members of a free society but to turn out loyal, unquestioning subjects of the Pahlavi dynasty, taught young Iranians only to read, write, and memorize facts, and left their minds untouched. Young Persians learned that unthinking obedience to authority was a virtue, that critical discussion was both rude and dangerous, and that to prosper they must not show initiative but, on the contrary, must attach themselves to an influential mentor. The schools gave them neither trust nor responsibility, nor did students learn, as they do in societies where citizens are accustomed to participation in political decision making, to understand the logic of principles that went beyond personal ambition and family. Not only for our work, but for any future that democracy might have in our country, one of the most important tasks the School of Social Work would have would be educating Iranians to place loyalty to the community and helping strangers above their own comfort and interests.

To increase their understanding and love of our country, therefore, I was making them take courses in Iranian history and in Persian philosophy and culture. To equip them for the thoughtful, careful analysis necessary to examine social problems and write the studies that would serve as the basis for the legislation and the reforms we would have to fight for, they would study sociology, logic, statistics, research methods, Persian composition, and English, the main language of the literature in our field, without which they would have no access to the knowledge and ideas of colleagues in other countries. Finally, to help poor clients with legal problems, as well as to decide what legislation we should advocate and how best to promote it, they would need a working knowledge of government, political science, and our legal system.

Finding teachers for all these courses on my small stipend had not

Shazdeh as an officer at the Austrian Military Academy, Tehran.

Aghajun, Satti's maternal grandfather.

Shazdeh around the time of his marriage to Satti's mother in 1911, with some younger relatives and friends. At far right is Hadji Doktur Khan; the young man to Shazdeh's left is his nephew Mohammed Mossadegh.

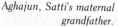

Shazdeh, at age fifty-seven, as governor-general of Fars Province during World War One.

*Some of Shazdeh's military staff, ca. 1907. The tall soldier in the
back row is Shazdeh's gunnery sergeant, Reza Khan, who later
became Reza Shah Pahlavi.*

*Shazdeh, at age sixty-six, with Satti (front row, second from left)
and some of the boys at a Friday inspection in his room.*

A summer outing in Shemiran. Seated in the back row are Satti's stepmother Fatimeh (far left), and Mashti and Khanom (center). In the foreground are Mashti's wife Korsum (at left) and stepmother Batul (at right).

Dr. and Mrs. Samuel M. Jordan in the 1930s, standing before their house in Tehran.

Satti, far right, as a bridesmaid at Jaby's wedding, 1935.

Nosratdoleh, Shazdeh, and Shazdeh's youngest son, Abdol Ali, at Jaby's wedding.

With some American friends and a tennis racket at USC in 1946.

Working at her desk at the Tehran School of Social Work in its early years.

As dame d'honneur, *with Jawaharlal Nehru, 1962.*

Satti with her mother in Khanom's garden.

Batul, Khanom, Jaby, and Fatimeh on an outing in Tehran.

Satti, flanked by two U.N. consultants in the second row, with members of the School's first class.

Dr. Mohammed Mossadegh in the early 1960s, under house arrest in his garden at Ahmadabad.

Satti and her eleven sisters.

RIGHT AND BELOW:
December 1978:
Revolutionaries who forced
their way into the School.

At Reswanieh: in Dadash's
rose garden for the last time.

been easy, but I had managed to scrape together a part-time faculty from Tehran University and the teachers' training college. My family, who enthusiastically supported what I was doing and had already come to my rescue with many donations of money, furniture, curtains, and other items we needed, proved a godsend. Twelve of my brothers now had Ph.D.s, and Fatimeh-Khanom's son Hafez, a professor of history at the University who had studied at Stanford, volunteered to teach my Persian history and culture course for free, while my brother Alah Verdi, a son of Hamdam-Khanom who also had a doctorate from Stanford and taught physiology at the University, was teaching the physical development and first aid course. Ghaffar's wife Jahan, whom my brother had met when he was studying engineering at Berkeley, was teaching the students to read English, and my sister Homy, whom my mother had sent to college in England, was translating articles about social work from English into Persian so that the students could begin reading professional literature right away.

Where to find trained social workers to help supervise the students' fieldwork almost stumped me. I had started organizing the School too late for Julia Henderson to send me any U.N. consultants for our opening year. However, again I was lucky: two American women in Tehran happened to have M.S.W.s, as did the program director of "the Joint," as it was known (the name was short for the International Joint Distribution Committee in Iran, the American Jewish war refugee organization that now served Iran's Jewish poor). When they heard what I was doing, all three volunteered to serve without pay as field supervisors. I gave thanks every night in my prayers for the kindness of these unselfish Americans, as well as for the generosity of my family and many friends who were helping us get off the ground.

We couldn't be a school if we didn't have a library. I had no money left for books, but I assembled all my old social work texts and the pamphlets I had collected in graduate school, borrowed fifty volumes on statistics, law, government, and public health from the University library, and lined everything up on some bookshelves in the room outside my alcove. It didn't look much like a library yet, but in the middle I placed a big dining table and twelve chairs that my mother had donated. Then I wrote to every social worker I knew and to all the booksellers and publishers of Tehran, begging them to donate publications of any kind. Gradually, books began trickling in: research studies in English from other schools of social work in the Middle East, as well as in India, Great Britain, and the United States; works on Iran; even Persian translations of Zola, Balzac, and Flaubert—not to mention a complete set of the works of Charles Dickens in Persian. Arlien Johnson, who was retiring as dean of the USC school, sent me her entire professional library, a gift that moved me deeply.

I had admitted about thirty of the forty men and women who had applied, all people in their early twenties, but fewer had appeared on the first day. As I required, they were all over twenty-one; the men had all performed their two years of military service and had held jobs of one sort or another, while the women, who were all the daughters of teachers, prosperous businessmen, and other educated people—no uneducated family, of course, would have encouraged a daughter to study a profession—were fashionably dressed, modern girls, eager to begin our work. Several minority students were among the candidates I had admitted—an Armenian and a Zoroastrian boy, and a Jewish and a Bahai girl. I was especially pleased by this. I wanted the Tehran School of Social Work to be an institution known for accepting and serving all Iranians, not just Moslems.

First, though, I would have to get my students to accept one another. Unlike the middle-class women, the young men were all from simple, working-class families, mostly in South Tehran. They kept their faces piously unshaven and often wore shabby suits and ties that were soiled and smelly. They were, in fact, precisely the kind of male student I was looking for: boys who, while anxious to better themselves, some-how felt drawn to a profession that promised to alleviate miseries they saw every day, often in their own lives. But at present they and the girls mixed about as easily as oil and water.

Far more than any young man from North Tehran, these boys were shocked to find themselves in a roomful of women—as aghast as the girls were at their male colleagues' scruffy, old-fashioned appearance. They would not sit near the women, nor would the women sit near them, and both groups carefully avoided looking at each other. The shyest boy, a husky farmer's son named Zamani who had come by bus all the way from a small provincial town near Qom to study at the School, cowered in the back, not daring to utter a word. Only one youth, a cheerful, curly-haired student named Kia, the son of a bazaar tailor, had the confidence to look at me instead of lowering his eyes gravely to the floor. Remembering my own shame in the presence of strange men on my first day in an American university, I sympathized. For the moment, there was little I could do to overcome this kind of mistrust.

I started by trying to teach the students other ways of seeing them-selves, and me. To encourage independence and initiative, I explained that I would expect them to contribute their views to our discussions—

something unknown in Persian schools—and would always give them absolute freedom to come and tell me whenever they had an idea for running our school in a better way. Not all criticism, I said, was rude and disrespectful, and I wanted them to become accustomed to developing their own ideas about how to help our people. My office door, I said, would never be locked, and I was always ready to hear their difficulties and complaints. If we were going to solve our nation's problems, we had to be able to talk about them without fear.

To establish more ease and trust between us, I also ran my classes according to the honor code. Naturally, at first the students believed neither the honor code nor my invitation to speak openly, but concluded that I was setting a trap to test them—which, in the schools they had attended, would not have been an unreasonable assumption. The first time I left them alone for an exam, saying that I was trusting them not to cheat, the curly-haired Kia had asked daringly, "With respect, Khanom, you won't even look through the keyhole?" When I showed them the library, whose books I said they could take home so long as they returned them, most of the students, who had never seen a library before, were astounded and asked me what was to prevent someone from stealing the books and selling them for food or rent money?

I replied that social workers could not work together unless they considered others' needs and not just their own. Their tuition and lunches were free, I said, and we could set up a common fund with money contributed by donors (for the moment these "donors" consisted of me, my family, and friends) for students who had financial emergencies, as well as for their fieldwork expenses, such as transportation and minor purchases to assist needy clients and their families. I would not require them to produce receipts for these expenses or prove that an emergency existed, and would simply assume that a student or client was speaking the truth. A madadkar, I said, always accepted the good faith of others unless and until there was reason to believe others unworthy of trust. Trust, I explained, was essential for accomplishing our goals. For this very reason, I added, if a madadkar ever betrayed a trust, I would counsel him to seek a different occupation as soon as possible.

I also insisted that men wear jackets and ties during field practice, and women long sleeves, skirts, and kerchiefs when they visited someone's home, which was how I myself dressed when in the field. A dress code, I explained, together with dignified and proper behavior on all occasions, would persuade strangers who did not know us, especially traditional people, that we were not callow young persons whose lack of gray hairs made our advice unworthy of respect, but serious men and women.

It was particularly important, I added, that a madadkar never under any circumstances accept "gifts" for helping people, or anything more than a cup of tea for hospitality's sake. This was the most fundamental rule of what was known as "professionalism." Taking bribes, I said, was not only dishonest but unprofessional: if we behaved like government officials or gendarmes, our clients wouldn't trust us because they would see that we were thinking only of ourselves and were not sincere when we said we wanted to help them. Therefore, if anyone violated this rule even once, I would instantly dismiss that person from the School and bar him or her from our profession forever.

I also told the students that social workers never refused to help because they didn't like someone's political views. We were society's physicians as doctors were physicians of the body, and like them we were politically neutral. Our sole concern was to learn how to help our people and humanity. For this reason the School of Social Work would never concern itself with politics, neither our own government's nor any other's. Nor did the religion or ethnic origin of others matter to us. We could not make progress by thinking in the closed-minded, dogmatic ways of ignorant people who feared anything new and different—if we did, how could we persuade our clients that learning new ways was to their advantage? A madadkar, I said, not only accepted people of the opposite sex as equals but individuals of every religion, ethnic group, and nationality. Then I told the students that as their first in-class assignment, I would ask our four colleagues from religious minorities to report to us about their beliefs and customs—and I expected, I added sharply, to hear plenty of questions from the rest of them. I would also invite representatives from the communities of the Christians, the Jews, and the Zoroastrians, so that we could learn more about these faiths.

In a short time the students had begun to accept their minority colleagues, and after a few weeks of adjusting to their new environment they also started growing more comfortable about offering "Khanom" their opinions. Men and women even began showing signs of reconsidering their complete avoidance of one another. Although they still did not converse socially and clustered separately in the dining room and the library, they were at least beginning to talk to each other in class.

The often shocking experiences of orientation were also helping to break down such barriers. I was taking everyone on visits to places of the sort they would work in, and much of what we saw was upsetting:

a dark factory filled with sick men laboring long hours, an overburdened public hospital, several city institutions for the needy, and some impoverished rural villages in the farming area of Varamin south of Tehran, whose elders and mullahs had uneasily agreed to accept some students to help with the villagers' problems. During this time several students had second thoughts and dropped out, leaving me only twenty in all. But those who remained were drawn closer by their passionate new desire to help the people we saw. These mostly city-bred students were also excited about their first real venture outside their own Tehran neighborhoods. They were fascinated not only by the colorful dress and picturesque customs of the villagers, but by the dignity and proud self-sufficiency of people who lived without electricity, running water, or medical care.

I remembered the villagers and nomads I had seen on my way to India, and realized that my students were discovering the same pride I had felt in the hardiness and adaptability that had made Iranians able to survive centuries of isolation, oppression, and natural disasters. No longer, I thought, would these young Persians think of themselves only as members of one family or clan, or as people from a certain town or tribe, or merely as subjects of the Shah. In their minds and hearts, they were also becoming citizens of a nation.

Early in November, at the end of the orientation period, we began fieldwork. I was anxious about this critical phase. The students' success in field practice and the impression they made on administrators who had never heard of social workers would be important in convincing Hossein Ala and my board of trustees that their enthusiasm and the government's small investment in the Tehran School of Social Work had not been a mistake.

In addition, I was nervous about the impact of field practice on the students themselves. Although many of the boys from South Tehran had known some degree of deprivation, none of the students, except perhaps the country lad, Zamani, had seen the kind of wretchedness all would encounter every time they went to the rural areas or the worst of the slums. Some of Tehran's institutions for the poor were literally no more than warehouses for unwanted human beings; their directors were not professionals but corrupt, tyrannical bureaucrats. City officials ignored these administrators, letting them run their domains like little satrapies. There, my students would be working with the most abject and abused people in our society.

This had already become clear to everyone during visits to two institutions that had shocked and horrified not only the students but even me, who in four years of social work in the Middle East had seen many shocking things. At the decaying city mental asylum, whose ragged, filthy inhabitants were cared for not by any doctors but by thuggish warders, the most troublesome inmates were chained in light-less basement cells that had not been cleaned for years. Even more horrifying, if possible, was a city orphanage on a large former farm in Aminabad, a village south of the capital. Here about three hundred abandoned children, from newborns to twelve-year-old girls, were put out of sight and mind, entrusted to illiterate, often brutal men and women who had been arrested for begging or prostitution and sent to work among these parentless and despised children in lieu of going to jail. In one of the dormitories, which were actually old farm store-houses, we had found dozens of silent, emaciated babies and tiny children sprawling on the floor. Thanks to the ignorance or indifference of their "nurses" and the orphanage administrator, they were so stunted from malnutrition and neglect that instead of walking they could only crawl.

These revelations had made us all sick with pity, disgust, and an-ger—not only me, the students, faculty, and my friend Forouq, but also our servants: a middle-aged couple named Mahmad and Motaram who were our caretakers, a poor woman named Zara, whom I had hired as a housekeeper, and Hossein, a young man who was now proudly in charge of our sole official vehicle, a battered Jeep station wagon loaned to me by the labor ministry. The day after the visit to the mental asylum, a young woman named Shala had come to my office in tears, asking, "Khanom, is *this* my country? Is this social work, all those miserable men not half an hour from my house? I can't stand to see any more—I came to say goodbye."

I was already afraid that many more students would leave before we had even begun, and I could not afford to lose Shala, a beautiful, intelligent, warmhearted girl whose father owned a textile factory, and of whom I had high hopes. But seeing the children had given me nightmares, and instead of trying to persuade her by reasoning with her, I exploded with my own anger at their plight. Did Shala, I demanded, think that quitting would help the people we had seen? "You are a young, healthy woman," I cried, "and from a good family. If we work hard and stick with our job we can *change* these things—stay and show what you, an Iranian woman, can do for this country!" She had gone home anyway, leaving me fuming and telling my broth-ers Hafez and Alah Verdi that the foreigners had been right when they had said after Mossadegh took over that we could never run an oil industry; we Iranians weren't even fit to clean up our own country!

We were all like Mashti, making excuses and telling ourselves we couldn't do anything and imagining that somebody stronger was going to come and take care of our problems—like the babies we had seen at the orphanage, who had never been taught to walk and didn't even know that God had given them legs!

Fortunately, the next day Shala came back, red-eyed and exhausted but saying that she wanted to be a madadkar after all. Her father, a devout Moslem, had found her crying in her room and urged her to return. Koran, he said, wanted us to help those weaker than ourselves, and if people like his daughter didn't save such human beings, who was going to? I was relieved at her return, but I was afraid that the strains of field practice might prove to be more than some of my twenty remaining students could tolerate. I knew from experience that my apprentices wouldn't see quick results. I badly wanted to do something about the orphanage and the asylum, but that was out of the question until impetuous recruits like Shala had a month or two of experience under their belts.

I had arranged for field placements mostly in Tehran itself, and in institutions where I had friends or knew people. Urban institutions could accommodate both men and women field-workers, but I could send only men, and Moslems, to villages, whose inhabitants would assume that any young woman I sent to work among them was a prostitute, and whose mullahs would never have allowed them to accept an Armenian or a Zoroastrian. Even sending Moslem men, in fact, was tricky, because the villagers would all be waiting for these young city slickers to steal someone's ox or try to corrupt his wife or daughter.

Drawing on my U.N. experience, I told the boys to just be helpful in whatever ways they could, and to have patience. If someone's roof needed fixing, they should offer to help. If somebody's children needed shoes in order to walk to school, they should get money from our fund for this. "Don't force your suggestions on people," I told them, "even if what you are learning in your classes makes you want to. Instead, first win everyone's trust with your virtuous behavior and humility, and by showing respect for the elders and for religion. Gradually the villagers will listen to your suggestions for purifying the water or cleaning the streets, and you will be able to show them that if they organize and cooperate with each other, they themselves can do something about their problems."

From working in Iraq, where the population is more than half Shi'a, I also knew that the first thing the students must do was go to the village mullah. Some mullahs, I explained to the boys, would welcome their help, while others would be suspicious and say that God meant villagers to suffer and live in the dirt, and that to question this was impious. If that happened, I said, they must not protest, because this would only make the mullah angry, and then he would go around telling everyone that they were government spies or tax collectors.

"Instead," I went on, "do all you can to win him over. If his wife needs medicine, bring it next time you come; if his daughter is about to give birth, arrange for transportation to take her to the maternity hospital in the city. Sooner or later the villagers will see that the holy man is taking favors from you and they will have to conclude that he doesn't think you are a spy or a tax collector. And if anyone says that it is impious to change the custom by cleaning the street or spraying the apple trees for worms, respectfully reply with the old saying, 'Help yourself, and God will help you twice.' Eventually, you will accomplish something."

The rest of the students all went to city institutions: the overcrowded public hospital at the University; Tehran's gigantic maternity hospital; a relatively decent orphanage run by the Red Lion and Sun Society (the Iranian equivalent of the Red Cross) for the children of disaster victims; a health clinic at the NIOC for oil workers; and a Jewish children's home and a hospital run by the Joint in the ghetto. Here, their clients would be both the individuals in these places and their families at home.

For a while I had been uncertain about what to do with Zamani, the strapping, tongue-tied rustic who sat in the back of the room. He was a true Iranian villager, generous and compassionate but apt to think with his fists, not his brain. A city placement would smooth his rough edges, but if provoked, he was primitive enough to land both himself and me in a lot of trouble. Finally I sent him to the men's section of the University hospital, where many patients were rural immigrants who would appreciate his blunt, honest simplicity. My apprehension turned out to be well founded. Not many weeks into November, I had a surprise visit from his volunteer supervisor—a gentle, middle-aged medical social worker whose husband was a Fulbright scholar at the University—who told me in great distress that Zamani had become angry at catching two orderlies trying to steal food intended for a patient, and had dragged them out to the hospital garden and beaten them nearly senseless.

I at once telephoned the outraged hospital administrator to apologize, then had Hossein get the station wagon and haul Zamani back to my office, where I asked him as calmly as I could what made him think he could assault those men. Zamani, looking aggrieved, replied virtuously that I was always saying in class that a madadkar must show initiative in thinking of solutions to social problems. Where he came from, beating somebody up was the solution they had for stealing.

It was some moments before I could get control of my face and explain soberly that this wasn't what I had in mind when I told the students to use "initiative." Social workers, I said, were not blown about by their emotions, like immature, illogical people with no education, but used their heads. Perhaps, I pointed out, the orderlies themselves had hungry families at home, and if so, they would only steal again after Zamani beat them, whereas if he talked with them instead of hitting them to find out why they had taken the food, he might be able to solve not only his patient's problem but also theirs and their families'. Solving social problems, I said, meant looking for causes first and solutions second—*constructive* solutions, I added hastily.

Soon I had my hands full trying to keep everyone's enthusiasm from flagging. Two boys whom I had sent to the NIOC's health clinic appeared in my office bruised, frightened, and covered with dirt; a rumor had spread that they were SAVAK informers sent to spy on the oil workers and an angry mob had attacked them at the gate. I worried constantly not only about the physical safety of the boys in the villages but also of the other male students, because if a madadkar became too eager to help the family of a hospital patient or a laborer and visited a client's wife and children without first making sure that a male relative was present, he might be badly beaten.

Hardly an evening passed without a student's appearing in my office to cry on my shoulder. The bright, emotional Shala, whom I had placed at the Joint's hospital in the Jewish ghetto, came all the time to complain that Mr. Seymour, her supervisor, would not let her give her families money and clothing—why couldn't she buy them things with money from our fund, she wailed, instead of limiting herself to finding someone to teach a husband job skills or arranging for a cousin to care for the younger children so that the older ones could go to school? She wanted to do something for people *now*. Everyone else, too, wept and complained about being unable to offer help instantly to unemployed men, sick women, and undernourished children, of overcrowding, of the indifference or impatience of physicians and of corrupt administrators. The students talked often and with angry frustration of the children in Aminabad. The hostility of the director had made me afraid even to try placing field-workers there—although Zamani had offered to go out to the orphanage, learn who was starving those little babies, and turn everybody into crow's meat.

I tried to comfort them and lift their spirits by explaining that we would help people most not with quick solutions like punishments or charity, which would only make them depend on us for alms without solving the causes of their poverty, but by working patiently to help them improve their income and their living conditions themselves. As for the orphanage and the asylum, I said, when the time came, we would help our clients there, too. But real, lasting social change was the product of careful thought. It came not overnight, through violence or revolution, but by educating people. Above all, it came from working as hard as you could and sticking to your job—no matter for how long, and no matter what happened to discourage you.

Toward the end of the first semester I felt that the class had enough experience to begin doing something about the asylum and the orphanage. During our visit to Aminabad, I told them, we had seen several unused buildings. Disturbed people would certainly be better off than they were now in the fresh air and open grounds of this old farm, which contained a large, pleasant garden. Why not transfer the asylum inmates there, find them medical supervision, clean and repair the asylum, and move the youngsters to the city? Then the children would not be far away and we could begin supervising their rehabilitation.

The students were enthusiastic, so I said that, since our first task would be persuading the city to back us, I would take this plan to the mayor of Tehran, who was a member of the School's board.

The name of the mayor at that moment—in Iran, high government officials were usually the Shah's appointees, and they came and went like the flowers of April—was Musa Moham. He was on my board, but I didn't know anything about him, except that neither he nor any of his predecessors had ever set foot in a single city institution for the poor, and that he had never come to a board meeting. A day or so later, I went to his grand office at the City Hall. The room was full of clerks and rows of men waiting with petitions along the walls. What I saw looked unpromising. Moham was about sixty-five, bald and fat, with an unhealthy pallor. He had the look, at least, of a true Persian politician: someone who, dispensing favors from behind a huge desk with a lot of papers on it, seemed unlikely to feel under any urgent compulsion to pay attention to human beings in whom he had no direct interest. I wondered how I was going to get him to listen to me.

However, I got straight to the point. Moham clearly had no idea who I was, so I introduced myself and said politely that I and the students of my school had discovered that certain social institutions for which he was responsible were in an appalling state—a fact of which I was sure he had not been informed, for the city was paying a substantial amount of money for their upkeep and he would certainly want to help us rectify the situation.

The mayor stared at me with incomprehension. "What institutions?" he asked blankly.

"For instance, Agha, the municipal home for small children in Aminabad, which you have never honored with a visit. Ah," I sighed as though the thought had just entered my head, "how I wish that you could see these children yourself! Then," I said sweetly, trying to soak the trap I was setting in as much honey as I could, "the subject would mean so much more to you."

Moham nodded amiably. "Certainly," he said, "I will go and see them sometime." Then he began signing papers on his desk. I sat stubbornly where I was, saying nothing. After a minute he looked up, startled that I was still there.

"Why can't you go tomorrow morning?" I demanded.

An odd expression crept across the mayor's face. For a moment he was silent, uncertain whether to be annoyed or curious at the odd spectacle of an evidently well-bred woman refusing to leave when a man told her to. Then a slow gleam of interest appeared in his eye. "Very well," he said magnanimously, "I'll go tomorrow morning."

This was a promise I was not about to leave to its own devices. "Good," I said, "I'll go, too—I have business there tomorrow. Can I accompany you?"

Realizing that he had been outwitted, he scowled but saw that he couldn't back out. "Come back here at ten tomorrow," he answered sulkily. "I'll take you in one of my limousines."

"Oh, no, Agha," I said, "I will take *you*, in my Volkswagen. If you really want to do something for these children, you will go with me alone, without a fancy retinue to tell the whole city you are going to Aminabad, so that your director has time to tidy things up. I want this to be a big surprise."

He was so irritated at my ruse that I half-expected him not to show up, but the next morning when Hossein and I arrived he was waiting as he had promised. At Aminabad the gatekeeper ran to notify the office of our arrival and the director, followed by several flunkies, hurried out amid cries of, "The mayor is here!" Moham, who to my surprise had listened with melancholy attention on the journey from the city as I recounted what we had seen on the earlier visit, said that he wanted to inspect the children's quarters. Glaring at me, the director complied, and we were escorted first to a dormitory for little boys who were so thin that their arms and wrists looked like twigs dangling from the sleeves of their gray uniforms. Then we went to the hall where the students and I had seen the infants. About forty of them sprawled before us now on a thin kilim rug—the babies trying to crawl about on shrunken limbs while the toddlers sat and rocked back and forth, staring into space like miniature old people with huge eyes sunk deep in bony little faces, heads gigantic above the skeletal frames and grotesquely protruding bellies of famished children.

Even for me, seeing this again was like a blow. Holding back my tears, I turned to look at the mayor and saw with alarm that his fleshy neck and bald head had gone crimson. For several long moments he stood, rigid with shock, gaping at the starving infants. Then he reached up and began beating his head in disbelief and anguish. Tears coursed down his sagging cheeks. He made no sound, but rocked back and forth like the children, smiting his head again and again. I was petrified. I saw that Moham had truly had no notion of how these places were run and was overcome not only with shock but shame. I had dragged this poor old man out here and forced him to confront his failure; what would I do if he had a heart attack or a stroke?

At last the mayor recovered his self-possession and mopped his face with a big white handerchief. Hastily I suggested that we return to the city. At first, as we drove along, Moham sat moodily, saying nothing. However, when I told him our plan and explained how, with his backing, my students and I could help the children, he swore that we would have all we needed. I pointed out that the two directors would be very angry and that I feared for the physical safety of my students, but Moham promised that he would frighten them into leaving us alone and letting us help our clients.

The following day I assigned Hossein to take two women students to Aminabad to assist a medical doctor and some nurses who were coming to examine the children while the rest of us began the transfer of the asylum inmates to Aminabad. Within a few days Moham's office had located a woman nutritionist assigned by the U.N. Food and Agriculture Organization to the Iranian government. She agreed to move into the orphanage at once with several assistants until the babies had gained enough weight to be moved, and I placed an ad in the newspapers inviting women who had at least an elementary school education and who were fond of children to apply for a free training program in modern child care that the School would give them. Upon completing it they would have a steady job and the official title of "Mother" to the children whose new home we were preparing.

Cleaning and fixing up the asylum took nearly three months. I went every day to supervise the work. All twenty of the students came whenever they were not in class or at field practice, and even the healthier inmates pitched in when they heard what we wanted to do for the children. The worst work was in the basement, where the violent ones had lain in small cells whose floors were lined with a solid cover of rock-hard dirt and excrement a foot thick. At first we nearly despaired, but after a few days someone came to our rescue: a dedicated Persian-Jewish sanitation engineer named Nasser Sumech, who had been trained in London and now worked for the Joint. Mr. Sumech and two other men from the Joint came every afternoon to soak the floor in gallons of liquid disinfectant, which they let stand overnight; then they would come back the next morning with shovels to clean out the muck. The stench was so horrible that I thought I would lose every one of my recruits, but when Zamani, Kia, and the other men saw what the Jewish volunteers were willing to do, they too waded in with boots and shovels, then washed down the cells with soap and water until the monstrous thing that had been there was gone and the building was fit for the children to inhabit.

Meanwhile, upstairs, our women field-workers and Forouq scrubbed, painted, and scoured until the whole place was spotless. Everyone's friends and relatives donated new rugs for the floors, pictures for the walls, and curtains for the windows, and when masons whom Moham sent had finished repairing the crumbling courtyard, the students and our caretaker Mahmad planted trees and flowers in it for the children. In the spring we moved them into their new home. As yet, Moham had no one to replace the orphanage's director, but he had found a qualified neuropsychiatrist at the University, a Dr. Nezam, to run the new asylum at Aminabad, and we replaced the children's incompetent nurses and keepers with the kindly "mothers" we had trained.

I had hoped that once the children were in the city we would be able to locate some of their relatives, but unfortunately the orphanage had kept no records, and most of the children had been brought to Aminabad too young to know their names or families. This was an enormous problem, because without names and birth certificates we couldn't send any of them to school in the fall. In addition, without a known father or mother the girls would be unmarriageable. The most shocking aspect of this anonymity was that their sullen keepers, who had resented having to serve in Aminabad, had contemptuously bestowed on them the names of animals, so that the children knew themselves only as "Rabbit," "Dog," or "Rat." We had also discovered that besides suffering from lice, stomach worms, tuberculosis, trachoma, and every other disease of dirt, malnutrition, and neglect, the children had been permitted neither to play nor to talk, and most literally did not know how to do either.

The suffering of these children kept me awake for many long nights. I remembered how Shazdeh had always taken care of every child in our compound, whether his own or another's. To him, every individual had been important—God, my father always said, had a place for everyone. But because those who ran our country ignored the welfare of human beings, these children had been turned into animals.

As soon as they were settled, therefore, I arranged for the state registry bureau to work with us to devise an identity for every single child, and for two whole months the registry officials sat at a table in the garden writing up birth certificates, with a doctor examining the children's teeth and determining their approximate ages. Then, for every boy and girl, our students would invent a father, a mother, and a birthday. Thus "Dog" became "Abbas, four years old, son of Sakineh and Hassan," and "Rat" became "Leila, seven, daughter of Robab and Ali." By midsummer, every child had an age, a name, and parents, and the students and I knew that from then on, no matter what happened, the children of Aminabad could prove that God had meant them to have a family. They, at least, would not have to go through life thinking that they were nobody.

Success had altered my students, too. What we had been through together at the asylum had swept away their remaining shyness, and all of us had come to feel like one family. At school men and women now talked and joked among themselves like cousins and treated each other as comrades. They no longer sat apart, and took great pride in what they had achieved.

Kia had played a major role in this new ease and confidence. During the worst of the cleanup he had joked continually, keeping up everyone's spirits and even working up a comic little routine in which he pretended to be Moham trying to climb into my little Volkswagen. In the end he had charmed the girls out of their snobbishness toward the other working-class boys, while the boys, seeing that Kia was not afraid to talk to their female colleagues, had gradually begun to follow his lead. The men's hygiene was also improving markedly—as part of our dress code I insisted that anyone who didn't have running water at home use our basement showers and laundry facilities once a week, and I noticed now that they often consulted Kia, the tailor's son, for hints on grooming. All the students were now very conscious of "professionalism" and of maintaining our high standards, and I took great pleasure in being in charge of such clean, competent, modern young social workers. More than anything it was a joy for me that year and the next to watch this expansion of my students' confidence as they discovered that they could accomplish things of which only a short time before they would not have dreamed themselves capable. This was important because the first classes would serve as models for those that followed—and indeed, later classes nicknamed the first two "the Bulldozers."

In our second year my faculty shortage eased a bit. Julia Henderson was sending me temporary teachers and supervisors and the American Fulbright Commission was providing us with foreign scholars to teach the students how to do social research so that we could begin determining what kinds of social programs Iranians needed. I was now devoting much time and energy to arranging for positions for the students after they graduated. I had already worked out an excellent wage and benefits scale with the Iranian civil service that would give the madadkar the financial security and prestige of a professional: by law, our graduates would automatically receive salaries and benefits that ranked just above a high school teacher's, a position which carried considerable status in our society. But there was still the tedious task (infinitely more exhausting, I thought, than working in a slum) of convincing scores of skeptical and distrustful administrators, provincial officials, business executives, and assorted bureaucrats to give social work a chance and hire a "director of social services" for their institution, provincial administration, or factory.

Right in the middle of this drudgery, something happened to infuriate me: several indignant students came to me with the news that both the city government and one of the charitable societies sponsored by the royal family—our country's equivalent of a private welfare organization—were starting "social work schools" of their own. These entities were letting it be known that they would turn anybody into a social worker with just a few weeks of training. This so-called "professional," presumably, could then expect to receive the same rewards as *my* well-trained graduates!

I was as angry as I have ever been in my life. All this time my students and I were killing ourselves to establish the highest possible standards for our profession, and now that word was circulating that Khanom Farman Farmaian was arranging for her people to have good salaries and titles like "Director" (we Persians always crave titles like "Director"), everybody wanted to climb up into the tree and feather his nest—after I had collected the straw!

This mimicry, I knew, was an example of a love of imitation for which Persians are famous throughout the Middle East—and which is a product, in turn, of our famous Persian survival instinct. It made me think of a little story my mother used to tell us about how Hadji the Pilgrim found a treasure on his way back from Mecca. As he was returning home, weary and thirsty after long months of hardship and danger in the wilderness, a fellow who had been sitting by the road when he had set out noticed the newly rich man's caravan coming back and said, "Hey, I'm very impressed with your success! I'm joining up with you." "But all this time you just sat in the desert doing nothing," said Hadji. "What have you done to be part of this?" Replied the new follower: "Didn't fate set me here, in the path of a winner? I'm with you—I'm going to be wealthy and successful, too!"

Fortunately, here was an instance in which my connections served me well: I at once put a stop to these enterprising new "schools" by arranging for the justice minister to have a law passed defining a madadkar exclusively as someone who had studied at an accredited school of social work, whether in our country or elsewhere. After that I received no more reports of imitation schools of social work. We Iranians, I reflected irritably, were nothing but opportunists—mere parrots, always watching for the main chance! And I made myself a solemn promise that no matter how large or successful we became, I would never lower my standards for any reason, nor allow anything to distract me from the work of building the School and advancing its reputation with the very best candidates available: sincere, unselfish, dedicated men and women—people who were loyal and devoted; people like the ones I had now.

By the end of our second academic year I had arranged for good salaries and positions for the first year's class, and in June of 1960 we held our first commencement.

Normally, nobody was allowed to shine in public except the Shah, his ministers, and the royal family, but I wanted to make certain that for just one day in their careers, my hardworking students got all the public honor they deserved. I decided to entrust all the speechmaking to them, save for a one-sentence introduction from me, a benediction by the dean of theology at the University, Professor Meshkat, and a speech by Hossein Ala, our guest of honor. I printed the program with the name of every person on our staff, from the faculty and our volunteer professionals right down to our servants. Since several students had written up their research on the problems of villagers, I had their reports printed for the guests—I wanted everyone to know what we were doing, and to see how diligent and thorough my students' work was.

To ensure a large and distinguished gathering, I sent invitations to every board and council member and government dignitary I knew, as well as to people like Abol Hassan Ebtehaj—who by that time was no longer the head of the Plan Organization but who had warmly supported the School from the start—and to everyone else I knew in good society, including all my family and personal friends. On the day of the ceremony, our garden, filled with Mahmad's June roses, was packed with officials, from the ministers on my board to foreign ambassadors who were my friends or my family's.

I don't believe I have ever been prouder than I was on that day. As students like Zamani, Shala, and Kia stood before the eyes of all their relatives and basked in the limelight, I was certain that never before in Persian history had so many distinguished personages sat respectfully for a whole hour to applaud the sons and daughters of common shopkeepers, small factory owners, craftsmen, and peasant farmers—people whose fathers they had never heard of! Never before had average young men and women and their happy families come to a reception and shaken hands with so many government directors, ministers, and ambassadors, or had their pictures taken with them. Best of all, when I saw the papers the next day, there were my students, smiling excitedly behind a beaming Hossein Ala. Seeing their pride and delight and that of their families, I decided that I would always make our commencements exactly like this one.

Needless to say, I had also extended an invitation to Musa Moham. He had retired as mayor, but before doing so had succeeded in replacing the orphanage's corrupt director with a man named Ahour, who had a degree in education from the University (and who afterward proved to be an able, dedicated administrator). Moham had toured the new children's home the moment it was ready. When he saw the boys and girls dressed in clean clothes, playing in the garden with their "mothers," I thought he would burst out dancing and singing. While still in office he had called me at least once a week, asking, "Is there anything you or your students need? Is there anything I can do for you?"

Indeed, like a number of government officials I had come to know well because of their support for our work, Moham had become a good friend, and often confided to me what he was thinking. As it was considered unsafe for any Iranian politician to say what he really thought to anyone outside his family—even in those days everyone was scared to death of SAVAK—I was always touched and honored by this trust.

One day around the time of our first commencement, as we were talking about the country's countless problems, Moham suddenly leaned forward. "You know," he said in a low voice, "we are all standing on a bridge over nothing."

A little puzzled, but speaking respectfully because of his age, I asked what he meant. "I mean," he said, almost in a whisper, "that our society is a bridge without foundations. There is no justice and everyone is only for himself and the future of his family. I don't know how we have survived until now. How will it end? It's a miracle that we're still here, that the bridge hasn't fallen down."

I was baffled by the ominous sound of this. I certainly didn't like our politics, but what my friend was implying surprised even me. The Shah had the army, SAVAK, and the all-important favor of the Americans. He had vanquished or tamed all his opponents. Who on earth was going to throw out the Pahlavis? Needless to say, I would have been the last to deny that the government was shamefully indifferent to human welfare, or that the absence of any political voice for millions of people was a tragedy for everyone. But it seemed to me that the political state of the country nowadays called more for sadness than alarm. And so far as I or anyone could see in this modern, new Iran, the Shah's power was totally secure.

Besides, in my own sphere I was more optimistic than I had ever been in my life. Now that the School was growing, I had more field-workers, and we were starting new research projects and lobbying for social legislation to give women and children more legal rights and protections. Within six months of my return we had started the country's first family planning clinic, and during the second year we had lauched programs for the welfare of poor prisoners, their families, and imprisoned juveniles, and made headway toward improving conditions in the prostitutes' quarter and the state workhouses, which I planned to transform from prisons for the destitute into trade schools. At Amin-abad, Dr. Nezam had installed a staff of trained nurses and the patients there had started a truck farm. At the home in the city the school-age children were doing well and the babies had achieved normal health and growth. The dedicated FAO nutritionist who had nursed them had even presented us with a photo album she had compiled of the infants' progress. After observing the students' joy at this incontrovertible evidence that our problems had practical solutions, I had said to myself, "Here are Iranians who know what we can do in this country if we only try—here are twenty people who believe in something!"

Moham, I decided, was too pessimistic. I had learned that if one only avoided politics, one *could* achieve something constructive, and I was happy now, brimming with faith and hope. The evidence of my own eyes told me that at last time was on our side, and I felt that I had been proven right in coming back. Gradually I would expand the School and educate more young Iranians, Persians who believed in themselves and the good of the nation, in the principles of concern and community, and who, in turn, would teach others to believe. We, Iran's social workers, were going to show our people how to become a truly modern, truly enlightened nation. The madadkar was going to give this country something solid and real. We were building the bridge's foundations.

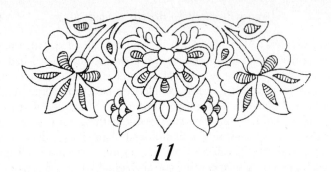

11

TREMORS

*They are dead. They just don't know it. I don't care what
revolution it is. Somebody is going to get those fellows. They are
out. It is just a matter of time.*

—Senator Hubert H. Humphrey, discussing the government
of the Shah of Iran at a meeting of the Senate Foreign
Relations Committee, June 15, 1961

*T*HE SEVEN OR EIGHT YEARS THAT FOLLOWED OUR FIRST COM-
mencement were at once the most satisfying and the most
arduous I had yet known. During this time we launched numerous
pilot services and programs, social research projects, and legislative
drives, especially to improve prison conditions and laws affecting the
legal age of marriage and the welfare of women and children. The
School, of course, could not tackle our country's massive problems of
poverty, overcrowding, and backwardness on a large scale all by itself.
But it could show how to deal with them on a small one. And as we
did it became clear that Iranians, so famous for their mistrust and
cynicism, welcomed the knowledge that by working together people
could not only solve problems but could create possibilities they had
never imagined might exist for them.

In the spring of 1961, for example, a record-breaking snowmelt in
the Alborz caused a flood that all but destroyed a shantytown called
Javadieh, where thousands of poor villagers from the countryside had

settled. I took a number of students there to help with the relief work. In a short time we had established a day-care center for the victims' children while their families were being resettled, and after a while somebody gave us a small house to make this program permanent, so that our field-workers and some volunteers could begin offering the children's mothers tips on child care. Soon the field-workers were giving rudimentary information about diet, hygiene, and birth control.

Hearing that someone could tell them how to improve their families' lives and their own, hundreds of women began flocking to the day-care center. Soon the students and I were approaching city officials, businessmen, and wealthy individuals about contributions for a full-fledged neighborhood community welfare center, and donations began pouring in. The current mayor gave us an empty lot for a new building. Twenty-two-year-old Queen Farah, the Shah's new wife, who had already visited several of the municipal institutions where we were introducing reforms, saw to it that we received enough money to pay for a full-time professional staff. Owners of construction companies announced that they would provide free of charge the cement, bricks, tiles, and doors the new center needed; merchants supplied furniture, curtains, and kitchen equipment; grocers promised regular contributions of food. Before long, the leaders of adjacent neighborhoods were asking us to build community welfare centers for them, and individuals I barely knew or had never heard of were coming to the School to contribute money, to offer us land or bricks, or to establish stipends to support poor social work students who needed help.

Slowly but steadily my students and graduates were making themselves known for something that was all but unique in our country: complete honesty and a willingness to undertake even hard, dirty jobs to help other human beings. This reputation was enhanced after 1962, when a terrible earthquake leveled communities around the city of Qazvin, northwest of the capital, and my entire student body went to help the rescue workers pull people from the rubble, count the hundreds of dead, tend to the injured and homeless, and care for the orphaned. Shala, Zamani, and many of my other graduates also took leaves of absence from their jobs to go and labor alongside our other volunteers; Zamani remained in one village for an entire year, supervising a reconstruction project funded by a European youth organization headed by Princess Beatrix of the Netherlands, partly to make sure none of the funds would be misappropriated. (Remembering with amusement his initial approach to social problem solving, I was sure they would not be.) I was especially touched when Shala, who was now the head of social services for the girls' section of the orphanage, visited my office after returning from the quake zone to show me a beautiful necklace her father had given her—to show his pride, she said, that she was proving that a woman could serve the country as well as a man.

I never had enough time to do all that needed doing. The families of our graduates were now boasting to their relatives and friends that their kinfolk had good salaries and titles like "Director," and that ministers and even the mother of Queen Farah herself came to our commencement ceremonies. (I had begun inviting Madame Farideh Diba, as she was known, to hand out the diplomas. She was a warm, motherly, wholly unpretentious woman whom the students loved, and who enjoyed eating ice cream with our graduates after the ceremony and having her picture taken with the students as much as they enjoyed being photographed with the mother of the Queen.) In 1962 I inaugurated a four-year program leading to the equivalent of a bachelor's degree, an internationally accredited professional licentiate in social work, and soon we began receiving more applications than I could accept.

I had long since been compelled to hire a secretary; she was a gentle and devoted young woman named Esther, whose Iraqi-Jewish family had been driven out of Baghdad by anti-Semitic persecution there. In addition I had to find many more temporary faculty from other countries to teach the additional courses a four-year program demanded. I was also traveling to conferences elsewhere in the Middle East to present papers on topics like child welfare and women in developing nations, entertaining many foreign professional visitors and former U.N. colleagues, and corresponding with schools of social work and universities in various Middle Eastern countries, India, the Philippines, Europe, and the United States. More than anything, I wanted to be able to staff our school with full-time, permanent, native Iranian social workers, and I was assiduously cultivating these international contacts so that I could send our graduates abroad for advanced training. In addition to my regular tasks at work, I was also now occasionally being required to serve as *dame d'honneur*, or escort, to visiting heads of state, for the Shah's government was eager to show that Iran now had women professionals. In this way I met many interesting and glamorous figures, including Jawaharlal Nehru and his daughter, Indira Gandhi. I was so awed at finding myself talking to the statesman who had led India to independence from England that for once I couldn't say a word until Mr. Nehru, taking pity on me, finally struck up the conversation himself. I was so busy that there were days when I wondered how I would get around to eating or sleeping.

I had settled down in a comfortable two-story house at Tajrish, with a garden, a pool, one womanservant, and a daytime gardener. The house stood surrounded by an iron fence on a dirt road deep inside the old Reswanieh estate, far from the noise of the main thoroughfare and the Tajrish bazaar outside. Except on Fridays, I left for work nearly every day at the crack of dawn or earlier, arrived at school at seven, and didn't return to Tajrish until eight or nine at night.

I had known when I returned in 1958 that I probably would not remarry. For one thing, I could not have carried out the many social duties of an upper-class Iranian wife and still have run the School. There was another compelling reason as well: if I married, sooner or later some enemy—naturally, given the nature of the School's work, we had enemies—would be sure to accuse me of using government connections to advance a husband's business or career interests at Court. If this happened, I could never again tell my students not to accept bribes. Naturally, it went without saying that any personal friendship with an unmarried man who was not my relative was out of the question. Even my innocent and highly public visit to Moham's office and the excursion to Aminabad in my car had not gone unremarked: Dadash had taken me to task for it, pointing out solemnly that in our country a woman could not simply go where she wished and do as she pleased, as in the West. I chafed at his reprimand, but I realized that I must submit to my brother's advice. A scandal, or even an unfounded rumor that I had been seen dancing at a Western-style nightclub, would cost me the credibility of my students and graduates forever. I had chosen the life of a woman alone, and I must accept the consequences.

I did, however, have an active social life. It was like any other Iranian woman's social life, meaning that it took place mostly at the family lunches, dinners, visits, birthdays, engagement parties, weddings, funerals, and thousand other occasions on which Persians reassure themselves that they are still embraced by the all-encompassing walls of the family.

Surrounded once more by people who loved and cared about me, I wondered more than ever how I had lived for ten years without this most essential part of myself, my family. Dadash had recently been sent to Saigon by the World Health Organization to direct its office there, but Farough had come back to Iran with Jean and their children and settled at Tajrish. So had our youngest brother, Rashid, who had started an engineering company with him. Ghaffar and his wife Jahan and my married sisters Homy and Sory lived elsewhere, but Khorshid and her husband had made their home on Shazdeh's old estate, as had four of Fatimeh-Khanom's five sons: Ali-Naghi and Ali-Dad, who had gone to school with me; Kaveh, who had started a telecommunications company with Ghaffar; and Hafez, whose American wife Jody—they had met while Hafez was at Stanford—was a talented artist and made many contributions to the School. Together with me, my stepmother Fatimeh-Khanom, who had lived at Reswanieh ever since the destruction of the compound, and Hamdam-Khanom's son, Khodadad, who also lived at Tajrish with *his* American wife, Joanna, there were now no less than eight Farman Farmaians and their families in this new "compound." Thus I had literally dozens of brothers, sisters, and sisters-in-law to whom I could talk or pour out my troubles whenever I felt the need.

Mitra, who was doing well at her English school, was now in her early teens, a petite, raven-haired, graceful beauty with huge, dark eyes. She was as tranquil and sweet-natured as when she was little. On her visits during the summer she went about everywhere with my brothers and sisters, her grandmother, and her cousins. In August she and I would drive together across the mountains to the Caspian to attend a gigantic family reunion organized by Farough and Homy, where everyone spent two weeks living in tents, talking, swimming, walking on the beach, playing bridge, and watching how their children were growing up. Mitra had become a favorite of the whole family, and Farough and Ghaffar in particular behaved more like her fathers than her uncles. It had been an enormous relief to see that she felt as happy and loved by my brothers as any child could feel by an actual father. Arun and I had not written since the divorce; I considered that chapter in my life utterly closed. I had long ago promised myself that if Mitra ever wished it, one day I would give her the chance to meet him, but I had no desire to hear from him. Rather, I dreamed wistfully of the day when Mitra would come back to Tajrish to live with me permanently.

My own mother was now past sixty. She had moved out of the old "railroad house" on Sepah Avenue the year before my return. In her new home she had begun the practice of holding huge luncheon buffets on Saturdays, the first day of the workweek, for any of Shazdeh's children who wanted to stop by. As she lived not far from school, I lunched with her almost every day. By this time there had been several divorces in the family besides mine, and Khanom now seemed resigned to my unmarried state. While I was certain that she would rather I had remarried, I also knew that she was proud that I had been the first Iranian woman to act as a consultant to a foreign government, and she doted on Mitra. Only once had she inquired, with seeming casualness, about my husband's religion. I had replied cheerfully that we had "shared the same beliefs," and my mother, with equal tact, had never mentioned Arun again.

I had never seen her so good-humored and satisfied with life. She occupied her days with tea and family gossip and shopping, going to shrines with Fatimeh-Khanom (Batul, of course, still adamantly refused to go), visiting her children and grandchildren, and cooking up big pots of rice for her servants' poor relatives. The new house, which my brothers had built for her, had a spacious kitchen for her to prepare her big Saturday buffets, and she even had a small pool in her bedroom so that she no longer had to go down to the courtyard five times a day to wash her hands before each of her prayers. Best of all, the new house was square. To Khanom, a square house measured the distance between past loss and present possession, helplessness and self-respect. She no longer needed to ask what God would send her next. She had never forgiven Reza Shah for his assaults on the veil, and looked back on his cruelty with sad shakes of the head. Nevertheless, she often said that one had to admit, in simple fairness, that the Pahlavis hadn't turned out as badly as one had thought they would. Even Reza Shah, she said, had done a lot of good: under the Qajars, you couldn't take two steps in any direction without worrying about soldiers and bandits. Reza had put a stop to that, and with all these new roads his son was building, she could visit any shrine she liked in perfect safety. Young people nowadays couldn't understand what it meant to have the whole country suffering from chaos and *harj-o-marj*.

I was amazed at how much she, like the country, seemed to have changed. She laughed and joked all the time, never scolded anyone, and was proud of us all. "How I wish Shazdeh could have lived to see what you children have done with your education," she would say to us. "I will read Koran for him tonight." Such tremendous alterations had taken place since I first departed for America, and especially in the lives of women, that things that had once bewildered and upset my mother no longer appeared to disturb her in the least. She found it quite acceptable that young women should study abroad, travel alone, and take up professions, and was constantly urging her friends and women relatives to send their daughters to me so I could turn them into social workers. Men and even girls in our circles now chose marriage partners whom their families had not picked for them, and although some of my brothers and half brothers had married foreigners and non-Moslems, my mother, who got along very well with her foreign daughters-in-law, said that she didn't think this new fashion was any better or worse than the old. People, she pointed out, still seemed to be getting along or not at about the same rate they always had. The chief thing was for husbands and wives to be happy together, as she and Shazdeh had been.

She and I got along so well these days, in fact, that the only source of friction between us had been her initial dark suspicion, formed shortly after my return from Iraq, that I was trying to thwart God's will by keeping husbands and wives from natural relations. This was how my mother had at first interpreted my efforts to introduce birth control to our country.

Iran's birthrate was one of the highest on earth, and I knew that population growth was the most important social problem we faced. Fathers and mothers, made desperate by the arrival of babies they couldn't afford, would send their children out into the streets to beg or shift for themselves, or abandon them at the doors of mosques, whence they would be sent to places like Aminabad. Some Tehran neighborhoods swarmed so thick with children who had no place else to play that streets were literally impassable. But even though it was vital that Iranian women learn to postpone the arrival of new babies until they and their husbands could afford them, and thus gain a chance to lift themselves out of the cycle of poverty, Iran, unlike several other Moslem countries such as Egypt and Pakistan, had never seriously addressed this fundamental problem or made any attempt to develop a national family planning program. In the Middle East, feelings about the importance of having many children are extremely strong, and it was difficult to convince old-fashioned, traditional Persians like my mother that birth control was not against God's law.

From the opening of our first semester, I had been sending a married field-worker from the School—a steady, responsible young woman named Minou, who had two children of her own—to assist a new organization I had helped found, the Family Planning Association of Iran, in starting a clinic at the Tehran maternity hospital to teach new mothers how to manage the size of their families in the future; we were getting help from an organization called the Pathfinder Fund, which assisted such programs in developing countries. Our association had to be extremely discreet about its work, and to do everything in accordance with Islamic law. Since 1953 the clerical community had been compelled to refrain from publicly opposing the government, so that to a superficial eye, the influence of religion in our society, especially in more "Western"-looking places like North Tehran, might seem to have diminished. However, no one in daily contact with ordinary people (which meant everyone who employed a servant) could be unaware of the power that Iran's mullahs still held over the lives and minds of millions of Iranians in every city neighborhood, bazaar, and village.

Recently, however, Al Azhar University in Cairo, the greatest institution of Islamic learning in the world, had issued a ruling on birth control, citing passages from the Koran in which the Prophet commanded believers to care for the health and welfare of women and children. This ruling stated that birth control was in accordance with Islamic law, because the planning and spacing of children promoted the health of women and the financial well-being of the entire family. I was therefore informing my students and graduates of the Al Azhar ruling, and as a result we had encountered no objections from any clerics. But at first, when I had tried to convince my mother that birth control was lawful according to religion, she had not believed me. Family planning, she declared, flouted God's will. Men and women had been commanded to marry so that they would have children, and I was trying to prevent this. "'He who gave you teeth will give you bread,'" she kept saying, quoting her favorite proverb at me for the ten thousandth time. "If a woman is supposed to have a child, she will, and it's a sin to try and interfere." She had been outraged when she began hearing me suggest to her maidservants that they go to the clinic to get the new birth control pills that had just become available. "You want my servants," she told me in an accusing tone, "not to get close with their husbands."

"She isn't saying that your servants shouldn't 'get close,'" Batul-Khanom would put in impatiently. "She's saying that now, with this little white pill, they can get close *better*, because they won't have to worry." And if my mother left the room for a moment, my stepmother would turn to me and whisper in triumph, "I understand *exactly* what you are trying to do. Do you know what my great regret is? That I'm not young enough to come and help you!"

"Well," my mother would grumble as soon as her old friend was gone, "she can say what she likes, and you can hand out as many little white pills as you want, but they won't work. If God wants a woman to have a baby, she will. Even if she takes a little white pill." Yet even in this critical area my mother's natural good sense and her native Persian pragmatism had eventually conquered her distrust of a new idea. After all, she finally observed one day, it was a good thing if women didn't have to have ten or twelve children and lose their looks and their health. "Shazdeh," she added affectionately, "always told us that having lots of babies made women more radiant. That was just like him—he didn't have to have them himself. So maybe the pill, too, is part of God's plan."

Nevertheless, beyond a certain point my mother's ability to change her views ground to a halt before the wall of her orthodoxy. For instance, despite her strong approval of my "school to help the poor" and the generous donations she made, she never attended our commencements. Though she knew that I would have loved her to come, she could not bring herself to sit among men even in a chador. I understood her feelings, but they made me a little sad. Mohammed Reza Shah allowed women to wear the veil or not, as they wished, and I didn't want to force new attitudes on anyone. Yet too much zeal, I thought, was fanatical and constricting, a mentality that confined not only women but all Persians to the past and prevented us from moving ahead.

Even during my workday I remained in the midst of my family. Hafez and Alah Verdi had continued to teach courses for me, while Homy, Sory, and Jahan still did translations and interpreting for our foreign faculty. Jaby, whose kind and completely selfless nature hadn't changed since our childhood, was always raising money among her friends for our emergency fund, or collecting clothing for the school servants, or finding furniture we needed for our community centers. Very often Homy and Sory, by arranging handsome lunches for my foreign professional guests at their homes near the School, also relieved me of what would have been the great burden of providing this mandatory element of Persian hospitality myself.

Ever since 1958 my family and friends had been donating money to keep us afloat, and I was continually worrying about the School's financial situation. The house we occupied on Takhteh-Jamshid Avenue was both costly and too small for the eighty students we had now, although Hossein Ala had gotten the army to put up some barracks as classrooms. But I couldn't afford to rent anything larger— my small subsidy from the welfare agency council, which wasn't a regular government budget allocation but just a hodgepodge of whatever monthly contributions the council members were willing to make, barely covered our present rent, supplies, and the nominal wages I paid the full-time faculty, myself, and servants like my driver Hossein. I had always been forced to go around trying to raise funds from wealthy people I knew in high society, and as I quickly discovered, separating the rich from their money wasn't easy when nobody had ever heard of a "madadkar." The ad hoc nature of our funding was a continual reminder of the shaky foundations on which social work still rested in my country. Despite the luster a four-year program gave us and the warm support of individual officials like Hossein Ala or some of my friends in the ministries, as yet neither the School nor my profession had any real standing with the government, and I was afraid that if we stepped on too many big tails, even the funds we had would be withdrawn and the School would have to shut down. I always felt as though I were walking on eggs—a sensation with which I had first become acquainted only a month or two into the School's first semester.

One morning in the fall of 1958 I had been startled while teaching class to receive a telephone summons from Hossein Ala's secretary. When I hurried to the court ministry, my mentor, smiling reassuringly, explained that the Shah had become curious about the School, of whose activities, as Mr. Ala diplomatically put it, he had recently been made cognizant. I was to appear at the Marble Palace at ten o'clock the next morning for an interview.

I stood there dismayed. I had always assumed that Hossein Ala's backing and that of my trustees would be enough to ensure that our bit of funding wouldn't dry up. Not liking to think much about the possibility that I might one day have to go to Mohammed Reza Shah for support, I had ignored it. Now I realized that if I didn't impress him favorably, the survival of the School would be jeopardized. The prospect of meeting him filled me with alarm.

I was, of course, used to conversing with ministers and diplomats like Mr. Ala, many of whom I saw informally on family occasions, and no one in my immediate family held any grudge against the younger Shah for his father's confiscations and murders. But I knew nothing of him personally (in Iran we did not have television interviewers like Barbara Walters to show us what kinds of personalities our king and queen had). In Iran, the king stood at the very pinnacle of society. Generals and courtiers fought for the privilege of groveling at his feet and kissing his shoes; in letters he was addressed by such titles as "Shadow of God" and "Refuge of the Universe." His power wasn't ceremonial as in England, but real—since 1953, Mohammed Reza Shah had made himself not just theoretically but literally responsible for running the country. He supervised all important details of the government and the military himself, and no one dared to act except at his command or that of someone immediately below him, like

Hossein Ala. Nothing important happened in Iran unless he ordered it or specifically endorsed it. He was as powerful as his father had been, and I well remembered my one glimpse of Reza Shah the day he strode into our compound from the Marble Palace in his military cloak to watch Shazdeh's house burn.

However, one did not choose to obey or disobey a summons from the Marble Palace. Anxiously I asked Hossein Ala what, exactly, an interview with the Shah meant?

Mr. Ala, a small, kindly man, famous for his humor and his gift of putting people at ease, looked amused and said that it meant I would have to wear a hat.

Perhaps because of the memory of my mother's introduction to Western hats under Reza Shah, I do not wear them. I replied nervously that I disliked hats and had never owned one, not even when I worked in America. The Persian word for hat is *kola*, and as puns are highly prized among Iranians, the court minister looked delighted at the opening I had given him: "Surely," he answered with relish, "you own at least a Coca-kola?" Seeing that this mild jest had made me laugh as he intended, he added that the only requirement was to explain to the Shah what I was doing, and answer the questions he would put to me.

The next morning I had Hossein drive me to the Marble Palace, which Mohammed Reza Shah had taken over when his father abdicated. The court ministry was actually in its precincts, and I always passed through its gate when going to see Mr. Ala. However, I had never set foot in the palace itself, and that morning I was filled with many conflicting emotions. I knew that Mohammed Reza Shah wanted progress, but his father had thought of "progress" as buildings, roads, and Iranians dressed in Western clothing, not educating people to lift themselves out of dirt and ignorance, or teaching them to think like responsible citizens. The king was known to brook no criticism of his policies, and if Mohammed Reza Shah was truly like his father, I thought, I didn't see how I could make him see the need for human as well as technological advancement. At most, I could expect only three or four minutes of his time—Mr. Ala himself never gave me more than five—and in a conversation with the Shah, one did not speak unless spoken to. I had no idea how one was supposed to talk to the monarch, but I did know this much: if I blurted out the wrong thing, Hossein Ala would have to abandon his support of us. Then the School, and social work, would fade into oblivion, as did most new ideas in our country.

The blue flag of the Pahlavis was flying above the gate beside the green, white, and red flag of Iran. I waited while the gatekeeper, holding his silver staff of office in his hand, consulted his roster to admit me. Nearby, in the shadow of two massive gilt statues representing palace guards from the time of Darius the Great, stood the tall Imperial Guards, the regiment whose task was to protect the person of the monarch; they were known as "the Immortals," and wore a special neck scarf of the same Pahlavi blue as the flag to show that they belonged to the Shah's military elite. They reminded me of Reza Shah, who had chosen the Imperial Guard from the finest specimens of Aryan manhood (being real "Aryans," of course, they didn't have blond hair and blue eyes, but black hair and dark skins). A servant in a blue suit conducted me about a hundred yards along flower-lined walks and rows of cypresses. For the first time I passed through what had once been Shazdeh's and Ezzatdoleh's garden.

After walking through long white corridors past dozens of large and small offices and conference rooms, we came to an antechamber, where I was told to wait. I sat down on an embroidered sofa facing a pair of huge doors—the Shah's office. On either side stood two handsome young men wearing the most beautiful silk suits I had ever seen. They were members of the Shah's elite corps of adjutants, a group of about a dozen honor companions especially selected from the cream of society to guard the Shah's door one day a week and accompany him on state visits. One was the son of a great Azerbaijani landowning family we knew. He stared straight ahead, giving no sign that he had ever seen me before. I remembered how I had decided after seeing Hossein Ala the previous day that I was not going to run out and buy a hat.

All at once, my family's past began rushing back with such speed and clarity that I began to worry that my powerful emotions were going to make me lose control of myself when I came into the Shah's presence. Memories of Shazdeh, of my mother's stories, of our life in the compound, welled up in me, and I found that I could not stop them. All my old pain and anger came back. Suddenly tears rose in my throat and choked me. I thought of Shazdeh's losses and ours after the coup—of his years under house arrest, the confiscation of this estate, the murder of Nosratdoleh, the destruction of our compound. For a few minutes, aversion at the coming interview threatened to overwhelm me.

Then, as I stared, unhappy and ill at ease, at the doors and the expressionless adjutants, the irony of the situation struck me with great force. Once my father had dwelt where I was sitting, wealthy and powerful. Then Reza Shah had built a sumptuous palace in my father's garden and lived in it for a few years. But he had been toppled, too, by the Allies, and now his son was using this place for office space.

How often it had happened in our history, I reflected, that destiny overturned and changed our lives: changed them utterly and completely. And I realized that sudden, violent change was the heart and soul of our Persian experience. Conquerors and foreigners came and went. Dynasties rose and fell, displacing one another like the repeating arabesques of a carpet. Clinging to thousands of years of culture, we Iranians had woven art, jokes, and poetry to forget our sorrows, held fast to our pride, and tried to survive the earthquakes as best we could. This carpet pattern of Persian history, ever-changing yet always the same, was why Shazdeh had feared for his children, and why the art that Iranians knew best was the art of survival, whether we were shazdehs or villagers, learned ayatollahs or illiterate tentmakers, great merchants or naked beggars. It was the reason my father had insisted that even his daughters learn to swim.

Now I was "Khanom" to a profession that needed me to give it its start. Shazdeh, I reminded myself, had always taught us to do what we had set out to do, and not to waste time bickering with fate or feeling angry over the wrongs done to us by Reza Shah. I was doing only what I must. I, Shazdeh's daughter, had come to this spot to ask Reza Shah's son to use his power to help create something good for our people, or at least not to oppose it. And if Reza Shah's son wanted to see me, I thought, he would have to accept me for what I was. I could not flatter him, but I could will myself to think only of my goal, and allow nothing to interfere with that.

After ten or fifteen minutes the doors opened and I was ushered into a huge, magnificent office with walls and curtains of cream and light jade. On the floor were enormous carpets from Isfahan in uncommon and exquisite designs. Elaborately framed Persian and European paintings hung on the walls; polished flower vases and precious antiques graced every inlaid cabinet and taboret. In the center of the room was a conversational island consisting of a long inlaid coffee table with sofas and an armchair at either end. A spectacular bouquet of autumn roses stood in the middle. For an instant I felt as if I had been transported straight back in time to Shazdeh's office, and my recent self-control almost deserted me; as I moved blindly forward into the beautiful room, I could almost hear my mother and stepmothers shushing us as we filed in for our Friday inspection. Then I saw Mohammed Reza Shah. He was standing near his desk in front of a window at the opposite end of the room.

Seeing me enter, he moved toward the table. Crossing my arms over my chest I bowed slightly but respectfully, as we had been taught to do with Shazdeh. "Salaam—" I began, then stopped in consternation as I realized that I was not sure what to call him: Hossein Ala had said nothing about that. Quickly I added, "Your Majesty."

He nodded and beckoned me to approach. Tensely, I crossed the room. The Shah took a seat at the end of the table nearest his desk and gestured to the armchair at the other end. I sat down and found myself looking across the flowers at a slender man of about forty, with graying hair and an erect carriage. With astonishment I saw that he was not in the military uniform he always wore in public, but had on an ordinary business suit of charcoal gray wool, meticulously tailored; absently I noticed that it was not quite as good as the one the landowner's son outside in the antechamber was wearing.

The Shah smiled slightly and said in a soft, courteous voice, "I am told that you have returned from studying in America." I was amazed. It was the voice and manner of any gentleman. Without thinking about it, I had been preparing myself to meet a coarse, despotic, semieducated soldier's son—now I saw with surprise that Mohammed Reza Shah was just like my own brothers, well-spoken and urbane. I was so startled, and so distracted by my recent emotions, that for a moment I was nearly speechless. "Yes, Your Majesty," I managed to reply. "Before I worked for the United Nations, I studied how to provide people with social services."

"Ah." The Shah leaned idly back in his chair and paused, evidently pondering his next question. After several seconds, he said, "I am told that you have opened a school for social service here."

"Yes, that is correct."

He raised an eyebrow. "But is it necessary?" he asked pleasantly. "In Iran we already have institutions to provide social services. The city of Tehran has hospitals and orphanages and so on. My family itself already oversees a great deal of social service."

For a moment I was flustered. Then I understood his confusion: the School's actual name, in Persian, was "Tehran School for Social Service." "Yes, Your Majesty," I replied, choosing my words with care. "But my institution's purpose is to *train* personnel who can work in the royal and city institutions, and who can care for and help needy people in general."

I paused uneasily, then saw that he was waiting for me to elaborate. Suddenly I plunged ahead, so anxious to use my time well that I forgot to address him as "Your Majesty." "You see, Agha," I rattled on, as though he were any ordinary minister, "it is important that we have men and women scientifically educated to help the inmates of these institutions. The skills a madadkar requires are complex, and careful training is necessary. For example, in our orphanages and other facilities—"

Alarmed, I stopped short. In a single instant the Shah's affable demeanor had vanished, and his eyes had narrowed ominously. Lifting his chin, he frowned. "The orphanages?" he demanded. "What is wrong with the orphanages? They tell me that our orphanages are excellent."

I had blundered into a minefield. The wives of high-ranking ministers and generals vied with each other to please the Queen or the Shah's sisters, Princess Ashraf and Princess Shams, by donating money to the hospitals and orphanages sponsored by the Pahlavi charitable societies. "They" might well be the women of the royal family, and I hardly wanted to imply that enterprises that they oversaw were improperly run. By the same token, if I were frank about conditions in the city institutions, the news that I had criticized these establishments to the Shah would have every official in town screaming to have the School shut down.

Just as I was wondering what to say next, we were interrupted by the entrance of a distinguished old servant carrying a towel and wearing white gloves. He advanced toward the Shah with a tray bearing a single glass of tea, placed this before the king, and bowed deeply. The tea glass holder and saucer, I saw, were of pure, smooth gold, the tray the famous worked gold of Isfahan. Beside the saucer lay a pair of tiny, exquisite gold prongs and a golden sugar holder. The Shah paused to drop one or two lumps into the glass, then began stirring the tea with a tiny golden spoon.

I tried to use the pause to collect myself. Looking at this beautiful tea set, which was probably worth more than most rural villagers earned in ten years, I asked myself if anyone ever told Mohammed Reza Shah an unpleasant truth about anything. It was appalling to think that my next words could destroy the School. Yet I must answer his question about the orphanages. I would simply have to tell him the truth as diplomatically as I could. I waited until he raised the glass, then took a deep breath. "No, Your Majesty," I said firmly, "unfortunately our orphanages are not excellent. Indeed, they are far from what they might be, for it is impossible to have social services and institutions of excellence without trained personnel. At present, most of these children are not looked after by anyone who understands their care. Nor is anyone seeing that they go to school or learn skills, so that many of these children leave the orphanages only to become beggars."

I stopped, too apprehensive to continue. I had no idea how my words were affecting him.

Still frowning, the Shah put down his glass. There was another long pause. Uncertain whether this indicated displeasure or not, I waited at the edge of my chair, prepared to rise and flee if he angrily dismissed me.

"Ha," he murmured at last, his tone quite mild again, "isn't that interesting? They told me that the children would be much better off in an orphanage than in their own homes."

I replied that it was indeed better for the children to have a roof over their heads than to sleep in the streets. But would it not be better still to care for them in a proper, scientific manner, teach their parents how to manage the size of their families, and give men and women the skills to earn money to support these offspring instead of abandoning them? There was much, I said, that trained people could accomplish, and in the long run not only would the children, their families, and society all be better off, but the state would save a great deal of money on their upkeep.

At my last words the Shah's expression grew even more thoughtful. Restlessly, he began asking one question after another. From time to time he would stop for several minutes to digest what I was saying and I would simply sit and wait until he decided to go on. His questions were apt and intelligent, and it was almost as astonishing and heartening to find him interested in the answers as it was to see him in a business suit. Nevertheless, I remained poised on the edge of my seat, ready to bolt from the room if necessary.

All at once the Shah jumped up impatiently, turned, and strode back to his desk. Flustered, I jumped up, too, fearing that I had stayed too long. The king, however, merely went to his telephone and picked up the receiver. Without waiting for a response, he ordered the listener at the other end to see that in the future the Tehran School of Social Work received twenty thousand rials a month; I realized that he was talking to the man who served as his personal treasurer. Returning to his armchair, he asked another question or two, then abruptly rose again. He nodded.

Hastily I got up, bowed, and left the room, following the servant in the antechamber back down the long corridors again. I felt exuberant. Twenty thousand rials a month was only about three hundred dollars, an insignificant sum to a man who sipped his tea from solid gold, but to me it was more than ten percent of our monthly budget, and its psychological value was beyond price. I could hardly wait to begin saying smoothly to reluctant donors at dinner parties, "The Shah himself is already supporting our work generously." I had achieved what Mr. Ala had sent me for! I looked at my watch and saw with surprise that the interview had lasted nearly forty-five minutes. This was far more time than I had ever imagined the Shah would devote to such a topic.

I followed the servant back through the garden to the gate in a state of elation. Not for the first time in my life, I thanked God for my father's staunchly forward-looking and practical temperament, which had so often inspired me to trust my instincts and move ahead. By nature and by professional training, I was an optimist. Social work stood for giving people a chance to do something with their lives, and Mohammed Reza Shah had decided to give social work that same chance. I felt happy, relieved, and grateful. When I was sitting in the antechamber I had seen that my father wanted me to set my face forward, not backward to a history that was over and done with. I had chosen the right course. The School's future lay ahead of me, and in pursuing my goal I was going to look neither to the left nor to the right. I was determined to disregard the past.

One afternoon in January of 1962, my brother Hafez arrived at school badly shaken. That morning, he said, the Shah's security forces had invaded the campus of Tehran University, where students were peacefully demonstrating to protest the arrest of three of their number for criticizing the government. Army commandos had entered the buildings and gone on a rampage. Hafez's car, which had been parked in front of the history department, had been wrecked in the melee. The soldiers had destroyed furniture, books, and equipment, assaulted women students in the classrooms, and beaten some male students almost to death. My brother had made up his mind to take Jody and the children to America as soon as he could line up a teaching post. How could you work or teach in a country, he said, where you didn't know when your own army was going to attack you for saying what you thought?

I was terribly upset by his news, as well as saddened to learn that we were going to lose him and my sister-in-law Jody, of whom I was very fond. But I knew that leaving was the only thing Hafez could do if he wanted to live in a place where he could work, write, and speak freely. As a result of the army's attack, Alah Verdi also decided to emigrate.

Mohammed Reza Shah, I thought in sorrow and dismay, was genuinely willing for us to have better orphanages, hospitals, and vocational programs. Then why did he not understand that we needed to be able to speak our minds and criticize him without being assaulted or jailed? Surely, if he could see the importance of paying attention to human beings, he could also see that if we wanted to solve our problems, we had to be able to talk about them freely!

Indeed, about two years after my one and only private meeting with him, it had begun to appear that the Shah might start allowing more of the freedom of expression and true political participation that Iranians like me were hoping for. Although our two political parties—which the monarch had created himself in 1957—were popularly known as the "Yes Party" and the "Yes, Sir, Party," in 1960 the Shah had publicly declared that he was in favor of democracy, and most recently he had actually seemed disposed to allow open elections and more freedom of speech. The National Front had even been able to get a representative elected to the Majlis again.

Through friends and relatives in parliament and from the international press (since our own press was censored, everybody got their political information from the grapevine and the American, English, and other foreign magazines and newspapers that were readily available), we knew that the American government was pressing the Shah for reforms to counter the influence of communism. In May of 1961 the king appointed Dr. Ali Amini, an independent, progressive politician, to oversee a land redistribution program—which, the American government hoped, would turn our illiterate, poverty-stricken villagers into agrarian capitalists, and thus make them less susceptible to a Soviet-style revolution. The Shah disliked Dr. Amini (who was a Qajar cousin of ours), and most people believed that he had made him premier only because he felt that the Americans were pressuring him to do so.

Recently, however, both middle-class people and the working poor had been plagued by escalating prices, government wage freezes, and other economic woes, and strikes and protests were on the rise. Many educated Iranians, among them university students and academics like my brother, remembered how much freer and more democratic life had been under Mossadegh, and the country's mood was angry and restless. Everyone hated the stifling political atmosphere, the corruption that was allowed to flourish in government, and the repressiveness of SAVAK, which jailed as a "Communist" anyone who advocated a strike or protested something the government had done.

The brutality of the raid on the University made me shudder. Like everyone else, I knew quite well that the price of protest in our society was being labeled "subversive," or worse. A year or two earlier, the Shah's displeasure had fallen heavily on the honest and reform-minded Abol Hassan Ebtehaj, who had publicly criticized Iran's heavy dependence on American aid. This respected man, whom I had liked and admired so much when I had met him in Baghdad, had been arrested and imprisoned without trial on unspecified charges for seven months before finally being freed. I knew that if I or my students became involved in political protest, the School would be closed at once and social workers, who were already viewed with mistrust by officials who thought we were trying to interfere in their domains, would be labeled political troublemakers and refused jobs. Without jobs or—worse yet—from exile or jail, I and my graduates could do nothing to help Iranians have better nutrition, better housing and sanitation, skills and incomes. In horror I imagined the commandos coming and firing on *my* students.

The university raid made it even more obvious to me that I must keep us out of politics. In the classroom I told students that we must, of course, talk about social problems, or we could do nothing about them. But we could only change the system, I said, from within—by working patiently to help raise people's living standard, by the research we were publishing to make the government more aware of the problems, and by educating officials about their responsibility to others. None of us was strong enough to go against guns or the secret police. If we tried, we would simply be crushed.

Dr. Amini lasted about eighteen months. The Shah was said to detest him because, nearly a decade after the fall of Mossadegh, he was still haunted by the specter of someone arising to threaten him. When Dr. Amini proved unable either to deal with the discontent or to stay in the good graces of President Kennedy's administration, the Shah gladly replaced him as prime minister with Asadollah Alam, one of his oldest friends and closest advisers.

Then, suddenly, in January 1963, the king began trying for the first time to win the support of the people as a whole. He announced a sweeping new reform program to be called "the White Revolution." Among its first provisions were the vote for women, electoral reforms, land redistribution, profit sharing for factory workers, and a rural teachers' corps to combat illiteracy.

I myself was overjoyed. At last, I thought, the government was beginning a major human development campaign, a program to build not only roads but people! With this official policy and the money that would be behind it, in no more than a decade we might have health insurance and social security, rural hospitals and job training, legal protections for women and families—in a single generation, we would catch up with the West!

My first euphoria, however, quickly lost its glow. The Shah arrested the entire National Front leadership—who were protesting that the reforms did nothing for social justice, freedom of speech, or parliamentary democracy—and threw them into jail for urging a boycott of the nationwide referendum the government called to approve the White Revolution. Then, when the referendum took place, the government claimed that the margin of victory was ninety-nine percent. This result was so improbable that nobody believed it was anything but a barefaced lie to impress the foreign press, especially the American media.

I felt angry, frustrated, and confused. Though I knew that the reform program was in part an effort to preempt the National Front, I did not want to forego so much potential good for our country and had voted in favor of it—the first time I, a woman, had ever been allowed to vote for anything. But why was it necessary for the Shah to jail his opposition, or falsify the results of a vote on reforms that the great majority of Iranians supported? The program's centerpiece, which was the phasing out of our outmoded and unjust system of land ownership, was popular even among old landowning families like mine. Couldn't the Shah and Premier Alam see that people couldn't help but distrust a government that lied and cheated even when lying and cheating were patently unnecessary?

One day early in May 1963, Hossein said excitedly as we were driving somewhere, "You know, Khanom, that holy man has stood up in Qom again and is preaching against the Shah."

Recently, several young seminarians had been killed in a violent government raid on the famous theological school in Qom, the Feyziyeh, after protests there against land reform (some of the biggest landholders in Iran were religious institutions). Though such things were never reported in the press, even illiterate people like Hossein and the School's other servants, as well as many of our students, knew all about them anyway, not only from relatives in Qom, but from their own mosques and from talking to friends and family in the pious enclaves of the bazaar and in the teahouses of South Tehran. Once or twice Hossein had mentioned a mullah by the name of Khomeini. All I knew of him was that he was an elderly cleric who taught at the Feyziyeh, and that, like many traditional clerics, he had opposed both land reform and the vote for women. One thing about him was obvious, however: he had more than his share of courage.

For a few weeks we heard nothing more about him. Then, early in

June, the Ashura festival took place—the final, climactic days of mourning in the month of Moharram over the martyrdom of Imam Hossein—and Ruhollah Khomeini preached a scorching sermon against the Shah. Reza Shah's son, he said, was the tool of foreigners and a conspiracy of the Bahais and Israel to destroy Islam. He actually hinted that if the king continued in his impious course he would be deposed. The next day, the elderly cleric was arrested and brought to Tehran.

The news that the government had arrested a venerated mullah from the Feyziyeh raced through the bazaar like a brushfire. Within hours, mullahs, theology students, and guild leaders had plastered the walls with his picture and organized thousands of tradesmen, craftsmen, vendors, and others to march in a demonstration and shout anti-government slogans. Military security units moved in at once. Not believing that Iranian soldiers would shoot at them, the protestors kept marching. The army, under orders to shoot to kill, mowed them down.

The riots that followed in the capital and in other cities for the next three days were the worst of modern times. The government's brutality unleashed all the pent-up rage that had been growing and festering ever since the Shah had been returned to power in 1953. Not only tradesmen, peddlers, and young seminarians but teachers, factory workers, office clerks, university students, and National Front activists—most of whom, I am sure, had never even heard of Khomeini—poured into the streets to hurl sticks and stones at the police and soldiers. They attacked government buildings and desecrated the Armenian cemetery. At school a few miles north of the bazaar, I and our faculty, students, and servants waited in horror for the sketchy reports that came in from people who had relatives where the fighting was. The central city was a battle zone. Nobody knew how many were being injured or killed.

Everyone was not only sickened by what was happening, but utterly bewildered. I didn't know anyone who didn't believe that SAVAK and the security forces had the country totally under control. Furthermore, from a political standpoint, the government's horrifying violence made no sense whatever. The Shah had always tried to cultivate the support of the bazaar, and the new reform program was meant to win him the love of ordinary Iranians—the very ones his officers were now massacring. Could he really think that bazaar marchers calling for an old mullah's release were "subversives"? Our field-workers in the area of the shooting had reported that many of the dead and injured lying in the streets were evidently villagers who had come into the city to sell baskets of fruit at the market and spontaneously joined the protest.

These were not paid ruffians or political extremists—merely simple, credulous people convinced that the government was endangering religion by arresting a respected mullah. How could a king who loved to talk of his "divine mission" to his people and of himself as the nation's "father" have so little understanding of their feelings, or be so unwilling simply to let them express what they felt?

On the third and last day of the rioting, I heard to my sorrow that Hossein Ala had abruptly forfeited the Shah's favor by trying to persuade him to tell the army to stop firing on fellow Iranians. I soon learned what lay behind his sudden disgrace. On the second night of the rioting—so went the story I heard—Mr. Ala had summoned eight of the Shah's most loyal advisers to his home, where they all swore an oath to go to the king the next day and beg him to order the army to stop shooting. One general, however, to ingratiate himself with the Shah rushed to the royal residence at five in the morning and waited outside the Shah's bedroom to tell him of the "conspiracy" when he awoke. All the "plotters" were placed under arrest immediately, including my kindly, elderly mentor. I was profoundly shocked by such ingratitude for the venerable service of a man whose devotion to his monarch was beyond suspicion. His spirit broken as a result of this disgraceful treatment, Mr. Ala died within a few months.

The cabinet itself, however, realized at once that the 1963 riots had been a political disaster, and a day or two after they ended, I was surprised to receive a telephone call from Premier Alam, with whom I had previously had little to do. He explained that his regime wanted to compensate the victims and their families for their losses, and had formed a committee of ministers and one respected merchant, Hadji-Agha Magd, who had been chosen by the men of the bazaar themselves to represent them and the Tehran community at large. According to Hadji-Agha Magd, Mr. Alam said, the people of South Tehran trusted no one but Khanom Farman Farmaian's social workers.

At least, I thought sadly, they trusted somebody. Every student in school that year volunteered to work on the investigation, which took twelve months to complete. With Hadji-Agha Magd spreading the word in the bazaar and the slums, we began looking into hundreds of cases. Every week I submitted my students' reports to the justice ministry, carefully itemizing each family's monthly needs and expenses, how many children had to be supported, and how much money we wanted the government to pay. Sometimes a minister would demur, suggesting that a family might subsist on less than we were asking, and Hadji-Agha Magd would tell him grimly, "Your Excellency, pay what Khanom Farman Farmaian says." Not a single recommendation we made was turned down, and I guessed from this that the ministers themselves were profoundly ashamed of what the regime had done. Yet no one in the meetings spoke a word against either the Shah or the shootings, and publicly the government continued to insist that the riots had been provoked by subversives and "reactionary clerics." The Persian press gave the number of casualties as a mere two hundred, while Premier Alam told the foreign press that eighty-six had died and a hundred and fifty had been injured. The School, however, investigated and authenticated the claims of over a thousand families, and we were certain that the number would have been twice that, had the victims' relatives not been afraid of their names ending up in the files of SAVAK if they came forward.

Sometimes I thought about the exquisite golden tea service the Shah had used when I was in his office. It had made him seem so far above the lives and concerns of ordinary people, so removed from unpleasant criticism—truths that no one dared to utter in his presence, just as they had been afraid to say them to his father. If only, I thought, someone could say to Mohammed Reza Shah, "You don't need to have your government injure people or lie to them. Just let us say what we think, and listen to the voices of the weak, as a Moslem prince is required to do. Help your people instead of hurting them, and they will love you as you wish."

But I had no idea what went on in the Shah's heart. My views were only the simple, uninformed opinions of an average person. And if anyone thought now of telling the Shah what his people felt, the fate of Hossein Ala and the demonstrators showed clearly enough where that would lead.

These tragic events, however, brought an unexpected windfall to the School, for my students' excellent work had opened the government's eyes to the value of social workers. At last I was able to get us a regular budget, and in 1964 I moved us triumphantly into a brand new three-story building on a large tract of land in a pleasant residential district close to the foothills at the northern edge of the city. With this new campus, we would be able to accept not just dozens of future applicants but hundreds. The building had a lovely Persian-style facade of blue latticework that I had designed myself and included a student cafeteria, a real library, plenty of classrooms and faculty offices, and a copying and printing shop, so that we could publish all the facts we were learning about the country's social needs. I also drew up plans for an auditorium and another building to house the Family Planning Association and the administration of our community welfare centers, and had flower beds and saplings planted among the stone benches and fountains in our gardens, which would be open to the public. Thinking of the generations of Iranian students, graduate teachers, and visiting international scholars who would work and study together at this beautiful new school, I understood why Shazdeh had so loved the construction of public works.

I had carefully arranged for my office in the main building to face north, so that I could look at the mountains when I glanced out the window. After returning from Iraq, to have some exercise during my long workday I had joined a fancy new country club called the "Imperial Sports Club" and went there as often as I could to walk on the handsomely landscaped grounds or to play tennis.

In addition, from our first semester I had extended an open invitation to any students who loved hiking, as I did, to go with me on Fridays to the mountains above Shemiran. There, in the high passes and long valleys, were many remote hamlets, typical Persian villages of thirty, forty, or a hundred families, who could be reached only by pack animal or on foot. We could learn a great deal this way about the needs of the isolated rural villages that made up seventy percent of our population. Zamani, who missed the fresh country air, had been the first to volunteer, and two other male graduates also joined me regularly. Every Friday at six in the morning, we four, and often a few others, would set off along the dusty road with a tea thermos, a water jug, and a lunch I had packed until, after a few hours, we reached a tiny village where we would sit down under a willow tree, offer to share our food and drink with the friendly, curious villagers, and strike up conversations. Thus, every weekend, we learned much that was interesting and valuable: how many babies had died in the past year, how many men had been forced to go to the city to look for work, how many children could not attend school.

By this time, graduates like Zamani and my other hiking companions, my secretary Esther, and servants like Hossein had come to seem like members of my own family. Indeed, many of my students and graduates as well as the servants frequently solicited my advice or confided in me their personal or financial woes, and often I knew their hopes and troubles better than those of my oldest acquaintances. I never ignored anyone's problem and always made sure that everyone received what he needed, for I knew that this help often made the difference between somebody's relatives' having enough to eat or going hungry. Although I never asked any of our municipal or ministerial contacts to do anything for me personally, I was always happy to use my own and the School's connections whenever necessary, not only to advance the School itself but to assist anyone connected with us who was in need. I wanted everyone to see that those for whom I was responsible could rely on me to help them.

Thus the bonds of bread and salt among us grew stronger by the year. I knew that I enjoyed the love and gratitude of these colleagues and my staff and their families, while I, in turn, trusted these faithful friends and followers as I would have my own relatives.

When Mitra came in the summer, I would take her hiking with us, too, and we would visit the desert provinces south of Tehran and the villages there. Once, during the August vacation, she and I hiked with Zamani and our two other Friday regulars in the desert region where he came from and stayed overnight with his family, all of us sleeping on the floor of his mother's living room. Zamani was from Khomein, where the famous cleric whose arrest had triggered the 1963 riots had been born; Mr. Khomeini had taken his surname from his hometown.

After the disaster of the riots, everything had become very quiet. Ruhollah Khomeini had been detained for eight months, until the spring of 1964, and SAVAK had rounded up hundreds of political activists, trying and imprisoning them in secret. The National Front leaders jailed before the reform referendum had finally been released, but most abandoned all political activity and withdrew to their homes, resigned and demoralized. It was quite evident that there would be no more Mossadeghs, and that the Shah's long journey toward unchallengeable power was complete. He changed officials at whim, and there was scarcely a minister or politician in Iran now who didn't remind himself at least once a day, "Today I am somebody, but tomorrow I may be nobody; better to make no decisions, say nothing, do nothing." Not even the greatly trusted Asadollah Alam had lasted long as premier—one day the Shah, for no apparent reason, replaced him and packed him off to Fars to take up the politically insignificant post of president of the University of Shiraz, so that for a while, even he became a nobody.

Needless to say, since 1953 the Shah's and the government's repressiveness had been connected in our minds with the nation that had restored him to power and enabled him to achieve absolute supremacy. America was providing our government with aid for development, but it was also selling the Shah a great deal of military equipment, and the security services who put down demonstrations rode around in American jeeps with a picture of clasped hands symbolizing Iranian-American friendship. Many people, of course, had American friends, or sent their sons and daughters to the United States to study. People still liked Americans as individuals, for many were generous and compassionate—the American Women's Club of Tehran, for instance, had provided several volunteers for the School of Social Work and had made welcome contributions. But for every Iranian, including me, the great, paramount fact about the U.S. government was that it had overthrown Mossadegh, helped to create a terrifying secret police, and, as we saw it, used its immense power to control our monarch for its own purposes, just as the British always had. Furthermore, Iranian university students, who were too young to remember the missionaries, saw the United States only as a harsh, militaristic power that was intervening in Vietnam, a small, weak nation like our own. America was also the chief supporter of Israel, a state that most Iranians held responsible for the suffering of their fellow Moslems, the Palestinians, in terrible refugee camps. Just as people had once been convinced that Reza Shah could do nothing that was not ordered by the British, so they felt now that his son did nothing without U.S. government approval.

In October of 1964, the Majlis, at American insistence, passed a bill extending full diplomatic immunity to all American military personnel and their dependents in Iran. The bill outraged everyone except its sponsors. Both Mossadegh and Reza Shah had worked hard to abolish similar agreements that the British, the Russians, and other nations had forced on us. Some deputies were so angry that they actually took the extraordinary step of defying the regime, and boycotted the voting. Not long afterward, the Majlis accepted a two hundred million dollar American bank loan. To us, it seemed obvious that, as had happened so often before, Iranian sovereignty had been bartered for foreigners' money. Within twenty-four hours, the elderly Khomeini, who had been silent since his release from detention, was denouncing the immunity agreement as contrary to Islamic law, and heaping scorn on shameless politicians who traded justice for dollars.

This time there were no demonstrations—everybody was too scared. But the mosques distributed leaflets of the inflammatory remarks and the bazaars sold tape recordings (quite a few people now had the new cassette recorders) so that the illiterate would know what Mr. Khomeini had said in his sermon. Hossein, who had heard the tape at a friend's, told me angrily in the car one day that this holy man had explained what the immunity law meant: American soldiers could now run over the Shah in the street and no one would punish them. But if he, Hossein, an Iranian, hit some American's dog, he would be hanged at once.

The sermon made Khomeini a hero again. This time SAVAK decided to make sure that the vexatious old fanatic would no longer trouble the regime with his barbs. It arrested him once more and conveyed him unceremoniously across the border to Turkey. After that, there were no more public protests by mullahs for a long time, and people like me heard scarcely a whisper of the name Khomeini.

In the fall of 1966, we opened the new Javadieh Community Welfare Center we had been building. Here our field-workers and volunteers, supervised by a director who was one of the School's own graduates, would teach literacy, child care, nutrition, women's health and hygiene, and handicrafts with which women could earn money and improve the family income. The new facility also contained an expanded, modern family planning clinic, with a full-time woman doctor and nurses trained by the International Planned Parenthood Federation, which provided medication and educational materials, and to which the School now belonged.

That same year, Queen Farah, who had donated funds, paid an official visit to Javadieh and its family planning center. Shocked at the dozens of emaciated women who, cradling newborns in their arms and surrounded by scores of toddlers, were waiting to see the doctor, she turned impulsively to me and asked what she could do to help. I explained that I thought the best help she could give us and these women was to advance the cause of birth control in our country. Thus, thanks in large part to her support, in 1967 the Iranian government finally established a national family planning program. It was to be run by the health ministry and was endorsed by a humane and highly regarded cleric, Ayatollah Shariat-Madari. This national program could do what the School itself could never have done: bring the benefits of family planning to millions of women, especially in the rural areas. From this time on the Queen also began taking a strong personal interest in our other community welfare centers and health clinics, as well as in the School itself.

The community welfare centers were now expanding as rapidly as we could build and staff them, and I was being offered enough land for dozens of centers in the urban slums and the provinces. Through each one that we built we were able to touch thousands of lives with health, nutrition, day-care programs, vocational training, family planning, and educational and recreation programs for youngsters. Minou, my graduate who was now directing social services for the maternity hospital, designed a program that sent women field-workers out into poor neighborhoods to persuade young wives and mothers to come and take advantage of our centers and health clinics. Male field-workers were going out into shantytowns and villages to teach the inhabitants how to organize to get paved streets, piped water, and electricity.

The enthusiasm and goodwill our activities and reputation for integrity inspired continued to amaze even me. It was no longer unusual for complete strangers to walk into my office, say that they were from such-and-such a town or province, and, telling me, "Here, Khanom, please have your students spend this," casually place a check for a million rials on my desk.

Such gestures never ceased to move me. I knew the donor didn't mean simply that he trusted me not to embezzle his gift of money or land. He meant that my students and graduates were showing people that things didn't have to be the same as they had always been. We Iranians, I thought, were beginning to understand that we could do something about the way things were, and have a say in our own destinies.

The man who had once inspired so many of us with the faith that our nation could control its destiny was now in his late eighties, and suffering from throat cancer as well as his old complaint of stomach ulcers. By early 1967 it was apparent that Dr. Mossadegh, who had not been allowed to leave his house at Ahmadabad since his release from prison more than ten years before, was declining rapidly, and the government consented to let our cousins Gholam and Dr. Mossadegh's eldest son Ahmad, an engineer, bring him to Tehran for treatments at the hospital his mother Najmeh-Saltaneh had founded. After a month or two it became obvious that nothing could be done for him, and Ahmad and Gholam brought him back to the family home on Kakh Avenue, where he was installed in his grandson Hamid's room with a twenty-four-hour nurse. Even now, so fearful did the Shah appear of the man who had threatened his power that Gholam's wife, Malak, was obliged to feed and house four SAVAK agents posted to watch that part of the house so that they could report to the government who his visitors were.

Dr. Mossadegh's wife, Zia-Saltaneh, had been a good friend of my mother's until her death two years earlier, and of course Gholam was a close friend of Dadash's, so that during the years since my return I had continued to see my cousins regularly. Zia-Saltaneh and Gholam had always told us warmly that Dr. Mossadegh had loved and revered

Shazdeh as his favorite uncle; in him, they said, the premier had seen an Iranian who looked to the future, not the past. But I could never enter their house on Kakh Avenue without remembering the past— that day in New York when I had read in the newspapers how the house had been shelled and sacked by a lynch mob. Unlike every other aristocratic old Persian household, at Gholam's there were no old family rugs, no antiques that had been handed down for generations: everything was shiny, inexpensive, and new. The restoration of their home spoke more tellingly than any words could have of the tragic, violent change that had overtaken the Mossadegh family.

Aware of the terrible mental torment of Dr. Mossadegh's isolation, I had often wished that I could visit him at Ahmadabad, not only for the honor of setting eyes on him again for the first time since my youth, but also to ease his loneliness a little. Sometimes I had begged Ahmad to let me go along when he and the others visited that week— we could pretend, I said, that I was a sister—but Ahmad had always replied that SAVAK knew who everyone was, and that it would be useless to try. In March 1967, however, he told me that I might come to Gholam's house and pay my last respects.

The next day I went to Kakh Avenue, and Ahmad took me up the stairs to his father's darkened room. Dr. Mossadegh was propped up in a hospital bed, the white sheet pulled up to his chest and a table full of sweetish-smelling medicines beside him. We stood at the bedside and my cousin said, "Father, I have brought Sattareh, who has been asking to see you."

I almost wept. His long, humorous, kindly face, the face that to Iranians like me had symbolized our pride in ourselves and our country, was so emaciated from illness and imprisonment that its skin looked like canvas stretched too tightly on a frame. The long and famous Mossadegh nose now protruded like a mountain rising above a rocky landscape, and the shadows around his eyes were like caves. I saw that the dust of death was on him.

With a great effort he lifted himself a little to greet me with a kiss. Unable to trust my voice, I leaned forward. He smiled. "*Dochter-da'i*," he said deliberately, "Daughter of my uncle, I am happy to see you."

I looked at him and saw that although his voice was a hoarse whisper, his speech was firm and clear, his eyes alert and sparkling. They were still alive and full of his old energy, and in astonishment I realized that inside, he hadn't changed at all.

"Do you remember, Father," said Ahmad with a smile, "how Satti wrote all those letters to Abbas telling you not to be so stubborn with the British?" Dr. Mossadegh chuckled and said that he did. He asked me what I was doing now. In a sentence or two I told him about the School of Social Work and what we were trying to accomplish. He nodded, but I saw that he was too weak to carry on a conversation. I took his hand and held it for a minute or two without speaking, wanting only to show how I loved and venerated him. Then I left.

He died the following week, at the beginning of No Ruz. I do not remember that his death was announced in the press; rather, as I recall, people learned of it the same way they had learned about his trial: in the Persian manner, from family to family, servant to servant, relative to relative. No public funeral or mourning rites were allowed, and although in his will Dr. Mossadegh had asked to be buried in Tehran, among the graves of Iranians who had died in the protests at his attempted removal in 1952, the Shah refused to allow this, knowing that it would provide a focus for opposition. Ahmad and Gholam buried their father at Ahmadabad.

What, I wondered bitterly, did the Shah have left to worry about? Not only was Dr. Mossadegh himself dead, but in the fourteen years since his overthrow it had become clear that all his sacrifices on behalf of our independence and the Iranian constitution had been for nothing. Anyone who showed evidence of leadership was jailed, banished, or silenced, and not even the Shah's most trusted advisers dared to contradict him. The king had made sure that no popular leader would ever have a chance to develop a following again. It was nearly unbearable for me to realize that Mohammed Mossadegh had died knowing that his fight had been for nothing, his struggle aborted, the faith he had given us rendered useless. The eyes I had looked into on Kakh Avenue had not been those of someone who believed that his life had been wasted. But my own heart was full of sorrow, regret, and anger.

12

THE BRIDGE OVER NOTHING

A ruler given to tyranny undermines his own sovereignty.
—Sa'adi

*B*Y THE END OF THAT DECADE, HOWEVER, THE "WHITE REVO-lution" seemed to be a resounding success. Our oil revenue had more than doubled in ten years, and we appeared to have entered into a kind of Golden Age in which we were rushing toward the future at breakneck speed. Small plots of land had been distributed to millions of villagers. New factories were producing everything from helicopters to textiles. Improved health services were enabling countless more babies that might once have died of malnutrition and disease to survive infancy. In addition to roads, dams, railways, airports, and hospitals, new schools were being built to educate the millions of average young men—boys just like Zamani, my hiking companions, and all the shy, hopeful youths I had first recruited—who were growing up and study-ing in the new universities or going abroad on government scholarships to seek the much-coveted degree that would elevate them to the ranks of teachers, engineers, and other middle-class professionals. Millions of young men with illiterate fathers and mothers now envisioned for themselves a prosperity, standing, and respect among their kinsmen that their parents had never dreamed of. All my students, graduates, and faculty looked forward with impatience to being able to live in a Western-style apartment with a shower and an indoor bathroom and to taking their vacations on the Riviera or in Paris.

An almost delirious admiration for things Western had seized the country. Everywhere in North Tehran one saw liquor stores, fancy international hotels, and signs advertising Gucci clothes or Kentucky Fried Chicken, as well as Western movie theaters and discos where young people could dance and drink on Thursday night until all hours. Everyone, especially the young, was avid for European or American clothes, films, music.

Such developments might not have seemed disturbing in the West, but in our country, propriety and filial obedience provided the glue that held families together, and hence society itself. Many people felt that we were not only trying to catch up with the West, but to *become* the West, while an entire older generation of parents, even among Persians of my class, was shocked and outraged at what these Western ways were doing to their children, culture, and what Iranians considered moral behavior. I had always believed that we could learn from Western methods of solving social problems, and of course I wanted my country to have such things as sewage plants and factories that produced consumer goods. But I, too, felt distressed by our wholesale embrace of Western products, Western culture, Western life-styles. Even the poor immigrants in the Tehran shantytowns, who deeply disapproved of the garish billboards and—to us—risqué cinema posters displaying the faces and limbs of Western movie actresses, craved Pepsi-Cola and Levi's. One acquaintance of mine, a man named Jalal Al Ahmad, who was a former country school principal and a writer of books about rural life that I greatly admired, had coined a phrase for Iranians who seemed to be relegating our own culture and traditions to the dustbin. He called them "Western-stricken" (some people have translated this with the awkward term "West-toxicated"). The phrase had become famous.

One day in 1967 or 1968, Jalal Al Ahmad was among a group of friends I had invited for tea who were arguing heatedly about what to do about the "Western-stricken," and I asked the author of this famous expression what he proposed as a solution to the problem.

Al Ahmad, a handsome, gray-haired man who liked to cover his strong feelings with a cynical, engaging grin, smiled and held his tea glass a little above his saucer, which was protruding over the edge of my coffee table. "Look," he said, "I don't like where this cup is sitting." He moved it to the part of the saucer that was sticking out over the edge. "I want to put it *here*."

I felt an alarm that had nothing to do with my teacup. "But it will fall!" I exclaimed. "Do you mean that you want to destroy everything you don't like?"

"Yes," he said with satisfaction. "That is my solution."

"No," I cried, "That's no solution, to smash everything. If we don't like the way things are, we must work—work until we find a way to make them better."

This conversation bothered me a great deal. Our country needed to believe in something constructive in this new, modern, urban world we were building so rapidly. We seemed to be losing the traditional values that had always sustained us, replacing them with nothing but material things—cars, blue jeans, and hamburgers. Yet nobody since Mossadegh had come up with a positive program. Iranians only complained: about the Shah's repressiveness, the government's corruption, the lack of freedom in the press, the "Western intoxication." Everyone seemed to be getting ahead, yet everyone wanted more than they had. Inflation was high, and even the spate of newly minted university graduates had to struggle to keep up with the price of food and housing. A sour anger and discontent, not only with the government but with many aspects of life in our country, had been seething for years—and while fear of SAVAK and the army had stifled it, it had never disappeared. Increasingly, with so many yearning for the new material goods and thinking only of how the country's growing wealth could benefit *them*, Iranians were more inclined to envy and resent those who had achieved success than to emulate people who wanted to do something for their community, and this envy was growing stronger all the time. I was reminded unhappily of the spiteful, divisive atmosphere that had ruled after Reza Shah's abdication. How, I wondered, were we going to make progress with our enormous social problems if even brilliant intellectuals like Al Ahmad had no positive solutions, only complaints? Just smashing teacups was no answer at all.

By now the School had opened or was building nearly two dozen community welfare and family planning centers in Tehran and the provinces, and a degree from the School of Social Work—which now had around two hundred students and screened several times that number of applicants each year—was growing more prestigious all the time. In 1970 I had begun a two-year, internationally accredited master's degree program, and more of our students than ever were going abroad for advanced training. I was proud that many old graduates, like Zamani, who had returned to Tehran from the provinces and was now working at one of the ministries and was also on my faculty, were providing us with the skilled and competent native Iranian social workers I had always wanted to staff the centers and teach at the School for us.

I was a little concerned, however, about the School's increasing size. I wanted us to keep on growing so that we could expand our programs and networks. But inevitably, expansion meant that I could not know all our students personally, or make sure as easily as I once had of the unselfishness and dedication of those we admitted. I accepted only applicants who scored in the top five percent of the university entrance exams, and had established a committee made up of Zamani and a number of other experienced faculty members to conduct interviews to screen out opportunists. Nevertheless, I worried that the growing materialism of Persian society in general was affecting the School as well. Many of our incoming male students, who came from modest backgrounds, tended to start their studies on the assumption that the School's purpose was not to educate them to think or train them to help the poor but to give them lunch every day, send them abroad to study, and eventually use the connections that our illustrious board of trustees afforded to get them a lucrative job when they graduated. As I became less and less able to know each student personally— and as they had less opportunity to know me—I was having to rely more on our curriculum than on my personal example to teach them their responsibility to others besides themselves.

Unfortunately also, by this time many students and even a number of my younger faculty members, knowing how highly the government and my board of directors esteemed us, and aware that I extended help to those around me, believed that "Khanom" had unlimited power to grant anyone's desires, and that, at the very least, I should pay a beginning assistant professor or a welfare center social worker a salary that would enable him to buy himself a house and a car. In an advanced, already industrialized society such expectations would not have been unreasonable, but in our country these were things that most people could not usually afford until they were well established, and often not then. Some of the more ambitious of the boys from poor families were perfectly certain, and expected, that my grand connections were going to help me land them a rich general's daughter to marry when they graduated.

I worked tirelessly to help my male students better their lot in life, but sometimes I felt my temper wearing thin over this Iranian obsession with being "somebody." For instance, almost no semester passed without someone's complaining that our name should be not "School of Social Work" but "University of Social Work." Naturally, I had stuck to my original policy of encouraging people to come to me with suggestions for change. But to this request I always replied—and with growing impatience as the complaint persisted year after year—that as we gave a degree in only one subject, we had to remain a "school," and that I couldn't make us a "university" simply by changing our name. My repeated explanations fell on deaf ears, and by now the grumbling about our being "only a school," when we were as distinguished an institution of professional education as any in Iran, got on my nerves. All these status-seeking Persians, I thought irritably, should be proud of what we had accomplished instead of complaining that I was denying them the prestige of a degree from a "university." But I reminded myself that this silly preoccupation with our own importance came from our ancient insecurity—the old, desperate need to feel that we and our families would survive.

As time went on, the self-centeredness I had noticed began to seem more disturbing. I was unhappy at a feeling that as the materialism of Iranians was increasing, so was ingratitude and disloyalty among us. I considered this most apparent in the cases of students and graduates whom I had arranged to send to foreign universities for advanced degrees—and who, after I had singled them out for this enormous personal advantage, refused to come back and repay their debt to the School and to their country by doing the work it had been understood they would return to do. I might add that arranging for someone from the School to study at a foreign institution involved a great outlay not only of government money but also of time and effort on my part, and I detested nothing so much as disloyalty.

One particularly foolish and ignoble example made a lasting impression on me. In 1971 or 1972, one of these newly returned graduates, whom I had sent to America on full scholarship and to whom I had written to offer a teaching post, arrived in my office at the beginning of the fall semester.

Previously, I had believed myself to know this individual well. I considered him an average, rather undistinguished young man from a typical working-class family. I had sent him abroad to acquire an advanced degree and had been counting on his accepting the post. He entered my office, however, startlingly decked out in a very American suit of bright red plaid. And when I greeted him, using his last name— which I still did even with close friends like Zamani—I was taken aback to hear from him that he had changed it: it was no longer that of the poor village his family came from, but something that sounded more distinguished. Looking about my office in disdain, he announced haughtily that he could not accept the post I was offering. He had studied in America for two years and spoke English. He had a master's degree now; he was somebody. Why should *he* stay here and train people to work in a slum? And with that, he left.

I was nearly speechless with anger. When I got home to Tajrish that night, I went straight to the house of my brother Khody, Hamdam's son, who at the time was with the Plan Organization, the governmental office that was responsible for sending students abroad. Arriving in his living room so indignant that I was practically in tears, I begged my brother to tell me why this was happening. Was I such a poor teacher? Had I failed so miserably to educate some people? Didn't our students believe any longer in helping their country? Or perhaps there was something about *me* that was causing them not to come back! Was I ever unkind? Wasn't I killing myself to help people like *them*! Their welfare was my only concern—yet they deserted me, and Iran!

Khody got up and hugged me. Patting my back, he said, "Dear, don't take it personally. Every year at the Plan Organization we send not one or two who don't come back, but hundreds. The government is educating our young people to build dams and work in hospitals. But it's not educating their minds. All they hear about in school is loyalty to the Shah, not the country, and all they see is a government that thinks only of itself. Why should they do otherwise than the government?"

Kia, who worked at the boys' orphanage, just laughed when I told him about this incident. "Listen, Khanom," he said lightly, "didn't anybody ever tell you about Iranians? We go where the wind blows us. That fellow in the red suit is a typical modern Persian patriot— he wants the wind to blow him back to America, where he can have a much nicer life than you can give him."

I answered firmly that, however true this might be of some people, I would never accept that I could not teach people to look further than their own narrow point of view. He and all the other "Bulldozers" were proof that we *could* train people's minds. I was as convinced now that I was right about this, I told Kia, as I had been at the beginning. Nevertheless, I could never recall this incident without every bit of my fury returning.

As time passed, I was feeling a pressing need to retreat from the strains of my work and from crowded, polluted Tehran. Even Tajrish, once a rural market village, had been absorbed into the northward-creeping city. The sports club I belonged to offered me exercise but no privacy, and I longed for someplace quiet, where I could really get away. In 1968 I had purchased an acre or two of land in a village called Galandwak, about a forty-five-minute drive from school. It lay in a wide mountain valley among orchards and wheat fields. I began clearing the land of stones and started an orchard, planting trees that would give big, golden Lebanese apples when mature. As soon as I had saved enough money, I built a small one-bedroom house for myself, along with a house for a gardener and his family to take care of the property while I was away. I was now going there every weekend and as often as I could during the week. I loved my young apple orchard and small house, from whose windows I could see, beyond the flat tin roofs of the village with its tiny mosque, the snow-capped mountains that to me signified home. Here I could relax from my work, enjoy my orchard, and hike with the Friday regulars.

Sometimes I asked Zamani if anyone in his family ever heard anything about their illustrious fellow citizen, the cleric Khomeini—who, I gathered, had come to be accorded the status of an ayatollah. Not a word, of course, had appeared about him in our censored press since his deportation to Turkey in 1964. He seemed to have vanished into the air—though, of course, nonpolitical Iranians like me who traveled in completely secular circles rarely heard about imprisoned or exiled clerics. Zamani only shook his head and shrugged, replying that he had heard the old fellow had gone to Iraq.

In October of 1971, the king, who several years earlier had crowned himself "Shahinshah," or "Emperor," held a lavish celebration at Persepolis to commemorate twenty-five hundred years of the Iranian monarchy and glorify his reign. The party, which attracted the attention of the entire world, was reported to cost more than one hundred million dollars. A few days after this event, Hossein informed me that the mullah at his neighborhood mosque had circulated a scathing blast from Ayatollah Khomeini against the Shah.

Since his banishment, the exiled cleric had been living and teaching in the Shiite holy city of Najaf in Iraq. From there, his followers smuggled his sermons back into Iran's mosques, so that his words actually reached as many Iranians from exile as if he had been preaching at the Feyziyeh. His sermon against the Persepolis celebration excoriated the Shah, whom he called an enemy of Islam, a man who ignored the fact that Iranians were starving and who sold oil to Israel, Islam's greatest enemy. Time and again, said the old cleric, the shahs of Iran had turned the pages of Iranian history black with their crimes. Islam was fundamentally opposed to monarchy.

This was the first time that Ayatollah Khomeini had attacked the monarchy itself. Indeed, even the American press, which normally never uttered a word of criticism of the Shah, looked askance at the celebration's staggering cost. But our growing oil income, the apparent successes of the White Revolution, and Iran's increasing military strength all seemed to be making the Shah more and more confident of his own position. He ignored the sermon and dismissed the foreign criticism. In the same year as the Persepolis celebration, for the first time we began to hear reports and rumors of guerrilla activity, and opposition to the Shah among Iranian students abroad was gaining strength. The Shah was watering Khomeini like a slow-growing tree and making him the religious opposition's uncontested champion. But Iranians like me didn't know that. In my circles, talk of the sermon died away quickly, and so, once again, did the name of Khomeini.

My own frustration with the government did not come from its in-clination to pomp (Iran had, after all, a glorious past, and I thought that a case could be made for spending what amounted to a rather small fraction of our gigantic oil income to show our pride in that), but rather from the impossibility of making public the facts our research established about Iran's social problems, or bringing anyone in the government to admit the truth about the White Revolution.

Even though everything about the Shah's program looked rosy on the surface—and we were certainly making genuine advances, not just in technology but also in literacy, rights and protections for women and children, and other areas that affected the well-being of millions— reality had never measured up to the government's lofty claims for what it called the "Shah-People Revolution." Two-thirds of the pop-ulation still earned less than seventy dollars a month. Health care in most rural areas was virtually nonexistent. At the same time the flow of immigrants from the countryside into the shantytowns was increasing every year, with the result that South Tehran's housing problems were worse than ever. The capital especially had overwhelming numbers of both working and unemployed poor.

The School of Social Work often published studies to show that not enough jobs, housing, health, educational, and social services were being created to accommodate this influx. For instance, the very fact that urban health care for the poor had improved meant that fewer babies died and more children needed schools. But these schools were not being built because the government did not want to admit that in solving some problems it was creating others—to do so would have been to risk displeasing the Shah, and the Shah's displeasure meant disgrace and perhaps jail. By intimidating and censoring the press, the government kept everyone in a kind of informational fog, a miasma of governmental lies, promises, propaganda, and grandiose claims that no one could disprove even if they wanted to try because the newspapers dared not publish the information. In Iran, no one could ever be quite sure of anything, except that it wasn't what the government said it was.

Even in the government itself, no one paid the slightest attention to our research. Many of the ministers or undersecretaries I knew warmly supported our work, but if I tried to press the facts on them, I ran smack into a wall. In 1965, the Shah had appointed as premier a former foreign ministry official named Amir Abbas Hoveyda (the man who had replaced Asadollah Alam had been assassinated). Hoveyda was a cozy, witty, pipe-smoking politician who ruthlessly eliminated all potential rivals for the Shah's favor and showed signs of becoming the most durable premier in our modern history. He claimed that the number of Iranians opposed to the Shah came to a mere fourteen hundred disgruntled persons, and he had so frightened almost everyone in government who might oppose his policies that when one parliamentary deputy had the temerity to inquire about a matter in a proposal, the premier cowed him into silence merely by remarking ominously, "Listen, mister, I'm not *your* prime minister, I'm His Majesty's prime minister."

Once, discussing the plight of the rural areas with a certain individual who held very high office in the health ministry—someone of education and culture whom I had known for years—I asked why he refused to pass on to Hoveyda some information I had given him. "Aren't you the same man I used to know," I demanded, "who always talked of what he wanted to do for the rural areas? You know that our medical graduates refuse to work in the countryside. Why don't you just *tell* the Shah or Hoveyda that in the whole country, there isn't a single village with permanent health workers or a medical clinic of its own?"

"Look here, Khanom," said my friend, "do you see this piece of furniture I'm sitting on? This chair, which is that of a very high official in the health ministry, does something to the person who sits in it: it compels him never to do anything but bow and say, 'Yes, Your Majesty.' Whoever does not sit in this chair, let *him* go and tell the Shah and Hoveyda the truth."

I felt that Queen Farah was the only one who really wanted to know what was going on in the lives of common people. I was now on the boards of a number of charitable organizations that she sponsored, and often met with her at her office to discuss the new welfare centers we were building and the School's other activities. She never expected flattery and was never angry just because I told her the truth about something. She was always available if a problem arose at one of our centers that she could help with, and she always attended the opening of every welfare center we built, no matter how distant the province. This was of enormous importance to us, because it not only bolstered the morale of the staff and all my students but let the public know about the work we were doing—since the Persepolis celebrations, getting a story into the newspapers had been growing more and more difficult unless the Shah, the prime minister, or a member of the royal family was the subject.

Unfortunately, our ministers were no more anxious to speak openly to the Queen than to the Shah or Hoveyda. In board meetings, they often told her blatant lies. This made me very angry, because I knew that she wanted to be told the truth. I would always come armed with documents and statistics, so that whenever somebody said that the population growth in Tehran had dropped to two percent the previous year, I could pass a note to her saying that it was really *three* point two percent, which of course was an enormous difference. The queen would then inquire why the minister had given her a wrong statistic. This, of course, would not endear me to the furious official, who would try to have me thrown off the board.

By this time I had become rather well known (or notorious, as some people felt) for not making speeches and not using many words when I did, and my reluctance to show more enthusiasm worried some people in my family. After every commencement, Shazdeh—our eldest brother, Mohammed Vali Mirza—would take me aside and tell me very seriously, "Satti, you *must* praise the Shah and the royal family; SAVAK will get after you if you don't." But I couldn't bring myself to do this. I wanted to keep the School untainted by politics. Besides, I loathed the kinds of speeches Persian officials made. I blushed just to think of the Queen's opinion of me if I were to say at the opening of one of our centers, "O Queen, your husband is wonderful, your children are wonderful, you yourself are wonderful." As for praising the Shah, I thought we had enough nightingales in Iran.

Everyone was so terrified of SAVAK by now that hardly anyone even thought it possible to oppose the government. Although we knew that terrorist incidents occurred, people had been amazed when the press, in the winter of 1971, reported the capture and execution of thirteen armed guerrillas who had dared to raid a police station on the Caspian and kill three of the gendarmes. My students, faculty, and I all took very seriously the dark joke that wherever three Iranians gathered, one was from SAVAK. The secret police, now under the directorship of General Nassiri, had an informer in every classroom, students who were paid or blackmailed into reporting what the teacher and other students said, and reported anyone who discussed things honestly as a "subversive" or an "agitator." I now told my own students expressly at the beginning of every semester that, as we knew not everyone was trustworthy, our discussions of social problems must remain completely nonpolitical, and I made it clear that we would never discuss either the Shah or the regime. Since the mere mention of the Shah was enough to make any student freeze and look over his shoulder, I never had to repeat this warning.

Once in a while, a letter from SAVAK would arrive addressed to me personally, marked "Confidential" and containing a warning that So-and-So, whom I was about to hire, was considered "not adequately loyal." I always ignored these letters and went ahead with whatever I was going to do, but then a few days later some man in a dark suit would come to my office to warn me in person that this individual was "dangerous to the national security." Somehow I always managed to keep my temper, send for tea and cookies, and reply that I was pleased to hear that SAVAK was concerned about the national security. I, too, I said, was working for the national security—I was showing people how to improve their lives and give them some hope and faith in the future. I was hiring the person in question because he knew his subject, and he wasn't going to talk about politics, and did SAVAK by some chance think that *my* loyalty to the country was in question?

By this time I would have gotten really angry, and after saying hastily, Oh, yes, yes, to be sure, everyone knew what Khanom Farman Farmaian was doing for the country, this anonymous fellow would just finish his tea quickly and leave me to fume. The same one never came back twice, which I thought was very inefficient of them. But I had no illusions about either my immunity or the School's. The Queen's patronage gave us some protection, as did Asadollah Alam, who considered us valuable—and who, having been made minister of court, was now my chairman. But SAVAK was now more powerful than anyone except the prime minister and the Shah himself. It didn't take any trouble with us only because we were too small a fish to bother frying.

Once (I think it must have been around the time the thirteen guerrillas were captured and executed), SAVAK came to school late in the evening and arrested a group of graduate students who had been studying in the library. Horrified and outraged, I got in my car and drove as fast as I could to the court minister's home, where I begged his confidential assistant, a man named Pedram, to tell Mr. Alam that I needed to talk to him urgently. To my dismay, Mr. Pedram informed me that the court minister was spending the evening with the Shah. A few minutes later, however, Mr. Alam called in. Very upset, I begged him to get my students released and returned to their families. Half an hour later, he called again. General Nassiri, he said, had known nothing of the matter—it was all just a mistake by a subordinate. He gave me a number to call, and said that I must tell the person who answered that the students were to be freed at once. I was to say that "the agents had been given false information." I did as he told me, and my students were released the same night.

I was frightened by this incident. I held myself entirely responsible for my students' safety, and I certainly didn't want the School to start having trouble from this quarter. Several months later I managed to learn through a relative who knew the right people that SAVAK had been looking for someone who was believed to have terrorist connections and had been making calls from the School. I was not surprised that SAVAK tapped anyone's phones, but I was shocked by the news that someone at our institution had fallen under suspicion. Finally, though, I reminded myself that, as I kept the School's grounds and garden open to the public at all times, anybody, really, could have entered one of the buildings and used a telephone there. This reassured me a little, but I did not want the School's neutrality violated again. I began making even more of a point of reminding both my students and my faculty that social work must not become politicized.

Nevertheless, there could be no doubt that more revolutionary views than mine, spurred by the growing anti-Shah student movement abroad, were gaining ground at all institutions of higher education. Recently a gifted and charismatic young intellectual named Dr. Ali Shariati had been winning enormous popularity among young people, including many of my own students. Dr. Shariati, who had studied Marxism, said that Shiism was actually a revolutionary creed that should inspire Moslems to rise against injustice, oppression, Western imperialism, international Zionism, and the degrading "Western intoxication." Shariati's new explanation of the meaning of Islam was giving educated young Iranians in the schools and universities a fresh and exciting way of expressing the deep frustration millions of people felt with the direction that our society had taken under the Pahlavis. Cassette recordings of his talks were appearing even in rural villages.

I was curious about Shariati myself, and at the students' urging I invited him to speak in our auditorium. Shariati's works were not banned, and in my view staying clear of politics did not include preventing people from hearing whom they wished to hear. In his talk, Dr. Shariati was careful not to preach openly against the government;

he expounded his message instead through allegories and examples from history. I found him an impressive speaker. Soon, however, SAVAK had enough, and not long afterward it arrested and jailed him and banned his writings.

The students left a poster advertising the event on the pillar at the entrance of the main building as a permanent memorial of his visit, and now I saw it every time I entered there. Sometimes I wondered again who it was that SAVAK had wanted to arrest. Social work stood for building, not destroying, and it wasn't sticking my head in the sand, I thought, to hope that the person had not been one of *our* students or graduates. In our country, everything was dangerous now. We could not even say something as simple and harmless as "I am not against the monarchy, but I am against the suppression of our constitution, the corruption and injustice in our government and the courts of law, the destruction of our political rights and freedoms, and the drowning of our ancient Persian culture in a mindless imitation of the West. And I want these things to stop."

Ever since my return to Iran more than a decade earlier, my chief personal concern had always been Mitra's education. She had graduated from her English school in 1966 and gone on to attend a small college in Florida. She was now a lovely young woman, graceful and sensible, but rather quiet. I had been a little anxious about her studying in the United States, but I need not have worried. Mitra, beneath her soft manner, was as capable of taking care of herself as I had been at her age.

She made friends wherever she went, and even brought some of them, both men and women, home to Tehran during the summers to meet me and all her other "parents." I often dreamed that one day she would finish her studies and return to Iran to begin a career; I planned to fix up part of my house in Tajrish so that she could have her own quarters at Reswanieh. I was therefore delighted when she graduated in June of 1970 and decided to study early childhood education at Indiana University. She had spent time during several of her summers as a volunteer at one of our centers, and now I could dare to hope that one day she would return home and use her knowledge to work with us.

I was concerned, however, that her schooling had been so completely Western—I didn't want her to forget that her first heritage had been Eastern, and I wanted her to be aware that not all that was worth knowing flowed from the West, nor was all the West had given the world good. As a graduation present, therefore, I told her that I would take her on a six-week trip to the Orient, where I had to attend a conference in Tokyo. We would visit New Delhi, Nepal, Bangkok, Hong Kong, Manila, and Japan, where I thought it especially important to see the hospital in Hiroshima where many survivors of the first atomic bomb had spent nearly their entire lives.

I was nervous about going to India. Mitra and I had never discussed her father, but I decided that I could no longer evade the question that had haunted me for eighteen years. I still had an old Calcutta address for Arun, and I put it in my handbag. When we arrived in our hotel in New Delhi, I took a deep breath and observed to Mitra that, as her father lived in Calcutta, we might go there to visit him. "You know that he loves you," I began awkwardly, "and I'm sure that he would like to see you—"

"No, Mummy," said Mitra with gentle firmness, "that's not necessary. If he had loved me he would have stayed with me." Greatly relieved, I saw that my daughter knew her own mind. I felt very proud of her maturity, and of my family, too, because now I was certain that all of us together had been able to give her what she needed.

By the time Mitra had almost finished with her two years of graduate school in the spring of 1972, I was making excited plans for her to come home for good and begin working at one of our welfare centers. Every time I went to the bazaar and saw a lovely old Persian antique— a bit of tile, a length of hand-loomed fabric, a brass candelabrum, things that our "Western mad" society was throwing out or selling for a song—I would think, "Mitra could use this when she comes to live in Tajrish," or, "That rug would be nice for Mitra's bedroom."

In June, however, my fantasies came to a rude awakening when my daughter called and told me joyously that her own plans for herself revolved entirely around a tall, handsome American graduate student in her own field, and that she wanted to marry him in September. She reminded me that she had brought Mike home one summer to meet us all, and that we had all liked him. She felt I would approve of her decision.

For just a moment I could barely grasp the phone. I could not for the life of me remember who "Mike" was—Mitra had brought so many friends to visit us, both male and female, and, happy that she was home and busy with my work while she entertained her friends, I had never realized that one of them meant more to her than the others. When my first shock passed, I was dismayed. She had always talked of traveling, of having a profession; why did she want to give all that up and get married? I said after a moment that I did remember Mike, and thought that he was a nice young man. But did she really want to settle down so soon? Didn't she want to use two or three years to do all the things she had dreamed of doing? But Mitra had made up her mind, and, remembering my own struggle to live my life as I had wanted to live it and not as tradition dictated, I decided that I must not try to dissuade her.

So instead of welcoming my daughter home again, a few months later I flew to Bloomington, Indiana, to meet my future son-in-law again. I insisted on only one thing, that Mitra be married, as an Iranian daughter should be, in the presence of her family. I managed to round up three representatives of our clan: my brother Rashid, who was going to be in New York that summer; Jody, Hafez's wife, who could come from Austin, where Hafez was teaching at the University of Texas; and my niece Susu, Farough and Jean's middle daughter, who was studying at the University of Georgia. Standing under a big tree in a garden before a smiling woman justice of the peace who performed the ceremony, I was happy to see my lovely daughter's joy. But the flight home was a long one, and I had many hours for the knowledge to sink in that she would never be my companion in Tajrish or take part in the School's work.

I remembered how Khanom had suffered when I had left to go to a country at the end of the earth, and I knew that the pain she had felt then was what I was feeling now. All this time, I realized, I had unconsciously beguiled myself with a vision of Mitra beside me in my old age, lunching with me in the middle of her workday, as I still did with Khanom. That had not been Mitra's destiny, nor mine, and I— wanting to, perhaps—had deluded myself. Now I wondered: if I had stayed home in the andarun and married, like the proper Persian daughter my mother raised me to be, would I have been rewarded by having a child who stayed close by me? But then that child would not have been Mitra.

I thought of the Frenchwomen Dadash had told me about so long ago on that bright March day in 1944 in the café on the Avenue Lalezar—women who sat alone at small tables in the cafés in Paris, taking their meals by themselves. At the time I had understood only that he was telling me I must not be shy about appearing in public, or be afraid to move in a world of men. A generation later, I understood that my brother had also been trying to warn me of the loneliness that could come to someone who chose not to live the life of an ordinary woman.

*   *   *

On my return, I gladly threw myself back into my work, blocking out my personal cares, as I had always been able to do when I had tasks to accomplish. We now had enough donations of money and land for fifty or sixty welfare centers around the country. Moreover, the School by this time was something of a showcase in the Middle East, and I had to receive many visitors and travel a great deal. I was also on the board of the International Association of Schools of Social Work and held a second volunteer position as a vice president of International Planned Parenthood. Furthermore, I was appearing on a weekly radio program discussing social issues, representing the International Social Service in Iran—this was still another voluntary position, in which I tried to help resolve individual cases of an international nature, especially adoption cases and the agonizing problems of international child custody disputes—and acting, as always, as the School's chief fund-raiser, mentor, cheerleader, family problem solver, and mother confessor.

In addition, around 1972 I had started a program through the ministry of education to send social workers into high schools and elementary schools, to teach children about civic responsibility, an area in which the schools were still failing badly. I knew that we couldn't do anything about SAVAK or the government's lies, but I felt that we could try to instill in young Iranians a feeling of obligation to their society.

Unfortunately, the whole climate of that society was now evolving rapidly in a way that continually undermined these efforts. In 1973, both OPEC and the Shah announced the enormous price increases that led to what the West called "the oil crisis" but which, from our point of view, could best be described as what has been termed "the Middle Eastern Gold Rush." This was a phenomenon produced by the combination of virtually unlimited petrodollars, which were flowing into the public treasury by the billions every year, and the Shah's insatiable appetite for buying Western military hardware. Extraordinary amounts of the oil money—almost forty percent of the government's budget—went to purchasing American weapons for his army. Additional wealth was going into fancy development projects, many of which we didn't need, such as nuclear power plants.

Traditionally, there had never been any distinction in Iran between the public purse and the monarch's private wealth, and the Shah now treated the national income as though it were his to spend as he pleased, with virtually everyone in government following suit. Hundreds of people used connections in high places, especially connections with the Shah's royal relatives, to swing "commissions" of hundreds of thousands of dollars for brokering government contracts for the Western corporations that rushed to take advantage of the spending spree. Millions were made overnight on rake-offs from loans from someone in the royal family or the government to build factories and luxury office buildings. A new class of Iranian nouveaux riches was born, and the Avenue Lalezar suddenly swarmed with big European limousines that blocked the traffic in front of Charles Jourdan and Cartier. Men nobody had heard of six months before flocked to North Tehran's French restaurants and danced all night, drinking champagne, in its nightclubs. Their wives flew to Paris to get their hair done and brought back crateloads of designer clothes. They gave parties with Russian vodka and imported delicacies from Maxim's, and flew to Saint-Moritz or Monte Carlo for weekend vacations.

To average people such as my students, faculty, and graduates, this ostentatious spending was like a heady, explosive inhalant. We were a poor people, and while old landowning families like mine had been wealthy, when they spent in public it was to endow seminaries and hospitals. Iranians were dazzled by the sight of this new and conspicuous consumption, in which it was obvious that the spenders hadn't come by their money selling magazine subscriptions. If the government could make these people, whose fathers no one had ever heard of, rich overnight just because they had the right connections, why shouldn't it do the same for everyone else?

This preoccupation with riches became wedded to the simmering discontent of twenty years. I began to wonder what was going to happen when all these highly wrought expectations were disappointed, as sooner or later they must be. Government spending on development and construction was creating factories and windfall jobs for laborers, and more poor were streaming into Tehran from the provinces than ever before. But this spending was also sending inflation wildly out of control, while much of the work connected with weapons maintenance or other military contracts went to foreign workers, for not enough Iranians had the necessary technical skills. Nobody could keep up with inflation, yet those who did not have everything they wanted—and people now wanted *everything*—sulked and gnawed themselves in envy, feeling that they were not getting their due.

These mounting tensions were being further exacerbated by what I can only term a government campaign of psychological degradation of our people, at all levels of society. The Shah now boasted that Iran was on its way to becoming the "fifth power" in the world, and the Hoveyda government acted as though all Iranians should bow their heads in gratitude for the benefits their government and their king, the Light of the Aryans, was bestowing on them. No anniversary of significance to the Pahlavis, whether it was the Shah's birthday, his father's birthday, or the anniversary of his escape from an assassination attempt in 1965, could pass without a "festival of national thanksgiving" at the city stadium. I was expected to send a quota of students and faculty to march in the parade. Needless to say, nobody wanted to attend, and since not going meant drawing the unwelcome attentions of SAVAK, Esther and I always had to go around asking the cafeteria staff, gardeners, drivers, and the other servants to attend the rallies in place of our students, in exchange for the day off.

One day in March of 1975, the Shah announced that he had just abolished our two-party political system. From now on, there would be only one party. He was calling it the "Resurgence" Party, and Premier Hoveyda would run it. Everybody was expected to join, and anyone who didn't feel like doing so could go to the foreign ministry, get a passport, and leave the country. When I asked Mr. Alam if my school had to join, too, he said yes, everybody had to prove their loyalty by signing up. He was enormously pleased with the whole idea. The old parties had never done anything; this one was really going to get things organized.

Humiliated and resentful like everyone else, I got a group membership application form, signed my name to it, and placed it unhappily on a table in front of the library for the students and faculty. In 1960, I thought, Mohammed Reza Shah had told us that he believed in democracy and the two-party system. Why was he doing this to us now?

Kia, when I said this to him, shrugged ironically. Why not, if the government had only fourteen hundred opponents, as Hoveyda claimed? By the way, he quipped, had I heard the new slogan in the last royal birthday parade? The marchers hadn't chanted *Javid Shah*— "Long live the Shah"—but *chapid Shah*: "The Shah is running off with our money." The government couldn't tell the difference.

It quickly became obvious, however, that whatever liberty of thought or expression had remained to us was no longer being tolerated. Aided by SAVAK, the new party at once began intruding itself into every aspect of life. No longer was it possible to stay out of jail just by refraining from open criticism. Writers, poets, teachers, intellectuals, and artists who failed to glorify the White Revolution sufficiently were beaten or jailed, tortured for being "Marxists," and forced to "confess" their errors in public. Dozens of prominent clerics were banished or imprisoned. Everybody now had a family member, or a friend, or a friend of a friend who had mysteriously disappeared.

By this time I was living almost exclusively in my small house at Galandwak, to which I retreated every evening. The house had become my sanctuary. I loved the clean air and peace of its orchard, where, in winter, gazelles and bighorn sheep came down to nibble at the snow-covered apple trees. Living there, however, also gave me an excuse to refuse invitations to nightclubs and to parties of the fashionable set, which revolved around the inner circle of the imperial court and which were attended by foreign nationals and embassy personnel; SAVAK kept a careful eye on anyone who talked to Americans or other foreigners.

In the School's early years I had tried to spend time with foreigners, and especially Americans. Despite the role the CIA had played in overthrowing Mossadegh, I always hoped that my opinions and those of other Iranians unconnected with the court would somehow get back to the American Embassy or the Iran-America Society. If the U.S. State Department, I reasoned, only knew how much resentment people felt and how many problems were simmering beneath the smooth surface Westerners saw when they visited Iran, the American government might compel the Shah to permit genuine political freedom. I felt that if I could be honest with anyone about the government's repressiveness, it was with Americans.

But American visitors were not interested in our political problems. "Oh," they would say when I tried to tell them how much was wrong, "but the Shah is doing so much for your country! You're making such progress!"

By this time I finally understood that every nation saw every other nation solely from the standpoint of its own interest. But I was increasingly baffled and angry that Americans simply refused to face facts that every Iranian knew. The Pahlavi Foundation, officially a charity organization, was a conduit for siphoning off the oil money into royal business ventures, court patronage, and leverage schemes. The greed of the Shah's relatives was so outrageous that it embarrassed even the officials and businessmen who participated in the corruption. Many of our government's statistics about the White Revolution and the internal opposition were barefaced, transparent lies—yet everyone who read the international press could see that American newspapers and the U.S. government were swallowing this propaganda hook, line, and sinker. Why, I wondered, were Americans so credulous and blind? Why didn't the American press write about the way things really functioned in Iran, and say what we didn't dare say because of SAVAK— were they all so afraid of losing their visas? Why didn't the United States government at least *try* to find out what was really going on?

Only my occasional meetings with Queen Farah provided a measure of relief from the constant anger and frustration I now felt about every aspect of our political situation. I had grown to love and admire the Queen for her warmth and intelligence, her honest nature, and her absolute commitment to the welfare of her most vulnerable subjects, especially women; I felt a deep personal gratitude not only for her support of our work but for her willingness to listen to the truth. Furthermore, while the Shah seemed to be removing himself more and more from the current of the people's feeling, she remained one of the few with direct access to him. Although I knew that her ability to sway him was limited—she fought an endless, losing battle for influence with his sisters—I nevertheless hoped that some of the information I planted in her ear would find its way to him.

Once, at the opening of a new community welfare center in one of the shantytowns, we went up to the roof and I pointed out the single asphalted road running among the squalid shacks. Did she realize, I asked her, that this road was paved only two days ago, in honor of her visit? "Perhaps," she murmured dryly, "I should come more often." "Yes, Your Majesty," I said, "you *should* come more often. Because any progress we make in this country is only for the eyes of you and your husband."

The year after the invention of the Resurgence Party, I, along with millions of other Iranians, woke up one morning and learned that the Shah had just abolished the Moslem calendar. Effective immediately, everything in Iran—birthdays, religious holidays, historical events—would be dated not from the year of the Prophet's flight to Medina but from the beginning of the Persian monarchy three thousand years ago. We were no longer living in the Moslem year 1355, but the "monarchial" year 3225.

Actually, the new calendar was an attack on the clergy—in effect, the Shah was declaring that the Moslem calendar was irrelevant to his modern new society. It was exactly as though the American president or the British monarch had announced that the Christian calendar was no longer valid and that it was not 1976, but some year nobody had ever heard of. In which millennium, I wondered, had I been born? In which "monarchial" year would my passport expire? In what century were my students supposed to receive their degrees? The Shah, who treated Iran as his toy, had so lost touch with the reality of our feelings that he was entering the domain of the surreal and recasting time itself.

Reality, however, was pressing upon us like a slowly rising tide. To halt the runaway inflation the government's spending had caused, the

Resurgence Party was now cutting back—not on military expenditures or showy nuclear power plants, but on basic development projects and new building construction. This left many businesses stranded and forced to lay off workers. In the meantime, the props of the White Revolution, insufficiently supported at the base, were beginning to crack. Dams constructed at extraordinary expense did not distribute water or electricity to the places that needed them. Modern factories built without any thought as to whether a sufficient market existed for their products were becoming choked with inventory, and workers who had been promised a share of company profits found that the profits were nonexistent. Shipping and transportation facilities were inadequate to process deliveries of food and consumer goods, which waited for months at the docks. As the ordinary necessities of life became harder to obtain, prices rose still further. There were shortages of goods, fuel, and power.

One of the most tragic failures was that of land reform, which had been run by men who neither knew nor cared about villagers and farming. The plots distributed had not been large enough to yield a living, while primitive peasants dependent for centuries on landlords had been given neither the means nor the knowledge to succeed as modern farmers, and in many cases the few cooperative banks that had been set up to help them were plundered by the villagers themselves. Hence, millions of able-bodied Iranians, having spent a few years watching new tractors they couldn't repair rust in their small fields, had pulled up stakes and made their way to the cities with their families. Migration had become a flood: fully a tenth of Iran's population had moved to the capital and other towns. This was a catastrophe, for while formerly we had been able to grow just enough to feed our population, now we were importing great quantities of food from foreign countries, and thousands of Iranian villages were empty and dying.

Meantime, the government, preoccupied with paying for American weapons and an army vastly greater than any conceivable threat could justify, was still unable to provide enough jobs, housing, schools, medical, and sanitation services to keep up with the giant population of the slums and shantytowns. Four million of Tehran's five million inhabitants, most of them illiterate or barely educated and nearly all of them deeply disappointed in their visions of a better life in the city, now lived in South Tehran, where many dwelt in rat-infested hovels and worried about their children. These children had no place to play, often no schools to attend, and either went to work or got into mischief in the immoral city—a place full of shameless Western advertisements, cinemas, liquor stores, nightclubs, and discos where Moslem daughters wore clothes that left their limbs naked and strange boys and girls danced together publicly. Relatives who found jobs working for rich people and foreigners in North Tehran came home in the evenings with stories of parties where men and women mixed together, drank wine, and smoked opium. For these uprooted poor especially, the Shah's modern society was atheistic, an anathema.

Our newly created white-collar class had also been deeply disappointed in its aspirations. Few of its members had realized the hopes of fabulous wealth that the oil boom had produced, and with the economy suddenly contracting again because of the government's efforts to control inflation, Iranians found their dazzling expectations of cars, houses, and European vacations vanishing like a mirage. To many rank-and-file Persians, in fact, the only real beneficiaries of the oil wealth were the thousands of foreigners they saw shopping and living in North Tehran—not only the engineers and skilled workers imported from India, Korea, the Philippines, and other developing countries to fill the gap caused by the lack of similarly skilled Iranians, but, first and foremost, Americans.

Most of the thousands of Americans now working in Tehran had come as technical advisers and consultants to the U.S. military or international corporations. To the eyes of any average Iranian, they lived like kings, in a separate community that had its own school, radio and television station, and country club. Most Persians considered a stroll through any good neighborhood in North Tehran evidence enough that the Pahlavi Shah had once again sold out the country's hopes to foreigners. What better proof of Iran's enslavement to American interests could there be, people said, than the fact that Richard Helms, the former director of the same CIA that had helped to overthrow Mossadegh and create SAVAK, was now the American ambassador, appointed in order that Washington might better relay instructions to its stooge?

Thus, disappointment, envy, repression, and the government's lies, corruption, and injustice were building an explosive, poisonous resentment that had no outlet. The illiterate, apolitical poor could barely make sense of the radio speeches given by the Shah and his false-hearted, fancy-talking ministers. They were seeking solace and explanations for their miseries from the person who, back home in the village, had always stood for simple righteousness and God's will, the mullah in the Friday mosque. But abroad and in the universities and technical colleges and among factory workers, an active, secret underground was spreading, fueled by Ayatollah Khomeini's steadfast opposition from abroad and inspired by Dr. Ali Shariati's message that Islam was against the oppression and economic exploitation of the masses.

When a dam begins to crumble high in the mountains, the people in the lowlands are unaware; they go about their business in ignorance. Like the vast majority of educated Iranians, I knew no more than what I read in the foreign press about anti-Shah demonstrations abroad, or the faint rumors that reached us of an underground opposition movement to whose members the Shah loosely and contemptuously referred as "Islamic Marxists." But we did know that even people at the imperial court themselves were disgusted with the corruption, injustice, and stagnation of Pahlavi society.

Often, these days, I wished that I had possessed my sagacious father's ability to discern the future. Recently, while serving as dame d'honneur during a state visit by the president of Mexico at that time, Luis Echeverría Alvarez, I had been reminded of Shazdeh in a most unexpected and moving way. The Echeverrías' party had been lodged at Golestan Palace, the museum and the former residence of the Qajar shahs, and the first evening, when my duties were over, I began strolling about the chamber to which I had been assigned, lost in admiration at the beauty of its magnificent antiques. One particularly handsome carpet, of exceptional richness and value, caught my eye. In accordance with ancient custom, the anonymous weavers had woven into the design the identity of the nobleman who had commissioned it. As I bent down to see whether I knew the name, I suddenly found myself following a script that was familiar and dear to me, for the carpet had belonged to one of the Qajar estates confiscated to build the Marble Palace, and the name was my father's.

As if by magic, I felt Shazdeh's presence surrounding me, urging me to persevere as he had done. Neither the loss of material possessions nor political or personal calamity had ever weakened his spirit. The carpet's design was woven with his name as permanently and indelibly as change and turmoil were woven into Persian history. Remembering his indomitable will, in that moment I felt comforted and encouraged. No matter what happened, I thought, I would always carry on the School's work.

In the spring of 1976, Shala, who had married a young man active in the Marxist underground, told me that she was leaving to go with her husband to the United States, where he would be out of danger of arrest. Kia, too, had decided to leave. For years he had been frustrated and bitter over corruption at the orphanage and the difficulty of changing anything, and now he told me that he couldn't stand it anymore. He was going to go to America and open a clothing store. If it hadn't been for my example, he said, he would never have stayed this long. The Shah and our leaders were only for themselves and the future of their families, our politicians all belonged to the party of the wind, and our society was rotten through and through.

The loss of two graduates I was so fond of was a great blow. Sorrowfully, I replied that I didn't blame Kia for leaving. But, I said, I still had hope. I still believed that if we only set our shoulders to the wheel and worked even harder, we could overcome our problems, and I would never give up. We were expanding. The School was admitting more and more students—next year I expected over five thousand applicants—and I intended to expand our community and family planning programs; as our people's lives became easier, we could start teaching more of them about the importance of social and civic responsibility, as we had begun doing in the schools. We *could* make a difference, and I was just going to put my head down and forge ahead. "Dearest Khanom," said Kia sadly, "with all respect, I wouldn't be so optimistic about changing the nature of our countrymen. Don't put your head down too far, or you won't be able to see anything."

Nevertheless, in some ways 1976 was a banner year for me: in June, Mitra, Mike, and my infant grandson, Kayvon, came to live in Iran for nine months while my son-in-law wrote his doctoral dissertation. I moved most of my belongings to Galandwak so that they could have the entire house at Tajrish. Mitra trained field-workers in child education at one of our day-care centers. In the summer we all visited the provinces, traveled, and hiked together. It was a brief but very happy fulfillment of my dreams, especially when I saw how much Mitra still loved Iran.

Even when they returned to the United States in February 1977, I was not despondent: Mitra was pregnant again, and her child was due in August. In the spring, still glowing from the recent visit, I took my savings and made a down payment on a three-bedroom apartment under construction in North Tehran, then wrote to Mitra that it would be for her if one day she and Mike ever wanted to come and live with the children in Iran. If not, Kayvon and her next child could have it when they were older. I wanted my grandchildren to learn about the country whose history and culture would be their Persian grandmother's legacy to them. I wanted them to know its past and feel assured of a place in its future. I was certain that I would never leave my country. I wanted only to live and die in Iran.

13

THE MAN WITH THE MICROPHONE

A new dynasty gains domination over the ruling dynasty
through perseverance, and not through sudden action.

—Ibn Khaldun, fourteenth-century Arab historian

*J*UST AS EVERYONE'S ANGER AND FRUSTRATION WAS HUMMING in the air like a high-voltage wire, early in 1977 the political situation underwent an abrupt and hopeful change. The well-publicized statements on human rights by the new American president Jimmy Carter appeared to imply that regimes which suppressed political freedoms might be deprived of American arms and foreign aid. That, at any rate, was how both the Shah and his domestic opponents interpreted the American position.

All at once, the Shah began initiating small reforms, with the promise of more to come. Press censorship was relaxed enough to permit criticism of his ministers, if not of the king personally. In the prisons, where we could send social workers but had never been allowed to meet or talk with political prisoners, the International Red Cross was allowed to conduct inspections.

In May, the American secretary of state, Cyrus Vance, visited Iran, and it was whispered that he had told the Shah that if he didn't obey

Mr. Carter's wishes and allow greater freedom of speech, the Americans would remove him from the very throne to which they had restored him in 1953. Soon after this a few courageous people decided to risk a test of the new political waters. One brave journalist, Hadj-Sayyid Javadi, wrote an open letter to Premier Hoveyda asking why, if the opposition was only fourteen hundred people, Hoveyda's lying government had spent millions on SAVAK and the other security forces? In June, Dr. Shapour Bakhtiar and two more of the National Front's most respected leaders published an open letter to the Shah personally, stating flatly that our country was threatening to plunge into chaos because of economic mismanagement, corruption, immorality, sycophancy, official brutality, and the government's contempt for Iranians' rights and dignity. They warned him to release political prisoners and establish a regime based on a popular plurality, and demanded other reforms as well. Otherwise, they warned the Shah, he and his government were doomed.

These brave letters filled me and all liberal Iranians with amazement and joy. At last somebody had told the Shah that he must recognize the will of his own people. Bakhtiar and his colleagues were heroes. We were even more astonished when, instead of arresting the letter writers, the Shah removed Hoveyda, shifting him to the post of minister of court, and appointed as prime minister Jamshid Amouzegar, an honest, independent man who had been Hoveyda's interior minister but had had the courage to oppose his policies. I could hardly contain my elation, though I was less elated with the fact that Hoveyda was now the chairman of my board. Soon other letters began to circulate, signed by lawyers, writers, politicians, and intellectuals, and human rights groups began to form.

I hoped that now the Shah would appoint Bakhtiar to head a task force to investigate the wrongs done to the nation and recommend reforms—that, I felt, was what a real leader would do: pay attention to how ordinary people felt and acknowledge that he could no longer simply ignore legitimate criticism.

However, while it was now obvious that the Shah could not return to the total censorship and repression of the past few years, if he had been hoping that loosening restrictions would take the edge off the discontent, the effect was just the opposite, and it was an alarming one. Allowed to rise to the surface, and fed by long-suppressed resentment and the dashed hopes and setbacks of the past two years, people's anger was churning like magma in a crater. Communists and other radical groups had begun actively recruiting followers at the University and elsewhere. Demonstrations by mullahs and seminarians to bring back Ayatollah Khomeini took place in Qom and in the vicinity of the capital. Everyone began to worry about the potential for violence. Homy, Sory, and Ghaffar's wife Jahan, who all had teenage children in school in Europe, decided not to bring them home for the summer as usual, but to visit them abroad. Men and women belonging to peaceful opposition groups were attacked and beaten; bombs went off in the homes and offices of people who had signed open letters. Then, late in the summer, there was an attack on Princess Ashraf's car. SAVAK cracked down at once.

By this time I had gone on a visit to the United States. I had been uneasy about going away at such a critical juncture. During the summer Shariati had died in exile in London; his death had been blamed on SAVAK, and university students had rioted. But Mitra had just given birth to a little girl, to whom she and Mike gave the Persian name of Juni. I had never missed the beginning of a semester before, but she had had a difficult pregnancy and as I had not visited her when Kayvon was born, I had promised myself that this time I would not let work deprive me of the joy of seeing my second grandchild as a newborn; whatever happened, for once I was going to spend some time with my daughter.

When I returned, almost two months after the beginning of the fall semester, I found that my uneasiness about leaving had been justified. The streets seemed full of a simmering rage. In only a few months the doctrines of "Islamic Marxism" had gained enormous strength and visibility at the University and on other campuses. More young men than I had ever seen were wearing the facial stubble or beards that renounced "Westernism" and demonstrated Islamic zeal. At my own school many male undergraduates were wearing buttoned shirts without ties to emphasize that they were not "Westernizers." From colleagues at the University, where violent demonstrations had continued, I learned that at the beginning of the semester many women students had defiantly put on the black chador or black clothes to show their support for both Islam and Marxist economic theory, as well as their sympathy with the Palestine Liberation Organization, which they felt to be a kindred revolutionary cause. Radical Islamic students at the University were demanding the segregation of men and women on the campus. And when I walked into my introductory course for the first time that fall, I was startled to see, huddled among the usual bright, pretty dresses of the freshmen women, one young woman who had covered herself head to foot in black. She wore a black sweater, black skirt, and thick black stockings. Her hair was tucked severely under a tight black kerchief and her pale, unadorned face was at once anonymous and accusatory, like a fanatical nun's.

I had no intention of forbidding anyone to wear what they wished, but I felt as though I had been struck in the face. This young woman was educated and wanted to study a modern profession, yet she was shrouding herself in the garments of orthodoxy, covering her head like an illiterate villager or a woman of my mother's generation. The last thing we needed in Iran, I thought, was a narrow fanaticism that rejected personal freedom and new ideas. This girl was announcing that she didn't want to go forward, but backward. "Let us smash this evil society," my new student's face proclaimed. "We don't need to think of a plan for repairing and healing it if we destroy it. We don't have to worry about being tainted by the corrupt, modern West if we close ourselves off to it and reject everything it has to offer us, good and bad equally."

The mood of rage suffused daily life. The very air seemed to have become poisoned by all the frustration and anger, and I and everyone else felt constantly on edge. From our servants to my faculty, everybody was tense and ready to explode at the slightest provocation. One day, halfway through the semester, my director of academic affairs abruptly failed to appear at work. When I asked Esther and then Zamani where he was, I learned that he had taken offense at a minor criticism I had expressed in a meeting. A few days later I was amazed to receive a brief letter from him saying that he was resigning his position.

This man had been one of my three regular hiking companions for the past twenty years, and I had believed him to be one of my closest friends. He had been one of my very first students, and my protégé. I had helped his family when they were in difficulties and after I had sent him to study in America, I had comforted him on the phone when he had called me, weeping with homesickness for Iran. Now he had deserted me in the middle of this turbulent semester without even an explanation. I was hurt and shocked. But everyone, I thought with a shrug, was hypersensitive these days. I had never had any use for people who abandoned me, and I did not call him and ask him to reconsider his decision.

I believe it is safe to say that, in the fall of 1977, not a single person in Iran thought that the Shah's overthrow was even a remote possibility. He had an army of more than half a million men run by dozens of highly paid, loyal generals, and spearheaded by thousands of elite "Immortals," the Imperial Guard, who had sworn to fight for him to the death. While we knew that our government continually bombarded us with propaganda and lies about the greatness of our military and its commander-in-chief, nevertheless it was hard not to think that at least some of the propaganda must be true, especially when we were always learning from the American and other foreign media what a strong military power we were. Mohammed Reza Shah seemed as invincible as any god-king who ever sat on the throne of Cyrus.

Iran was like a parched stand of trees in summer, waiting for lightning to strike and set the mountainside on fire. The black dress was now being worn by two or three more women at the School, and they and several male students came to my office and asked to use the auditorium for their daily prayers. Guessing that they wanted to use it as a meeting place to organize and plan demonstrations, I said that they were welcome to use two large classrooms instead, but not the auditorium. I was not anxious for any of our students to be arrested, imprisoned, and tortured by SAVAK.

Of the country's explosive mood, there had still been scarcely a hint in the Shah's public statements or the international press. But that fall, for the first time the Shah's image of invincibility was suddenly smashed. In November, he and Queen Farah went to Washington for the first of an exchange of visits with President Carter and his wife, and several hundred Iranian students and other anti-Shah activists demonstrated as the Carters were receiving the royal couple on the White House lawn. American police dispersed the students with tear gas, which the wind blew into the faces of the Shah, the President, and their wives. The next day we were astounded to see the international newspapers filled with pictures of the Shah wiping away tears with his handkerchief.

This sight was a profound shock to Iranians. I was personally sorry to see our nation lose face by the inadvertent humiliation of our ruler, but the image in these photographs shook even the Shah's most ardent opponents. It was as if the smooth and glittering surface of a mirror had cracked. For a quarter of a century the Shah had cloaked himself in pageantry and military pomp, had made people tremble in fear of his army and his ferocious security forces. Suddenly a handful of students had reduced him to tears. For the first time, people realized that the Shah was not a god, but a human being, vulnerable to an effective opposition.

The great question in everyone's mind now was: what would the U.S. attitude toward Iran be after President Carter's return visit? We believed that the Shah would always do what the American government wanted. Despite the new American leader's stand on human rights, his administration had continued to allow American companies to go on selling weapons to our government. But many Iranians, including me, were hoping and expecting that when the Carters came to Tehran at the end of December for the Western New Year, the Shah and the President would use the occasion to announce at last the beginning of a new political era, with a free press and an open system of government. Many even hoped that the Shah might be forced eventually to yield the real power to the cabinet and the Majlis, as in Mossadegh's day, and to give up his position as commander-in-chief of the military.

On December 31, 1977, millions of people turned on their radios to hear the live broadcast of the dinner speeches being made by the two heads of state. But we heard no announcement of a new era. President Carter simply praised the Shah for his "great leadership," which, he said, had won our monarch the love and admiration of his people and had made our country "an island of stability" in our troubled region of the world.

Iranians were at first incredulous, then contemptuous and outraged. How could the United States, everyone asked, be so ignorant, so utterly unaware of the truth? Didn't the Americans *know?*

I reminded myself that nations saw other nations only through the blinding light of their own interests. But my God, I thought, if this is "an island of stability," what are the other places like?

President Carter's speech, far from compelling the Shah to announce a restoration of democracy, seemed to imply that his policies had the full approval of the American government, and that he had done all he needed to satisfy the United States. The Shah, not unnaturally, appeared to conclude that since he had loosened the reins of repression with the left hand, he could now tighten them with the right, and the Iranian government felt itself once again free to go on the offensive against its enemies. Its first target would be the religious opposition. Through the network of the neighborhood mosques, tape recordings of Ayatollah Khomeini's inflammatory sermons from Najaf were now available to a vast audience inside the country. The Shah, who saw danger only in international communism and "Islamic Marxism," had long since dismissed the traditional clergy as irrelevant. Still, Ayatollah Khomeini had been a thorn in the government's side for a long time. All these years he had been hammering away at the same theme: the Shah must go.

A week after Mr. and Mrs. Carter's departure, on January 7, 1978, an article supposed to have been written by the Shah's minister of information appeared in a Tehran newspaper. It accused the clergy of working with international communism to destroy the White Revolution. It also grossly slandered Ayatollah Khomeini, accusing him of immorality and of being a British agent. The next day, a large crowd of religious leaders, students, and citizens in Qom marched in protest. The government, no longer concerned about American pressure, ordered the police to break up the demonstration with gunfire. Dozens of people were killed and many more were wounded; many of the victims were mullahs and seminarians. For the first time since 1963, rioting took place not on the university campuses but in the streets of an Iranian city.

It was as if a tremor had passed through the entire land. Surely, I thought, after this terrible event the Shah would begin taking people's feelings seriously, and not try to brush off the unrest on "subversives" anymore, but appoint an honest commission to look into the causes of our discontent. But he only came home from a visit to President Sadat in Egypt blaming the disorders on "Marxist terrorists" again. Soon after, Hoveyda, as court minister, gave a lavish party celebrating the publication of a book the Shah had written. The news of this callousness reached the people of South Tehran instantly, spread by Hoveyda's own servants. Yet the very next day the Resurgence Party organized three million of its members to march "voluntarily" in a demonstration in support of the monarch.

I felt sick. People had been killed and injured. The dead had scarcely been buried by their relatives and Hoveyda was toasting his master in champagne and handing out copies of his book. Didn't he, at least, realize that the life and death of a country was more important than maintaining appearances? It was as though the imperial court were festooning the bier for its own funeral.

That winter and spring, a cycle of violence, mourning, and renewed violence began such as our country had never known in modern times. As with any deaths, our Moslem religion required that the January killings be commemorated after forty days, and in February there were massive memorial protests in a dozen towns, protests in which even women and children took part. In Tabriz, rioting broke out, and when local police refused to fire on the rioters, the government summoned troops and tanks, injuring and killing many. These dead were mourned and memorialized in their turn by further protests forty days later, in March, and these demonstrations became large-scale riots in which protestors fought with police and religious fanatics attacked or set fire to every symbol of "Westernization" that they could find: foreign banks, luxury hotels, liquor stores, Western movie houses. Hundreds were killed and thousands injured, and every death not only furnished a reason for another demonstration forty days later, but drove the families of the dead and thousands of sympathizers into the arms of the religious opposition. People had seen that the stern mullahs and brave seminarians, inspired by the exiled Ayatollah Khomeini, had the will to stand openly against the invincible Shah and his government. They alone had shown the courage to do in broad daylight what no one besides a small number of radicals and leftist guerrillas had even imagined possible in secret. They were steadfast even when that meant imprisonment, torture, and death.

And at times, their leadership seemed to be having the desired effect. In the late spring the Shah removed General Nassiri as head of SAVAK. He announced that the next Majlis elections would be free and open and promised more reforms. He still insisted, however, that subversion was behind the memorial demonstrations, and refused even to deal with the National Front, to whom he now referred as "traitors." Moreover, even while making some concessions he began cracking down on the opposition again. Thus he appeared sometimes weak, sometimes harsh, but never consistent or truly decisive. His vacillation was all the more alarming to moderate people like me because as the size of the funeral processions and memorial demonstrations increased, every month made it clearer that the authority of the mullahs was growing and spreading, bolstered by Ayatollah Khomeini's powerful sermons and by an increasingly well-organized network of mosques, neighborhood committees, and urban guerrilla groups.

At our welfare centers we could get little work done and conducting classes was almost impossible, so in May I held abbreviated examinations and, after a shorter than usual commencement, adjourned us for the summer. Especially for my students and younger faculty, the sheer excitement of what was happening was too overwhelming. Millions of Iranians had grown up since the Shah's return to power in 1953, and ever since they could remember, he and SAVAK had been omnipotent. Now someone was defying that great force.

One morning at the end of May, Hossein, as we were driving somewhere, handed me a tape recording of one of Ayatollah Khomeini's sermons. "You must listen to what Agha says, Khanom," he said excitedly. (Ayatollah Khomeini's admirers now referred to him simply as "Agha," or "Master.") "It's what I've been telling you— Agha says we have to get rid of the Shah!"

He gave me an innocent, knowing look. Like most ordinary people, Hossein was a firm member of the party of the wind. His views on politics were not so much neutral as strictly noncommittal. He and the School's other servants talked about Khomeini's views, but without expressing an opinion one way or the other; they were waiting to see which way the wind blew. Even so, they, like our students and younger faculty members, found it thrilling to hear someone openly defying the Shah.

I was, of course, very curious to hear Ayatollah Khomeini at last, and when I got home that night I listened to the tape. It had been played so often that some places were almost too scratchy to make out, but what I could understand was powerful, impressive, and disturbing. The Ayatollah divided humanity into two classes, the oppressors and the dispossessed. The chief oppressor was the West, occupying with its imperialistic war machine a land that needed not fancy hotels, indecent cinemas, and liquor stores, but food and housing. And while the West forced its immoral ways on us, its illegitimate, atheistic instrument, the Shah sold our oil to these same imperialists and to Israel, conniving with Jews and Bahais to destroy Islam. He exploited the downtrodden, suppressed our constitution, and denied the people justice. The people must rise up and overthrow him and his Western-stricken society.

I was confused, shocked, and alarmed. I certainly wanted justice, but I didn't want the destruction of *everything* the Shah had created, for in some areas we had made real progress—what I wanted was a more open, honest, responsible government and a democratic society in which everyone could participate. I was repelled by the bigotry in the sermon, which I considered utterly alien to the spirit of toleration that had always been part of our country's history and religious tradition. But what disturbed me most was that Ayatollah Khomeini seemed to offer no constructive program. What, specifically, did he want to put in place of what we had? It was one thing, I thought, for Al Ahmad to talk about smashing my teacup, or for my students to put on black clothes to show their support for Islam or the Marxists. It was another to actively seek the destruction of a government with no plan for replacing it.

And yet I was also deeply impressed by the sermon, whose genius lay in its simple eloquence. Ayatollah Khomeini clearly knew exactly how to address the concerns of "the dispossessed." When the Shah or the prime minister spoke to the nation, they did so in language that two-thirds of the country couldn't understand. Ayatollah Khomeini talked like any village mullah. He spoke in words intelligible to any laborer or housewife. Of course, it was impossible for someone like me not to be glad to hear that he was sympathetic to the needs of ordinary people, and that he supported our constitution and a just system of government. But I saw now that it was more than this that made Hossein and our other servants so enthusiastic. Here was a man like them who was simple, stern, and incorruptible, and whose basic message everyone could understand: the nobodies of Iran had been deprived of their fair share for too long. And this old man, who in all those years had never flinched or wavered in his purpose for a single moment, was demanding that they overthrow their oppressor, and take their fair share.

However, in June and July the streets were calm, apparently as a result of the Shah's concessions. No classes were held in summer on our campus, since this period was always devoted entirely to fieldwork, and there were few students around. I therefore turned to the chief business at hand, which was interviewing applicants for the fall. In the fall semester, for the first time the Tehran School of Social Work would be able to boast over a thousand students—that is, if we had a fall semester. It was not long before I began to doubt that we would.

To stem inflation and thus remove some of the incentive for unrest, the Shah had allowed Premier Amouzegar to cut back on government spending. Unfortunately, as also happens in more stable and highly developed countries than mine, slashing the budget produced massive layoffs and hence more discontent. Suddenly, hundreds of thousands if not millions of workers and transplanted villagers who depended on the government's urban development and construction projects for their daily bread found that jobs and money were scarce. During the summer, strikes and work stoppages began in electrical plants, water-works, textile factories, auto assembly plants, and other industries. Workers and laborers in Tehran and the major towns rioted, leftist and Islamic guerrilla groups attacked and set fire to Western cinemas and other hated symbols of Pahlavi rule, and police and army troops shot into the crowds, killed demonstrators, and imposed martial law. The worst massacres were in Isfahan, but the most horrifying incident of that summer occurred in Abadan. There, on August nineteenth, the twenty-fifth anniversary of the Shah's return to power, nearly four hundred people, mostly women and children, died in a fire set in a movie theater whose exit doors had been mysteriously locked.

A shock wave swept the nation. The government insisted that religious fanatics were responsible, but the radicals had only burned empty cinemas, and of course no one believed anything the government said. Few people doubted that anybody but SAVAK could have committed such a horrible crime. In the mass funeral that followed, ten thousand relatives of the victims and other mourners shouted for the destruction of the Shah and his dynasty.

Once again, the Shah blamed the unrest on others. Not for the first time, he tried to lay the nation's troubles at the door of the West— which, he told French television three days after the fire, was no longer supporting him but was instead instigating his enemies; if he went, the Shah threatened, the Americans and the British would lose their oil. However, again he appeared to retreat, replacing Premier Amouzegar with an old crony named Jaffar Sharif-Emami. I myself was unhappy with this dubious choice. Sharif-Emami had been the head of the notorious Pahlavi Foundation; people called him "Mr. Five Percent" for the commissions he charged Western companies to get them government contracts. Nevertheless, the king now promised that we would soon have free elections and parliamentary rule again. Many political prisoners were granted amnesty, while the press was permitted to discuss labor disputes and the opposition, and the new premier worked at trying to reach an accommodation with the National Front.

At the same time, to please the devout he also abolished the hated "monarchial" calendar and the women's affairs ministry. Moreover, to ingratiate himself with the orthodox whose prejudices were being inflamed by Ayatollah Khomeini's sermons, he started a campaign to get rid of prominent people known or rumored to be Bahais. One of these was Hoveyda, whose father was supposed to have been a Bahai. He was summarily dismissed as court minister, having finally come to the end of his usefulness.

For a week or two, however, these distasteful stratagems seemed to have an effect, and it looked as though the government, the National Front, and the moderate religious leadership might actually be able to work together to avoid more strikes and bloodshed, and even move the country gradually toward the democratic elections the Shah had promised. Then another tragedy occurred that made the Abadan fire only a prelude.

On September 4, in observance of a religious holiday, a series of peaceful demonstrations began in the capital, larger than any in the past. The crowds were gigantic, composed of men and women from every class and political viewpoint, with tens of thousands of people chanting in unison the best-known slogan of the opposition movement: "Allahu akbar, Khomeini rahbar": "God is great, Khomeini is our leader." Over the next three days, despite the calls of the National Front and the moderate religious opposition for restraint, these peaceful demonstrations became larger and more radical-sounding, until over half a million people were shouting slogans calling for the downfall of the Shah, an end to America's presence in our country, the return of Ayatollah Khomeini from exile—and, for the first time, an Islamic republic. Scrawled messages appeared on walls, in doorways, and on banners that the crowds waved: "Death to the Shah and the Imperialists," "Bring back Ayatollah Khomeini," "We want an Islamic republic."

On Friday, September 8, unaware that on the previous evening the Shah had forced the cabinet to declare martial law, an enormous crowd estimated to be somewhere between five and twenty thousand people staged a sit-down protest in Jaleh Square in South Tehran. Ordered to leave by the troops of the general who had just been appointed governor of the capital—the same man who had ordered the shooting of protestors in June 1963—they refused, and with that the soldiers began pumping round after round of bullets into the defenseless crowd. Soon Jaleh Square looked like a slaughterhouse, with blood running on the pavement and prone bodies piled up one on top of the other, wherever they had been sitting or standing. The killing went on all day. Army helicopter gunships hunted down demonstrators who fled. Not even the riots of 1963 had seen such deliberate and dreadful slaughter. September 8 became known to Iranians as "Black Friday."

This horrible event shattered any hope of gradual political progress, or even of a return to normal life. The government had destroyed all possibility of compromise between itself and the moderate opposition. The moderate Ayatollah Shariat-Madari, who had been patiently calling for a return to constitutional rule, declared that he would no longer deal with a government headed by the Shah. In every town and city, neighborhood *komitehs*, or committees, of bearded young men, organized through the mosques, went from house to house, urging people to join the protests, handing out pamphlets and cassettes of Ayatollah Khomeini's sermons. Strikes spread through the country to oilfields and refineries, chemical works, and other important industries. The mass demonstrations continued without interruption.

The numbers and fearlessness of the protestors were now growing every day. Not shaving, or wearing a shirt without a tie, or a black dress and an "Islamic" scarf, had become badges that showed one was on the right side. Gradually over the past nine months people had lost their fear of SAVAK, and one day a student brought a cousin to school to show him around, proudly introducing him to me as a member of the Mojahedin guerrilla organization who had just been released after six months in jail. The police were increasingly reluctant to arrest arsonists, while firemen would not put out the fires in banks or liquor stores. The civil courts were refusing to jail rioters. Instinct made people want to side with the winners, not the losers, and it was becoming apparent that the winners would not be those presently in power. As the scales became weighted more and more in favor of the mullahs and the guerrillas, Iranians were waiting to see what happened, and which side to come down on.

Of course, with hundreds of thousands of civil servants and private employees striking and pouring into the streets to join the demonstrations, the country was at a standstill and there could be no question of holding classes. Only a couple of our welfare and family planning centers were able to function at all. Anxious at the evident success of Premier Sharif-Emami's hate campaign against the Bahais, soon after Black Friday I had told the one or two Bahais we employed that until the wave of animosity against their faith had subsided, it would be safer for them not to come to school—indeed, I urged them to go abroad for a while if they could. I was less concerned about Esther, who was the only Jewish staff member. All the students and faculty were extremely fond of her, and in spite of Ayatollah Khomeini's rabble-rousing about Israel and Zionist conspiracies against Islam, I doubted that she would become a target. However, for safety's sake I told her and several Armenian faculty and staff members that I was putting them on paid leaves of absence until things settled down again.

I also sent home an American researcher who had just come to the School as a Fulbright scholar, paying his salary for the full year. I did not think I could guarantee the physical safety of Americans any longer. On the day following the massacre, President Carter had telephoned the Shah to assure him in person of America's friendship and future support. Rightly or not, many Iranians had concluded from this gesture that the United States government approved of the killings—most, in fact, were convinced that the CIA and the British had ordered them. "Throw out the hireling of America," the crowds were chanting. "Fifty years of monarchy, fifty years of treachery! God is great, Khomeini is our leader!"

Early in October, in an action as shortsighted as the article that had started the rioting in January, the Iranian government, hoping to stem the deluge of cassettes and sermons from Najaf, persuaded President Saddam Hussein of Iraq to deport Ayatollah Khomeini. The Iranian government was indifferent as to where he went, so he went to France and settled down with his household in a village outside Paris. From there, through the Western media, he began preaching his message not only to Iran but to the entire world.

Now the common people could actually see photographs of Ayatollah Khomeini sitting in an austerely furnished room on a simple prayer rug in his plain gray cassock and black robe and turban, a broadcasting microphone before him. His message was implacable and unchanging. He was calling for the establishment of an Islamic government. When corruption, Western imperialism, and Zionism had been uprooted and we were governed by the Koran and the law of God, Ayatollah Khomeini promised, everyone except the Bahai heretics would have religious and political freedom. Best of all, in the new society the poor would be given all the things they needed for a good life—free water, free rent, free gasoline and electricity, even free public transportation. Iranian members of the opposition in Paris streamed to the rented house in Neauphle-le-Château to pay their respects, then returned home extolling Ayatollah Khomeini's simplicity, his extreme piety, his unwavering commitment to the destruction of imperialism, injustice, and corruption. In Iran, everyone could now listen to the interviews he gave on the BBC's Persian-language radio— which, to our government's outrage, was broadcasting uncensored, openly pro-opposition reports about the strikes and riots.

Near the end of October the attacks on cinemas, liquor stores, and other signs of Pahlavi and "imperialist" corruption spread to the smaller towns. Many more oil workers went on strike, and oil production dropped well below what the country would need for fuel that winter. The Shah, realizing that Premier Sharif-Emami could not regain control of the situation, began casting around for someone with whom to replace him, and I learned from rumors in the city that the king was about to offer the premiership to Dr. Ali Amini, whom he had appointed prime minister in 1961. This was the first really encouraging news I had heard in months. Obviously the Shah had decided to bow to the inevitable at last. Dr. Amini was honest and generally popular. He was thought to be acceptable to the Americans but was also well liked by clerics. The Shah invited him to the palace for a conference, and Dr. Amini told him that, with the country on its knees, he could accept the premiership only on condition that the Shah acknowledge his responsibility for what had happened and withdraw from politics. He must liquidate the Pahlavi Foundation, use the state's lands and assets for national development, and step aside as commander-in-chief of the military, turning power over to the cabinet and parliament, as our constitution required.

This news was reported in the press almost as soon as Dr. Amini emerged from the palace, and for a brief moment I thought the miracle would actually occur. Surely the Shah would grab this chance to yield power gracefully, in a dignified manner that would save the country

from further turmoil. Dr. Amini was said to want the Shah to appoint
a regency council and abdicate in favor of his son. This seemed to me
the best solution to our problems. All these hopes, however, were soon
dashed. The Shah refused Amini's conditions.

I hid my face in my hands when I heard this. What would happen
next? The Shah was both rigid and weak, and I saw us without any
leaders at all. Ordinary people wanted to wash the government away;
they blamed the Shah and America not only for repression and corruption but for all their frustrations. Now Ayatollah Khomeini's
speeches were encouraging them to expect miracles from someone
else, but how were these miracles to come about? Being a cleric,
Khomeini was naturally inexperienced in matters like taxes and civil
administration, and how were all the free houses and bus rides he was
promising to be financed? This stern old mullah sitting on a prayer
rug with just his little microphone before him was surpassing anything
the government or the Americans or the British, with all their spies
and informers, had ever done to win the hearts of Iranians. The
rhymed, rhythmic chanting in the streets, which I heard now wherever
I went in the city, was so powerful that it swept all before it. "Who
got the oil?" the crowds chanted. "America! Who swallowed the oil
money? Pahlavi! We are followers of the Koran, not the Shah!" But
no one, including the Ayatollah himself, seemed to have a real plan.

The School was nearly deserted, but I was determined to show that
social workers stuck to their job, and was driving in every day from
Galandwak to be in the office as usual. I had to stay in touch with
the community welfare centers in Tehran and the provinces that were
still operating. Esther, who claimed to be bored at home, insisted on
coming to work in case I needed help. Hossein was usually around as
well, along with our night watchman and our custodian, Zabi, a skinny
but industrious young villager who lived in one of the shantytowns,
and for whom I had always brought clothing to take home; Zabi
considered it part of his job to bring me tea and fuss whenever he
thought I was working too hard. One of the gardeners came as well,
a crusty old fellow who grumbled that if bullets didn't scare Khanom
they weren't going to keep him away, either. Occasionally Zamani,
whose ministry was closed, and Minou, whose department at the
maternity hospital couldn't function, would drop by to give me any
news they had heard.

Since Black Friday a group of ten or a dozen undergraduate men had also been coming to the School regularly to help me raise funds to buy medicine and bandages for the city's hospitals, which we delivered ourselves to the crowded emergency rooms in one of the School's five Land Rovers. One afternoon around the first of November I received an urgent telephone call from a welfare center we had established for the women of the red-light district—it was known as the "Ghaleh," or fortress, because it was enclosed by a wall. The frantic director told me that a crowd of "beards"—the nickname for the most fanatical of the clerics' supporters—was threatening to burn down the entire Ghaleh, and the police and fire department refused to help.

Horrified, I ran out of my office and, getting Zabi to help me round up some of the students who were hanging around, packed six or seven into my own car, a station wagon, and drove as fast as I could past shuttered stores, street barricades, and occasional clusters of chanting demonstrators to the Ghaleh, which was nearly half an hour away in South Tehran. By the time we arrived at the welfare center, black smoke was rising from a few wretched little houses nearby. Several women stood in the street, screeching with rage and fear and cursing their persecutors. The rioters, a couple of dozen bearded young men in black shirts carrying torches and cans of kerosene, had moved on to the next house and were shouting threats and insults at a few gaudily clad teenagers who watched, paralyzed with terror, from an upstairs window.

I was appalled. The women of the Ghaleh were illiterate and most were addicted to opium and arak. Many were wives or village girls who had been lured or abducted from their homes and sold into the brothels, so that they were beyond the pale of respectable society and could never return to their families. These pathetic women were defenseless, the poorest and most unpolitical creatures in Iran. How could anyone imagine that it served God to burn them alive? The government's weakness and the growing authority of the mullahs had evidently emboldened these strutting fanatics to show their power by punishing a few miserable women for the sins of the "imperialists." When the fires spread, the dilapidated mud-brick buildings would collapse as their wooden doors and flammable contents began burning. Several thousand people—the women, the children who came to work with them, the peddlers and street vendors of the district—were in danger.

A police station and a fire station stood just outside the walls, but not a uniform was in sight. Nearly beside myself, I realized that the police and the fire department had decided that it was better to let the Ghaleh burn than to antagonize the "beards."

The students and the male staff from the welfare center had fetched some buckets and were escorting more women out of the nearest buildings. I ran on foot to the police station outside and found its shamefaced captain, whom I begged and berated to go into the Ghaleh with his men: those women, I pleaded, might be guilty of a sin in the eyes of religion, but surely they and all the others inside didn't deserve to die on that account, as the women and children in Abadan had.

The captain, looking embarrassed, said that he wanted to help, but he was afraid that his men might accuse him of being in favor of immorality and corruption. I knew that he was lying, and was only afraid that the rioters might be there on orders from some important opposition figure, who might have him fired when fate revealed who the winner was. "You know that isn't right," I screamed. "If you and your men are God-fearing and religious, you have to *help* the weak, regardless of what those poor women do for a living! You're supposed to protect people in danger, no matter *who* the government is!" At last he agreed to send some officers.

Meanwhile, I ran next door to the fire station and insisted that its reluctant chief let me take a couple of his men back inside with me. When we arrived, the students, the director, and the staff were working enthusiastically with their buckets and had almost put out the fire in the first house. Shamed at last, the firemen ran back to the station house for their equipment. Blue police uniforms had also appeared by now, and the rioters were fleeing. "You scum!" a woman standing in the street yelled after them. "What are we doing today that hasn't been a sin for a thousand years?" I yelled at the policemen to follow and arrest the fanatics, but they ignored me. Finally, after about four hours, all the fires the mob had set had been put out and I drove the exhausted students back to the School. I had a feeling that they knew the political group the rioters belonged to, for all of them were South Tehran boys. But by now so many of our students idolized Khomeini, even those I knew weren't religious, that I didn't think it would be prudent to ask if these thugs were his followers.

A day or two later, I was alarmed to receive a telephone call from the assistant of a high-ranking cleric whose name was unfamiliar to me but who, the caller explained, had heard about the incident in the Ghaleh. "Ayatollah Mahmoud Taleqani," he said, "commends you highly for your deed. It was a good and courageous act."

Surprised and a little embarrassed, I murmured something polite and hung up the phone. I did not know what to think of this call. Like most unpolitical and secular people, I knew absolutely nothing about the leadership of the religious opposition, except for Ayatollah Khomeini and Ayatollah Shariat-Madari. I asked Dadash at lunch that day who Taleqani was (my brother had returned from Saigon a few years earlier to become the director of the Pasteur Institute, the public health institute that Shazdeh had founded, and had since retired), but Dadash didn't know either. Abbas, however, who was from a clerical family, said that Ayatollah Taleqani was the most popular and humane of all the mullahs, and although he was presently associated in some way with the radical Mojahedin, he had been a loyal follower of Mossadegh and the National Front—Ahmad Mossadegh, in fact, knew him well. He had just been released from political imprisonment.

Surprised, I wondered how Taleqani had heard about the business in the Ghaleh—in view of everything else that was happening, it was a minor episode. But by now everyone wanted to be in favor with the clerics, and there were many ways such news could come to an aya-tollah.

On November fourth, the worst violence Tehran had seen yet began when the army fired into a crowd of students at the University who, to mark the fourteenth anniversary of Ayatollah Khomeini's exile to Iraq, were trying to pull down a statue of the Shah. The next day, hundreds of thousands of people demonstrated in the center of the city, and smoke rose from the European shops on the Avenue Lalezar and every other business associated with the West, luxury, and im-perialism. Foreign banks and the British Embassy were set ablaze and barricades of tires, rubble from construction sites, and abandoned cars were erected to block the way of the tanks that ground along the streets, and from which soldiers fired on unarmed demonstrators.

Late that afternoon, the Shah flew over the city in his helicopter to view the charred husks of high-rise hotels, cinemas, stores, and the Embassy building. He was reported to be distraught, close to a nervous breakdown, because the Americans would not tell him what to do about the demonstrations. The next day, however, the government announced that the Shah would take decisive measures to deal with the crisis. Once again, people felt relieved, expecting that at last the Shah understood that he must relinquish power.

That evening, November sixth, the king went on television. Weep-ing and in a breaking voice, he declared that the wave of strikes was justified. The people, he said, had risen against oppression and cor-ruption, and he, their king—before he had always referred to himself as Iran's "emperor"—had heard their "revolutionary message" and supported it. The monarchy was "a gift entrusted to him by the constitution and the people," and he, our king, would rectify "past mistakes." He had dismissed Sharif-Emami and was installing a military government. The new premier was to be General Gholam Reza Azhari.

Even now, I thought, this man could not be a leader. I was in despair. The Shah wept to see that we no longer wanted him, but he would give up nothing. This new military government was doomed. General Azhari was an old man, sick with a heart condition; he could never stand up to the mullahs, the Shah's jealous generals, or the Shah himself. Refusing the conditions of Dr. Amini had been an act of suicide. The Shah had to go. He had no choice but to appoint someone like Shapour Bakhtiar or some other National Front leader to the premiership, and then withdraw and live quietly outside the capital. If he abdicated, there was still time to save the country. I only hoped that he would not flee again in a time of crisis, as he had once before.

Naturally, this still left the great question of whether Ayatollah Khomeini would accept a regency. Personally, I hoped that Khomeini would compromise. Recently a rumor had been circulating that the Shah was seriously ill, and his manner and appearance during the speech had certainly suggested this. The Koran commanded all Moslems to be compassionate, and an ayatollah was a man of the highest religious principles. Besides, Iranians were always compassionate to the sick.

To the Shah's speech, Khomeini at once replied from Paris that the Shah must abdicate and be tried by an Islamic court. The people must continue their fight until the monarchy was destroyed. Two of the most respected National Front leaders, Mehdi Bazargan and Karim Sanjabi, flew to Paris to see him. From there they joined the voice of the National Front to the clerics' demands for the establishment of a democratic, Islamic system of government in place of the monarchy. The National Front would expel any member who continued to support the Shah and the present government.

Meanwhile, the king was "fighting corruption and oppression" by having numerous government officials arrested, including the infamous General Nassiri, as well as the Shah's loyal old servant, Hoveyda. I thought that Hoveyda had been a bad prime minister and had wasted twelve precious years, but I found this action contemptible. Instead of giving up power, the Shah was trying to make his servants the scapegoats. He was utterly blind, unable to see that we wanted him to do something about the master, not the lackeys. He had shut his ears for so long that he was as unable to understand the point of Iranians' "revolutionary message" as a man who had lain in a sickbed for years was capable of getting up in an earthquake and holding up the walls of his house with his bare hands. When Sanjabi and Bazargan came back to Tehran, he had them arrested, too, for treason.

All year, many of the nation's highest officials, seeing the writing on the wall, had been transferring huge fortunes to banks outside the country, and many of those who had profited from the waste and corruption of the oil boom had already left. After the Shah's speech of November sixth, this exodus increased greatly, and now other kinds of people were leaving in large numbers, too—doctors, industrialists, and especially European-trained professionals. A week or two after the broadcast a dear friend of mine, a physician who had been instrumental in helping to establish family planning, told me that he had sold his house and was joining his English wife and their children in London. He urged me to sell whatever property I owned and leave the country as well.

Amazed, I protested that he couldn't go. He hadn't done anything wrong, and neither had I.

My friend replied that what we had done or not done would soon be irrelevant. He had been trained in England, and in the eyes of many who wanted an Islamic republic, he was "Western-stricken," the agent of imperialists and Zionists, and so was I. "Perhaps," he added, "Khanom Farman Farmaian's heroic labors on behalf of the poor will carry more weight with Agha than the career of a mere physician. But I don't think I want to live in the Iran he wants to create. Believe me, Satti, the time has come to get out."

This really shocked me—I couldn't believe that he was serious in telling *me* to leave. Many women in our family were away with their children in Europe, but only until the country stabilized. I had no intention of going. All my own brothers and our youngest sister Khorshid and all my stepmothers' sons were staying. The Farman Farmaians had never sent money out of the country, or invested it anywhere but in our homeland; we were an old family, and we had responsibilities. I couldn't abandon the School, while Farough, Ghaffar, Rashid, and my other brothers with large businesses had to take care of their workers. People like us didn't run off to the Riviera when things got tough, and leave those who depended on us to shift for themselves, like these craven officials and corrupt nouveaux riches trying to save their money and their skins. As for my being "anti-Islamic," I thought indignantly,

I certainly had nothing to fear on that score. Who would want to hurt *me*? I had devoted my whole life to caring for "the dispossessed." If social work wasn't "Islamic," then what was?

More and more, however, I felt that our family was disintegrating. I missed our women who were away and I missed Mitra, Kavyon, and my new little granddaughter. It was as if an unseen guerrilla army were sniping at the foundations of our existence as a family, chipping away a few bricks at a time. And recently we had realized that we would soon lose Khanom.

The health and spirits of my mother, who was now more than eighty, had been declining for several years. Batul-Khanom had passed away in 1975 after an illness, and since her death my mother had never been the same. She saw Fatimeh-Khanom often—my stepmother was still in excellent health—but she was happy only when she could talk of the friend with whom she had had so many disputes about mullahs, and who had always made her laugh.

Khanom's bereavement had gradually undermined her heart, and recently she had grown too weak to leave her bed. Jaby began sleeping at her house, and Dadash and the rest of us were going there every day to have lunch and see her. To relieve Jaby, instead of driving back to Galandwak I spent the night there once or twice a week. Sometimes the sound of car horns blaring in a demonstration would reach my mother's bedroom. Once, when some of us were there, she had asked what the noise was. "Don't worry, Khanom," said Jaby soothingly, "it's just a demonstration—you know, to get rid of the Shah."

"Yes," someone said to her teasingly, "Ayatollah Khomeini is going to come back and run the country. The poor will get free gas and everyone will get a train ticket to Qom. That should please you, Khanom."

My mother looked troubled. "God forbid that mullahs should come to power," she said after a moment. "Religion should remain religion."

Toward the end of November her condition grew worse. Dadash, realizing that the end was not far off, decided to move her to Pars Hospital, a private hospital that was still functioning reasonably well and where she could have better care than we could give her at home. Dadash and Jaby visited her there every day, and I went as often as I could. Her room overlooked Elizabeth Boulevard, a major thoroughfare, and here we heard the chanting of "God is great, Khomeini is our leader" all the time. From the window next to the bed we could see smoke billowing into the winter air from burning buildings, like a black fog rising from some hellish lake of fire.

Sometimes, when Khanom heard the noise outside, anxiety would appear in her eyes and she would mutter anxiously, "What do those people want?" Dadash would try to calm her, telling her that they were unhappy, but that everything would soon calm down. He understood that her fear was not for herself, but for the country. She was remembering the harj-o-marj she had lived through when she was first married to Shazdeh, the time of anarchy. Dadash, Jaby, I, or another of us would sit with her so that someone would always be there when she woke from her doze.

One afternoon during the lunch hour, when things seemed quiet around school, I went to see her and found her sleeping. I sat down by the bed, feeling grateful that she had had some years to enjoy her life. She had never had jewels from Shazdeh, but because we had all been educated and because my brothers had been able to make her comfortable in her old age, in the end she had been content with what God had given her. Sometimes, when she heard some rich younger relative boasting of her presents from her husband, she would raise her chin and said proudly, but with a twinkle in her eye, "Yes, young lady, you have all those rings, but Shazdeh has given me much finer jewelry than that. Sabbar," she would say, pointing to Dadash, "is my diamond. Jaby is my pious green emerald, the Prophet's color, and Satti is my fiery ruby. Farough and Ghaffar and Rashid are my garnets and opals, Homy and Sory and Khorshid are my pearls and my sapphires. You see? I, too, am loaded with jewels."

The car horns blasting outside wrenched me from my reverie. I feared that the racket would upset her. At that moment Khanom awoke and looked weakly up at me. Instead of showing alarm, however, her eyes moved to the amulet I had put on with my clothes that day. It was one that I had bought on a trip to Egypt several years before: a black onyx set with tiny diamonds in Arabic script. As it was among the few pieces of jewelry I had ever purchased, she had seen it often.

"That's so pretty," said Khanom, and smiled at me.

A day or so later she fell into a coma, and died without regaining consciousness. Dadash telephoned to say that she was gone, and we held a quiet funeral, keeping the rites as simple as possible—the Shah's nervous troops had been known to fire on funeral processions. It wasn't until long afterward that I remembered her noticing the amulet, and realized that its thin line of stones must have been the last writing that my mother, who had so loved to read her Koran, had seen before God took her. The little jewels formed the word "Allah."

PART FOUR

EARTHQUAKE

14

BLACK FOG AND FIRE

*It is when the Persian is inspired by that enthusiasm for a
person, a doctrine, or a cause of which he is so susceptible
that his heroism becomes transcendental.*

—Sir Edward Granville Browne, *The Persian Revolution
of 1905–1909* (published 1910)

*O*N DECEMBER 2, 1978, MOHARRAM ARRIVED AND DURING ITS TEN
days the violence increased again. Ayatollah Khomeini exhorted everyone to unite and sacrifice themselves in blood like Imam
Hossein, until the soldiers threw away their arms to join the people's
cause. Crowds large and small filled the streets, angry men and black-
veiled women with waving fists and bulging eyes. Neighborhood organizers and the "beards" kept the protests disciplined, but it was
impossible to go near a crowd without fearing that it might turn into
a lynch mob. To set foot in the city was like getting caught in a slow-
moving cyclone. A million people would move along Shahreza Avenue, the main artery across the city, stretching from one side of
Tehran to the other, carrying banners and shouting slogans, a thick,
black, living river. On every street one saw shuttered, empty, burned-
out stores, broken pavements, flashing police lights, overturned cars
and trucks. The smells of burning buildings and rubber tires, billowing
smoke, and tear gas pervaded the chilly air.

General Azhari's military government was helpless against Khomeini, whose propaganda was a marvel. His messages mesmerized the poor, but many professionals and other middle-class people were also drawn into the vortex. Even I, despite my deep reservations, could not but be grazed by the excitement. This frail-looking old man with the common touch, who had proven his strength and sincerity by his years of sacrifice and his implacable hatred for the Pahlavis, seemed to speak at last for the Hosseins, the Zabis, the Mashtis. Iran had only a few somebodies, but it had millions of nobodies, and not since Mohammed Mossadegh had any Persian leader spoken with such conviction, steadfastness, and fire on their behalf. Don't sit down and be quiet in your homes, Agha said to them; whoever leaves the streets is a traitor. Don't believe what the Shah and the government said yesterday in that speech: the government is lying to you. When the Islamic republic is established, there will be no more injustice, the constitution will be restored, the government will take care of you instead of exploiting and oppressing you, and you will have all you need for nothing.

There were terrible street battles. At night, hundreds of thousands of people, even in Tajrish, stood in the cold on their roofs crying, "God is great!" Thousands more, dressed in white shrouds, defied the curfew the military government had imposed and, in emulation of Imam Hossein and his family, marched through the streets, offering themselves for slaughter as martyrs for the Khomeini revolution. On Ashura, the last day of Moharram, Karim Sanjabi and Ayatollah Taleqani led a march of two million people through the city, proclaiming Ayatollah Khomeini's leadership and demanding the abolition of the monarchy, an Islamic government, and social justice. Hossein told me in the greatest excitement that the mosques had announced that as a special sign of God's favor Agha's face would appear on the moon, and on the appointed night, millions of Iranians climbed to their rooftops to bear witness. I did not contradict Hossein when he described the marvel he had seen. Even in little Galandwak people marched through the square in front of the mosque and chanted: "Death to the Shah, we want Khomeini."

The sound of gunfire had become commonplace everywhere as the army fired into the churning crowds. But whenever the tanks and infantry approached them, the demonstrators threw carnations at the troops. "Brothers in the army," they chanted, "why are you killing your brothers?" Hearing these spine-chilling words, issuing from a million throats that spoke as one, was like hearing the ocean speak. Ayatollah Khomeini had been right: weeping young village draftees of eighteen or nineteen, sickened at killing other Iranians, would tear off their military insignia, stumble into the crowds, and give their guns to the demonstrators even as their comrades kept on shooting them. I was not surprised to hear that desertions from the armed forces were increasing every week.

The surreal atmosphere was heightened because in recent months many tough-looking hit squads had appeared, swirling gangs of armed young men who roamed the streets and attacked isolated army patrols or small police constabularies. Unlike the band of thugs who had invaded the Ghaleh, these had a vaguely military appearance. Some appeared to have gotten hold of army patrol vehicles, and many wore thick green parkas, camouflage jackets like the army, or Che Guevara–style berets or headbands, while others had on motorcycle helmets, ski masks, sunglasses, or woolen caps pulled low to conceal their features. I had heard rumors that some had trained outside the country with the Palestine Liberation Organization in Syria, Libya, and Eastern Europe, and even in China and North Korea. Others, who kept their faces heavily swathed in masks or white shawls—like actors, I thought, in a Hollywood film about terrorists—actually looked vaguely foreign themselves. It was said that a number were not Iranians at all but from the PLO, but I did not know whether this was true or not.

Nobody could say who the guerrillas were or where they came from. By now we were hearing the names of dozens of underground organizations—Tudeh, Mojahedin, Fedayan, Hezbollah, as well as all manner of radical student groups—and it was impossible for an ordinary onlooker to tell which group each guerrilla gang belonged to or what its mission was, so I just thought of them as "the street people." All carried rifles or submachine guns, and felt that this entitled them to go where they wished and do as they pleased. These days, on our nearly empty campus, I would sometimes enter the cafeteria or auditorium to discover several armed young men holding a meeting. I resented this, but since I had a feeling that some of my students knew who they were, and since they weren't causing any trouble, I decided not to create any.

One afternoon I was in my office doing some paperwork when I heard gunfire outside. Since this was no longer unusual, I was not really alarmed. I always kept a small camera with me during my workday in case I needed to photograph conditions I wanted us to study, and I picked it up and went out into the hall, where Zabi, the night watchman, and several excited undergraduates had gathered to look out the glass doors at what was happening on the street. A few small pickup trucks were parked in front, with four or five armed men around each. I was about to go back into my office when three of them strode in the front entrance of our building. Without speaking they shoved past us and made their way up the stairs to the roof. Four more took up positions outside the entrance, pointing semiautomatic rifles at the street, with one kneeling right in front of the door where we stood, beside the column with the poster memorializing Ali Shariati's visit to the School.

I hesitated. I was about to protest that they couldn't simply barge in without so much as a "Salaam, who's the boss around here?" when I stopped myself. These men had guns, and it would hardly be wise to risk everyone's safety. At the same time, my students were watching me, waiting to see what I was going to do. I was their teacher. They looked to me for leadership, to know how to behave. I did not want them to think that social workers could take sides: we didn't even know who these people were shooting at. I felt like a parent whose home had been invaded by robbers—I had to do something to show my children that I was not helpless in my own household, but what?

Then, as I stood there, astonished and angry, I realized that I had no way of knowing whose side any of these students were really on. Whether or not they knew who the guerrillas were, they might approve of them as freedom fighters. Even Zabi, who was devoted to me, I reflected, probably wouldn't like it if I told supporters of Ayatollah Khomeini to leave our building.

Suddenly I felt beset by doubts. I no longer knew most of the students, nor did they know me. How did such boys see me? As a social worker who had been on the side of the "dispossessed" since she could walk and talk? Or merely as the director of a large and flourishing institution connected with the very government that Ayatollah Khomeini wanted to bring down—someone whose sole purpose, in their minds, was to furnish them with a degree that would enable them to make good money and take a vacation abroad once a year? Possibly they even welcomed this invasion!

On an impulse, I turned quickly and hurried up the stairwell after the guerrillas. Turning to look back, I saw, rather to my relief, that none of the students was following. That was just as well, I thought— they could assume what they liked; at least this way it wouldn't look as though I were being shoved aside in my own school.

I stepped onto the roof. The guerrillas were kneeling at the end with their guns trained on an apartment building across the street, but not firing. I felt no special fear: they were after someone else, not me. I went up behind them and watched for a few minutes, still angry but also curious. Then, because it seemed the natural thing to do, I began reflexively snapping pictures of them with the camera I had in my hand. One, hearing the shutter clicking, glanced around, but seeing only a woman with a camera, he returned indifferently to his task. I took some more pictures, then waited about fifteen minutes. Nothing happened. Finally, tired of the inaction, I went back downstairs and out to the front, where I took pictures of the man kneeling before the poster of Shariati and of those on the street. After that, I returned to my office. Doing something useful always made me feel better.

After a few hours the gunfire in the area stopped and the guerrillas drove away. Zabi came in with some tea, saying that he had heard the men telling the students that they were after somebody, but not who it was. I wondered whether they had succeeded in catching the person. One day, I thought grimly, when things finally got back to normal, I would have some interesting mementos to show Mitra and my grandchildren.

By mid-December the violence was completely out of control and the situation in the city was desperate. The hospitals and clinics were short of doctors, nurses, supplies, and medicines, while the emergency rooms were overflowing. Everywhere on the streets one saw men with bandages and crutches. Like everyone else, the police now stayed indoors, refusing to act, since anyone they arrested might be connected with a mosque or a revolutionary group, and nobody could say who was going to come out on top. The courtyards of every neighborhood police constabulary had become way stations for the injured, who were brought there by someone until their families came and took them to the hospital, and for the bodies of the dead, who were collected by the military or by one of the local mosques or komitehs after being identified by their families or taken to the morgue. Many of the dead and injured were mere boys of twelve or thirteen, for the mosques, guerrilla bands, and komitehs were all linked by the people of the neighborhood, who collected news and then had their young sons carry messages and information to the organizers. These children had become the little foot soldiers of the revolution—having grown up in overcrowded, depressing homes, with nowhere to play but muddy alleyways and garbage dumps, they had become addicted to the wild and exciting atmosphere of the streets.

Thus, whenever we learned that a riot or gun battle was taking place, my students and I would jump into a Land Rover and I would drive us pell-mell to where the fighting was, with one of the students waving a white flag to show everybody that we were rescue workers and keep them from shooting at our vehicle. Frequently, by the time I had maneuvered the Land Rover through streets blocked by rubble and barricades, the crowd of demonstrators outside the bank or cinema would have fled, with two or three people lying bleeding or dying on the pavement until we or someone else collected them. Often they would be dead or wounded teenage runners, whom we had to take to the police yard and then find their parents to give them the terrible news. I was still in full mourning for my mother, and my black clothing seemed dreadfully appropriate for the nation as well. The hearts of millions of Persians were now filled with black rage at the Shah and his foreign sponsors—who, Agha told the people, would be called to account for the sorrow and sacrifice of all these martyrs.

All during this time there were constant reports in both the Iranian and foreign press that the Shah was talking every day to the ambassadors of the United States and Great Britain, asking them what to do. I wanted to scream with frustration at these reports. Didn't he realize that the Americans didn't care who was king, as long as the oil kept flowing? Furthermore, at this critical juncture we were reading that Ambassador William Sullivan, Secretary of State Vance, and Zbigniew Brzezinski, the director of the National Security Council, were quarreling among themselves, just like the Shah's own generals, about what he should do. The vacillation of the American government—which seemed to be giving its old friend no help at all—was almost as distressing as the Shah's inability to give up power. The United States, having foisted on us a leader who had never allowed any other leaders to develop, seemed to have no policy for dealing with the eventuality that he might not survive. If the State Department didn't know enough by now to decide on what position to take, I wondered, what had the CIA been doing in our country all those years, with its big American Embassy and its helpful Iranian businessmen and its many dear friends at the imperial court and in General Nassiri's office? America now appeared as blind, confused, and desperate as the Shah himself.

Anti-American sentiment was growing worse with every week of increasing violence, and private American companies, worried about the hostility and harassment individual Americans were now encountering in the bazaars and even from their own servants, had already evacuated many of their employees. The anger at the United States was also affecting our family. Hafez and Jody, of course, had left years ago, and my sister-in-law Joanna, Khody's wife, was in London. But Jean was still in the country: one of her daughters had married a physician and lived in Tehran, and she and Farough had moved out of Tajrish into an apartment in the city. Farough, who was going to spend the Christmas holidays with their youngest daughter in London, was worried about how vulnerable Jean would be on her own.

By late December the whole country was on strike and sabotage was taking place at the army and air force bases. The strike by oil workers meant that the city's fuel reserves were almost gone, and merchants and shopkeepers began hiding food and other basic supplies for fear of looting. The riots, bonfires, and gun battles were growing steadily worse. Army desertions were now into the hundreds each day, and the young deserters were handing over their weapons to the Ayatollah's forces. The Shah, unwilling to risk an actual bloodbath, had now ordered the soldiers not to shoot protestors. His army generals, who asked why they were sending troops into the streets if not to control the riots, were growing daily more desperate over the indecisiveness of the monarch, who was deeply depressed over the fighting and hardly stirred from his chambers.

It was impossible not to pity him. The most ruthless generals wanted him to order an all-out attack by the army, and I did not believe the Shah personally capable of letting them kill hundreds of thousands, perhaps millions, of Iranians. The greatest pain of my heart, however, was for Queen Farah, who was said to be trying to rally her husband's spirits and infuse him with the will to embark on a constructive course of action.

The Shah and Ambassador Sullivan were still talking. The United States wanted a civilian prime minister and a regency council to take charge. Everyone was sure that it could not be much longer before the Americans made the Shah install such a regime and abdicate— he clearly had no alternative but to step aside and appoint someone like Shapour Bakhtiar or Karim Sanjabi, whom he had released from jail with Mehdi Bazargan. But the Shah could not find any National Front leader who would accept the premiership so long as he retained control of the military. Suddenly, on December 28, the army opened fire on the mourners in a huge funeral procession led by Sanjabi. People were killed on both sides. Everywhere, as we drove around the city, the students and I could hear sirens and gunfire and smell tear gas. At long last, on December 29, the Shah announced that he was replacing General Azhari with Shapour Bakhtiar, pending ratification of the appointment by the Majlis.

For the first time in months, I and all my family felt relieved and genuinely hopeful. But the great question now was, who would unify the country? Thanks to the Shah's relentless jealousy all these years of men with leadership ability, moderate people like us had no strong, magnetic leader like Khomeini. Bakhtiar and the other National Front politicians were decent, honorable men, but none was a second Mossadegh, a populist whom both educated and illiterate could follow. By now, even to people like me, the return of Ayatollah Khomeini seemed to hold out some genuine advantages. Many of his views were disturbing or simply impractical, but he was unquestionably a man of unshakable religious conviction who believed in the welfare of the poor. Recently, he had been attacking the Shah for destroying the constitution, and contrary to what I had heard of his views in 1963, he now seemed to advocate political participation for women. He had said publicly that the clergy did not wish to rule the country, and was clearly casting himself in the role of spiritual leader, not of a political figure.

I thought of what my mother had said before she died about religion remaining religion. Devout Iranians like her all felt that participation in politics was bound to contaminate spiritual purity, and Ayatollah Khomeini undoubtedly believed this as well. But even I, along with many other moderate, secular people, was beginning to think that if it was what fate had in store for us, his return as Iran's spiritual leader might act as the strong, binding force the country so desperately needed to recover, not only from the present disorder but from the moral confusion of many years. I began telling myself that perhaps the inevitable would not be as bad as I had feared.

Karim Sanjabi, Mehdi Bazargan, and the other leaders of the National Front at once carried out their promise to Khomeini to expel any National Front member who cooperated with the Shah. The next evening, however, Bakhtiar went on the radio and gave a beautiful, stirring speech that lasted over an hour. He announced that he had accepted the premiership on the condition that the Shah sever himself from the nation's affairs and absent himself for a rest—Bakhtiar did not specify how long the rest would be, nor where the Shah was going on the "vacation" he would be taking, but we assumed that he was going to the country somewhere. The new premier also told the nation that before Dr. Mossadegh's fall he, Bakhtiar, had sworn to the premier to fight for the rest of his life for the unity and security of Iranians. He reminded the country of the many times he himself had been in prison and of other personal sacrifices he had made during decades of opposition to corruption, oppression, and the government's hollow, jerry-built economic policies. He pleaded eloquently for the peaceful cooperation of Iranians during this period of transition, in which his government would immediately free all political prisoners, restore total press freedom and the rights of individuals and political parties, and dissolve SAVAK.

Bakhtiar's speech moved me and thousands of other Iranians to tears. This was exactly what we had wanted for a quarter of a century. No Persian prime minister had been able to utter words like these for twenty-five years. At last Iran's wounds could begin to heal. We had returned to a path that could lead to becoming a truly modern, truly democratic nation. In the emotion of that moment, it hardly seemed to matter that the Shah had not formally abdicated; the fact that he had agreed physically to leave the capital meant that he was at last relinquishing control of the army.

I realize now that, as my mother used to say, the vegetables cooking in the *awsh*-pot don't always know they've started boiling. They can't get out of the stew and see, as the cook can, what's happening to them. Like stewing vegetables, Iranians who thought the way I did were already boiling in the cauldron Ayatollah Khomeini's little microphone had made of Iran. We couldn't climb out and see how late it was, or that the flames he had lighted had already ignited the country beyond all hope of compromise.

Bakhtiar immediately announced that Ayatollah Khomeini was free to return to Iran, but the National Front merely reiterated its demand for the Shah's formal abdication and Khomeini exhorted his followers to more strikes and protests. He had vowed not to set foot in Iran until the Pahlavi monarchy was gone, "thrown into the dustbin of history." Obeying Bakhtiar, the Shah's new servant, he declared, was the same as obeying the master, and the master was still Satan.

Meanwhile, the Shah was still in his palace, protected by his "Immortals," the Imperial Guard, and no one knew exactly what he meant to do. I found it tragic that Khomeini and the National Front refused to support Bakhtiar, which left the new government almost no chance of survival: to anyone who saw the continuing demonstrations, it was quite obvious that without Khomeini's support Bakhtiar had no chance at all. Every day thousands of people gathered and marched to demand his resignation, the Shah's abdication, and Khomeini's return. However, I retained a wistful hope that Khomeini might yet recognize Bakhtiar's virtues and change his views so that the National Front could change its position.

In the first days of January General Robert Huyser, the deputy commander of the Supreme Allied Command in Europe, arrived in Iran to talk to the Shah's generals, presumably to tell them not to support the Shah anymore. Only a few days after Bakhtiar's appointment, President Carter had met with the European allies on the island of Guadeloupe for a summit conference, and in the course of the conference President Giscard d'Estaing of France had persuaded the American president that it was no longer in the Western allies' interest to back the Shah instead of Khomeini. To us, it seemed as though a law of nature had suddenly reversed itself—only last week the American government had still been declaring its support for its ally of twenty-five years; now it was deserting him and sending Huyser to us for some mysterious purpose.

All this news threw everyone into even more confusion and turmoil. Whom was the United States going to support now? Khomeini? Bakhtiar? Or had Huyser been sent to arrange a military coup to install somebody else, and if so, whom? The Imperial Guard, forty thousand strong, had sworn to defend the Shah until death. If it did, we would certainly have civil war. On December thirtieth the State Department had finally given the American embassy leave to encourage all U.S. dependents in Iran to return home. They were getting out as fast as they could, but the pro-Khomeini air traffic controllers at the airport had announced that U.S. and Israeli airplanes would no longer be allowed to land. There had already been attacks on individual Americans—a few weeks earlier, an oil executive in Tehran had been assassinated—and American citizens working for foreign companies, at the military bases, or the Embassy were now afraid of their house servants, their drivers, their Iranian neighbors. By this time Farough had gone off on his trip to London, and I was worried about Jean, who, like everyone else, was staying indoors as much as possible. My sister-in-law, however, wouldn't consider leaving Iran. Where else should she go? she asked. She and Farough had been here for twenty years. Iran was her home now.

Nobody went anywhere these days without a good reason. Looting had begun as rioters realized that no one was going to interfere with their getting something for themselves. I continued to go to school every day and to have lunch with Dadash, Jaby, and others in the family, but apart from meeting my relatives and our rescue expeditions, I stayed safely inside my office or at Galandwak. Whenever I went to have lunch with Ghaffar or Rashid, whose offices were near the American Embassy, I saw moving tanks, soldiers pursuing rioters, fighting, burning buildings.

Tuesday, January 16, had been the date set for the Majlis to approve the Bakhtiar government. On that day I was to have lunch with Dadash at an upstairs restaurant in the center of town that we liked. That morning, to my surprise, the students and I were not called out by any reports of fighting or riots, and when I went to meet Dadash, I noticed that the streets were strangely quiet. Tanks and trucks lined the boulevard as usual, but the helmeted soldiers were simply standing around, doing nothing. Astonished at this unnatural inactivity, I went upstairs to the restaurant, met Dadash, and sat with him at a window table overlooking the broad boulevard below. As we ate, I kept staring in disbelief at the street. The quiet, after four months of demonstrations, honking horns, and gunfire, was eerie.

All at once, at about one o'clock, we heard shouting. Looking out the window at the street, we saw young soldiers jumping up and down, kissing and embracing each other, shouting, weeping. At that moment the restaurant manager, who had turned on the radio to hear the outcome in the Majlis, cried out for everyone to listen. He turned up the volume and we heard the voice of the announcer saying that the Shah had left—he, the Queen, and a small entourage had departed from the airport about a half hour ago. Their destination was unknown.

Everyone in the restaurant was silent, taking in this awesome statement. Though the Shah's "vacation" had been announced, no one could believe that he was actually gone.

I looked down at the street again. Grinning newsboys were running toward the soldiers, waving a gigantic black two-word headline that covered the whole front page: *"SHAH RAFT!"* — "The Shah Is Gone!"

Suddenly a fashionably dressed, middle-aged woman sitting not far away jumped up and rushed over to our table. Taking my hand in hers, she squeezed it warmly. "Congratulations, Khanom Farman Farmaian!" she cried. Her expression was ecstatic.

I stared at her blankly. I was sure I had never met this lady. I exchanged a glance with Dadash; he was just as baffled as I was. "Congratulations?" I asked in astonishment. "What on earth, Khanom, is there to congratulate *me* about?"

"Why, Khanom," she smiled, her eyes glistening, "everything will be different now. This Ayatollah is going to come back! Corruption will no longer exist, we will have compassion and justice, the poor and destitute will be taken care of—we will be a new people, a truly Islamic society! This Imam will appreciate all that *you* have tried to do for the masses. Who doesn't know of your struggles for a better life for them? Everyone has heard of you and your school, everyone used to read in the paper how the Queen helped you and visited your welfare centers. You'll be able to do so much more now, because Ayatollah Khomeini will help you. You must be very happy. Congratulations, Khanom, congratulations!"

Dadash and I looked at each other again as she went back to her table, then resumed our meal without a word. I felt uncomfortable and unhappy. I did not want this woman's sincere but thoughtless compliments. After everything the Queen had done to help the very work this lady admired, she considered it only natural to run up and congratulate me on the Pahlavis' downfall—after all, I had ended up on the winning side! I thought of the enormous pain the Queen must have gone through, and still had ahead of her. I didn't like people thinking I had joined the party of the wind.

I knew that Dadash shared my discomfort with this well-meaning woman's effusiveness. Our feelings were not of gaiety, but of deep solemnity and uncertainty. How would the country deal with this momentous turning point in its history and the changes that lay ahead? Iran had been a monarchy for three thousand years, and Persians respected no leaders but strong ones. The army generals, the Imperial Guards, the commanders of the royal air force, had been trained for decades to look to no one but the Shah for orders. He had been their sole and absolute authority. Dadash and I both remembered the soldiers and officers who had run away from the Allied invasion in 1941. Could this new generation of orphaned generals now transfer its loyalty to an abstract thing called a nation, and obey Bakhtiar?

When we left the restaurant, however, everyone in the street was celebrating. On the scarred, littered boulevard, protestors, students, and armed guerrillas triumphantly brandishing rifles were shaking their fists in victory and yelling, hurtling along in cars and riding on the hoods and fenders. Demonstrators and passersby cheered and waved pictures of Ayatollah Khomeini. They hugged each other and the smiling soldiers, who stuck the carnations people thrust at them into the barrels of their guns. I saw one well-dressed man of about sixty coming out of an office building, grinning and gleefully holding up a big framed color portrait of the Shah that he had torn from a wall and mutilated. Looking at his good clothes and prosperous appearance, I could not help wondering what he would have done with that portrait a year ago. People like that were like Mashti's watermelon, I thought— you couldn't tell from the outside what was inside their hearts.

Later the same afternoon it was announced that the Shah and Queen had gone to visit President Sadat in Egypt. At the airport, when asked how long he would remain away, the Shah had replied that he had been tired for some time and wanted to rest, and that he was unable to say precisely when he would return. It depended on his health. Dadash, I, and everyone else in our family were surprised, disappointed, and dismayed by the news that the Shah, as it now appeared, was not abdicating at all, but was only leaving the country again, as he had in 1953. It grieved me very much that he was not courageously stepping forward and announcing openly that he was giving up power, or departing in a way that would leave the country in no doubt that he was gone for good.

In the end, I thought, he had not behaved like a king. But no doubt he was watching out for his own interests, not ours, and still hoped that the Americans would bring him back as they had the last time he quit the country during a crisis. Of course, for all we knew, the Americans planned to do just that, if it suited them. Neither he nor they had given us a strong leader. When all was said and done, Mohammed Reza Shah, who had styled himself "the father of the nation," had simply gone off and left his children holding the bag.

It was less than a month before Bakhtiar's government fell. The Shah's generals, bereft of their commander-in-chief, were stunned by their leader's departure. A vacuum suddenly existed where none had been, and they did not know what to fill it with.

Bakhtiar warned of the danger of a military takeover and tried to maintain calm, but three days after the Shah left, a million people marched in Tehran to demand his resignation and Khomeini's return. There were demonstrations in favor of the government, but they could not compare to those in favor of Khomeini. Army officers themselves were rebelling and taking command of their posts. People were afraid to leave home at all. In Galandwak as in the city, life was at a standstill. The villagers huddled indoors, emerging only when the local komiteh organized a demonstration in the village square.

The looting in Tehran had grown worse and spread to the countryside. When a huge army base in the mountains called Lashkarak fell into the hands of the revolutionaries, the teenage sons of the Galandwak villagers who were on the komiteh led a party to help sack it. For two days, the happy villagers came home with wheelbarrows full of shoes, radios, and guns, until there was nothing left to take.

Late in January, Mehdi Bazargan, the National Front leader, flew to Paris again to see Khomeini. He brought back a written declaration that upon returning to Iran, Ayatollah Khomeini intended to withdraw to Qom and resume his teaching and studies. This statement indicated that his role would be one of a guide and mediator, rather than a political force, and that, like all his predecessors in the position of supreme spiritual leader, he intended to remove himself from the contamination of the political scene.

This message, conveyed by the liberal Bazargan, an extremely devout and honest man who had been one of Mossadegh's most faithful followers, was immensely reassuring. Bazargan had spent years in prison for opposing the Shah's suppression of the constitution and human rights, and everyone knew that he would never lie. Delivered by so respected an envoy, Ayatollah Khomeini's statement made Iranians like me feel that he meant what he said about restoring the constitution. I was sorry that he was against Bakhtiar, but since the present government's defeat was clearly inevitable, the country would certainly not be badly off under the leadership of a good, honest man like Mehdi Bazargan.

To keep order and prevent a military countercoup, Bakhtiar implored Khomeini not to return to Iran yet and closed the airports to prevent this. But his authority was already too weak to sustain such a move. At Khomeini's orders, the employees of government ministries were refusing to allow the new ministers to enter their own offices. Furthermore, not only had pro-Khomeini sentiment completely pervaded the rank-and-file military, but the revolutionaries had penetrated deeply into the officer corps. There was even a rumor that the pilot who flew the Shah to Egypt had been a member of the Mojahedin.

In the final days of January, thirty people were killed when fighting broke out during a protest over the closing of the airport. And on January 29, Bakhtiar announced that Ayatollah Khomeini would be permitted to return to Iran.

Not in almost thirty years, since the nationalization of our oil by Mossadegh, had Iranians felt so joyous, so united in a common emotion, as at this moment. An extraordinary euphoria flooded the entire nation. Suddenly everyone, including me, was able to believe with the lady in the restaurant that we would be redeemed. Without being able to say quite how, we felt that Ayatollah Khomeini's return would make us a better people. The numerous papers and magazines that had proliferated since the lifting of press restrictions printed poems that compared the return of Ayatollah Khomeini to the coming of the Messiah, the Mahdi, the Hidden Imam. Embezzling the country's money, stealing the food of orphans, neglecting the destitute, would become things of the past. Envy, selfishness, treachery, and filial disobedience would cease to be. Everybody would be able to realize their most decent, unselfish goals and aspirations. The era of the party of the wind would be over, and a new age would begin.

On the first day of February, 1979, the Ayatollah's chartered Air France jumbo jet landed at Mehrabad Airport. February is a very cold

month in Tehran, but more than a million people had gathered there
to welcome him, and another million lined his motorcade route, which
had been washed in his honor. Tens of thousands of villagers had
walked miles and slept in open fields, like pilgrims, in order to be
there to greet him.

I went to a neighbor's house to watch the arrival on their television
set. Because of the mountains, however, the reception was so poor
that nothing of the form of Ayatollah Khomeini could be seen but a
snowy black-and-gray blur. After a short time I gave up and went
home. I would rather wait to see what Ayatollah Khomeini actually
did, I felt, than to see him on television. The following day I found
out that the broadcast had been interrupted anyway because someone
had managed to cut it off and fill the screen with a portrait of the
Shah.

It seemed, however, that Ayatollah Khomeini was not returning
immediately to Qom. Instead, after he had visited the cemetery to pay
his respects to those who had been martyred in his cause, his followers
spirited him off to a temporary headquarters in the eastern part of the
city, an old school called Alavi School, not far from the Majlis and
Jaleh Square—now hallowed ground for the revolutionaries. From
here, Agha instructed the people to continue their demonstrations until
Bakhtiar resigned and warned Iranians to be vigilant against the activities of the American Embassy, lest the CIA attempt to restore the
Shah once again. A few days after his arrival, he also told Mehdi
Bazargan to form a provisional government.

By this time it was obvious that Ayatollah Khomeini's supporters
had, for all practical purposes, already won. Bakhtiar's government
was all but nonexistent. Not only his regime but the whole state
bureaucracy had collapsed. The ministries were empty of employees.
Many former ministers, officials, and parliamentary deputies had fled
into exile or were in prison, where they had been put by the Shah
himself during his anti-corruption campaign in November; their numbers included Nassiri and Hoveyda, whom the king had not thought
to have released before his departure. The civil servants, like everyone
else, were on strike. The city's neighborhoods were in the hands of
the Mojahedin, radical Islamic student groups, Tudeh, and other
armed organizations, and were run and supplied by the komitehs,
which reported to the mullahs. The Imperial Guard was still loyal to
the government, but the leaderless generals were disputing among
themselves about whether to keep on supporting Bakhtiar or reach an
understanding with Ayatollah Khomeini. The commander-in-chief of

the air force himself had supplied the helicopter that had taken Ayatollah Khomeini on his visit to the cemetery. Soldiers were now deserting by the thousands.

Bakhtiar courageously continued to call for the rule of law. But on the evening of Friday, February 9, when the Imperial Guard attempted to crush a mutiny by air force cadets and technicians on their base near Jaleh Square, the street bands and other underground organizations sprang to arms to help the mutineers. After a few hours, finally demoralized by the killing of fellow soldiers and other Iranians, the Imperial Guards withdrew. The mutineers and revolutionaries distributed truckloads of guns to the neighborhood and to students at the University and set up street barricades from one side of the city to the other. Then, for two days, they broke open prisons and led mobs in attacks on police stations and armories. By Sunday, February 11, not only the guerrillas but every male in Tehran who was old enough to walk had a rifle or a machine gun, and the barracks of the Imperial Guards and the main army bases were under attack.

That afternoon, the generals of the Supreme Military Council declared the army neutral in the conflict, and we learned over the radio on the news that evening that Iran now belonged to the forces of the Islamic revolution. I was relieved to hear that although the broadcaster assured listeners that he was being pursued, the unfortunate Bakhtiar had somehow managed to escape from his office. I wished that he might not be caught and killed.

The mullahs, the guerrilla groups, the students, the marchers, the young boys running messages in the streets, had won. It had taken them two days to bring down the world's fifth-largest army—a day less than the Allies had needed to defeat Reza Shah's forces in 1941.

On Monday, the twelfth of February, Ayatollah Khomeini formally named Mehdi Bazargan prime minister of the new government and over the radio urged an end to the disorders. Moslems must discipline themselves, he said, and not take the law into their own hands. The time had come for everyone to stop looting and flying at one another's throats. He called for the faithful to return to work next Saturday, February seventeenth. On that day, declared Ayatollah Khomeini, all banks, offices, and shops would reopen; all schools and universities would resume their normal schedule of classes. Everyone was to turn in their guns.

During the next few days this speech was broadcast over and over again, and I felt a great rush of relief and hope. If Bazargan had the complete support of "Agha" and the backing of both the army and

Khomeini's own followers in restoring security and order, I thought, the new dawn of cooperation and harmony that everyone longed for could begin.

Between then and Saturday, however, little sign appeared of either cooperation or a new dawn. The burning and looting continued. Many blocks were completely boarded up or stood in ruins, with charred pavement and burned-out buildings everywhere. The excited guerrilla and radical student groups, who were now dressed in motley captured army and air force uniforms and military helmets, rampaged through the center of town, fighting with each other for control of the streets at the barricades that had been set up to stop government tanks. The Khomeini forces had triumphed, but it was still impossible for mere bystanders to tell who was who. At one point we read in the newspaper that one of these groups—nobody knew which one—had stormed the American Embassy and taken hostages, after which another group had mounted a counterattack and saved the American staff.

The revolutionaries, upon breaking into the prisons and finding Hoveyda and Nassiri among those the Shah had left behind, charged Nassiri as well as three other generals they captured with "causing corruption on earth" and "fighting against God." They gave them mock trials and executed them. On Friday evening, February sixteenth, a photograph of Nassiri's body, its head bandaged from the beatings and torture he had undergone, appeared on television and in all the newspapers so that people could exult at his fate. I had detested Nassiri, but I was nauseated by this cruelty. Were we now to become as savage as SAVAK itself, torturing and executing people without proper trials? I hoped that Bazargan and Ayatollah Khomeini could restore order quickly.

Vengeance was becoming the order of the day. One of my neighbors in Galandwak, a Moslem, had already been denounced to the komiteh by his cook as a secret Bahai. Another told me that a servant whom he had dismissed for stealing ten years before had come back and threatened that if his former master did not give him money, he would tell the komiteh that my neighbor drank wine. In Tajrish, rival guerrilla groups were shooting at each other in the market square outside Reswanieh.

I thought of the snipers who had barged into my school to hunt down their enemies. These young men from the bazaars and poor neighborhoods, whose relatives had been killed or injured by the Shah's troops and whose little brothers had been shot carrying messages, had just won a great revolution, defeating the combined might of a half-million-man army and SAVAK. Before, their hopes had been frustrated, their aspirations denied, but this revolution was their liberation from a dull, shabby existence, a ticket to a new life in which anything might be possible—wealth, respect, revenge on those who had held them down and ignored them. They saw themselves as Che Guevaras, and they were growing used to victory, to a sense of power, to feeling like somebodies. They didn't want that feeling to stop but to go on and on. Each separate group convinced itself that it alone had won, and that the revolution belonged to it and no other.

I was dismayed at the spirit of vengefulness, cruel destructiveness, and opportunism that had arisen. Tomorrow, however, was Saturday, the seventeenth, and everything might start returning to normal. There was still almost a full semester left. I wanted to get the School and the community welfare centers functioning again quickly, as well as do what I could for our servants who had lost property or had family members injured or wounded in the demonstrations. There was money in the emergency fund, and I had been able to continue paying the faculty and staff during the disorders. We could get along well enough until I found out who would be overseeing us in the new government.

I wondered to whom I would report in the future. It was unsettling to realize that I no longer had a board of trustees—all the officials who had been on it besides Hoveyda were either in exile or in hiding. I knew no one in the new regime; it was almost like starting over from scratch. Nevertheless, I was eager to begin rebuilding. I longed to get back to work, to take up my task again. I wanted to be among people who believed in something. I only hoped that on Saturday, Iranians would begin to heed the words of Ayatollah Khomeini.

15

THE PARTY OF THE WIND

That black smoke that rose from the roof—
    that was our black smoke. It came from us.
That burning fire that swayed left and right—
    that was our fire. It came from us.
Do not denounce the foreigner, or lament anyone but us.
This is the heart of the matter—our affliction came from us.

                                 —Anonymous Iranian poet, 1989

*T*HE NEXT MORNING, CHEERFUL AT THE PROSPECT OF RETURNING
to work and hence in an optimistic frame of mind, I rose well
before dawn. Half a foot of snow had fallen during the night, covering
the leafless branches of the apple trees and the tin roofs of the villagers'
houses. I hurried out to start my car so that it could warm up. As I
dressed, I listened for the ordinary dawn sounds of the village, the
bustle of farmers taking their cows for milking at the dairy stable. But
the dirt lane outside my wall was filled only with snow-muffled silence.

Uneasy, I dressed as quickly as I could, swallowing a cup of coffee
as I put on the black clothes I was still wearing in mourning for my
mother. Hurriedly I threw on a light black coat and kerchief to keep
me warm until I reached the office, grabbed my handbag, and went
outside to my car. It was bitterly cold, but as I threaded along the dark
lane I was relieved to see a few farmers trudging just ahead. The main

road had been cleared, and this, too, seemed a good omen. As the sun rose I passed the giant looted army base of Lashkarak, where three unsmiling revolutionaries in assorted garb and different-colored helmets stood before the gate. They waved their rifles and machine guns at me in excitement, shaking their fists solemnly and shouting, "Allahu akbar!" My hands tensed on the steering wheel. But at least, I thought, to judge from this the warring factions were working together now instead of killing each other. So far, Ayatollah Khomeini's call for order seemed to be a success.

In the village of Niavaran, where the royal family had lived, I drove by the palace. Even at this hour there was a crowd in front of it, but the tall Imperial Guardsmen who had always stood there were gone. Nervously, I speeded up a little to avoid the crowd. I wondered what would be done with the palace—perhaps it would become a museum, like Golestan, the palace of the Qajars. Reaching the city's northern outskirts, I was encouraged to see people standing on the sidewalks waiting for buses, while others looked as though they were walking to work, maneuvering around the still-standing barricades and the hulks of burned cars and army equipment. I felt better. Perhaps things would be calm enough by summer for our women and children who were abroad to return, and then we could be a real family again.

I arrived shortly after seven and left the car in the parking lot by the side of the main building; Hossein or one of the other drivers would park it when they came to work later. I glanced around to see who else was there. Normally Zabi, our several gardeners, and the other servants started working at seven, too—Zabi considered it his job to carry my briefcase, books, and camera to my office for me—but I saw no one. Indeed, the parking lot, garden, and buildings seemed deserted, almost eerily quiet.

Suddenly, as I started up the stairs, Zabi dashed out of a side entrance and ran toward me. His face was ashen, and I wondered what was the matter. "Good morning, Zabi," I called cheerfully. "Is everything all right?"

He hurried close to me. There was terror in his eyes. Barely moving his lips, he whispered, "No, Khanom. There are students inside with guns, waiting to kill you."

I stared. Had he suddenly taken leave of his senses? "But why would any students be here before eight?" I asked stupidly. "Classes don't start till then."

"Please, Khanom," he begged, "you must leave. They are serious. I don't want them to see me talking to you."

I hesitated. "Where are these students?"

"In front of the library. They are blocking the way to your office."

Still I could not believe him. "Are you sure they are social work students? *Our* students?"

"Oh, yes, Khanom. One of them used to go with you in the Land Rover to wave the white flag. There are three others as well. They say they are going to kill you."

I paused to collect my thoughts. I could think only that this was a student notion of a prank that I didn't think was funny. "Well," I said, "take my things from the car and I'll go and talk to them."

With Zabi faltering behind me, I marched up the stairs to the glass doors and turned into the corridor that led to the library and my office. Sure enough, four boys in jackets and tieless shirts were standing there. One was a junior named Isadi who had often come with me to pick up victims of the fighting; another was a skinny, pockmarked senior named Ashari. There was also a sophomore, Kharmandar, and another second-year boy whose name I couldn't remember. All four carried semiautomatic machine guns. Two or three other students clustered behind them looking frightened; they did not appear to be with them. I saw no other servants besides Zabi, and realized that they must all be hiding. Zabi had shown great courage in slipping out to warn me. Well, I thought, if these boys were trying to give Khanom a scare, they were going to be disappointed. I wasn't going to scream and drop dead just because somebody pointed a gun at me.

I walked forward. Ashari, who was evidently their leader, quickly stepped to the center of the corridor to bar my way. The other three, still grasping their weapons, clasped hands behind him to form a barricade. "What's this all about?" I demanded coldly.

"You wouldn't send me to Bombay last year," the one whose name I didn't know said in a sulky voice. Isadi chimed in loudly but uncertainly: "You were always asking the mother of the Queen to our commencement ceremonies. You are an imperialist." Kharmandar's complaint was that he had failed his sociology exam the previous semester and had had to spend the summer studying to retake it.

"Ayatollah Khomeini says that the time has come for all the dispossessed to throw out their oppressors," Ashari said. "You are with the oppressors. You were trained in the imperialist country of America. You are one of them, and this school has been serving the imperialists and the CIA. We are taking you to Ayatollah Khomeini to ask him to execute you."

When I stared at him, too astonished to react at once, he frowned heavily. "We are going to ask Ayatollah Khomeini to execute you," he repeated. "He is going to kill you."

Suddenly I realized that I had better do something quickly. There was a tiny room opposite the library that we used as our information office. It had a telephone. Swiftly, without giving the students time to think, I dashed across the hall and, darting into the room, slammed the door and locked it. Since the government was gone, calling the police was probably useless. I decided to call Ahmad Mossadegh, who was a friend of Premier Bazargan.

Hastily, I dialed my cousin's office. To my relief, he was there. Assuring me that the students could not arrest me without a warrant, Ahmad urged me to call Ayatollah Mahmoud Taleqani. Taleqani, he said, was one of Khomeini's closest advisers, and was a reasonable man. Along with telephone numbers for Taleqani's office and home, Ahmad gave me Bazargan's office number, where he said Taleqani might also be found.

Hastily thanking him, I hung up and dialed the office number at once. A sympathetic assistant said that the Ayatollah was not in. However, he confirmed that the students could not arrest me without a warrant. All arrest warrants were issued only from revolutionary head-quarters, and they were only for the apprehension of the Shah's high generals and for former officials, SAVAK men, and notorious police informers. "Make them show you their warrant," he urged me. "They must have one in their hands to arrest you."

Gratefully I hung up, about to go outside again. Then it occurred to me that the students might cut the telephone wires. I always went to Jaby's for lunch on Saturday; I had better let her know what was happening. I picked up the phone again. The line had gone dead.

Furious, I put back the receiver. What was going on? I vaguely remembered that the boy who talked about going to Bombay had wanted to go there for an International Planned Parenthood Federation training course—the IPPF itself had turned him down because he couldn't speak English. Kharmandar was angry because I had refused to override his professor's decision to flunk him. Apparently, in the spirit of the moment, they were tagging along with the other two for revenge. But why were Ashari and Isadi trying to make me out to be an "oppressor"? Isadi had always cheerfully volunteered to go along to gather the dead and wounded. Ashari was a dull, depressed youth who had been imprisoned by SAVAK for two years. Zamani and my director of academic affairs, who were on the screening committee, had reported that he was too self-absorbed and introverted to make a good social worker, but his grades had been acceptable and I had felt that anyone who had been a victim of SAVAK should be given a chance; besides, prison must have made his emotional problems worse, and perhaps studying social work would help him. I had not only admitted him, but given him financial support. He wouldn't be standing there now, I thought contemptuously, if I hadn't felt sorry for him.

I suppressed my emotions and tried to think. I was fairly certain that these students weren't religious zealots or even committed radicals— they were what the oil boom years and the disappointments that followed had produced: immature, bitter, resentful young men who felt that society had failed to give them what it had promised, and whose version of Marxist theory was that if somebody owned what they wanted, he should give it to them instead of keeping it for himself. With the School grown so big, it had been hard to keep such boys out. There were many young men like Ashari now, who felt entitled to a reward for having chosen the winning side. No one would take their accusations seriously, but they had guns, and it was just possible, I realized, that they were doing this at the behest of someone in the new regime. I had no one now who could tell me who that might be. All my family's and the School's connections were gone, swept away with the old order. Of everyone I knew, only Ahmad might be able to find out, and now I couldn't reach him. I would just have to go back and ask the students calmly for their warrant. Displaying impatience or trying to defend myself would only increase the danger to me and any others in the hallway.

I unlocked the door and stepped outside again. Zabi had vanished in terror. Ashari was looking disgruntled at my temporary escape, which had undercut his moment of victory. Speaking in as neutral a voice as I could command, I asked him if they had a proper warrant.

"We have a warrant," said Isadi, and grinned, patting his gun. "Here it is."

Taken aback, I wondered what to do next. More students were filing into the building from the other end of the corridor, and so were teachers and field supervisors. They were smiling and talking as they arrived, as happy to be returning to work as I had been. God only knew, I thought, what Ashari and the others might do with those guns. It would be best to go along with them, and insist on the legalities later. But if enough people arrived in the meantime, perhaps they would be intimidated into reconsidering what might simply be a vicious but unplanned and impulsive act of malice.

"Well, then," I said, stalling, "what are you going to do?"

"We are going to take you to Ayatollah Khomeini," Ashari repeated sullenly. "He will execute you." I thought briefly of trying to talk him out of it, then gave up the idea. He would only take it as an insult and get angrier. There was no way I could reason with boys like this.

We stood about awkwardly for a minute or two. More people were arriving, men and women who had been with me for years, some since the beginning—teachers, supervisors, clerical staff. I didn't see Esther, but Zamani's wife, who was on my research faculty, had just walked in with a field supervisor who had often come on our Friday hikes. I waited for someone else to start talking to the students, for someone to ask why they were arresting me. All my graduates had been taught how to defuse tense situations and knew what to say to make people less angry and defensive. Each moment that Ashari hesitated would make him less likely to persist.

But minutes seemed to pass and no one spoke. I stared at the faces behind the students in surprise, then in growing alarm. I didn't expect anyone to defy the students or attempt to disarm them, but when someone was talking about killing me, was no one even going to ask what I had done?

Just then three more people came in through the front entrance. I glanced around. One was not a social worker but a part-time professor of research who taught at several other colleges in the city. But the other two, who served as directors of two of our welfare centers in South Tehran, were my own graduates—conscientious, hardworking men who had been among my first students, and whom I had known well for twenty years. They would certainly understand how to talk to Ashari and his gang.

The students looked over my shoulder and saw them, too. Suddenly galvanized into action, they began pushing excitedly toward them to surround them, exclaiming that they worked for an exploiter of the people and must meet the same fate as she. Shocked, the research professor tried to explain that he had merely come to give his weekly lecture. The two directors looked first at the guns, then at me. A kind of recognition seemed to dawn in their eyes. They glanced at me in fright, then at the students who surrounded us. Then one of them, with an imploring expression, looked at Ashari, pressed his hands flat against his breast, and gave me a sidelong look that said more clearly than any speech, "Surely you do not think that *I* am an oppressor, like her? I am on *your* side." The other director nodded in agreement with the unspoken words. Thirty people behind Ashari watched in silence, their faces impassive.

Suddenly Ashari turned around, unsmiling but triumphant. "I have important news!" he shouted. "The Islamic revolutionary fighters have won. Now it is we who will run this place! We are taking the director and these members of her staff to Ayatollah Khomeini to be executed!"

There was a pause of no more than a heartbeat. Then somebody called out, "Allahu akbar!" At once, other voices joined in. "Allahu akbar," they cried, "God is great—hurrah!"

In disbelief I looked first at one face, then another. It was as if we were all in a bad movie together and everything was happening in slow motion. I felt as though someone had driven a knife between my ribs, but as yet there was only shock, not pain. I could understand that they might all be afraid to protest, but why, I wondered dully, were they cheering? I saw staff members and graduates I had taught fifteen or twenty years ago. They were people whom I had coaxed and comforted through fieldwork, had sent abroad to study and found good jobs, whose families I had helped in emergencies, who had consulted me on everything from financial problems to the choice of a marriage partner. Twenty years passed before my eyes, twenty years of hard, unending labor on behalf of our profession and of these people, for whom I had felt responsible. They and I had shared bread and salt. Now not one was raising a word in my defense.

I looked at Ashari again. His eyes looked back at me with feral distrust. The idea that such a creature was planning to run the School of Social Work was so disgusting that I felt almost physically ill. Without trying to disguise the contempt I felt, I said, "Well, if that is what you are going to do, then let us go and do it."

We went outside to the parking lot where one of the Land Rovers was waiting. The students had selected a driver named Zarabadi. He was a man of about forty, whom I had hired when he told me that his wife and children were sick for lack of proper food, and who often came now to tell me how well his family was doing. I was sorry that the students were forcing him to drive.

The students bundled us into the big vehicle, I in the second row between the professor of research and Kharmandar, and the two directors in the back seat with the fourth student, who held his gun on us to make sure we didn't try to jump out and run away. Isadi and Ashari, handing Zarabadi a large white handkerchief to wave, climbed in front and we set off southward toward Shahreza Avenue. The road was cluttered with burned and scattered wreckage, sandbags, and hunks of cement.

Zarabadi drove slowly and carefully, avoiding the rubble, while Ashari stuck his arm out the window, waving his own handkerchief importantly. At the intersections farther into town, traffic was being directed not by the regular blue-uniformed city police but by pairs of bearded or stubble-faced young men in the odd assortment of paramilitary gear we had been seeing ever since the army's surrender. A few wore Arab headdress, and once, when we stopped near a couple, I heard them talking to each other in Arabic. I wondered in passing why Arabs were directing traffic in Tehran. Where were the ordinary police? At all these intersections, the students leaned out and yelled triumphantly, "Allahu akbar! We are taking traitors to Ayatollah Khomeini to be executed!" The men outside did not smile, but nodded and solemnly shook their fists in congratulations.

When we reached Shahreza Avenue, Zarabadi suddenly rolled down his window, too. "Hey," he yelled, laughing, "look what I have—I am taking four traitors to Ayatollah Khomeini! These people will soon be shot!" The guard waved him on. Still laughing, Zarabadi turned left onto Shahreza. I could hardly believe my ears. His joy sounded completely authentic. He was sincerely glad that I was about to die.

It seemed a long, long drive. We proceeded slowly, through a strange phantasmagoria. Along some walls, beneath old white scrawls of "Death to the Shah" and "Death to America," red flowers now lay in the doorways or on the sidewalk beneath red inscriptions: "Here a martyr died." Rubbish of all kinds littered the road, including office file cards and papers where mobs had invaded government buildings or police stations. It looked as though the police had simply vanished and been replaced by these street gangs. Had they gone the same way as Bakhtiar's government? Then I saw what looked like a blue police tunic caught overhead in the lower branches of a leafless tree. Both its sleeves seemed to have been ripped off, and it was encrusted with a dark substance that looked like dried blood. I closed my eyes in horror. If the police no longer existed, who was in charge of the country now? Suddenly it occurred to me that maybe the new government had begun arresting ordinary people, too, not just men like Nassiri, Hoveyda, and the Shah's generals. Did Ashari actually have grounds for believing that my arrest might be taken seriously by those under Ayatollah Khomeini?

We turned right and headed south toward the area of the Majlis and the old bazaar. Forty-five minutes after our departure from the school, Zarabadi pulled up in front of a small police station. The students ordered us to get out and walk ahead of them into the station yard. Ashari and Isadi vanished into the building. Here, too, there were many revolutionaries, and the same confusion of costume. All the faces had an eager, serious, exalted expression, a look of intense purpose. A few minutes later the students came out and told us brusquely to go inside.

Apprehensively we went into the building. The students did not follow. Several junior police officers were inside, all in regulation uniforms. This was the first sign of order and sanity I had seen all morning, and I nearly gasped with relief. Just then the station captain came out of his office. He stared in astonishment at us—a respectable-looking woman carrying her handbag and three middle-aged men wearing neat suits and ties—and I felt even more encouraged. It was clear from his expression that no one like us had been brought to him before. Obviously Ayatollah Taleqani's assistant had told the truth: the new government wasn't arresting civilians. I asked the captain what we were supposed to do, and he replied, with courteous sympathy, that he did not yet know, but why didn't we sit down and rest for a while? I thanked him, and the four of us sat down on some chairs along the wall. The captain said something in a low voice to one of the junior officers, who left the room. We waited. Looking through the front window, I saw the students in the station yard being questioned by several uniformed police and one or two men in plain clothes.

Finally, after a considerable time, the captain emerged from his office again. I looked up expectantly. Very politely, he said, "Khanom, I am having someone call the headquarters of Ayatollah Khomeini to find out where you must go now."

For an instant my mind went blank. Then my heart began to pound. Until this moment I had not seriously entertained the idea that anyone in the new government had an interest in this. But if not, why would the police need to involve Khomeini's headquarters? One of the men next to me began to sweat with fright.

His anxiety brought me to myself. I reminded myself that the men who had been taken with me had families to consider, and had simply found themselves in the wrong place at the wrong time. I got up, went over to the captain, and explained that I was the only one the students had accused. As the director of the School of Social Work, I bore sole responsibility for its policies, and if there was anything that I or my institution had done wrong, I would take the blame. These men were not connected with my administration. I would go willingly to Ayatollah Khomeini, I said, but I asked that my colleagues be released. The captain agreed to release the men, provided that my associates agreed to sign papers promising to return if necessary. He would have to send to "the Central Committee" for these documents.

We returned to our seats. As we passed the window I noticed that Ashari and his gang were still outside. Ashari was holding a pink folder which I recognized as a School of Social Work file. I wondered how it had arrived at the police station, for I had not noticed it in the car. Nearly all our files were open, and none held any dark secrets. The folder could contain nothing but the most innocuous correspondence. Even so, a chill passed through me as I realized that it had evidently been snatched from my office to help corroborate whatever I was supposed to have done.

The captain, who saw that it was nearly ten o'clock, had considerately ordered a plate of food to be brought in for us. I felt no hunger even though I had left home with only a cup of coffee in my stomach, but my neighbors swallowed the food in nervous haste. A few minutes later, the captain reappeared and summoned them, saying that the forms had just arrived. Without glancing at me they rushed into his office to fill out the documents. While they were there I fumbled in my handbag for some notepaper and hastily wrote down Jaby's telephone number. When they came out, chattering thanks to the captain, I gave the note to one of the men, imploring him to telephone my sister and let her know where I was. Then, once more, I sat down to wait. I felt baffled and scared. What could the School have done, what had someone accused me of? It was as if rules that I had followed correctly all my life had changed overnight. I had the sensation of having taken a step and suddenly, inexplicably, found myself walking on empty air.

I tried hard to think clearly, but my mind felt as though it were being dragged down by a whirlpool. I had always kept the School completely neutral, committed only to helping the weak. But since the surrender of Bakhtiar's government and for months before that, people who had committed no crime at all had been shot down in the streets. The whole city seemed to be in the hands of these angry, bearded young toughs with guns. I looked out again and saw that Ashari and the others were no longer there. I hoped that they had seized me of their own volition, without a warrant. But being rid of them was no comfort if I were now to face unknown accusers without even a chance to learn what I was supposed to have done.

At last, after what seemed a very long time, the captain came into the room with a bearded young man in gray trousers, a black shirt buttoned to the collar, and a black leather jacket. He was holding the pink file folder from the School. My heart sank. I felt as if I were caught in the wheels of some horrible machinery from which I could not extricate myself. "Khanom," said the captain, "I am placing you in the custody of this man. He will take you to Ayatollah Khomeini."

Outside stood a very small two-door Fiat. Another "beard" stood beside it, a rifle in his hand and a bulge under his jacket that looked like a pistol. With my two guards sitting in the front we began heading south. Hesitantly I asked the first man, who was driving, where we were going. To the Imam's Tehran residence, he said curtly. It wasn't far from the bazaar. We would be there shortly.

We headed south, into the crooked byways beyond the bazaar. This was the heart of the old city, and the farther we went, the more congested the twisting street became. It was jammed with great numbers of darkly dressed, unshaven men, women in black chadors, and even children, all moving swiftly along in the same direction as we, and I realized that they, too, were trying to reach the Alavi School where Ayatollah Khomeini was. Not far ahead I could hear voices roaring, "Allahu akbar, Khomeini rahbar!"

The Fiat slowed to a crawl and the driver honked furiously. Moving only a foot at a time, he turned into a dead-end alley barely wide enough for the tiny car. The Alavi School's outer wall and large gate were clearly visible at the other end. But the road was so thick with the surging crowd of pilgrims and well-wishers that we stopped completely, unable to move at all.

For fifteen minutes we sat. The crowd streamed past, chanting ecstatically, fists waving in delirious excitement, the younger men pushing forward so that they could reach the gate or touch the walls where Ayatollah Khomeini was. The tiny car swayed with their shoving, and the guard who was driving leaned on the horn until I thought it would break.

At last I could stand it no longer. I wanted only to get this over with. Politely, I suggested that we try to reach the gate on foot, promising I would not attempt to escape. After a moment's hesitation the driver agreed and we got out, pushing and shoving our way along the alley wall. I clutched my handbag to my chest and inched along between the two men, fearing that the crowd's weight would shift at any moment and cause me to fall and be crushed in a slow stampede. At last we reached the big wooden gate, which a number of men were trying to break down. The driver spoke to the chief of the dozen or so guards who were fighting back the crowd, and this man unlocked a low door inside the gate, gesturing to me to jump inside. Seeing the door open, the mob roared and surged forward. I ducked my head and half stepped, half fell through the opening. Two of the gate guards jumped in after me, one holding the pink file folder the driver had given him. The door slammed shut behind us, and I heard the key turn in the big metal lock.

I looked around. We were inside the compound of the revolution's headquarters, at the edge of an open stretch of snow-patched, muddy land. A good hundred and fifty yards away was a long wall behind which, under the leaden winter sky, rose the three-story school building. For a minute I could not understand what the bleak expanse of land was, then realized that it had been the school's playing field.

Avoiding puddles, we crossed the field to the wall, where, as we approached, I saw a small, elderly gatekeeper sitting with his back to us on a low stool, looking through an open wooden door in the gate to the inner courtyard. He wore an old striped woolen jacket and had a transistor radio clasped to one ear. Evidently he found watching any activity going on in the courtyard less dull than watching the empty playing field. The guard who was holding the pink folder went up to him. As the other guard held his rifle muzzle a few inches from my face, he showed the file to the gatekeeper and announced importantly that they had to take me inside.

The gatekeeper squinted dubiously and put down his radio. I saw that he was just an old villager with a big nose, a scruffy beard, and a patch over one eye. He grunted, shook his head, and got to his feet. They couldn't take a woman inside, he said. I would have to wait out here. He took the folder and disappeared with it into the courtyard. After about ten minutes, he came back. The guard said something that I couldn't hear. The gatekeeper shrugged and nodded at the wall next to the doorway, as if to say, "Just let her stand there; where do you think she's going to run to?"

Uncertainly, the second guard standing beside me lowered his gun. Then, with suspicious backward glances, both men moved off in the direction of a big canvas army tent about a hundred feet away. Glad not to have guns pointed at my face any longer, I stood with my back to the wall near the doorway, holding my light coat together and shivering a little. I had no idea how long I was going to have to wait. Apparently I was the only woman in the place.

I looked around. I hoped that someone would come out soon and talk to me. There was no place to sit. The tent, where some guards were unloading boxes from a wagon, was the only thing I saw on the playing field. Guards were constantly coming and going to and from the main gate, escorting male arrivals. Both visitors and guards had the exalted, purposeful look of the revolutionaries I had seen at the police station and on the streets. Our day has arrived, their movements seemed to say. From the alley outside the main gate came loud chants of "Long live Khomeini" and "Death to America." I felt as if a giant hand had suddenly plucked me from the real world and set me on an alien planet. Why was I in this frightening place?

I looked again at the gatekeeper, who had closed the gate after admitting another group of visitors and was listening to his radio again. He was just an old day-servant, one of many that a prominent cleric would have about. From the tinny little instrument a familiar voice was rasping; Agha's gatekeeper was whiling away the long hours by listening to rebroadcasts of his master's sermons. I would have liked to learn who inside the building had my file, but a servant of this level wouldn't even know where to begin. He was merely a lowly toiler in Ayatollah Khomeini's large household.

Even so, his presence steadied me. Among all these cold, bearded faces, a simple old servant of Ayatollah Khomeini seemed almost a friend. I yearned for a voice that sounded familiar and human. He must be very bored, I thought—I might get a bit of useful information out of him.

I edged closer to the doorway. "Salaam," I said, bowing slightly. I was afraid he would think a woman could only have been brought in because she had been unchaste; I was glad that my head was covered and that I was still wearing mourning clothes.

The old man hesitated. Then, furtively, he nodded. "Salaam," he mumbled.

"You are listening to Agha's speeches?" I coaxed.

He nodded again, shyly, picking up his stool and opening both doors of the gate to let in five or six servants who were carrying several enormous covered pots of food. As they passed through, he sneaked another glance at me out of his good eye, flattered that a woman with an educated accent had shown respect by being the first to speak.

"Who were those men?" I tried to keep my voice deferential.

"They have come to wait in the courtyard until my master appears there this afternoon," he said with great pride. "Many have already come to pay their respects, and many more are waiting inside now." Still keeping his eyes averted, he sat down again with his back to me, looking into the courtyard. "Who are you?" he demanded, consumed by curiosity.

"I am a teacher," I said humbly. "I have a school. My students arrested me and I was brought here, but I do not know why."

To my surprise the old man slapped his forehead. "Such unruly young rowdies," he cried, shaking his head. "They've brought another one! All this undisciplined behavior, it makes you sorry for the poor country." As I waited hopefully, we were interrupted by two frightened older men in hats and coats, escorted by a couple of the rifle-bearing guards. Uneasily, I backed off. The guards spoke to the gatekeeper and the old man admitted them, then stood watching as they went into the courtyard. That, the old man said disapprovingly as they all disappeared through the gate, was what he meant. Those men had been denounced as imperialists and fighters against God—heaven knew by whom; an ungrateful employee, perhaps. These cases were coming to Agha all the time now, and he had plenty to do without them. Agha had asked everyone to stop this sort of thing, but people didn't listen to his wisdom.

Shaken, I leaned back against the wall. Terms like "imperialist" and "fighter against God" were being used to denounce those accused of opposing the revolution—"fighter against God" especially was the term used for people like Nassiri and the SAVAK generals, and was among the most damning terms possible for clerics to use of a Moslem. If the police had seen fit to send me here and the revolutionaries had accepted my arrest as legitimate, the charges were being taken seriously. I must at all costs stay alert and calm.

Trying hard to shut out the sight of the muddy field, the guards, the noise of the chanting mob, and with an effort to keep my anxiety from being heard in my voice, I asked the gatekeeper if he had served Ayatollah Khomeini for a long time. At my question, his grizzled face lit up. He told me with pride that he had been Agha's household servant for many years, both at home and in exile; his name, he added courteously, was Hadji Dulabi of Qom.

I felt that I had to find a way of ingratiating myself with my new acquaintance, to make him understand that I was not a "fighter against God" or an enemy of the revolution. If someone inside that building had an interest in me, he might ask this old man about me—for Hadji Dulabi, although lowly, was clearly a trusted servant. I must make a good impression on him.

Seizing my chance as he paused, I asked in a respectful voice whether he remembered the riots that had occurred many years ago, when Agha was still in Qom and was first arrested for speaking against the Shah?

He frowned, trying to recall. I waited tensely. Then he said that he remembered.

"I and the students of my school, Hadji," I said eagerly, being careful to address him by his title, "arranged for the families of the dead and injured protestors to be paid for the wrongs they suffered."

He nodded, vaguely courteous, not comprehending. Ah, he said after a moment, no doubt that had been a pious, godly thing to do. Agha was always saying that unruly behavior was bad. *He* did not want all this disorder. It was a shame, he added kindly, that I couldn't go inside, but with all the visitors and prisoners they had no room where they could keep a woman.

I sank back against the wall in despair. Apart from the cold-eyed guards, this old man was the only person with any connection to whoever in that building had concerned himself with me—and we were speaking across a vast gulf. The boundaries of his world were the teahouse, the wheat field, the village mosque. Hadji Dulabi of Qom didn't care if a woman had a profession or even whether she was a fighter against God. To him she was just a "zaifeh," as anonymous as though she were wearing a chador. In this revolutionary new order I was merely a creature they had to leave outside until they could decide what to do with her.

Noticing my sudden weariness, Hadji Dulabi generously asked whether I would like to sit down and rest. The thought of depriving an old man of his seat made me pull myself together. I thanked him and said that I would prefer to stretch my legs a little and get warm. He shrugged, but when the next group went inside, he called, "Khanom, the guards say you can walk back and forth between here and that storage tent over there. You can get warm that way."

I thanked him and walked toward the tent, rubbing and slapping my arms. I was in a state of shock, and I wanted to stay alert. What offense could I or the School possibly have committed? The students' words in the corridor had told me little, though their motives were clear enough: they thought that if they had me killed, the new government would give them the running of a large, prestigious institution. That was idiotic, but I knew that these four "Islamic freedom fighters" were just young Iranians who, like many others, had passed through a school system that had never taught them to think beyond their own emotions. They were no different from the man in my mother's little story who sat in the desert and demanded a piece of the treasure someone else had brought back from Mecca—they wanted a share, too, and the mere fact that they wanted it made them think they deserved it.

I was to die, I thought, because they hated and envied me for having what they desired for themselves. As for those who had cheered my arrest, I must try not to remember that. I could not afford to let that memory interfere with clear thinking.

I racked my mind for clues in what the students had said that would tell me what anyone here could hold against me or the School. I could think of nothing. Ashari and Isadi obviously wanted to link me with "imperialism" and "the CIA," but the students themselves had always wanted Madame Diba at our commencements; she wasn't a Pahlavi, nor had she ever been accused of corruption. As for my studying in America, so had tens of thousands of Iranians by now—so many that Premier Bazargan and even Ayatollah Khomeini probably had some among their own advisers. Ashari and the others, I thought, must have just improvised this whole thing, without thinking through what they were going to say. Surely no one would issue a warrant on the basis of such accusations.

It was now early afternoon. The temperature must be in the low forties, and in a few hours would begin dropping fast. I didn't dare request any of the hostile-looking guards to ask when someone was coming for me, nor did I dare approach any of the visitors. I might only antagonize someone who could speak ill of me to whoever was in charge of my case.

When I reached the doorway again Hadji asked me if I wanted to go and rest inside the storage tent. Gratefully, I replied that I would have a look inside. As I walked toward the tent once more, I realized that I was beginning to feel light-headed from shock and hunger. I thought of giving Hadji money to get me some tea or food, but was sure that if this kindly old man tried to smuggle something out of the kitchen he would only get into trouble himself. There was nothing to do but wait. I tried to walk briskly, as I usually did. However long I had to be here, I did not want to lose control of myself.

Reaching the tent, I stepped inside and drew a sharp breath of surprise. The huge space was crammed floor to ceiling with loot: piles of expensive carpets, gilt-framed mirrors, fine furniture, framed oil paintings, books, clothes, silk tapestries—a mountain of goods on both sides, separated only by a narrow aisle about three feet wide that had been left for access to the things at the rear. There was no room for even one more piece of booty.

I looked around, but saw no chairs amid all the spoils. Since there seemed to be nothing to sit on, I closed the flap and walked back to Hadji Dulabi again. "There's no room in there," I said. "It's full of stuff."

"It's what I was telling you," he grumbled. "Everyone is denouncing and looting his neighbor." Agha, he said, had asked the police and the Islamic revolutionary fighters to bring in whatever they caught people with, to discourage them. "You can see for yourself," Hadji

Dulabi added indignantly, "that he has put these things in a tent to keep the snow and rain off them. He is protecting people's property."

I walked back toward the tent again, shocked and saddened. Why did we always undermine ourselves with opportunism and vengefulness? Iranians had united to rid themselves of a dictatorship, and now that unity was falling apart again, just as it had when Reza Shah left and we had turned from fleeing the Allies to reviling his memory and arguing. When would we begin putting the nation's good before our own?

Suddenly I saw before me, as sharply as though it were happening, the faces in the hallway. What had happened to Reza Shah had happened to me, too. As soon as everyone saw that I had fallen, not a single voice had been raised in my favor.

I stared, numb and unseeing, at the playing field. Once, when I was a child, Mashti had told me that after the coup, when Shazdeh was arrested and imprisoned in the Qasr-e-Qajar, Sayyid Ziya had had Hadji Doktur Khan tortured to make him reveal the location of my father's private papers. Shazdeh's old friend had refused to reveal where the papers were, and his hands had been palsied from the torture for the rest of his life. I wondered how many Persians would do the same thing for an employer today. The old bonds of bread and salt had dissolved amid modern urban life and the materialism, fear, and greed the Shah's policies had encouraged. His rule had destroyed our struggling democracy while at the same time educating us in no principles except the age-old one of survival. That, I thought, must have been why my colleagues had so easily joined the party of the wind.

Walking back to Hadji again, I saw a group of prisoners approaching the gate, stumbling along with their hands on the guards' shoulders. They had been blindfolded with women's head scarves. Unnerved, I waited until they had gone inside, then went up and asked who they were. He said grimly that they had worked for SAVAK—"very bad people, Khanom." Such men, he explained to me, had been informers who had ruined whole families and worked for America and the British and Israel. Now they were being brought to justice.

Nervously, hoping to discover something about my own fate, I asked what was done with them. Did judges try them?

"No," said Hadji with satisfaction. "Agha's councillors and revolutionary guards question them. Then they put them to death at night, up there on the roof."

My knees grew weak and I placed my trembling hand against the wall for support. Trapped out here with no one to intercede for me,

I was nobody—invisible, impotent. What would become of me in this lawless place? How long before this would be over?

Hours dragged by, and still no one came. I passed the time and distracted myself from my terror by pacing, chatting with Hadji, and watching the groups of visitors, guards, and prisoners going in. The afternoon wore on, the air grew colder. I had nothing to do but wait and think. My mind went over and over the morning's events, my years at the School, the worry my disappearance would cause my family. I didn't know if the man to whom I had given my note at the police station had bothered to call Jaby, but even if he had, in this new order there was nothing my family could do.

Late in the afternoon a group of ten or fifteen young men in civilian clothes arrived. I watched curiously as they filed through the doorway into the inner courtyard. There was something familiar about them, but I couldn't put my finger on what it was. A few had a pious growth of new beard on their faces, yet they looked more like soldiers than pilgrims, being strikingly tall and muscular. Hadji peered after them eagerly. When I asked him who they were, he said proudly that they had belonged to the Imperial Guard. Not one week before, he added, those very same men had been killing their countrymen to protect the Shah. Now they had all sworn allegiance to Agha and were coming to pay their respects.

Hadji had been watching the courtyard with increasing excitement for some time. Suddenly he gestured to me urgently. "Come and see," he whispered loudly. "Agha is coming onto the balcony! Come and see him!"

I hurried over and stood at the top of the shallow steps, looking into the large courtyard for the first time. It was completely filled, for hundreds of men had arrived during the day and were now packed in shoulder to shoulder. The very stones seemed to vibrate with their suppressed excitement. On the third-floor balcony about a hundred feet from where we stood, two men were coming out, one in a black cloak and turban, the other in Arab headgear. A roar of "Allahu akbar!" went up from the crowd. The enthusiasm was so contagious that I myself felt caught by it.

Ayatollah Khomeini hung back a little, as if reluctant to appear. The other man, however, grinned and stepped forward, waving his arms above his head in a gesture of victory. I had recognized him at once, and felt baffled. Turning to Hadji, I asked what Yassir Arafat was doing there. The old man beamed. Arafat's organization Al Fatah, he explained proudly, had helped Agha by training the Islamic revolutionary fighters to use guns. Now Arafat was here to kiss Agha's hand and pay his respects.

In that surreal place I experienced only mild surprise that the rumors of the PLO's involvement in our revolution had been true. I felt concerned solely with Ayatollah Khomeini, who would decide my own fate. I kept my eyes fixed closely on the balcony, but both men soon withdrew. The shouting died away, yielding to the same hushed, expectant murmur as before.

A few minutes passed. Then Ayatollah Khomeini appeared alone, followed by half a dozen clerics in black and white robes. Slowly and with evident reluctance, he advanced to the center of the balcony again, his councillors trailing behind him, and stood with his eyes lowered, unmoving and unmoved in the thin winter light. Even from far away he looked forbidding—but then, I thought, so did most frowning, white-bearded mullahs in black robes. I had expected an aged, frail ascetic, and was surprised at how strong and fit he appeared. The audience waited breathlessly. After a moment, without any other motion, Ayatollah Khomeini moved his right forearm, raising his hand in the barest acknowledgment of the crowd's presence. So careful and deliberate was the motion that not even his robes seemed to stir.

A deafening shout of "Allahu akbar!" rent the air, a cry of allegiance. To these men, I saw, the country's true leader was not Mehdi Bazargan, but this uncompromising old man who had defied the West in the name of Islam and vanquished the Shah with the sheer power of his faith. His stony strength was now their firm pillar in a cracked universe. Yet it was strange to me, an Iranian, to see a scholarly cleric appearing on a balcony to receive the acclamation of the crowd, like a political leader; this was something quite new in our experience.

After a few moments he left the balcony, still moving slowly and deliberately, the others following reverently behind him. Quickly I stepped back from the doorway as the men in the courtyard began coming toward it to leave. I felt reassured for having seen Ayatollah Khomeini in person. Of course he looked severe, but this was no ignorant village mullah; this was a devout and learned man who stood at the pinnacle of the religious community. It was impossible that a cleric of this caliber would consider someone like me a "fighter against God." I felt sure now that if I were here for some other reason than an impulsive action by Ashari and his band, it was because somebody had lied about me. Now that Ayatollah Khomeini's audience was over, surely someone would come and question me, and I would be sent home.

By this time it was early evening, and the light was rapidly fading.

I watched the many groups of men move back across the field to the main gate so that they could get home and say their prayers by sunset. The chanting in the street that had been going on all day was weaker and more sporadic; all but the last diehards were leaving. Yet still no one came, and I slowly began to understand what I had already started to suspect and fear much earlier: being unable to bring a woman inside, my accusers had simply forgotten she was here.

The cold and gloom increased rapidly. I was by now very hungry and fatigued, as well as exhausted from having to walk and stand in the chilly air for hours on end. At about six o'clock Hadji moved his stool to let in several men who were herding a gigantic, bawling sheep through the gate. The sheep, he said, was to feed all the men inside— Agha and his councillors, the guards, and the prisoners.

At hearing this, a hot fury rose in me. It was obvious by this time that whoever was supposed to see me had gone home to supper.

For the past few hours I had been growing increasingly aware that in spite of having taken no more than a cup of coffee since early morning, because of the cold I would soon have to urinate. I was appalled at the necessity of having to ask anyone in this place whether I could use a bathroom, but finally I realized that I had no choice. Concealing my humiliation as best I could, I asked Hadji whether a toilet was available—unlike English, Persian has no face-saving euphemisms for this word—and he said I could ask a guard to take me inside the courtyard.

I went up to one of the two or three black-shirted young guards still on duty and spoke to him. Coldly, he turned and led me inside the courtyard, where a row of old-fashioned outhouses stood. They were no more than stinking holes with frame doors and an old water urn inside. As I closed the door I looked down and saw the guard's feet close by, and I realized that he could also see my feet and hear what I was doing. I felt the most excruciating shame and outrage. What fault had I committed, a woman of more than fifty, who had worked hard all her life to help Iran? I was being deprived of contact with my family, terrorized by the fear of what my detention might mean, and subjected to a physical discomfort that amounted to actual abuse. Whose idea of Islam, I asked myself, was this?

By seven, darkness had fallen. Tall floodlights were switched on and a dim electric bulb illuminated Hadji's doorway. Only a few guards were still patrolling. Occasionally a mullah or a man in civilian dress would enter at the main gate, cross the field, and go inside, but no one came out anymore.

I did not know what to do. It seemed too risky to ask a stranger to carry a message. But the cold was so intense now that I could no longer stand and chat with Hadji; I shook if I stood still for more than a few seconds. I paced relentlessly back and forth between the doorway and the tent, walking as fast as I could. By eight o'clock, except for a passing servant and a guard or two, the arrivals had stopped. Even the chanting in the street had died. I realized that I was going to be left here all night, and might freeze to death. It had been a mistake not to speak to someone sooner. In desperation I resolved that if anyone else came along, I would ask him to help me, no matter who it was.

Around nine o'clock I was walking near the wall when I saw two men coming across the field. In the white glare of the lights I could see that one wore a black cloak and turban—a mullah with his servant behind him. I hurried over to where Hadji sat huddled in his jacket, also trying to stay warm. Who was the man coming toward us, I asked, and was he staying here?

Hadji peered at the two figures. "Oh, that is Ayatollah Rabani-Shirazi," he said. "He is a big man, very respected."

I asked if I might request this cleric to take a message inside for me. Hadji nodded sympathetically. "Yes, yes, Khanom," he exclaimed, "hurry, go ask him to help you—he's one of Agha's most important advisers."

I stood a few feet back from the doorway and waited until he reached me, then stepped forward. "Agha, salaam," I said, bowing.

Astonished to see a woman approaching him in that place and at that hour of the night, the mullah paused in his rapid stride. Avoiding impurity, he bent his head and looked down at his shoes. "Salaam," he replied in a low voice, and waited. He was a small man, no taller than I was, taut and disciplined.

"Agha," I stuttered, my lips trembling with the cold, "I beg you to ask something of Ayatollah Khomeini for me." As soon as I stopped walking I had begun shivering so hard that I could scarcely speak.

He neither requested my name nor looked up. "Why are you here?" he said. He was obviously in a hurry and was poised to move on at once.

I gave him my name and explained what I knew of my circumstances. He frowned slightly, but I could not tell what he thought. "How long have you been here?"

"Since morning, Agha. I implore you to be so kind as to tell Ayatollah Khomeini that I am waiting. If I am to be imprisoned or—anything else, I would like it to be done quickly."

A shadow crossed his face, a fleeting emotion that I thought might be sympathy, but he instantly controlled it and began walking on. "I will do so," he said curtly, and was gone with his servant before I could thank him or say goodnight.

I went back to my pacing, glancing frequently toward the doorway and wondering what Ayatollah Rabani-Shirazi thought of a woman who had been arrested by her own students—probably that I had been detained for immoral conduct. But whatever he thought, he was my only hope. No one else was going to arrive at such an hour.

Half an hour later, when I had reached the tent again and turned around, I glanced toward the gate. With a shock I saw that it was closed, and that Hadji Dulabi was gone. I walked quickly back to where he had been. His stool and radio were gone, too. Hoping that he had not left for good, I resumed my pacing. Half an hour passed, then forty-five minutes, then an hour. Hadji Dulabi did not reappear, and I realized that he had gone to bed. We had not been exactly friends, but without him I felt more alone than I ever had in my life.

By now it was at least eleven and the playing field was completely deserted. Even the few guards had withdrawn to the main gate or had gone inside the building. Two hours had passed since I had spoken to Ayatollah Rabani-Shirazi. Maybe, I thought, he had been in too much of a hurry and had forgotten my plea. Or, more likely, he had decided not to bother Ayatollah Khomeini with a small matter like this.

I was now gripped by a cold and fear that seemed to have invaded every cell of my body, and although I could have eaten nothing, I was nauseated by hunger. The mud and slush had begun to freeze over, and I had to be careful where I stepped on the uneven ground. I now walked along the wall that fronted the courtyard, so that I could grab the rough bricks for support if I slipped. My legs ached with fatigue. But I struggled to keep going, reminding myself that I had often hiked in winter for hours at a time on an empty stomach. Memories of hikes with Shazdeh came back to me, and I could almost hear him shouting, "Keep marching, keep marching—no stopping to rest!" I thought how lucky it was that he had made us strong and enduring. I was so angry now that I felt as though I had a fire inside me. It couldn't warm me, but at least it would keep me upright until I could tell these people what I thought of their "Islamic" revolution, even if I died or were imprisoned for it.

More hours passed. As I hugged the wall and tried to keep moving in my thin clothing, memories of my mother, of the compound, of summers in Shemiran—Mashti taking us hunting for hidden springs under the willows, Shazdeh teaching us to swim—came and comforted me. At other times, the memory of the faces in the hallway recurred like a stinging flash of light. Even if I survived this night, I knew that I could never bear to see those faces again. Yet, inexplicably, I felt that I must be responsible for what was happening to me. I had tried to teach people to believe in trust and loyalty and personal responsibility, and I had failed. My mind kept turning over the stones of my past, trying to find beneath old mistakes and faults an explanation that made sense, as though guilt were a priceless jewel I had mislaid.

Suddenly, in the darkness, I heard shots, about thirty yards distant and coming from overhead. My heart racing, I stumbled toward the lighted gate as fast as I could. Another volley crackled from somewhere above me. I pressed myself tightly against the doors and waited to see if the gunfire would come closer. Then I remembered what Hadji had said: these were the firing squads, executing the SAVAKis and generals. I had heard no screams—the guards must have gagged their victims to keep them quiet. Or maybe they were too weak from whatever had been done to them earlier.

Terrified, I moved away from the building as quickly as I could and staggered blindly along the freezing mud, flinching at the intermittent shots. At times the gunfire came in volleys, like rain spitting from a momentary storm cloud; at other times I heard only a single bark that seemed to extinguish human terror like a curse. The possibility of my own death was now real and imminent, like a developing picture that had suddenly come into focus. My whole body was shaking with fear.

I had always believed that human beings ought to turn to God for help only when they had done all they could to help themselves. Now I began to pray. I had often wished that Mitra and my grandchildren lived in Iran. Now I gave God thanks that they did not, and that my mother was at peace and not suffering the anguish that she would have felt tonight if she had been alive. I also gave thanks for Shazdeh, who was the reason I was still on my feet and stumbling along this path and able to retain possession of myself. "O God of Abdol Hossein," I said, "please give me also a clear head and the strength for whatever is to come, so that I can keep my self-respect and not disgrace myself and my family and Shazdeh. If they decide to kill me, I want to go to my death in a worthy manner."

After this I lost track of time completely, and could concentrate only on staying upright, for I knew that if I sat down on the ground I might fall asleep and freeze. It occurred to me that I had never made out a will. But that didn't matter, I realized; by law, whatever I had would go to Mitra.

At last, after what must have been another couple of hours, as I was approaching the doorway I saw three men standing there, waiting for me. In the dim light I could not make out their faces, but they were wearing jackets and trousers, not cloaks and turbans. One, the tallest, stood a little ahead of the other two. He had a notebook in one hand and something tucked under his arm. As I approached, I saw that it was the School of Social Work file.

"Good evening, Khanom," the man said politely. Clearly he was the one in charge. "What is your name?"

I tried to speak distinctly, but my teeth were chattering so hard and my lips were so numb that he asked me to repeat the words. "My name, Agha, is Sattareh Farman Farmaian."

He nodded, obviously shocked at the condition I was in. "Yes, Khanom," he said. "I am sorry that we have come so late. We would like to speak with you. We have been sent by Ayatollah Khomeini."

16

THE TRUE BELIEVER

*It has been accepted by all Moslems in every epoch that at the
end of time a man from the family of the Prophet will without
fail make his appearance, one who will strengthen Islam and
make justice triumph.*

—Ibn Khaldun

I PEERED AT THE FEATURES OF THE MAN IN CHARGE. HE WAS ABOUT
fifty-five, with short black hair heavily sprinkled with gray and
a lined, weathered, amiable face with a little stubble. His clothes,
which appeared dark brown in the dim light, had an old-fashioned
look. With automatic courtesy he inquired whether I had eaten anything, adding that it was almost four in the morning. I said that I had
eaten nothing since I had been brought here, and he again looked
shocked. Would I, he asked, like to have something from Agha's
kitchen?

I shook my head. My nausea seemed to have disappeared for the
moment, but my stomach was so empty that the mere thought of a
bowl of rice brought it back again. Besides, nothing on earth, I thought,
was going to make me take favors from these people. Nevertheless, I
was glad to see that he seemed to be a decent and conscientious man,
who evidently wanted to do the right thing.

I looked carefully again at all three. Apparently the two who had not spoken were there to assist him. They were both clean-shaven and in their early thirties, dressed in lighter-colored, less conservative clothing than he. From his leathery skin I judged that he was a farmer, but a prosperous, moderately educated one. Perhaps, I thought, he had been one of the many bazaar merchants or other businessmen who, out of moral scruples, had withdrawn into farming or fruit growing during the last decade rather than participate in the graft and corruption necessary to do business under the Shah's regime. His eyes were not focused directly on my face, but he also had not ostentatiously lowered them to show his purity, as Hadji and the cleric had. I was now fairly certain that he was not a fanatic, just an ordinary person.

Sounding tired, the investigator explained that they had many cases to go through; that was why no one had come earlier. Momentarily at a loss as to where to conduct an inquiry, he looked around and saw the tent under one of the floodlights. "May I suggest," he said, "that we go and sit in there?"

I followed him to the tent, the two younger men walking behind me, and we stepped inside. With the tent flap open, the floodlight above it and the bulb just inside the entrance made it easily bright enough to see by. As he glanced around for a place where we could all sit, the chief investigator seemed nonplussed by the mountain of loot that jammed the huge space. The two younger men looked around in frank amusement. It was scarcely warmer inside the tent than outside and the dirt floor was wet. Finally, seeing a low wooden rifle box lying just inside the entrance, the older man took out his pocket handkerchief and carefully dusted it off. Then, as courteously as before, he asked me to sit down on this. Though my legs were almost too stiff to bend, I slowly managed to lower myself into a sitting position. Opposite the rifle box was a pile of several large carpets. The investigator hoisted himself onto the carpets and sat looking down at me, his long legs dangling and his knees at about the level of my face. The two assistants took up positions in the aisle, standing on either side of us with their arms folded deferentially, as a sign of respect for the tall investigator, who, though not a mullah, was plainly a man of considerable prestige in Ayatollah Khomeini's entourage.

I sat hunched awkwardly on the low box with the cold air at my back, looking up at the investigator, my legs drawn close to me to avoid touching his, which were only about a foot away. In this cramped position, surrounded by all the loot and with three big men towering over me, I felt oppressed and claustrophobic. My teeth were chattering less, but I was parched with thirst.

The investigator sighed and opened his notebook, evidently uncertain of the best way to begin. He looked as though he had had little experience at his job before tonight, and would just as soon not have had any. I would have liked to know who he and his assistants were, but he gave no sign of being about to introduce himself. I wondered if he was expecting to interrogate me only briefly, and whether this meant that I could expect to be released or, on the contrary, that I should prepare myself for the worst.

"Now, Khanom," he said finally, trying to make his tone authoritative, "why are you here?"

I looked up. I was absolutely astonished. Didn't *he* know? But I quickly concealed my surprise and resentment. The last thing I wanted was to antagonize my interrogator by making him lose face before his men. I answered cautiously that I had no idea what this was about, and could tell him only that I was a teacher, and that my students had arrested me and sent me here.

"Yes," he replied, looking relieved that I had given him a way to start. "I've been told about that. It is Agha's impression that those youngsters are extremely naive." Before I had time to feel happy at this encouraging remark, he took a pencil from his jacket, ripped a blank sheet of paper from his notebook, and handed both to me. "What is your name? Write it down for me, and also your father's name and your profession." Realizing that he did not want me to see that he knew so little about my case, I did as he bade me.

"Now," he said when I had finished, "please write down what you think of this revolution." I had the feeling that he did not know how to proceed and was stalling for time. Sitting back on the carpets, he took out the pink folder, leaned over, and muttered something to one of the assistants that I could not hear. The two younger men sat down next to him and peered over his shoulder as he quickly leafed through the papers inside. This was obviously the first chance he had had to read the file. After a moment or two the assistants rose again and, with ironic interest, began to occupy themselves by examining the nearby spoils.

I felt more confused and indignant than ever. What was I supposed to say about their revolution? That I saw all this looting and killing and thought it splendid, and that I hoped they wouldn't kill me as well? To hell with them, I thought. I'm not going to chew their food and swallow it for them, too. Taking the pencil, I wrote carefully that although at first I had believed that the revolution was meant to bring about democracy and justice, I was now seeing that innocent people were being arrested and detained. This was not the revolution I had hoped it would be, I wrote, and I did not believe this movement could succeed if citizens who had helped the country all their lives were detained and mistreated. Such a revolution, I finished, was certainly not one that *I* would back.

I handed the tall man the piece of paper. So much for that, I thought. He can show that to them and they can take me up on the roof and shoot me. At least I've finally given these people a piece of my mind.

The investigator took the paper and slowly read what I had written. As he read he looked more and more distressed. Suddenly he burst out, "No, no, Khanom, that's not so, what you say isn't what Agha wants! The disorder you are referring to is caused by troublemakers, street rabble! Ayatollah Khomeini doesn't believe in these things, he *wants* democracy and justice. The people themselves betray their cause—this is a good revolution, good for the masses!"

"That's not what *I* see!" I cried. I was incensed. I started to struggle to my feet, but I didn't have the strength, so I shouted from the rifle box, ignoring the exhaustion and thirst that made my words slur. "I see looting, confiscations of private property, executions without proper trials according to our laws, arrests of innocent civilians. Don't tell me that what I see with my own eyes isn't true! These things have been happening for a week, they've been happening right here, all day! Don't tell *me* about 'the people,'" I yelled. "I have built welfare centers that have helped millions of 'the people'! Hundreds of thousands of Iranian children are healthy and going to school and their mothers are learning skills and getting good medical care because of me! And you pretend that this is a good revolution, when you have arrested someone like *me*?" Then, emptied of strength, I sank back again.

"No, Khanom," he said with deep sincerity, "I must explain to you that you are mistaken! Didn't you hear Agha say on the radio the other day that everyone should stop looting and denouncing each other? *He* does not want this. The illiterate masses do this for their own purposes, and are not listening to his wisdom."

I was surprised at how genuinely troubled he seemed. Too spent to argue further, I didn't answer. I've said what I had to say, I thought, and now I'll keep my mouth shut, since I've upset him so much. He must be a true believer in this revolution. But I looked hard at the carpets he was sitting on.

He flushed darkly and, laying down the notebook, picked up the pink file that was lying next to him and took some papers from it. "Look here, Khanom," he went on almost beseechingly, "Ayatollah Khomeini didn't ask for your detention. It was not he who ordered your arrest. Your students are the ones who have accused you."

So Ashari and the others had been acting on their own, after all. As I digested this news, he held up a sheaf of papers from the folder. "They accuse you of eleven crimes, offenses that implicate you as an enemy of the revolution."

I sat stiff with shock. How had the students had a chance to work up such a long list of accusations? They certainly could not have done so if they had just dreamed up their coup this morning or last night. They had to have obtained the file in advance and gone through it carefully. How long had there been a plot at the School to get rid of me? Days? Weeks?

The investigator went on to explain that I would surely find many of these so-called crimes stupid—I must know how immature and illogical the young were. Ayatollah Khomeini had read the accusations himself, he continued, and had asked him to come and talk to me about them because he wanted justice done. However, Agha deemed many of the charges unworthy of serious consideration. This too should show me, said the investigator, that Ayatollah Khomeini did not condone irresponsible behavior.

His tone was soothing, but I was too stunned to care. Esther and I had never locked up anything—we had nothing to conceal, and apart from obviously confidential documents such as faculty references and student evaluations I had never seen any need for us to hide our files from anyone. My door had always been open to everybody, and every student committee had access to my office and correspondence. I was staggered by the degree to which Ashari and the others had abused my honor system, and how they had exploited the personal trust and responsibility I placed in the students not merely to depose me but to try to have me killed. Why had I not listened when someone like Kia warned me not to be blind, not to trust people? And he hadn't been the only one.

After a moment, with a great effort, I managed to collect my thoughts. I must forget about the students for the time being, I told myself, and try to keep my head. This man had been sent to examine me to see if I was against the revolution, and to find out whether there was a case against me. I was lucky that he seemed so reasonable. "Very well," I said more calmly. "I will be happy to listen to the charges. Please read them to me."

Holding the file on his lap, he leafed through the first few papers in it. "Let us begin, Khanom, with the first five charges. The students claim that you worked for SAVAK and they include five different documents to prove this." I listened anxiously while he began reading aloud from an administrative memorandum from SAVAK, warning all college and university libraries not to permit banned books. Realizing that this was just a form letter, he put it down on the carpet and began on the second one, which commanded the School of Social Work to produce two hundred students to attend the Shah's last birthday parade. This, too, was obviously just a memo, and with an annoyed expression he placed it on top of the first one and read through the third and fourth. The former was a letter informing all educational institutions that student agitators were planning to strike school cafeterias for serving frozen meat because it was against Islamic law; the latter warned schools of higher education not to tolerate anti-government activity.

Before I could respond to any of these, he shook his head in disgust. "How silly," he exclaimed to the assistant on the right. "These are just form letters. They must have been sent to dozens of institutions like that. The only thing they prove is the foolishness of these youngsters." The man he had addressed gave his colleague a superior smile of agreement. "Khanom, I'm sure you realize that this evidence is absurd—it proves nothing. I won't even bother to read the fifth document."

Still very upset, I bowed my head. The investigator shoved the memos aside and took up another piece of paper. He read through it quickly, then said in a severe voice, "The students charge, Khanom, that you are guilty of manipulating and stealing money from the School of Social Work. They say that this is proven by the fact that you arranged to construct buildings on land owned by your school and then embezzled the money provided to build them. You also built more than forty 'community welfare centers' and 'family planning centers' on land you owned all over the country, for which work you accepted bribes from the contractors. They have provided a letter to show this."

I looked up at him, speechless. I felt as though someone had just smeared my face with filth. In a shaking voice, I asked him to read me any letter that said I was a thief and had taken my own institution's money.

He picked up a piece of paper and handed it to me. It was written on Plan Organization stationery, and was a report, many years old, on the cost and progress of our auditorium—which had been finished in 1974—stating what the Plan Organization had paid the architect and contractor upon the completion of the second floor.

Barely able to hold back tears of anger and humiliation, I replied in a low but steady voice that the accusation was false and that the students, being inexperienced and unfamiliar with the workings of organizations, must have misunderstood the situation. Although our school as an institution owned a great deal of land that had been donated over the years for us to build numerous welfare centers for the poor, this land did not belong to me personally and I had nothing to gain by having buildings constructed on it to increase its value. Nor could I have manipulated a penny of the money to which the Plan Organization letter referred, since, as he could see from this very letter, all payments for construction of the auditorium had gone directly from the building department of the Plan Organization to the contractors and architects, not to me.

The tall man, clearly chagrined at having revealed that he had not had time to read the evidence beforehand, put the letter down. "Really," he said to his assistants, "these students must have been crazy to think that this would prove anything against her."

I bent my head again to hide my anguish, shame, and outrage. To pretend that I had "stolen money from the School" was a lie so egregious that even the most naive and fanatical student would have known it for one. I had always insisted that student committees play a strong role in running the School, and any student could have vouched for the fact that the only money under my direct control was the small emergency fund that I had set up in our very first semester. Moreover, not only was this fund run by the students themselves, but donations from me and members of my family accounted for most of it. Would I have stolen money from myself? If the accusation had not been so vile it would have been laughable.

I realized now that Ashari and the others must have believed that if they got rid of me, they themselves could skim off all this money and land they assumed I was helping myself to—that was what the Shah's officials had been notorious for doing. That they were so naive did not surprise me. But who had led them to think that the School would be placed in their hands? By this time I was certain that they themselves did not have the wit to plan this, and must have been working in concert with others. Who was really behind this?

The investigator was speaking again, and I forced myself to attend. "Khanom," he said, "I am embarrassed by the extreme stupidity of those who have brought such foolish charges against you. But Ayatollah Khomeini himself," he continued with great earnestness, "recognizes that the charges I just read to you are the result of youthful unruliness and folly. Does that not show you that what the students have done is contrary to what Agha wants? Above all he desires justice. Surely you can see that?"

I nodded wearily. Perhaps, I thought, what he was saying was true.

I was glad that Ayatollah Khomeini felt that the charges were ground-less. I had already heard more than half of the eleven accusations, and so far his investigator seemed, if anything, to be on my side. "Now, Khanom, the seventh charge—" He gave me a look that seemed more puzzled than anything else. "The students allege that you are responsible for the killing of five thousand infants."

"How can anyone say such a thing?" I cried.

He consulted the paper in his hand, talking as he read. "The students testify here that as part of their education they were required to attend courses on how to prevent the birth of children, and to work for a semester in clinics you started for this purpose. In these clinics, they say, doctors gave women medicine that prevented the births of at least five thousand children in the last year alone. You were responsible for bringing these activities to Iran, and if you had not started these clinics, millions of Iranians would have been alive to fight for Ayatollah Khomeini and support the revolution." He frowned. "I must tell you, Khanom, that I know that such medicine for women exists. I never heard anything bad of it, but if what the students say is true, the accusation is very serious."

"Perhaps," I said evenly, "you will permit me to clarify this matter a little. It is true that I am responsible for bringing what is known as family planning to Iran, because when I began my work I saw that parents had more children than they could feed or educate, and that women's health was endangered by having children every year." In an emotional voice I went on to explain how, with this medicine and other methods of contraception, our clinics enabled women to avoid conceiving until families could afford to care properly for the children they already had and the mother could recover her health from the last baby. Our movement, I said, enjoyed the endorsement of no less an Islamic authority than Ayatollah Shariat-Madari, whose learning and piety he must surely consider beyond reproach. "I am amazed and grieved," I finished, my voice trembling, "that these students could attend our school all this while and not have understood that. I am sure that all this was thoroughly explained to them in their courses."

He listened intently, watching my face closely for signs of falsehood or insincerity. When I fell silent, he became very thoughtful and said nothing for some minutes, glancing at me with great interest several times, as though he would have liked to ask me more about the subject. When he spoke again, it was in a tone that I felt was somehow ad-miring, but all he said was, "All right. I'll read you the next charge."

I listened, torn between relief that he didn't believe I had killed anyone and my growing dismay at the viciousness of the accusations.

By "misunderstanding" family planning, the students were trying to make me out to be a murderess—a SAVAK-style sadist like General Nassiri, someone who deserved death. I wondered whether whoever had plotted with them knew how poorly the work had been carried out. I remembered the armed revolutionaries I had seen in our cafeteria last fall, and how I had felt that some of the students knew their identity. No doubt some of those in the hallway, too, had been part of this, and had cheered my arrest for that reason. Sick at heart, I imagined the excited, secret discussions in the cafeteria or even my own classroom: How do we take over the School? What do we do about Khanom?

The investigator took a small card out of the file. I was startled to see that it was my membership card for the Imperial Sports Club, which I always kept in my desk drawer. "The students," he said sternly, "accuse you of being a member of this club."

I paused, uncertain and worried. "Yes," I said. "I was a founding member. I did not usually dine there, but I took walks and sometimes played tennis on the courts. Was there something wrong with that? What crime am I being accused of?"

"The students have pointed out," he said, giving the words special emphasis, "that it was an *imperial* sports club."

So that was it: they were arranging the "evidence" to build a case that I was in league with imperialists—first by suggesting that I worked with SAVAK, then by suggesting that I was implicated in the corruption of the Shah's regime and SAVAK's sadism, and now with this. That the proof they offered was silly or irrelevant wouldn't matter to them; I was guilty whether there was evidence or not, because in their minds I was by definition one of the "oppressors"—someone who had what they wanted for themselves. I was indeed lucky that this man was a rational, principled individual and not a fanatic, whom they might have taken in.

He was waiting for my response. I could think of nothing to say but what was true. "Yes," I replied, "that was certainly its name. Years ago, because I found that my work was exhausting me, I needed a place nearby where I could walk and keep fit, so I joined with some people I knew to start a sports club. It had to be called something that honored the monarchy, or we would not have been able to attract members. But the club was private and had nothing at all to do with the imperial court, the Shah, or the royal family." As I spoke I looked appealingly at the two assistants, anxious to enlist their sympathy. "The students, of course, can know nothing about that. However, anyone can tell you that what I have said is true." The two younger men smiled knowingly at each other, as if I had said something humorous.

The investigator shook his head. "These youngsters," he muttered again. "This doesn't prove the woman is an 'imperialist.' All their evidence is nonsense. What a waste of time!" Looking tired and annoyed, he returned the card to the folder. If things continued this way, I thought, he might dismiss the three charges that remained. Trying to make myself as unobtrusive as possible, I stared at the ground while he read the ninth accusation for himself.

"The students claim," he said finally, "that you graduated from a university in America and that you have had contact with this university and others in America since that time, and with universities in similar countries, and that you have sent many students to these countries to be educated. Furthermore, you have an imperialist secretary who types letters and documents for you in English and sends them to the CIA." Frowning, he put down the paper he was reading from and looked directly into my eyes. "What have you to say?"

It was fortunate, I thought, that Ashari's blustering in the corridor had prepared me for this. I answered carefully that it was absolutely true that over the last twenty years, in my capacity as this school's director I had sent some three hundred students and faculty members abroad. I had done so in order that they might be better educated and acquire a knowledge of what was going on in their profession in the outside world.

"As the students who have accused me know perfectly well," I went on, trying to catch the eyes of the assistants again and shaking my head to convey my incredulity at this youthful foolishness, "my secretary sends names, letters, and documents not to the CIA, but to foreign universities." I further explained that while many had indeed gone to the West for advanced training, I had also sent numerous students to schools in the East and to developing countries: India, Africa, Pakistan, the Philippines, Japan, and even Sri Lanka, as well as to our own neighbors in the Middle East. I employed an English-speaking secretary because someone with a knowledge of English was essential for answering and filing our correspondence.

The investigator was staring at me—not in disbelief but in amazement. "Did you really send students to India and the Philippines, Khanom?" he asked. "But what could they learn in places like that? Those countries aren't in the West."

If the situation hadn't been so serious, I thought, I could almost have laughed—or cried. Even this faithful revolutionary was "Western-stricken" and believed that education was only good if it came from the West! "Surely," I said politely, "the countries of the West are not the only places we can learn from? I sent my students everywhere there were good services in child care, community health, or other programs that could benefit our people, regardless of where they were. My students go wherever they can learn and become more enlightened, and that is not only the West. The School of Social Work itself has long been a place where people from many other countries come to learn, because they know that we in Iran have something to teach them, too."

At this speech he looked so pleased that for a moment I actually thought he was going to reach down and pat me on the head. Never before, I thought wryly, had I been so warmly received as an instructor by someone whose prisoner I was. However, he said nothing more, but merely turned his attention to the folder again.

Then, as he read the next words, a shadow crossed his face. It rapidly gave way to a frown of real anger. Surprised and perplexed, I looked down quickly. Finally he spoke, in a manner completely changed from before. "The tenth charge, Khanom, is a very serious one. You are accused of being a Zionist." His voice was harsh.

For the first time his tone really frightened me. If he and Ayatollah Khomeini somehow concluded that I was a political supporter of Israel, it would be the end of me. The revolutionaries were deeply indebted to Al Fatah; this man himself had undoubtedly broken bread that very evening with Yassir Arafat. But what could he possibly have in mind that would show I was a "Zionist"? I looked up and saw with great alarm that his eyes were blazing.

"You traveled to Israel, at the order of the Shah himself," he said accusingly.

I had no idea what he was referring to. I must have looked as confused as I felt, because he continued angrily, "I will read you a letter which proves that this is true." He unfolded a piece of paper. Addressed to me, it informed me that His Majesty had received a request from the Child Welfare Society of Israel asking that I attend a conference in Tel Aviv and give a paper on children's welfare in Iran. It concluded, "His Majesty wishes you to attend this conference."

My first panicky thought was that the students had somehow forged the letter. I had been to Israel twice for international conferences, but both visits had been so long ago that I no longer even remembered the dates. Trembling, I asked softly when this so-called letter was written, and the name of the person who had supposedly signed it.

He peered at the letter. It was signed, he said, by the minister of court, Hossein Ala. The date was March 1959.

"That letter is twenty years old!" I cried. "Am I being charged with something that happened *twenty years* ago?" I looked at the two assistants and caught the eye of the one on the left, who broke out in a laugh. The investigator reproved him sharply for his lack of seriousness. When the younger man had respectfully apologized, he turned back to me. All his former friendliness had disappeared.

"Do you not know, Khanom," he said coldly, "that Ayatollah Khomeini has said that all those who side with Israel are on the side of the Shah, and are enemies of Islam and the revolution? He is a man of absolute justice, and to him it is irrelevant when a severe offense was committed. In his eyes something that happened twenty years ago may be just as serious as something that happened yesterday.

"The students," he went on, "have charged you with being pro-Israel. They are only stupid, inexperienced children and should have brought better evidence. But the fact remains that you went to Israel. Worse, you did so at the bidding of the corrupt Shah, who was Israel's stooge, just as he was the stooge of the Americans, who have exploited us all these years and who, as everyone knows, are even now themselves merely the instruments of the British. Do you think, Khanom," he demanded in genuine fury, "that *that* exploitation and imperialism was not serious merely because some of it happened twenty years ago, or thirty, or even fifty? No matter how old the evidence against you is, you are still implicated."

I felt very frightened, but replied that neither I nor my school had ever had anything to do with the Israeli government or its policies. Like physicians, or organizations such as the Red Crescent and the Red Cross, we strove only to help human beings, and in all countries with which we had contact our interest was in education and social welfare alone, not politics.

He did not reply. I was horrified. I understood that in both Ayatollah Khomeini's eyes and his I was guilty by association. Unlike the students, this man had principles and could reason. But this touched upon a matter in which reason was useless. I knew that I could not possibly convince him that advocating a government's social programs was not the same as agreeing with its politics. The very fact that he was such a principled man made my arguments irrelevant: his own unexamined emotions pressed upon his principles as a deep lake presses upon the great dam that holds it back. I realized that I must prepare myself for the worst after all. Trembling, and fearing that I was going to faint, I waited for him to read the last charge.

This one seemed to give him some difficulty, and he beckoned to the other two to help him with it. They leaned over his shoulder and muttered together, half reading and half talking, but were evidently unable to decide exactly what the accusation was. The students, I thought, must not have been able to express themselves properly. I looked down, anxious not to be the witness of their embarrassment.

Finally the assistants stepped back and the chief investigator said, "Khanom, the students' last charge is that you raised the living standard of Iranians."

I stared at him as though in a stupor.

He went on irritably. "They say that you have been training Iranians at your school for twenty years, with the result that many were lifted out of poverty and led comfortable lives with good jobs, adequate housing, automobiles, and so forth. The students argue that by doing this, you made these Iranians complacent and content with their situation, and thus helped to delay the overthrow of the Shah by discouraging them from becoming soldiers in the cause of the Islamic revolution. Perhaps, Khanom, you can explain what these foolish young men have in mind?"

His face seemed to blur. My head was pounding with a pain that must have come from hunger, and which had been growing since I sat down on the rifle box. I was dizzy and nauseated again, and now I was filled with a growing terror of death. "I can only say," I replied weakly, "that I was the head of a school and it was my job to train students to be social workers. I didn't know that I was doing anything wrong."

With obvious disdain he replaced the paper in the folder. "The reasoning of this charge is as illogical and inexperienced as all the others," he said with a weary sigh. "Agha, who has read them, has acknowledged that they reveal the students to be immature and irresponsible.

"But the overall picture," he continued, "is clear. Ayatollah Khomeini takes the imputations of Zionism and imperialism very seriously. However foolish the particular accusations, the students were correct in one thing: there can be no doubt that for the last twenty years you cooperated with the Shah and worked with his corrupt, imperialistic regime, which sold our country to the Americans, the British, and Israel. Your associations connected you with that regime and what it stood for, which is everything that the revolution is against. This in itself is a crime requiring severe punishment. For this crime Ayatollah Khomeini believes that you should be brought to justice."

The objects around us in the tent began to swim and the air suddenly grew incredibly cold. My throbbing head seemed to expand to many times its size, and a roaring noise filled it. I was convinced now that I was going to die, and tried in vain to control my shaking. Piercing the noise in my head was the single thought that I must at all costs hold myself together when they took me up to the roof, so that I could end my life with dignity.

After a moment I realized that the investigator was still speaking. Automatically I forced myself to listen to the words.

" . . . However," he was saying, "we have received testimony from someone here who knows you personally, and who has spoken well of you to Agha. It was at his request that Agha sent us to question you and examine the particular circumstances of this case. Mr. Kazemi, please give me the letter."

The assistant on his right took a piece of paper from his jacket and handed it to the investigator.

"This letter," he went on, "is from Ayatollah Mahmoud Taleqani, who was present in the meeting when Ayatollah Rabani-Shirazi brought your case to Agha's attention. I will read it to you." He read the letter. It was very brief, saying simply that Ayatollah Taleqani was familiar with my work, had witnessed that I had helped many of our people, and knew me to be guiltless of any wrongdoing.

Very soberly, the investigator folded the letter again and laid it beside him on the carpet, next to the file. "Ayatollah Taleqani, whom the Shah imprisoned for many years because of his activities on behalf of justice and democracy, told us that during the time he was in the prison of Qasr-e-Qajar he often observed that you came there with your students to improve the lot of the prisoners, that you taught them skills, separated the sick from the well, and were the cause of many more such acts of compassion toward them and their families. He also informed us that recently you were personally responsible for saving the women of the Ghaleh district from being burned alive by a street mob.

"Because of these things," he continued, "Ayatollah Taleqani has praised you highly to Ayatollah Khomeini and has given us this letter as evidence of his own great favor toward you. Ayatollah Taleqani also warned Agha, in my hearing, that the revolution would not succeed if it devoured people like Khanom Farman Farmaian."

I was completely confused. I had absolutely no idea what to conclude from this, except that it looked as though they weren't going to take me out and shoot me after all. "But then," I said, "what are you going to do with me? How are you going to punish me? Am I going to prison?"

The investigator looked at me in surprise. "Why, we are going to release you, of course. Ayatollah Taleqani is a very important man."

Again I felt dizzy. It was as though what was in front of my eyes had suddenly transformed itself, changed its shape like a jinni into something harmless but unrecognizable.

"Agha instructed me," he went on, "to investigate the charges against you, and if Ayatollah Taleqani's intercession appeared to be justified, to send you back to your school, where you are to continue your excellent work. He is now extremely displeased with these foolish students, whose naiveté and lack of information has wasted the revolution's time. But he desires that, as a good Moslem, you will forgive them for what they have done and return to your job, as he has asked everyone to do. He acknowledges that you are a woman of some value, able to contribute much to this revolution."

I bowed my head. I was still trying to make myself understand that I was not going to die.

"Do you have a means of getting home?" the investigator asked.

I shook my head.

"Mr. Kazemi," he said, turning to the assistant again, "do you have a car to drive Khanom home?"

With a self-deprecating gesture, the younger man replied, "I'm afraid I don't." I was startled to hear him actually speak.

"It doesn't matter," I mumbled. "I'll get a taxi." I wanted only to get away from this terrible place as fast as I could, and find a phone booth where I could call my family.

"I'm sorry," the investigator said with sincere regret, "that we cannot assist you in returning home. Please escort Khanom to the gate," he said to Mr. Kazemi, "and find her a taxi." Mr. Kazemi and the other assistant hovered over me solicitously as I slowly and stiffly pushed myself to my feet with one hand, clutching my handbag in the other.

"Khanom," said the investigator warmly, "I must tell you that I personally am very pleased with this outcome. I give you my word that your students will soon learn how angry Agha is that they mistreated you."

I looked at him. I felt no resentment that he had had the letter all along. He had not toyed with me, but had been a fair and honest investigator. He had given me the chance to clear myself, and I was grateful to him and to Agha for sparing my life. I did not consider him a hypocrite merely because my having the favor of someone more important than himself washed away what he considered my crimes against the revolution. That only made him human. He and I both knew that in our country, if you weren't strong yourself and didn't have somebody strong to protect you, you were nobody, and you did not survive. I wished that I could know this good man's name. But I did not ask what it was. I only wanted to leave quickly and never set foot in this place again.

Outside, it was growing light. Mr. Kazemi escorted me across the muddy field to the gate. He spoke to the guards on duty and they opened the small door that led outside. The alley that had been filled with a mob the day before was deserted. Looking toward the main street, I saw people coming and going, as if life outside had been normal all along. It was as though I had dreamed the whole thing.

I turned to Mr. Kazemi, wetting my dry lips before I spoke. "Thank you for escorting me," I said. "You and your colleague have been standing for more than three hours, and I do not want to keep you from your rest any longer. I can easily find a taxi on the big street over there." The distance that had taken more than half an hour to cover yesterday in the mob was only about fifty yards.

He seemed relieved. "As you wish," he said politely. "However, there is one thing that I would like to tell you."

He lowered his voice, afraid of being overheard by the guards. "I too was in the room when Ayatollah Taleqani interceded for you. He told Agha that your students were rabble and that if you went back to your school, you would not survive. He said that if Mr. Ashrafy, the investigator, found you innocent of the charges it would be best for you to leave the country. I am convinced that he was hoping someone would give you this message. Take his advice, Khanom. Next time there may not be an Ayatollah Taleqani around to save you."

He turned and walked back across the playing field, and I stepped out of the gate and trudged slowly up the alley toward the street. I felt very happy to have learned the name of this sincere and uncorrupt Mr. Ashrafy, who believed so devoutly in the goodness of this revolution.

By this time it was nearly light. I could see a phone booth fifty yards from the mouth of the alley. My vision was blurred and my brain was spinning, and though my nausea was gone, my head ached as though it would split in two. All at once exhaustion seemed to catch up with me. Afraid that I might not make it, with what felt like my last ounce of strength I staggered up the street to the phone booth, collapsed on the seat, and yanked the door shut. Digging in my handbag, I found a few coins. I did not want to call Dadash, who had no car, and since Abbas was retired now, I thought I had better not awaken Jaby. I decided to call Khorshid and her husband Kayvon, who lived next door to Dadash. They would be up: Kayvon, who worked for the oil company, would be preparing to leave for the office. I hoped I could still reach them.

I dialed their number and my sister picked up the receiver on the first ring, giving a sharp cry of surprise and relief when she heard my voice. The whole family, she said, had been up all night. I gave her the name of the intersection where I was and she said that she and Kayvon would be there in less than an hour. I hung up. There was no place to sit on the street, so, hoping that no one would want to use the telephone, I sank back on the stool to rest in the booth until they came.

But my mind continued to race with frantic intensity, as though I were still sitting on the rifle box—my release had been so sudden and unexpected that I was unable to accept the fact that I was no longer in the tent. I kept thinking of ways to address the various charges. I was possessed by an almost manic need to find better answers with which to refute everything I had been accused of. Over and over, I replayed Ashrafy's questions in my mind, as if by doing so I could nullify the treachery of those who had robbed me of my life's work.

Like a great blast of light, the day and night of terror I had been through had both seared my eyes and opened them, revealing blinding truths. It was as if someone had taken me to a mountaintop where everything at last lay stretched out before me, illuminated as clearly as the sky on a bright day at No Ruz. My heart refused to accept that everything I had built had been destroyed in less than twenty-four hours, but that was what my mind told me, and I was astonished at how obvious everything now appeared, and how I had deluded myself before. What miserable, ungrateful wretches we Iranians were, and how foolish I had been! The Shah's overthrow had opened everyone's hand, and people were revealing their true nature. Surely no other race on earth was like us—unprincipled, conniving, and treacherous.

Persians, I thought bitterly, were constant only in their inconstancy, in lack of principle and the fine art of survival. All these years I had believed that I was changing our character, teaching loyalty and responsibility, building a new Iran, when I was just wasting time. I had refused to recognize the most basic truth about us—that in the twisting, tortuous pattern of Iran's history, we always bowed before the strongest, seized whatever the day offered, followed whoever promised us the most. My whole philosophy had been stupid, the very opposite of our ancient Persian wisdom: never trust anyone outside your own family. Willfully and intentionally, I had never *mis*trusted anyone, unless and until they proved that they did not deserve my trust. Where were those timeservers and conspirators, I wanted to cry out, where were those self-seekers and false friends, when I won us the backing of Hossein Ala, when I got the Queen to support social work, when I demanded that the Mayor pay attention to human beings?

Yet even in the anguish of that moment, I had to acknowledge what I had known since the day the beggarwoman defrauded my mother: that no one could afford to believe in anything but survival if he lived in a society that allowed him to think of little else. Perhaps, after all, Iranians were not unique in their faithlessness, merely human; other nations had been luckier in their history than we. Could I really turn my back on all that I had built? If I did, henceforth Ashari and his gang would run the School. How could I allow them to destroy social work's future, as would certainly happen if I did not go back and save our young profession? If it was the wish of Ayatollah Khomeini that I return, surely that would give me some protection.

But I had never begged anyone who did not want me to take me back, and I knew that I would never return to the School even if God himself told me to do so. I had lost a long, long battle I had never admitted I was fighting. I knew now, even if Ashrafy did not, that Persian history had beaten me.

17

HARJ-O-MARJ

My soul is grown weary of Pharaoh and his tyranny;
I desire the light of the countenance of Moses, son of Imran.
They said, "He is not to be found, we have sought him long."
A thing which is not to be found—that is my desire.

—Rumi

*J*ABY AND DADASH, AS I LEARNED FROM KHORSHID ON OUR WAY home, had been frantic with worry since the previous morning, when Ahmad had called Dadash and told him that I was being threatened with arrest. They had at once telephoned our family attorney, who, unable to get any information on the phone, had gone to the School and demanded to know where I had been taken. At last someone had told him, but neither he nor Dadash had been able to learn more. Other dreadful news had also reached the family the day before: one of our half brothers who had worked for the government had been arrested as well, and no one knew yet what had become of him.

I asked to stop by Jaby's house so that my sister could embrace me and see that I was alive. Then we went on to Reswanieh, where Khorshid got a spare bedroom ready for me. I called Mitra at once. I wanted to hear her voice, and also to make sure she knew I was safe in case someone in the family mentioned my arrest in a telephone call. However, to avoid alarming her, I said only that I had been briefly detained and questioned. Khorshid gave me some hot soup and a bath. Then Dadash came over, followed by aunts, cousins, nieces, and nephews equally anxious to lay eyes on me, hover over me, and reassure themselves that I was all right. I tried to nap, but was still in that keyed-up state in which one is too nervous and exhausted to sleep.

All of us were now tormented with worry for the family itself. None of us had committed any crime—nevertheless, as Ghaffar said when I was persuaded to venture out and go to his house for lunch a few days later, if they could take me, who of us was safe? We agreed that I could not go back to Galandwak, where I would be alone and at the mercy of my gardener. I would stay on at Khorshid's, where she or Kayvon could answer the door and say that I was not there if anyone came to arrest me again. We already knew that I dared not return to my house just down the road. As soon as he found out that I had been taken away, my gardener, whose son was on the local komiteh, had appropriated it and all my belongings for himself and his family.

I remained in a state of shock, and for several days was like someone who had not yet awakened from a nightmare. Ahmad and Gholam telephoned several times to learn how I was, and relatives and friends stopped by to visit and bring news of themselves and their own families. But I felt that there was no comfort anywhere. I was numb with disbelief, unprepared and unequipped for the thunderbolt I had received. Khorshid's house was close to the street, and I jumped whenever I heard a car backfire. I felt that my ability to judge human beings had proven horribly, disastrously inadequate. Often I feared that anyone and everyone outside our walls was my enemy. My familiar view of the world had disintegrated overnight and the whole universe had been inverted, turned inside out. I seemed horribly vulnerable, and was almost afraid to stir from the house or even to make a telephone call. The vindictiveness of the students and their accusations filled me with the terrifying feeling that someone from the School, which was only a ten-minute drive from Tajrish, might be watching me, waiting to follow me when I went out and take me back to Ayatollah Khomeini's headquarters.

I felt that I could trust no one who had any connection with the School, not even Esther. I berated myself continually for having spent the best years of my life working to benefit so many who had really cared nothing for me. The sacrifices I had made over the years for the sake of the School and social work now seemed mere follies for which I had only my own stupidity and blindness to blame. On these worthless human beings I had lavished my best years, denying myself a husband, a real family life, leisurely hours with the people I loved. What a fool I had been!

Sometimes I would fall prey to a strange but profound sense of guilt that made me search my soul as I had done on the playing field and ask myself where I had gone wrong. What tortured me most was wondering whether there was not a grain of truth in the students' absurd charge that I had failed to train revolutionaries. I often asked myself whether, as Ashrafy had implied when he seemed about to send me out to be executed, I was guilty for having cooperated with the Shah's regime. For the sake of bringing people such things as better health and incomes, clean water and birth control, I had agreed to work within a dictatorship. To keep the School safe and independent, I had carefully avoided civic protest. People like me had not harmed anyone and had tried to do good. But I could not deny that I, along with thousands of other educated, privileged Persians, had let the Shah do what he wanted. When I thought about this, I felt desperately confused, and asked myself whether, in failing actively to protest what I knew to be evil, I had supported oppression. At such times, I feared that I had lived my life all wrong.

I had naturally assumed that from now on, to anyone outside my family my arrest by the students would make me a nonperson, someone to be shunned. Before long, however, a few people began getting in touch with me. Two or three days after my return home Zamani called, trying to find out how I was. I knew that since he worked for a ministry it was dangerous for him to call me or associate with me. For a moment I was deeply touched by my bluff, honest old friend's concern—how could I ever distrust Zamani? Then it occurred to me that someone might have persuaded him to contact me in order to get me to say something for which I could be arrested again. Cautiously, I thanked him and assured him that I was well, but said that he must not endanger himself by telephoning me again. As I hung up, I wondered if he and his wife, who had witnessed my arrest, had argued about whether he should make the call. Hers was one of the few faces in the hallway that I could remember clearly. The others were becoming blurred, as if my memory were trying to erase them.

At about the same time Esther telephoned and, ignoring my protests that I might be watched, insisted that I allow her and Minou and four or five other men and women graduates to come to Khorshid's house. When they did, she said that many teachers at the University had been taken the same day as I. Ashari and the others were rumored to have been members of various left-wing groups who were acting on the orders of a man who worked as a counsellor at the University, and who was one of our graduates—he had been the revolutionaries' liaison with the School. Ashari and his cronies had taken over completely, although the students had voted one of my deputies in as acting director.

Esther, the faculty, and all the servants were frightened to death of the students, who had confiscated all my things: not only my car and my office furniture (it hurt me to hear this, because my desk, which I loved, was one that Ghaffar had presented me with as a gift when I started the School), but even my books and the paintings on my wall. However, she said, two days after my arrest, a man who said his name was Mr. Ashrafy had come and summoned the whole school to a meeting in the auditorium. He announced that he was a representative of Ayatollah Khomeini and that Agha was extremely displeased with the students' behavior and had ordered my reinstatement. Ashari and his gang had not dared to say anything to Mr. Ashrafy. Esther, Minou, and the others begged me to go back, saying that without my leadership the profession would die. Surely, they argued, there could be no danger if Ayatollah Khomeini himself had ordered them that I be taken back.

I listened in silence. Who the conspirators had been didn't really matter to me now. All that mattered was surviving. These people had spent the last few months indoors, safe in their homes in North Tehran. They had not seen the bloody clothing hanging from the trees or innocent people being shunted through Hadji Dulabi's little doorway, or heard the rifle shots on the roof. I now knew that the roof of Alavi School was where Nassiri had been executed, his vocal cords crushed first so that he could not scream. Hoveyda had just been executed as well; I had been unable to look at the television pictures of his tortured corpse. How, I asked myself, could I be sure that these old friends and colleagues were not here to trap me? I replied carefully that I was glad to see them all and was grateful for their love and devotion. But since I believed that others at the School would not ask me to come back of their own accord, I was not going to shove myself down anyone's throat with the help of Ayatollah Khomeini.

The next day someone else came to the door. When I opened it, there stood Zabi with tears in his eyes, holding out my camera, briefcase, and the other things he had taken from the car when I had arrived at the School on Saturday. Seeing him almost made me weep. I knew quite well that no one would send our simple custodian to trap me— he was risking his job to visit me and bring me my things. Soon after, Hossein and our cook also came to see me. The poorest people at the School, I thought, our illiterate servants, who were the ones with the most to lose, were risking the little they had to come and see me. Hossein reported that everyone feared and hated the revolutionary students. Only the old gardener wasn't scared of them: he had mortified Ashari and the others by announcing that I had been the only one in the whole place who had had what *they* should have had between the legs, and it was too bad what everybody was stuck with now. Hossein's words made me smile for the first time since my arrest.

Finally I realized that I must think about what to do next. I remembered Taleqani's message that I should leave the country, but I could not bring myself to consider that. I had the apartment I had bought for Mitra, and I would have enough income from my pension, my savings, and a few small investments over the years to live comfortably, if not luxuriously. The government would surely get the chaos under control sooner or later. Then I could teach or lecture, or just be happy with my family. With one of our brothers still in detention and so much uncertainty hanging over everybody, I felt that I must remain here.

To distract myself from depression I read a good deal. Press restrictions had vanished with the old regime, and, knowing that my future and the family's would depend on what happened to the country, I now read every newspaper I could lay my hands on. Sometimes, under the cover of night, I visited relatives. Occasionally I went to the Tajrish bazaar, and once or twice I even ventured into town during the daytime to go to the bank, but I was afraid to set foot too often in the city. My only real escape from numbness, pain, and anxiety was having a friend or relative drive me up to the hills so that I could hike to keep fit. There, where I had spent my childhood summers, every stone, every brook, every village was familiar and comforting. I needed the fresh air and the chance to think things over as I climbed the well-known trails. I suspected that the paths I must learn to climb in the future would be extremely crooked and rough.

About three weeks after my arrest and our half brother's disappearance, Rashid too was taken, and it became my turn to sit and wait with the rest of the family, distraught and anxious, for news of him. We could find out nothing definite, but assumed that both he and our other brother were in the Qasr-e-Qajar. Not long after this, yet another close male relative of ours, who had once held a high post in the government, was also imprisoned. We feared the worst.

In only a few weeks, the disunity, vengefulness, and bloodletting that had arisen after Bakhtiar's fall had become a madness. Ayatollah Khomeini's return had not lanced the rage and resentment of the Pahlavi years but made it explode. The country was submerged in poison. It had become a "sacred duty," a "holy act," to accuse someone of being connected with the old regime. My nearest neighbor in Galandwak came to Tajrish to warn me not to return to the village: the gardener there had not only taken over my property but had brought his relatives from the provinces to live in the house as well. I was heartsick at the loss of my cherished sanctuary and its apple orchard, but I knew how trivial a misfortune this was: my friend's elderly husband, a retired public figure, had been imprisoned and she feared that he would be executed. The newspapers were full of stories of foreign-trained doctors or engineers who had been denounced by servants in the mosque and arrested, of soldiers murdering their officers, of villagers killing landlords. Laborers were arresting factory managers and owners as "exploiters of the dispossessed" and taking over the plants. The clerics, declaring secular and professional education un-Islamic, had removed almost the entire faculty of Tehran University and every other institute of higher education, replacing all but the country's medical faculties with mullahs or bona fide revolutionaries, whom they pronounced as capable of training Iran's future professionals as any "Westernizer." Like the School of Social Work, the University had come under student control and the students were denouncing their former professors as SAVAK informers and American agents. Anyone tainted by association with the "great Satans"—America, Europe, the Soviet Union, and Israel—was in danger of being denounced as a fighter against God.

Each day the country seemed to sink further into chaos, vigilante rule, and harj-o-marj. The giant organism that had united for the purpose of dethroning the Shah had broken into many little cells. Thousands of komitehs had sprung up in the city and in the countryside, and these self-appointed "guardians of the people" and morality roamed the streets, arresting and sometimes killing anyone they suspected of "promoting Western ways," of "working for the CIA" or "serving foreigners and imperialists," or of moral impurity. Often this included anyone against whom some radical faction had a grudge, or whose property someone on the komiteh wanted. Simply walking around Tehran was frightening, for the neighborhoods now belonged to whoever got up earliest and had the most guns. The dozens of new parties and factions that had arisen since February were trying to enforce their supremacy in the streets, and it was common for huge traffic jams to form at large squares and intersections. Here, ten or twenty enraged young men from different parties would be trying to take control of traffic by shouting conflicting instructions at drivers and pedestrians, thoroughly confusing everybody while one or two blue-uniformed policemen peeped safely out from behind a nearby tree.

Summary executions, official and otherwise, were increasing rapidly. Within a month after my arrest dozens of civilians were being taken every day and imprisoned or killed. Premier Bazargan, a humane and deeply religious man, protested the growing practice of trying people before religious tribunals and executing them, but the radical Revolutionary Council, a new, secret body of clerics, knew that popular sentiment was with the radicals, and Bazargan was helpless to enforce his views. Chaos had come again, just as in my mother's time. Not until now had I truly understood why she had respected as well as hated the impious and brutal Reza Shah: he had put a stop to the harj-o-marj.

Sometimes, while walking in the mountains, I thought about how one of my brothers' lalehs used to chant the tale of the fabulous bird called the Simorgh, a wondrous creature with magnificent plumage that lived atop legendary Qaf Mountain and would swoop down to earth to protect the land of Iran from evil. I longed now for the Simorgh to spread its powerful wings and save Iran, my family, and me from the harj-o-marj. But all around I saw nothing but a black, burning fire.

On the first of March, Ayatollah Khomeini returned to Qom—keeping his promise, as we believed, to withdraw from political affairs and concern himself solely with spiritual matters. We hoped that this meant that now the cabinet would be permitted to direct the nation instead of the Revolutionary Council. Ayatollah Khomeini was still everybody's hero and the only strong figure in the country. If Bazargan had his backing, surely the premier would be able to gain control of the political situation and curb the excesses of the radicals. With the country drowning in the tidal wave of vengeance, I hoped that Ayatollah Khomeini, as a religious man, would demonstrate his belief in the Islamic principle of forgiveness. No Ruz was drawing near, an occasion for healing and rebirth, and perhaps he would see the holiday as an appropriate moment to declare an amnesty for Iranians who had worked for the previous government.

No Ruz, however, came and went without an amnesty. Things were growing steadily more chaotic because people with the experience to get the government functioning normally were in hiding or fleeing for their lives—by air, if they could (by this time the revolutionary authorities were no longer allowing God's enemies to depart from the airports), but if not, then by car or across the borders on foot. Half a dozen friends of mine had been arrested. Others had gone underground and were hiding in the homes of relatives until they could find a way to get out.

Ayatollah Khomeini believed in Islam, I thought bitterly—a religion of compassion as well as justice. Why then did he not show mercy? I had been hoping for a miracle, but my only solace was knowing that most of our women, Farough, and some of my other brothers were safely abroad. The Simorgh was not going to come and save Iran. By now, however, I understood how extraordinarily lucky I myself had been. My arrest had come so early in the game that the revolutionaries had not known what to do with their very first woman prisoner. Now the clerics were used to trying and executing women—usually for "immorality"—as well as the old men and children whom the komitehs sent them. If the students had taken me only a few days later, my judge would almost certainly have been not the honest, sympathetic Ashrafy but a religious tribunal that would have dealt with me far more expeditiously. Ironically, I was alive because the conspirators had made their move too soon.

Esther and Minou had visited me again once or twice, so that during the weeks since my release I had been getting a little news of the School, which was rife with disputes and quarrels. The man the students had voted in to replace me was timid and indecisive, and hardly any work was getting done. However, as soon as the students had felt sure that I was not coming back, they had announced that no "traitor" on the faculty—including, of course, the former director—would receive a pension. They were fighting among themselves, searching the School's and bank accounts to discover what I had stolen and how much I had embezzled. They had been astonished, Esther said contemptuously, to find that all the donations of money and land we had received, worth millions of rials, were untouched and intact.

All this was agony for me to hear. Twenty years of building a profession was being dismantled in the course of a few months. I was sure that the mullahs, with their scorn for professional education, would close down the School. Social work in Iran would be destroyed. Meanwhile, Bazargan and his ministers were shunting back and forth between Tehran and Qom, still in conflict with the Revolutionary Council but unable to do anything without the radicals' approval. It was obvious that the moderates could not run the country without support of the strong and charismatic Khomeini. In the final days of March, the country voted overwhelmingly in a national referendum to replace the old constitutional monarchy with an Islamic republic. Ayatollah Khomeini hailed the new order as "the government of God."

In a kind of sad bewilderment I wondered what was really taking place in people's hearts. Did all these Iranians—the woman who had congratulated me when the Shah left, the policemen who had stood by to let the Ghaleh burn, my colleagues who had cheered my arrest— really believe that if we called ourselves an Islamic republic, we would become a new people, like my students who insisted that if we only changed the School's name to "university," we would become one?

But like Mashti, I was not inside the watermelon, nor inside the souls of Iranians. I have no answer to the truth of all these things. I know only that when somebody stronger comes along, people side with him. I am simply telling you what happened.

I was feeling less convinced than before, however, that I had been utterly wrong about human beings. The courage and devotion of Esther, Minou, and our servants had moved me very much. Nevertheless, I finally asked them not to call on me again. "I know that you love me," I said, "but you have families to think of. If you want to know how I am, call Khorshid sometimes, but don't ask for me." I was afraid that the radicals were tapping the telephones. My friends reluctantly obeyed.

Late in March, a few days before the constitutional referendum, I went early one evening to the Tajrish market to buy some fruit for my sister. This was not entirely safe because people from the School often made the ten-minute drive there to buy fruits and vegetables, but it was crowded at the end of the day and as I rarely went there anymore, I thought the risk small. I was therefore startled and frightened when, just as I was about to make my way back across the square—where, as usual, different political organizations were shouting traffic directions at everyone and causing a mess—I heard a voice shouting, "Khanom!" and realized that somebody was running after me. I turned and saw Hossein. He ran up panting and said he had been on his way to my sister's house to see me.

"That isn't wise, Hossein," I said reproachfully. "Can't you telephone?"

"No, Khanom, I was afraid to. I have come to tell you that today I was taking the students somewhere and they were telling each other that since the Imam did not kill you, they ought to go and do it themselves."

Shaken, I thanked him for the warning and said that this time he must go and not come back again. I did not think twice about whether to take the threat seriously. Komiteh members, party thugs, and members of the Revolutionary Guards—a new though unofficial revolutionary militia appointed to protect members of the Revolutionary Council—might kill anyone with impunity and no one dared protest. There was nothing now to prevent the students from killing me any time they wished. They knew that I lived in Tajrish. If they decided to come after me, there would be nothing I could do to stop them.

I knew now that I must leave Iran—if not forever, then certainly for a few years. These days, somebody who had worked in a government building as a guard under the old regime could be dead within twenty-four hours for "collaborating with the Shah." Men were being arrested in the streets as traitors to the revolution for not having beards and for wearing neckties. Religious persecution—of which the Bahais, of course, had been the first targets—was intensifying and spreading to Jews, Christians, Zoroastrians, and other minorities who had been tolerated in Iran for centuries. The longer I waited, the more likely it was that even if the students didn't carry out their threat I would be rearrested by somebody. I could no longer live openly, I couldn't work, I had no home and no pension or even any possessions, save what had been in the car the day I was arrested and that Zabi had returned. To remain for my family's sake would only put Khorshid and anyone I lived with in danger and accomplish nothing for my brothers and other relatives who had been taken. I decided that I must find a way to accept what had once been unthinkable: exile.

To get an exit visa to leave Iran, one now had to have permission from the Revolutionary Council. Its membership was secret, but I decided to write to Ayatollah Taleqani, who was undoubtedly on it, and ask him to help me. It was impossible to know whether he would or not. By this time, I was sure, hundreds of people must be appealing to him for help in escaping. However, it was the only chance I had. I wrote a letter explaining that, as I could not work in Iran, I wished to look for employment outside my homeland. I begged Ayatollah Taleqani's help in getting an exit visa for my passport.

I mailed the letter, waited a few days, then dialed the number Ahmad had given me when I was arrested. I was relieved when the same assistant I had spoken to then told me cordially that my letter had arrived, and that Ayatollah Taleqani, recognizing the impossibility of my supporting myself in Iran, would arrange for the passport and exit visa. However, the assistant did not know how long this would take. I thanked him, gave him Khorshid's number, and said that the people there would let me know when he called to say the passport was ready. Then I instructed Khorshid to tell anyone else who called that I was visiting relatives in Isfahan.

I spent the next six or seven weeks living in the homes of different relatives, waiting anxiously for news that Taleqani's assistant had called and jumping violently every time the telephone rang. Now, just as in the days when I had wanted to go to America, I thought of nothing but getting out. I worried constantly about what was going to happen to my family. Dadash and Abbas were retired, so perhaps the radicals would leave them alone. But Ghaffar and all our half brothers had begun living in semiconcealment after Rashid's arrest, while Farough had called from abroad and decided with Jean—who had by now applied unsuccessfully for an exit permit—that he would not come back. Khorshid insisted that there was no reason for her to leave, but I feared that it would not be long before they went after Kayvon, as well as everyone who bore the name of Farman Farmaian.

I had decided to go to London, where Jahan was living, and where I might be able to find work with International Planned Parenthood at their headquarters there. If so, I could earn enough to get by. I comforted myself a little with the thought that this would give me a chance to see Jahan, Farough, my sisters, and the others who had already left. England, after all, was only a few hours' flight from my homeland; living there, I would not forget that I could easily return when the country got back to normal again.

Several times I called Taleqani's assistant, but each time there was no word. I was very nervous. I never stayed too long in one house and went outdoors only to move to another hiding place, or to venture up into the hills for a hike. Even this, I realized, entailed a small risk. But I knew that I would have to leave quickly, and these walks would be the last time I would set eyes on my beloved mountains for at least a few years. I began visiting the older members of our family, starting with Mohammed Vali Mirza, to see them one last time. I did not tell them this, because I was afraid to say that I was leaving in the hearing of their servants—many servants' sons were on komitehs or had become members of one radical organization or another, for this was the key to advancement in the new order.

I was of course very much afraid of going back to Galandwak. Nevertheless, one day in May I realized that I had always been so busy with work that I had never had time to take pictures of the house and orchard I had loved so much. Deciding that I could not leave my memories of them behind along with everything else that was dear to me, I took the camera Zabi had returned to me, put on hiking shoes, and had someone drive me to the mountains around the broad valley where Galandwak lay.

There was a high hill there above a dam that had been built in the mountains during the Shah's reign to provide more water for South Tehran and the villages below the capital. I climbed to the top of the hill and sat down on a spot above the dam from which I could look out over the reservoir and the valley. There were my house and orchard and the flat tin roofs of the rest of the village—the house of the farmer from whom I had bought my milk, the blacksmith who lived next door to me, my other neighbors, the teahouse, the mosque. I took five or six pictures, then sat for hours, just thinking and staring at the mountains.

I felt that I was looking down at my whole life, which now lay shattered like jagged shards of glass. Since the day of my arrest there had not been an hour when the pieces did not cut my mind and make it bleed, but out of this rubble I would have to construct a new existence.

I knew that I was lucky to be alive and I was determined to make the best of the years that remained to me. I didn't need much—after all, I had worked among Bedouin who lived in tents and owned nothing but a goat; I had seen families living under tables on the streets in India, and dug people out of the rubble of earthquakes that had made them homeless in a few seconds. Moreover, I could probably find some sort of useful work in England. But my whole being cried out in protest. Why did I have to quit my country? How did I deserve to leave my land, my home, my people? The wheat fields below were green with spring shoots, the apple and plum trees in the orchards were a cloud of white and pink blossoms. The reservoir below the dam sparkled under the warm sun and brilliant sky. The standing water was so still it breathed.

As I had hiked and pondered during the last months, I had thought long and hard about what had happened to our society and what role I had played in its failure. While I lived here the reservoir had always represented for me what had been good about Mohammed Reza Shah's reign. He had brought other benefits besides dams: he had built schools, improved the lot of women and minorities, even given social work a chance. For all these reasons, despite the wrongs he had done, I had not rejoiced to see him destroyed, or wanted all he had built swept away. But he had cared too much for developing highways and electric plants, and not enough for developing the minds of the Asharis and Isadis who filled the schools he built.

And now I understood how I had been part of this failure. Always believing that there was still plenty of time, I had procrastinated, saying to myself that I could teach Iranians about the importance of democracy, of having a genuine political process, of *making* our government listen to us, after I had raised the living standard. To this end, which I had believed to be the more urgent one, I had been willing to postpone speaking out until it was too late. Like other people who knew what was happening in our country and who understood the importance of political participation and freedom of expression, I had been afraid— afraid of prison, torture, and exile, afraid of sacrificing my ambitions and my cherished dreams. Iranians like me had missed our chance, neutralizing ourselves by keeping our mouths shut, withdrawing from the political process, letting the Shah do what he wanted.

This harj-o-marj was the ultimate fruit of that. It had happened because we, who should have been teachers of the ignorant, did not set an example of leadership, did not sacrifice ourselves, our careers, our cherished dreams, to protest what the Shah was doing to us. We did not speak out against his injustices and his lack of respect for the people's voice. Perhaps, since we had so few examples of courage and principle to imitate after Mossadegh, we couldn't be blamed for letting SAVAK intimidate us. Perhaps too, we could not have won human and political rights for the Iranian people no matter how brave and unselfish we were. But if the Shah had suffocated us, we had also let him. I felt now that if enough of us, the moderate, educated, reasonable people, had gotten together, spoken out, resigned from our jobs, gone to jail, and even died—as a few brave ones had—we might have had the leader we needed now.

And unlike us, the mullahs had had guts. They had endured jail and exile. They had let themselves be beaten, tortured, and killed to destroy the Shah. They had had no plan, no program, and almost nothing positive to suggest—only "The Shah must go!" But they had been brave. While we had waited to see what would happen and which way the wind blew, they had ridden the wave of the people's rage. Now they were stepping into the leadership vacuum the Shah had created, the vacuum we had let him create. They weren't taking control because they had planned to, or because it was "destined," but because people like me had no strong alternative to offer. There had been no more Mossadeghs. Once more, the long struggle for liberty was being aborted. But this time, I thought, we couldn't blame the foreigners. This time we, the fortunate Iranians, the educated ones, had aborted it ourselves.

* * *

The following week Taleqani's assistant called to say that my passport was ready and that I must go immediately to a certain place for instructions about where to pick it up. In frantic haste I put on a black kerchief—the revolutionaries had not yet begun detaining women for not wearing the chador—and, having arranged for someone to pick me up, hurried to the city. The address Khorshid had taken down was that of a nondescript former government building in a small street near Kakh Avenue. There a clerk who referred to Taleqani's assistant as "Brother" in the new style affected by many revolutionaries met me and said that I must go at once to the airport, where Ayatollah Taleqani's people maintained an office, to pick up my passport. The office was on the second floor of the terminal building, and I must ask for "Brother M." As I stood nervously memorizing the instructions and the name, he handed me a sealed envelope, adding sternly that I must leave within twenty-four hours. After that, Ayatollah Taleqani's office would not be responsible for my safety.

I blanched. It was Wednesday. No flights were permitted out at night. I would have to get a ticket before tomorrow morning to be sure of getting on a flight within twenty-four hours. If I could not do that, I would be trapped until Saturday morning because of the Friday holiday. Shakily, I pointed out that this left me no time to get a ticket or prepare for my departure. "Very well, then," he said, "protection will be extended until Saturday. But see that you go by then, because if you haven't left, your exit visa will be canceled and your name will appear on a list of collaborators forbidden to leave the country. Remember: after Saturday we cannot protect you."

It was already late in the afternoon. I was very frightened of going to Mehrabad Airport, which I had heard was crawling with vigilantes. One family friend who had tried to get out and failed had said that the border guards had orders to shoot on the spot anyone who "looked like an enemy of Islam." However, there was no alternative, and the airport was an hour away, so I would have to hurry. I rushed out to the street and asked the relative whose car we had taken to drive me home so that I could get a black chador. When I had put it on, we drove as fast as we could out to Mehrabad, afraid the whole time of running into a roadblock set up by some revolutionary faction or other. I wondered what I would do if the passport were not there, or if it turned out to be invalid. Even the new government's passports were not always honored by the different groups of revolutionaries who were controlling the exit points.

By now it was past seven and growing dark. From the airport parking lot I could see armored vehicles all along the building. Bearded, helmeted gangs of young men in miscellaneous and unidentifiable uniforms were driving along the access roads in jeeps or patrolling the front of the terminal on foot, hoping to snare people on their wanted lists as they tried to escape. The airport was a microcosm of what was happening to the country. I was terrified of being recognized. I had taught and lectured to audiences of countless people in the past few years alone, not only at the School but at Tehran University, other colleges in the city, and even the police academy. My name, appearance, and social position had been known to many. It was by no means impossible that someone among the hundreds of vigilantes and other people here would recognize my face. I was nearly paralyzed with fear that I would be arrested. I felt almost as though I had been transported back to Ayatollah Khomeini's headquarters again.

A huge crowd of travelers and others, many of them laden with luggage, was moving toward the terminal building where I was going, for whole families were escorting relatives to bid them farewell. I pulled down the black kerchief I was still wearing under the chador until it hid both my eyebrows. Then I drew the veil tight, covering my face almost completely except for one eye. Instinct made me want to rush past the jeeps and foot patrols as fast as I could, but I had enough presence of mind to realize that someone running in panic would attract attention faster than anything else. Feeling every moment as though I were seeing death itself before me, I advanced quickly into the hurrying crowds. Then, remembering that my students had always joked about the unusually swift pace I set them when we walked together, I forced myself to slow down to the shuffling gait of an old woman.

The whole world seemed to be pressing through the glass doors of the entrance. The inside of the long, deep terminal was jammed with people—guards with rifles, taxi drivers, parents and children, brothers and sisters, wives and husbands bidding each other farewell, together with every one of their relatives. Many people, knowing that they were saying goodbye to these dear ones for perhaps the last time, sobbed and wailed hysterically, beating their heads and smiting their breasts as if in a funeral procession. Over the din I could hear the last departures being announced: Paris, London, Vienna, Zurich. I plunged blindly ahead in the direction of the long corridors that led to the administrative offices on the second floor, unable to see much because of the chador, my heart pounding with a stifling fear. The terminal floors, once spotless, were filthy with paper and litter. Pictures of Ayatollah Khomeini had replaced the photographs of the Shah and his projects and monuments on the walls. The pillars were covered with grafitti and handbills: "The Revolution has succeeded," "The Traitor Shah is gone," "Join the Mojahedin," "Join the Tudeh," "Join the Hezbollah."

At last I found the stairway to the second floor. I was terrified of learning that the passport had been revoked, and that I would be trapped and arrested when I asked for "Brother M." However, I found the right office. Inside, two revolutionaries were sitting at a table scattered with papers, folders, and pots of tea. I asked for "Brother M." and showed them the envelope with his name on it.

"Brother M.? He's in there." The man to whom I had spoken pointed to a closed door. When I hesitated, he got up, opened it, and said, "Brother M., a woman is here to give you a letter." Someone inside called me to come in. A bearded, chubby, dirty man in his thirties was sitting behind a big metal desk covered with papers. He was reading a file, and did not look up.

"Salaam," I said. "Salaam," he muttered under his breath, avoiding my eyes. An empty chair stood before the desk, but I saw that he did not think it proper to invite a woman to sit in his office, so I merely passed him the sealed letter. Opening it, he read the contents without any expression, then opened a desk drawer crowded with thick white envelopes. Leafing through a clutch of them, he extracted one, and, still without looking at me, handed it across the desk. Barely moving his lips, he said, "They told you that you must depart tomorrow?"

"Yes, they told me," I said. I was afraid of elaborating.

"See that you do. Otherwise you might not be able to leave at all." He returned to what he was reading. I waited, unable to move for fear of doing or saying the wrong thing. Finally I whispered, "Agha, should I go now?" He nodded.

I didn't dare stop to open the envelope and look inside; I wanted only to get out of there before he changed his mind. Forgetting to move slowly, I fled from his office, bolted downstairs, and ran out the front entrance of the terminal past the vigilantes, jeeps, and armored trucks, holding the envelope close to me beneath my chador. By this time it was dark outside. I found the car and asked my relative to wait. Then I rolled up all the windows and opened the envelope. Inside was my familiar maroon-colored passport. I opened it trembling, dreading to find something wrong that would make me have to go back to Brother M. and explain that I could not leave until Saturday. But in the dim light of a streetlamp, I saw that an exit visa had been stamped inside.

* * *

The next morning I called every airline that flew to Europe, but all of them, from Air France to Swissair, were full for months to come. Finally I called Pakistan Airlines and learned that they had a Saturday flight going not to London, but in the opposite direction, from London to Karachi by way of Tehran. This would be much more expensive, but I had to get out at any price. I went at once to the airline office on Ferdowsi Square and booked a seat. As I waited for the clerk to issue the ticket, it occurred to me that I had once before had to reach the West by going east.

I spent the next day at Dadash's house, saying goodbye to those closest to me in his magnificent rose garden. I was so afraid of a servant's learning of my plans and reporting them to someone who might block my departure that I did not even tell him or my other brothers and sisters when I was leaving, but said simply that I had a passport and was going away soon. We all understood each other. Despite our grief, everyone in the family was happy that I was leaving. Soon most of them would try to do the same. The revolution was rending the threads that Shazdeh had knotted with such love and care, scattering us like rags in a great wind. We knew that none of us would ever be whole again. My last sight of my brothers and sisters at home in a country of our own was at what had once been Reswanieh, where we took the color snapshots that would help us cling to memory and to each other in years to come.

Very early on Saturday I was taken to the airport in the car of a family member whose driver both of us trusted. After my relative and I bade each other farewell, this loyal man escorted me to the glass-walled departure lounge and waited to make sure nothing went wrong. Before I could enter the departure lounge my single suitcase had to be inspected by the border guards for gold, currency, or jewelry in excess of the limits set by the revolutionary government. I had been careful to take no more than five hundred dollars, the maximum permitted, and to wear and pack only simple things that would not invite questions. We had heard stories of the border police or vigilantes dragging people off the plane before it departed. My mouth was dry, and my pulse thudded so hard as the border guard inspected my luggage that I thought he must be able to hear it.

Although I had arrived very early in the day, well in advance of the flight to Karachi, the departure lounge was overflowing. Like me, I thought, most people here would soon be refugees. Even now, wearing a kerchief and in a large crowd, I felt vulnerable, afraid that the revolutionaries might come in here looking for someone at the last minute, and that I would be detained. For the next hour or two I tried to calm my nerves by drinking a cup of tea in the café, browsing aimlessly and blindly in the duty free shop, and reading the newspapers lying on a table in the lounge. Just hold on for another few minutes, I told myself, and then everything will be all right. Then you can find a new country and make a new life for yourself.

Finally, the boarding for my flight was announced. Knowing now that I was almost out of danger, I ran to the telephone and spent my last minutes in Iran calling Jaby, Dadash, and Khorshid to say a real goodbye to them. I also called Esther, whom I had never told I was leaving, but who I knew would tell no one, not even Minou, until I wrote to her to say that I was safe. Her courage and that of the few true friends who had called or visited me had helped to restore a little of my faith in people.

I went to the gate. With alarm, I saw that I was the only one getting on the plane: was I attracting attention, or being followed to be arrested at the last moment? I showed my ticket to the flight attendant at the door, then glanced fearfully behind me. No one was there. I was simply the only person going from Tehran to Karachi that day.

How strange, I thought; hundreds of other people were trying in vain to book themselves on flights out of the country—the flights to Paris, Vienna, and Zurich had all had long waiting lists. Then I realized that, desperate though people were to get out, they saw salvation as lying exclusively in one direction. Even now it didn't occur to them that they could reach their destination by talking another route than the one leading due West.

Still jumpy, I sat down. Even after the plane lifted off, I clutched my handbag tightly on my lap. I could not relax until I knew we had left Persian airspace. At last, when I was sure that we were no longer over Iranian territory, I took off my black kerchief. It was like removing a heavy iron helmet.

I sank back in my seat exhausted, feeling as if the troubles of the past few years had drained me of my last emotional reserves. I wondered how, amid all the sorrows and upheavals—the fires and riots, my mother's death, my own ordeal and those of my relatives and friends— I had stayed sane. I felt that nothing could heal me or stop the slow bleeding that had been going on inside me for so long. I no longer had what I needed to sustain me. Every pillar of my existence except Mitra had fallen. Iran did not want me. My family was in prison, in hiding, or dispersed. Galandwak, Reswanieh, the School, my work, and my friends had vanished from my life just like the compound, like my childhood world. I no longer had a home, only the vague, lonely, insubstantial future of an exile.

I thought of the poem by Sa'adi that had comforted me as I set out on my journey to America so many years ago: "Although love of country is required by the Prophet, one should not live in misery merely because one was born in a certain land." It still rang as clearly in my memory as the little silver coins Shazdeh had given us for reciting poems about loving one's country, the importance of education, the necessity of helping our people. In those days, I remembered, I had wanted to leave the andarun and make a wider, more interesting life for myself—and marvel of marvels, Sa'adi, seven centuries before, had seemed to say that I was free to do so.

Only now, decades later, did I have the experience to realize what had really led him to write those words, and what he had meant to say to me. The harj-o-marj had happened to him, too, and to Hafez, and Ferdowsi, and Rumi, and to every other great Persian poet. Seven hundred years ago, a thousand, or yesterday—it made no difference. The harj-o-marj was in our veins, seared into our Persian souls.

I did what all those poems said to do, I thought bitterly. I fulfilled my mission. But I wasted my time. At least my father still had us after the coup, and the compound, and his country, whereas I'm not even going to get my pension. I might as well have married and stayed in the andarun and had a pleasant life, instead of losing my home and most of the people I love.

Then, as if I had been praying and my prayer had been heard, the bitterness subsided and in its place I felt, reluctantly, the slow beginnings of the acceptance that is born of necessity. My father, whose career was destroyed and whose property was confiscated, had educated us, raised us to be fit and healthy, and taught us to move ahead and look forward. My mother, who had also suffered the harj-o-marj, had learned to accept hardship and to make her peace with change. Because I was their daughter, and because I was an Iranian, I would survive.

I did what I had to do, I thought. Sa'adi has said that I do not have to tie myself to a single piece of earth, that I can make my own way and my own fate. I have trained others to be self-reliant, and now I have to use my skills to help myself. I will accept what must be, and try not to regret that I didn't see that this revolution was coming, or that we had no time left, or that I would be betrayed and dispossessed of what was mine. Once again, I will go to some other country as Sa'adi advises, and find a place there. And then I'll just have to see what happens next.

EPILOGUE

I STAYED OVERNIGHT IN KARACHI AND FLEW THE NEXT DAY TO London, where I moved in with Jahan. Her two-bedroom apartment had become home not only to her and her three children, but also to Khorshid's two daughters and my sister Sory. Their company was the medicine I needed for my inner wounds to begin healing a little. I wrote to Esther to let her know I was safe, and where she and my other friends could reach me.

Planned Parenthood had no full-time work for me, though they very kindly gave me some consulting to do. I longed to settle down to a normal, stable existence in London, where I was close to other members of my family. I soon realized, however, that earning a livelihood in London was going to be very difficult for a displaced, middle-aged Iranian social worker. In July I also realized that my hopes of returning to Iran after only a couple of years had been a mirage: the Iranian press announced that the property and assets of a number of well-known families had been confiscated, ours among them. My only chance of supporting myself now was in the United States, where I had the most professional connections. I thought of the many times I had visited the U.S. in the two and a half decades since my departure from New York in 1954. Despite all that had happened to change the relationship between our countries, I had never tired of breathing the free air of America. Never had I dreamed that one day I would go there as I did in that September of 1979: not as a free and independent woman but as an exhausted refugee, like millions who had come before her.

I had hoped to obtain a teaching post or a position with the United Nations, but the U.N.'s budget had been cut and all university teaching positions had already been filled. I thought sadly of Mr. Jones, with whom I had remained in touch until his death in a plane crash in 1962, and wished I had such a friend now. After a while, finding no work, I gave up temporarily and did what I really wanted to do, which was to fly to where Mitra and Mike were living and be reunited with them and my grandchildren.

By this time, the political situation in Iran was moving completely out of the control of Bazargan and the moderates. Ayatollah Khomeini alone had the support of the army. The radicals of the Revolutionary Council were working to eliminate erstwhile allies like the leftist Mojahedin and the liberal heirs of the National Front, and the Ayatollah was supporting a new constitution that would make a body of clerics the supreme authority in Iran. Bazargan's reluctance to destroy every tie with the past and the West was costing him popular support and making him a "traitor" to the radicals. He now complained publicly that he was like someone trying to rule with a knife that had no blade.

Near the end of October, the radicals' cause inadvertently received a great boost from the United States itself, when, taking compassion on an old ally, President Carter admitted the Shah and his family to the U.S. so that he could be treated in New York for the lymphatic cancer he had kept secret for so long. The action unleashed a wave of rage in Iran. Most people were convinced that the United States intended to restore the Shah as it had in 1953. Ayatollah Khomeini, calling the Shah's admission a plot, demanded that the U.S. hand over the former ruler, and used the opportunity to attack the moderates in Bazargan's government who favored retaining ties with the West.

On the morning of November fourth, the fifteenth anniversary of Khomeini's exile for opposing the 1964 immunity law, a gigantic demonstration took place outside the compound of the United States Embassy in support of the Ayatollah's position. Hundreds of militant students climbed the Embassy walls. In the space of a few hours, fifty-two Americans had been taken hostage.

In Iran, popular feeling was overwhelmingly on the side of the students. To the great mass of people, the students' action did not seem the lawless act of terrorism it was, but an assertion of the dignity and independence of Iran. Finally, Iranians felt, after all these years, somebody was expressing their anger, the anger of a people who felt that the great powers had never given them a voice in their own destiny. To most, the awful destructiveness of the expression did not matter. All that mattered was that the students seemed to have won a great victory over the world's most powerful triumvirate: the Americans, the British, and the Shah. Everyone now would have to feel the effects of a small, weak nation's fury.

The next day, Ayatollah Khomeini officially sanctioned the taking of the Embassy, which he called "a nest of spies." Twenty-four hours later, Mehdi Bazargan resigned. The long, agonizing crisis of four hundred and forty-four days had begun. Watching the terrible events unfold every night on the evening news, I felt sick with pity for the innocent hostages and their families and horrified at the lawless attitude of the radicals in the Iranian government.

Even now, knowing all that I knew, I had to ask myself again and again how relations between our two countries, which had begun in this century with such warmth and goodwill, had come to this tragic pass. All that these young students knew of America was that the United States had been the Shah's backer for twenty-six years. All that Americans could see on their television sets was a country which, recently an ally, now seemed to be populated exclusively by black-clad, screaming mobs obsessed with reviling and humiliating innocent Americans.

Ironically, just at this time a book called _Countercoup_ was published in the United States. In it, the author, a former CIA official named Kermit Roosevelt, triumphantly revealed to Americans what Iranians had realized for a quarter of a century: that his organization was responsible for the overthrow of Dr. Mossadegh. In cheerful tones, _Countercoup_ boasted that after the overthrow of Iran's premier, the Shah, addressing the book's author as America's representative, had said to him, "I owe my throne to God, my people, my army—and to you."

Would any of this book's American readers, I wondered, understand that a distant event about which few Americans had any curiosity at all had helped bring about the very scenes that they watched in outrage on television every night? Would anyone be able to see from Mr. Roosevelt's self-congratulatory account why citizens of small, unpowerful countries like ours often felt that coercion and violence were the only way they could make themselves heard by the rest of the world?

Although all the Americans in our family were now safe (not long after my own escape the Embassy had finally helped Jean obtain an exit visa), the hostage crisis made me very anxious for myself and other Iranians in the United States. In the eyes of Americans, Iranians had all become shouting, fist-waving, fanatical mobs of terrorists. As the weeks of the crisis dragged on and anger at Iran intensified, Iranian stores were boycotted and some businesses were vandalized. Now, whenever I stood in a supermarket line and someone heard my accent and asked me, in the friendly American fashion, where I came from, I was afraid to tell the truth. I feared that I would never get a job, and for a long time I thought that people like me might be rounded up and interned, like the Japanese-Americans I had worked with as a social worker in Los Angeles after the war. The most frightening thought of all was that I might be deported back to Iran. I had learned at last that nothing in life was certain—least of all the future.

Eventually, with the aid of some American friends, I found work in a part of the country not too distant from where my daughter and her family lived, and I have succeeded in taking Sa'adi's advice and making a new life for myself. I am still a social worker, and since my job is concerned with the welfare of families and children I can feel that I am of some use to people again. The United States has many problems now, and it hurts me to see that more of its citizens rather than fewer are suffering. Sometimes I think that America's leaders have lost all compassion for human beings. Yet I can never forget for a moment what it means to live in a country where one is free to say what one likes and read what one pleases, to protest injustice, and above all, to try to do something about the problems one sees.

As all the world knows, the years after the revolution were years of great suffering for my country. Power struggles and executions in Iran destroyed the clerics' internal opposition; a million young men were lost in the eight-year war with Iraq; the Iranian government became isolated from the rest of the world by aligning itself with hostage taking and terrorism. Such problems as inflation, unemployment, and failed economic programs were blamed on the old scapegoats of foreigners and conspiracies instead of on fanaticism, corruption, ineptitude, and the persecution of innocent people and inoffensive minorities.

Education was among the chief victims of this blindness, and the School quickly fell apart. Ashari and others, as I learned from those who still wrote to me after I left, soon tired of the person they had set in my place, and in the end the man whom I thought most likely to have engineered my downfall was appointed the School's director. He had good revolutionary credentials and was not incompetent, but he was killed by an assassin's bomb in June of 1981, and thereafter the

School was allowed to languish and finally to dissolve. For many years, social work in our country seemed to have come to an end.

Recently, however, I received a letter from a graduate of ours that has given me some hope. My former student wrote to me to say that after my departure, the men and women I had trained felt themselves to be orphaned, yet many still believed in the value of social work and tried to uphold our high professional standards. This student was unable to tell me more for fear that her letter—which was delivered by a relative visiting my city—would be read by the wrong eyes, but she assured me that social work was still alive in Iran, and that its practitioners were trying to defend it against those who sought its destruction.

So it seems that I did train some believers after all, and that the Tehran School of Social Work's twenty-one years of existence were not utterly in vain. In any case, I do not now regret the life I lived. I have seen and done many interesting things and met many remarkable and impressive people. Long ago I set out into the world with my arms wide open, and I am sure that if I had it to do all over again, I would. I could never have just stayed home in the andarun. Not if someone had offered me five diamond rings.

AFTERWORD

by Dona Munker

SEVEN YEARS AFTER SATTAREH FARMAN FARMAIAN RETURNED TO the United States, a mutual friend brought to my attention a manuscript she had written. In it, she had set down memories of her childhood and education, her years of labor on behalf of the poor, and her arrest and narrow escape from execution. It was a modest, practical account that brought to mind a photograph I had once seen of her: a handsome, aristocratic-looking woman whose taut bearing suggested a lifetime of self-discipline.

That same week, as it happened, the Iran-*contra* scandal had started to unfold. Once again, the nightly news was reminding Americans of the existence of an apparently baffling people, the Iranians—not as terrorists, this time, but as shadowy traffickers in an arms-for-hostages scheme. Reading Sattareh Farman Farmaian's manuscript, I wondered just how accurate these stereotyped images of an entire nation could be. Who *were* "the Iranians"? How did they think and feel, and what would they say if asked about all that had happened in their country? Plainly, Americans could learn a great deal from a full-scale portrait of and by an Iranian like Sattareh and from hearing her views about her country and ours.

I called her to suggest that Westerners who knew little about Iran would welcome a detailed account of her life, and we subsequently spent four and a half years talking, recording her thoughts and feelings, reading and checking facts, and exploring at length the issues and events in her own experience and Iran's modern evolution that she, as an Iranian, considered important. It is the hope of this American writer that Sattareh's first-person history of her life and country will remind Western readers that aquiring such knowledge is in our own interest—and help to recall the folly of policies founded, in the words of American historian Arthur M. Schlesinger, Jr., on the ignorance of our own ignorance.

INDEX

ABOUT THE AUTHORS

SATTAREH FARMAN FARMAIAN emigrated in 1979 to the United States, where she continued her career in social work. She lives in Los Angeles.

DONA MUNKER is a writer, editor, and teacher with a doctorate in English literature. She lives in New York City.

READER'S GROUP GUIDE

Questions for Discussion

1. Among the important emotional threads running through *Daughter of Persia* is Sattareh Farman Farmaian's lasting veneration for her distant but beloved father, to whom she refers simply as Shazdeh, "the prince." How did Shazdeh—or Satti's memory of Shazdeh—influence her life and career? What other people struck you as especially important to Satti in her adult life?

2. Did the depiction of Satti's childhood home change your impressions of a "harem compound"? In what ways was Shazdeh's compound a microcosm of Persian life as the author claims it existed for thousands of years? Why did Persians feel that having a protector was so critical to survival? Do you think the need for a "protector" is a universal experience or particular to the Persian culture?

3. The incident in which Satti's mother refused to go to the police after being cheated by a beggar was a crucial lesson for Satti in the Persian axiom that one must "never trust anyone outside the family." Are Americans generally taught to trust those outside the family? Are there circumstances in American culture in which it is considered unwise or even unethical to depend on "family"? Do all Western cultures emphasize independence from family?

4. How did Satti's descriptions of individual Persian women from childhood—her mother, Khanom; her stepmothers Batul and Fatimeh; Princess Ezzatdoleh; Neggar-Saltaneh (the wedding party hostess); or Shazdeh's strong-willed sister, Najmeh-Saltaneh, the mother of Dr. Mohammed Mossadegh—both support and contradict Western stereotypes of traditional Moslem women?

5. If Shazdeh had lived a year or two longer, he would have found Satti a husband. How do you think her life would have turned out if she had been married off by her father? Might she still have been able to fight for social reforms? Do you think she could still have found happiness if she had had a conventional Persian marriage?

6. Satti felt that a priceless lesson of her student years in America, "the land at the end of the earth," was the freedom to speak openly and criticize anyone, even teachers and the government. She believed that if Iranians could learn to speak freely, "we could solve our problems." For this reason, she decided that one day she would return to Iran and teach Persians the value of "constructive criticism." Do you see as much constructive criticism in American public life today as Satti did then? Is it possible to solve large-scale social problems without constructive criticism?

7. Another of Satti's observations as a student was that "America was a wasteful nation." Satti felt that her American friends threw away clothing and even food they did not want without realizing the luxury in which they lived compared to countries such as Iran. Do you think "Americans are wasteful"? In what sense? Do you think Satti could have been more sympathetic to her friends, since Americans' circumstances were different than Iranians'?

8. What was your reaction to the 1953 overthrow of Dr. Mohammed Massadegh, Iran's democratically elected premier, by supporters of Mohammed Reza Shah, the British intelligence service, and the American CIA? Were you surprised to learn that although it took more than a quarter of a century for Americans to learn of their government's involvement in the plot, Iranians learned the truth within days? Do you

think the United States should never become involved in the overthrow of a democratically elected regime in a foreign country? Or do you think it's politically naïve to believe we must never betray the principles of democracy?

9. Satti's "Bulldozers"—the young men and women she recruited and trained to go into South Teheran to clean up its orphanages, mental hospitals, workhouses, and prisons—had to deal with problems that are generally less common in developed countries. How was the social work Satti taught different from social work in the West, and how was it similar? Do American social workers ever have to deal with similar problems here, for instance, in times of natural catastrophe?

10. Satti also taught her Bulldozers that *social worker* in Persian translated into *madadkar,* "helping person," to make the point that social workers cared not only about themselves and their families but also about people with whom they had nothing to do, or who might belong to a different religion or class, or be unlike them in other ways. Do you think generally Americans are taught to care about those in need, despite their being from a different race, religion, or class? Do you think the United States has a strong government program, such as Satti was trying to build in Iran, to take care of people less fortunate?

11. In introducing international family planning and birth control to Iran, Satti emphasized that birth control enabled couples to postpone having children until women had recovered from previous childbearing and until families could afford to take care of their children financially. To persuade traditional Persians that family planning was in harmony with Islamic law, she enlisted the support of a prominent ayatollah, who issued a favorable ruling. Did you side with Satti or with her mother, Khanom, who maintained a more conservative stand on birth control? In what ways were Khanom's religious arguments similar to arguments made by other religious faiths against birth control?

12. Satti criticized the Shah's social and educational policies, yet in retrospect she realized that she had not fully understood what impact

those policies were having on the students of her own school. Why do you think she was blind to this at the time?

13. By the last months of the Shah's reign, many well-educated, democratic, religiously tolerant Iranians, including Satti, were convinced that the Ayatollah Khomeini would be a compassionate, democratizing influence on Iran and not a religious fanatic. What led them to feel this way about Khomeini and the changes he was demanding?

14. Satti's arrest by her own students was all the more devastating because no one on her faculty or staff, besides Zabi, attempted to prevent it. While she later learned that the students were motivated by ignorance and an undeserved sense of entitlement, she felt shattered by the behavior of those who refused to get involved. Why do you think no one stepped forward to help her? Have you ever witnessed or been the target of a similar betrayal of loyalty at a critical moment? How did you make sense of it?

15. Social work has always taught that it is only by solving society's problems through slow, long-term changes in behavior, legislation, and policy that permanent, positive social change comes about. However, this approach means cooperating with the existing system. After her release from detention, Satti wondered in anguish whether she had supported oppression by keeping the school apolitical and not actively speaking out against the government's human rights abuses. Do you think Satti's efforts benefited or ultimately hurt Iran? What would you have done in Satti's position?